America

Our Sacred Honor

And for the support of this Declaration, with a firm reliance on the protection of divine Providence, we mutually pledge to each other our Lives, our Fortunes and our sacred Honor.

Mary A. KARDES

ILLUSTRATIONS BY
JONATHAN YOUNG

LifeRich
PUBLISHING®

LifeRich Publishing is a registered trademark of The Reader's Digest Association, Inc.

LifeRich Publishing books may be ordered through booksellers or by contacting:

LifeRich Publishing
1663 Liberty Drive
Bloomington, IN 47403
www.liferichpublishing.com
1 (888) 238-8637

Because of the dynamic nature of the Internet, any web addresses or links contained in this book may have changed since publication and may no longer be valid. The views expressed in this work are solely those of the author and do not necessarily reflect the views of the publisher, and the publisher hereby disclaims any responsibility for them.

Any people depicted in stock imagery provided by Thinkstock are models, and such images are being used for illustrative purposes only.
Certain stock imagery © Thinkstock.

ISBN: 978-1-4897-0426-9 (sc)
ISBN: 978-1-4897-0427-6 (hc)
ISBN: 978-1-4897-0425-2 (e)

Library of Congress Control Number: 2015907760

Print information available on the last page.

LifeRich Publishing rev. date: 06/15/2015

*This book is dedicated in Loving Memory to my Father, Len;
a man true to his God, his Faith, his Family and his Country.
Teaching by example, he touched more lives than he ever could
have imagined. He was right – Angels do walk among us.*

CONTENTS

America Part 3: Where Do We Go from Here?

INTRODUCTION:
WHILE WE WERE SLEEPING

"One flag, one land, one heart, one hand, one Nation, evermore"

-Oliver Wendell Holmes, 1862

I believe millions of Americans are bewildered and dismayed with the current state of America. Economic crisis, the threat of terrorism, constitutional chaos, political corruption, Obamacare, media and academic bias, political correctness, national security, climate change, failing schools, and foreign relations disasters are issues we are bombarded with on a daily basis. It seems that our "history" is being revised to accommodate political objectives. How did we get to this point? How did it get so bad? Why did things change so drastically since our parents were children? Who is responsible for the current American crisis? **Weren't there any warning signs?**

America is at a crossroads and the road we choose to travel will either restore the spirit of America or continue to change our country forever. We the ordinary citizens must make fundamental decisions. There have been warnings, although muffled by media sources, special interest groups, foreigners, and others, the warning voices **are** growing louder. The voices of genuine concern come from within the United States and from abroad. We Americans need to listen to and take seriously what we are being told. We need to educate ourselves about American history; **real, unbiased history**. We need to know the Constitution, the cornerstone of our country. We need to hold our politicians and government leaders accountable. We need to remind them that they work for us – *The People*.

We need to reestablish our uniquely special identity. To the chagrin of the politically correct, I say America is "exceptional." It is unlike any country in history. Its success, prosperity, growth, standard of living, and its spiritual soul would not have been possible anywhere else or with any other peoples. We are Americans. We are proud and owe no apologies for who we are. We are the most generous people on earth and have done more good worldwide than any country, ever. Alexis de Tocqueville, a French journalist who traveled through America in the early nineteenth century stated, *"America is great because she is good, and if America ever ceases to be good, she will cease to be great."* For the world's sake, America must retain her "goodness." I reject generalized disparagement about America, even from some of our own countrymen. There are and have been legitimate criticisms of American behavior that should be addressed, but we cannot let those issues supplant the factual uprightness of America. And, of course there are fringe groups and guilt-ridden pro-globalists committed to recreating America to fit their global community vision, but most Americans, of diverse beliefs and heritages have a common fundamental belief in the America that was given life with the blood of our forefathers.

So, you say, who is going to fix this? We are – and failure is not an option. Americans have overcome challenges including a revolution, and in the name of liberty established this country; a civil war that nearly ripped this country apart; world wars, natural disasters, recessions, and the Great Depression. We can do it again. We Americans of all races, religions, political affiliations, and economic positions need to band together for the common cause of healing this great nation. It won't be easy; there are many distractions and detractors, but it can and must be done.

To protect this country our ancestors made significant sacrifices and overcame hardships unimaginable to us. No matter the crisis, when they became engaged, they never gave up, and their character and determination are in each of us. They left us a concise history of events that clearly highlight the fact that liberty and freedom must always be protected. The words of our ancestors, immigrants from around the world guide us. The words of our Forefathers are as relevant today as when they were spoken. Words of warning, you might say. Thomas Jefferson warned us when he said, *"Eternal vigilance is the price of liberty."*[1] Theodore Roosevelt warned us by saying, *"The things that will destroy America are prosperity-at-any-price, peace-at-any-price, safety-first instead of duty-first, the love of soft living and the get-rich-quick theory of life."*[2] Ralph Waldo Emerson's words from 1860 reach across time: *"Some men appear to feel they belong to a Pariah caste. They fear to offend, they bend and apologize, and walk through life with a timid step."*[3]

Complacency, appeasement, blind tolerance, and political correctness are historically proven to be temporary and fatal measures only masking problems and prolonging the inevitable. The very problems and threats we do not want to think about grow larger, more complex, and unfortunately, we do not take action until the situation becomes critical. It seems we have become complacent either because we believe

---

[1] *Great Quotes From Great Leaders*, Peggy Anderson, NJ: Career Press, 1997
[2] *American Presidents' Wit and Wisdom*, Edited by Joselyn Pine, New York: Dover Publications, Inc., 2002
[3] *Behavior, The Conduct of Life*, Ralph Waldo Emerson, 1860

we individually cannot have an effect on national events, or think more "qualified" people are taking care of the "important" issues. We have become appeasers paralyzed by political correctness under the guise of tolerance. And, many of us out of frustration have "tuned out" of national involvement purposely quieting our own voices of support and dissent in national issues and events. It is imperative we find our voices and we speak up for our constitutionally guaranteed rights, our fellow citizens, and our country which truly is, as Abraham Lincoln said in 1862, "*the last best hope of earth.*"

"Hope" and "change" are good, but beware the change you hope for. Hope will not unite this country. Hope will not protect us. Hope will not strengthen our economy and create jobs. Hope will not bring peace. Knowledge, cooperation, and action are the tools we must utilize to heal our nation and re-kindle the flame of goodness that has radiated around the globe. Americans must commit to reform on all levels; from our leaders in Washington to the average citizen found in every city and in every county across America. It is time we make our forefathers proud. It is time to get actively involved in our government and our communities. It is time to stand up and defend our rights and the rights of our fellow countrymen. It is time to face reality! We have squandered our freedoms and taken for granted the gifts of this nation. We owe our children a strong vibrant nation, not the shadow of liberty we walk in now. There are things we can do, there are organizations and people we can trust; people committed to America's best interest. If we all join forces, we can heal our country and she will remain the beacon of liberty and freedom.

We need the courage to identify significant problems, and not be distracted by trivial politics. We need the resolve to affect positive change. We cannot continue to be passive about political violations of our Constitution. The purpose of this book is to identify some of the problems plaguing our nation. I am not an idealistic fringe patriot calling for overthrow or impeachment (The current Senate will not even investigate blatant Constitutional breaches and gross mismanagement by administrative officials). I am a realist – a knowledge seeking citizen concerned that our children and grandchildren will never know the greatness of this country we were blessed to inherit.

I see now what is going on around me. I see discontent, uneasiness, and lack of confidence in our leaders. I see America slowly being re-designed into a country that looks nothing like the country our Forefathers gave us. Like many others I "woke up" on September 11, 2001 and realized how little I actually knew about what had been going on in my own country, and in the world around me.

On September 10<u>th</u> 2001:
- I did not know the Muslim Middle East was committed to global destruction.
- I did not know that Islamofascist terrorists had established cells around the globe. I certainly didn't know they were right here in the United States
- I did not know that Muslim centers and schools were sprouting up all over the country and that hatred of America was a core study.
- I did not know that Europe had been sinking into a socialist abyss.
- I did not know people from countries with national health care systems swarmed to the United States for medical care.
- I did not know our borders were so porous that millions of illegal aliens were in the country, and that the future murder of one of our border agents would be "no big deal."
- I did not know how inept our educational system was or how liberal professors have rewritten our history and higher education curriculum.
- I did not know China had easily stolen our nuclear technology and was building up her military strength at an unprecedented rate.
- I did not know the United Nations had totally derailed.
- I did not know that human rights were "selective." Christians were and continue to be massacred in Africa and the Middle East and slavery still exists in places like Sudan and Mauritania.
- I did not know that our Constitution and liberties would be under attack domestically from the very government sworn to protect them.

- I did not ever think that one day my government would be indifferent to and then cover-up the attack of a U.S. Embassy and the deaths of four Americans.
- I also did not ever think that the undeniable terrorist massacre of military personnel inside a U.S. fort would be labeled by the government as "workplace violence."
- I did not know that one of the most powerful U.S. agencies responsible for "revenue," would target specific political and religious groups on a national scale with the blessing of the Executive branch of government. And then that same incompetent agency would be put in charge of enforcing a national health care system.
- I did not know our intelligence community that had been degraded for a decade prior to 9/11 would one day be instructed to spy on American citizens.
- I did not know that all levels of our government, the military, police, and even our educational system were being infiltrated by enemies of America.
- I never would have imagined that a U.S. president would be as arrogant as to blame everyone else for his mistakes and dismiss serious and deadly government blunders as "phony scandals."
- **I certainly did not know that America was eroding morally from the inside out.**

Talk about a reality check! How did I miss all this? I had become complacent, assuming people smarter than I were at the helm guiding our country and keeping it safe. When I heard *Americans* lamenting that **we** must have done something to elicit the 9/11 attacks; that **we** brought this on ourselves; that America's chickens have come home to roost, I woke up. Watching celebrations across the Middle East over the deaths of thousands of people and hearing that this attack was "America's own fault," I became angry and set out on quest of sorts to find answers to these things I did not know. Nothing justifies murdering 3,000 people – nothing! The more I learned, the more I realized the enormity of our situation. We are in serious times with grave consequences.

The following pages identify critical issues. They also identify individuals and organizations committed to the noble preservation of this great nation. The problems we face are not Democrat or Republican; they are not Black or White; and they are not gender-specific; they are American. We have been warned and we are continually being warned. We need to listen and arm ourselves with knowledge.

We need to listen to John Adams, ***"We have been afraid to think... Let us dare to read, think, speak, and write."***[4] Those words spoken by Adams in 1765 are extremely relevant today. We need to unite under the banner of our own Constitution and work together to restore the dignity and the strength of America. Since our government in Washington D.C. cannot or will not protect our nation, it is the duty of all Americans to defend our sacred gifts of independence and freedom.

---

[4] *John Adams*, David McCullough, NY: Touchstone, 2001

America

PART I:
OUR HISTORY AND GOVERNMENT

Old North Bridge, Concord, Massachusetts

April 19, 1775: Site of the "first day of battle" in the war of independence following the deadly skirmish at Lexington earlier that morning. Ralph Waldo Emerson wrote that the American Revolution began here with *"the shot heard 'round the world."*

U.S. History and the Constitution

"I know of no way of judging the future but by the past." — Patrick Henry 1775

The very first thing we 21ˢᵗ century Americans need to do is take a look back to the "beginning" of **The United States of America**. We are all aware of the prominent people, events and the result of the American Revolution, but we need a brief refresher on what our Founding Fathers endured and what they **intended** America to become.

Think about the risks the colonials willingly accepted when they decided to break away from England, the "Mother Country." It was not a decision taken lightly. Colonials, from General George Washington to the lowliest soldier, members of the Constitutional Congress, every businessman, storeowner, and farmer supporting American independence risked all they had for freedom. If the revolution had failed, these people stood to lose everything; some would have even lost their lives. They embraced liberty and willingly accepted the risks. In 1776 as John Hancock summoned the delegates to sign the *Declaration of Independence*, the very founding document of freedom in America, he said, "*we must all hang together,*" to which Benjamin Franklin glibly replied, "*Yes, we must indeed all hang together, or most assuredly, we will hang separately.*"[5] How many people today would willingly accept such risk?

> "*The sacred rights of mankind are not to be rummaged for among old parchments of musty records. They are written, as with a sunbeam, in the whole volume of human nature, by the hand of the divinity itself, and can never be erased.*"
>
> - Alexander Hamilton,
> *The Farmer Refuted* (1775)

These brave and noble people had a clear vision and united purpose. The signers of the Declaration of Independence, the soldiers of the Continental Army, and the framers of our Constitution are our Founding Fathers. They gave us the gifts of freedom, liberty, and self-government. They created a unique country that grew into the envy of the world. These gifts must be cherished, honored and defended lest our great country become common, weak, and irrelevant.

The importance of the *Declaration of Independence* cannot be overstated. Its powerful words changed the history of the world. The Declaration clearly and concisely states that the Thirteen Colonies in union declare "*...that all men are created equal, that they are endowed by their Creator with certain unalienable Rights, that among these are Life, Liberty, and the pursuit of Happiness.*" It declared the individual Colonies, now "United" States had a right to separate from England

---

[5] Delegates gather to sign the *Declaration of Independence*, July 4, 1776. *America The Last Best Hope, Vol. 1*, William J. Bennett, Nashville, TN: Nelson Current, 2006.

and institute a new Government *by the people and for the people*. It specifically lists unaddressed grievances against the government of England. In conclusion, the Declaration of Independence declared the United States of America as an independent country, *"And for the support of this Declaration, with a firm reliance on the protection of Divine Providence, **we mutually pledge to each other our Lives, our Fortunes, and our Sacred Honor."***[6]

With these compelling words, "America" was born and would pay a high price in treasure and blood for having the audacity to believe that government derives its power from the consent of the governed. With the Declaration of Independence, Americans declared to the world that man's law must be based on a higher moral order – natural law also known as divine law.

The Revolutionary War 1775-1781

The Revolutionary War officially began on April 19, 1775 with the first shot fired at Lexington, Massachusetts. The war lasted six and a half years, ending on October 19, 1781 with the British surrender to General Washington at Yorktown, Virginia. It was a long and difficult struggle ending with the unimaginable – a new and free country.

Keep in mind, the colonists with a new, ill-equipped and inexperienced army supported by untrained and undisciplined civilian militias confronted the most powerful nation on earth. England had the world's most advanced navy and a well-funded professional army led by seasoned officers. What England did not have was an understanding of the "American spirit;" the determination to do right, to embrace liberty, to be successful, and to give future generations a better life, even at the expense of their own.

General George Washington addressed colonial troops around Boston in 1775: *"They are now the troops of the United Provinces of North America; that all the distinction of colonies will be laid aside, so that one and same spirit may animate the whole and the only contest be, who shall*

---

[6] *The Unanimous Declaration of the Thirteen United States of America*, July 4, 1776

render on this great and trying occasion the most essential service to the great and common course in which we are all engaged."[7]

The Colonials endured numerous defeats. Some faltered under the stress, but as a whole they never lost hope or faith in the righteousness of their cause. Imagine what many soldiers in the Continental Army experienced during the war: Old equipment, no ammunition, meager rations, starvation, sickness, ragged flea and tick infested clothing, worn-out shoes and in some cases, no shoes at all. Many soldiers only had canvas and burlap to wrap around their feet. For a clearer understanding of the miserable living conditions of the colonial soldiers, visit Valley Forge National Historic Park in eastern Pennsylvania to see first-hand how 11,000 continental soldiers survived the brutally cold winter of 1777-78.

Thomas Paine (*"These are the Times that try men's souls"*) wrote a series of articles during the Revolutionary War period. The collection of sixteen essays written between 1776 and 1783 expound Paine's resolute support for an independent and self-governing country. The first essay was read to Washington's troops at Valley Forge.

General Washington, whose leadership was a key factor to the success of the war for independence, was supported by officers and non-military men whose dedication and valor should not be forgotten. One of those men was General Nathanael Greene who played a major role in many battles and was appointed Quartermaster-General in March 1778 after the harsh winter at Valley Forge. Greene successfully pressured Congress for funds to purchase supplies and his efforts greatly improved living conditions for the soldiers. Robert Morris' commitment to the cause of freedom was so strong that he paid the American army payroll from his own funds on the eve of the great battle at Princeton, New Jersey in 1776.

Another was Ethan Allen who led a band of soldiers, *The Green Mountain Boys* from Vermont. They along with other colonials seized British forts at Ticonderoga and Crown Point in New York. The Ticonderoga National Historic Landmark (Fort and Museum) has been restored to its majestic 18th century appearance when it was a bastion

---

[7] "Washington's address to the troops, 1775." *Epochs of Modern History, The War of American Independence*, J.M. Ludlow, London: Longmans, Green, and Co., 1877

in the wilderness. A family trip to the fort is educational as well as "awesome."

John Paul Jones was a vibrant and dedicated officer in the infant United States Navy who executed daring raids on the British coast. He is famous for saying, *"I have not yet begun to fight!"* during a heated battle while his ship the *Bonhomme Richard* was on fire and taking on water. Jones also said, *"I wish to have no connection with any ship that does not sail fast for I intend to go in harm's way."* His valor is commendable. The list of patriots is long. Two more heroes are Dr. Joseph Warren and Daniel Morgan. General Warren was a popular Boston doctor who administered medical treatment to the injured at Lexington. Against the advice of his commanding officer, he chose to fight alongside the other Colonials at Breeds Hill. Warren was the first Colonial officer killed during the war. Daniel Morgan was a brilliant commander who fought valiantly throughout the war. His victory over Lieutenant-Colonel Banastre Tarleton at Cowpens, South Carolina in 1781 was a stunning example of his tactical prowess.

The concept of liberty and self-government and the determination of the American people to be free reached across the Atlantic and into the heart of Europe. Marquis de Lafayette, a very young and wealthy French nobleman was smitten with the "American cause" in 1775 after listening to the English Duke of Gloucester's sympathetic description of the American effort. Lafayette arrived in America in June 1777 to volunteer his services to General Washington without the approval or support of the king of France. Washington commissioned him a Major General and the two men established a life-long friendship. Lafayette returned to France and worked diligently to garnish French support for the war. When the French government finally approved military and financial support for the "United States," Lafayette returned to America in 1780 with French troops to assist General Washington and the colonials. His devotion to Washington, the American people and the concept of representative government were vital contributions to our new country.

Another foreigner who contributed significantly to the cause of American freedom was Baron Von Stueben, an experienced General Staff member in the Prussian Army. His endorsement by the

French Minister of War to Benjamin Franklin resulted in a letter of recommendation that slightly exaggerated Von Steuben's credentials to General Washington by identifying him as a Lieutenant General in the service of the Prussian King. What was not an exaggeration was Von Steuben's military knowledge that would turn the American Army into a victorious force. Von Steuben's system of training, drilling, battle protocol and sanitation turned the undisciplined Colonial Army into a well-trained and dependable fighting force. There is an interesting little book titled, "**Baron von Steuben's Revolutionary War Manual: A Facsimile Reprint of the 1794 Edition,** Frederick William Baron von Steuben published by Dover Publications, New York, 1985. You can read the Baron's actual instructions and training plan for the Continental Army.

Polish General Casimir Pulaski met Benjamin Franklin in Paris and enthusiastically volunteered to fight for America in the War of Independence. Pulaski was commissioned as Brigadier General of the American Cavalry and his valiant performance during the war earned him the title of "Father of the American Cavalry." General Pulaski was mortally wounded during the campaign to recapture Savannah in 1779. His contributions to the war effort and the ultimate sacrifice of his own life for <u>our</u> independence should never be forgotten. I wonder how many students off from school and adults off from work every year on the federal holiday of Casimir Pulaski Day even know who he was and why he is commemorated.

Approximately 217,000 Colonials served during the Revolutionary War. 4,435 gave their lives and 6,188 were wounded though other sources cite the number at 7,148 and even higher.[8] These numbers may seem small, but the population of the Thirteen Colonies was only 2.5 million people, which was even less than the 2012 population of Chicago,

---

[8] United States war casualties – Revolutionary War. http://www. americanfamilytraditions.com/war_casualties.htm
American War and Military Operations Casualties: Lists and Statistics, The Navy Department Library
Congressional Research Service Report for Congress, 7/13/2005, http://www. history.navy.mil/library/online. Sons of the American Revolution, http://www. revolutionarywararchives.org/warstats.html.

Illinois estimated by the U.S. Census Bureau to be 2,714,856.[9] Many are distinguished heroes, yet all were patriots deserving of our honor and gratitude. Their blood and sacrifice gave our country life.

The Freedom Trail in Boston, Massachusetts is a wonderful way to walk through the history of the Revolutionary period in America. Boston was a "hotbed" of activity and agitation prior to and throughout the war. The trail takes you to important historical sites including old meeting houses, churches, and cemeteries. Museums and historical markers bring our Forefathers to life with the story of the revolution.[10]

While Boston was the heart of the revolution, Philadelphia, Pennsylvania was its soul. The "Historic District" is like a 'time machine" allowing you to walk in the footsteps of our Founders. **Independence National Historical Park** encompasses: Independence Hall, Congress Hall, the National Constitution Center, the Liberty Bell, Franklin Institute, and many other historical buildings, museums, monuments, and parks all celebrating freedom and the founding of this great nation.

The Articles of Confederation: 1777

The Second Constitutional Convention drafted *The Articles of Confederation* in 1777 which was ratified by all thirteen States in 1781. The Articles of Confederation were in effect our "first" Constitution. The purpose of the Articles was unification of the thirteen sovereign Colonies – now officially named in Article One as *"The United States of America."* It was basically a wartime alliance containing thirteen Articles that united the separate states into a single voice and force for freedom and independence. There was no president, the federal government was weak and had no power to tax. The federal government had to "ask" the states for money. The states retained sovereign authority except in matters of national interest such as treaties or negotiations

---

[9] Population of Chicago, Illinois 2012, US Census Bureau State & County Quick Facts.
http://quickfacts.census.gov/qfd/states/17/1714000.html
[10] The Freedom Trail, Boston, MA. The Freedom Trail Foundation: http://www.thefreedomtrail.org

with other countries and war. One paragraph of Article IX states, "...*The United States in Congress assembled shall never engage in a war, nor grant letters of marquee or reprisal in time of peace, nor enter into any treaties or alliances, nor coin money, nor regulate the value thereof, nor ascertain the sums and expenses necessary for the defense and welfare of the United States, or any of them, nor emit bills, nor borrow money on the credit of the United States, nor appropriate money, nor agree upon the number of vessels of war, to be built or purchased, or the number of land or sea forces to be raised, nor appoint a commander in chief of the army or navy, unless nine States assent to the same: nor shall a question on any other point, except for adjourning from day to day be determined, unless by the votes of the majority of the United States in Congress assembled...*"[11]

Remarkably, Article XI provided authorization for Canada to join the United States if so desired and be granted full rights provided by the Articles. Why, you ask would the United States invite Canada to join the Union? Simply put, to undermine British authority in Canada and ensure the end of British presence in North America.

The Articles of Confederation is the foundation of the Constitution. It is a relatively short document and well worth reading.

1787 - *The Constitution*

> **WE THE PEOPLE of the United States, in order to form a more perfect Union, establish Justice, insure domestic Tranquility, provide for the common defense, promote the general Welfare, and secure the Blessings of Liberty to ourselves and our Posterity, do ordain and establish this Constitution for the United States of America.**
>
> Preamble - *The Constitution of the United States*

With independence won, the Founders' task at hand in 1787 was to create a new, effective, and lasting form of **government of the people,**

---

[11] *The Articles of Confederation*, [of the United States of America], November 15,1777; ratified March 1, 1781

for the people, and by the people. The Framers of the Constitution set out to improve the government created by the Articles of Confederation. They created the Constitution around the goals stated in the Preamble: **Justice, domestic peace, common defense, general welfare, and the "Blessings of Liberty," not just for their generation but for all posterity.**

Critics like to claim that the Founders were wealthy men whose priorities were personal financial interests. Many were wealthy men, but it is important to remember that the Founders were men from a broad field of financial, educational, and professional backgrounds. Most of them were "gentlemen," well-mannered men who valued honor, valor, duty and charity. The Founders were well educated in domestic and international matters. Colonial America had a high literacy rate; education was embraced and books were treasured. Americans knew the history of England including the British monarchy, and political, religious, and civil strife. They were familiar with France and Spain and their respective histories as well as the history of the ancient world. They knew that Rome established a great empire that replaced the Roman Republic, but by doing so they lost their "liberties" and eventually their empire. They considered Rome not just a great example, but also a great warning.

All but three of the Framers were Christians though no reference to Christianity is made in the Constitution. That was by design. The Framers' intent was not to establish a "civil" religion. Their intent was to create a practical mechanism of government not prejudiced to any particular Christian religious denomination. The United States Constitution is the result of the merger of common (man-made) law and natural (Divine) law. There was no need to identify or detail natural law in the Constitution. Natural law was "a given," meaning natural law had guided man's ethical, moral, and responsible personal behavior throughout history. There is no way around the fact that the Constitution of the United States of America was created from Judeo-Christian principles and those very principles define our laws. Since natural law was an intrinsic part of the Framers' lives, as well as most Americans' their focus was on defining common (civil) law.

The Founding intent was to keep religion out of politics NOT out of public life. For example, President George Washington's 1789 "Thanksgiving Proclamation" established a National Day of

Thanksgiving advocated by the Congress and the public. He instituted November 26 as a day *"to be devoted by the people of these States to the service of that great and glorious Being who is the beneficent author of all the good that was, that is, and what will be; that we may then all unite in rendering unto Him our sincere and humble thanks for His kind care and protection of the people of this country previous to their becoming a nation; for the signal and manifold mercies and the favorable interpositions of His providence in the course and conclusion of the late war; for the great degree of tranquility, union, and plenty which we since enjoyed...we may then unite in most humbly offering our prayers and supplications to the great Lord and Ruler of Nations and beseech Him to pardon our national and other transgressions...to enable us all, whether in public or private stations, to perform our several and relative duties properly and punctually; to render our National Government a blessing to all the people by constantly being a Government of wise, just, and constitutional laws, discreetly and faithfully executed and obeyed..."[12]* Does that sound like the total and paranoid "separation of church and state" that we now have?

The Declaration of Independence, the Articles of Confederation, and the Constitution form a complete treatise on free government. The Constitution was written to support the Declaration of Independence which was the theoretical basis of a government whose power comes **only** from the consent of the governed. The Constitution brought the philosophy of self-government to life by defining government structure, organization, and operation consistent with the principles of liberty as stated in the Declaration of Independence. This new government structure would become the cornerstone of a great nation. It would be powerful enough to guarantee the nation's future, yet not powerful enough to threaten the liberties of its people. Richard Brookhiser captured the Founders mindset in his book, *What Would the Founders Do? "The founders also knew that lists of rights were not enough. If the structure of government was not well designed, liberty would be undermined by politicians, overwhelmed by popular opinion, or lost in*

---

[12] "General Thanksgiving by the President of the United States of America, A Proclamation," George Washington, *The Massachusetts Sentinel*, Wednesday, October 4, 1789

chaos. Where liberty and law were concerned, the how was as important as the what."[13]

"Consent" of the governed included relinquishing a "portion" of their sovereignty to the government for the benefit of those governed – not the government's benefit. In a speech by Professor Edward J. Erier at a Hillsdale College National Leadership Seminar he explained this historic political principle. *"The fact that only a portion of sovereignty is ceded by the people is the origin of the idea of limited government. The people delegate only some of their sovereignty to government, and what is not granted is retained by the people..."[14]*

It is extremely important to remember that our government is a "Republic" <u>not</u> a "Democracy," though it is often described as a Democratic Republic. The Founders clearly referred to the founding of our government as a Republic. A Republic is representative government ruled by established law that recognizes and protects individual "inalienable" rights. A Democracy is direct government ruled exclusively by the majority and focuses exclusively on the will of that majority.

The differences between a Republic and a Democracy:

REPUBLIC	DEMOCRACY
Citizens <u>elect representatives</u> to govern and make decisions on their behalf	Citizens are involved in <u>ALL</u> <u>decisions</u>
Government of established set of laws	Government of majority rules
Individual and property rights are protected	Individual and property rights are not protected
Prevents tyranny and mob rule	Promotes mob rule, unrest and even violence
Best form of government for countries with large diverse populations - like the U.S.	Does not work in large countries with diverse populations - only works in small communities

[13] "What Would the Founders Do?" Richard Brookhiser, NY: Basic Books, 2006
[14] "The Constitution and Limited Government," Edward J. Erier, Professor of Political Science, California State University, September, 2011

Russell Kirk in his book, **Rights and Duties: Reflections on Our Conservative Constitution** makes a point to note that the Declaration of Independence and the Constitution *"were drawn up under different circumstances for quite different purposes: the first in the enthusiasm of revolution, the second in the restoration of order, and the men of 1787 were not the men of 1776."* The men who wrote the Constitution had lived the revolution and had centuries of English history and world government to draw upon.[15]

The Constitution consists of the original 1787 document and its amendments. The first ten amendments ratified December 15, 1791 are identified as the *Bill of Rights*. The Constitution specifically details government function and power. It provides checks and balances so no group or part of government can overwhelm any other part. It clearly separates government power into three distinct branches of government; the executive, the legislative, and the judicial. The Constitution explicitly defines the power and limits of power of each branch. The Framers worked diligently to ensure that this government would be honorable, just, and protect its citizens from threats, foreign, and domestic.

A crucial yet sometimes overlooked attribute of the Constitution is its "designed" ability to adapt; allow for changes without diminishing its core components. Amendments are added to the Constitution when necessary, <u>not</u> in place of it. The Framers wrote the Constitution with us, the future generations in mind.

The Constitution gives us a government chosen by the people. The "voice of the people" is expressed through elections. WE elect our representatives, and WE have the power <u>not</u> to re-elect representatives who do not measure up to our expectations or who take their positions for granted. The Constitution addresses the election, roles and limits of power of the president, vice president, and congress. It clearly defines how laws are to be created and gives no state power over another. It addresses taxes, the military, freedom of religion and speech, gun ownership, the court system, and the right for a speedy trial with an impartial jury.

---

[15] *Rights and Duties: Reflections on Our Conservative Constitution*, Russell Kirk, Dallas, TX: Spence Publishing Co., 1997

- **Article I** established "legislative powers" creating the Congress consisting of the Senate and House of Representatives, and defined the requirements, roles, and limits of power. Congressional authority among other topics included: Spending, commerce, naturalization, military support, and appropriations. Article I called for the creation of the District of Columbia to be the seat of government of the United States. It addressed titles of nobility, and set limits on States' rights.

- **Article II** established "executive power" defining the requirements, role, and responsibilities of the President including the title of "Commander In Chief" of the Army and Navy. It also instituted the Presidential Oath of Office which every President promises to uphold upon entering office. The oath affirms, *"I do solemnly swear that I will faithfully execute the Office of President of the United States, and will to the best of my Ability, preserve, protect, and defend the Constitution of the United States."*

- **Article III** established "judicial power" consisting of one Supreme Court and inferior courts. The role of judges is to apply the laws passed by Congress, not to make or alter laws. It also addressed "trial by jury" and defined treason: *"Treason against the United States, shall consist only in levying War against them, or in adhering to their Enemies, giving them Aid and Comfort."*

- **Article IV** makes it clear that citizens of each state are entitled to all "Privileges and Immunities" as citizens of the other states. It outlines the admission of states into the Union. And, it guarantees every State of the Union a Republican form of Government and the promise of protection from invasion.

- **Article V** is extremely important. It provides procedures for amending the Constitution – to continually improve it. [Not to diminish it]

- **Article VI** confirms the Constitution and the future laws empowered by it are the "Supreme Law of the Land." Federal Senators and Representatives as well as the State Legislators, and all executive and judicial officers of the United States and the individual States are **bound by oath to support this Constitution**.

During the temporary partial federal government shutdown in October 2013, it became evident how constitutionally illiterate some of our Congressional Representatives really are. For example:

◦ Representative David Scott spoke to the House explaining why they needed to end the shutdown: "*We take a solemn oath here to defend the federal government, to support the federal government, to uphold the federal government.*"[16] Mr. Scott, there is NO oath to defend and support the *federal government*. Your oath was to defend and support the Constitution. The federal government does not exist outside of the Constitution.

◦ Similarly Representative Barney Frank said "*government is simply the name we give to the things we choose to do together.*" How do you even respond to such a silly statement?

It is appalling to me that elected officials representing us in government do not even know the Constitution.

- **Article VII** identifies the signers and ratifies the Constitution.

The first Ten Amendments (**The Bill of Rights**) were added to the Constitution and ratified in 1791. Summary of the Bill of Rights:

- Amendment I guarantees the freedom of religion (and "the free exercise of"), freedom of the press, freedom of speech, the right to assemble, and the right to petition the government with grievances.
- Amendment II guarantees the right to bear arms, and sustain a "well regulated" militia.

---

[16] "I Solemnly Swear to Support the Government?" Rich Tucker, The Foundry – The Heritage Foundation, http://blog.heritage.org, November 7, 2013

- Amendment III forbids soldiers from being stationed in private homes without consent of the owner. Quartering soldiers in homes was a common practice of the British.
- Amendment IV protects people from unreasonable search and seizure of their property. A warrant based on "probable cause" must be issued.
- Amendment V establishes that with the exception of military personnel, a person accused of a capital crime must be indicted by a Grand Jury, no one can be tried for the same crime twice, no one can be a witness against himself, no one can be "deprived of life, liberty, or property, without due process of law," and private property cannot be taken for public use without "just" compensation.
- Amendment VI addresses criminal prosecutions: the right to a speedy trial by an impartial jury (in the state and district where the crime was committed), and the right to legal counsel (lawyer).
- Amendment VII guarantees trial by jury in common law suits
- Amendment VIII forbids excessive bail, fines, and "cruel and unusual punishment."
- Amendment IX though seemingly vague, is interesting. It states: ***The enumeration in the Constitution, of certain rights, shall not be construed to deny or disparage others retained by the people***. It tells us that **other rights though not specifically listed do exist.** And even though they are not listed, they can still be violated. I believe the Framers' vague language purposely left the door open for future discussion and amendment as evidenced by the subsequent Amendments.
- Amendment X states, ***"The powers not delegated to the United States, by the Constitution, nor prohibited by it to the states, are reserved to the states respectively, or to the people."*** Amendment X clearly puts the power of government in the hands of the people of the States – not a large, over-extended federal government.

Together the Ninth and Tenth Amendments are the Constitutional Sphinxes guarding our government. James Madison who drafted the Ninth Amendment explained the purpose [intent] of these two amendments. The main purpose of the Ninth was to "guard against latitude of interpretation," while the main purpose of the tenth "exclude[d] every source of power not within the constitution itself." Madison saw the need to protect the Constitution and its amendments from liberal and judicial interpretation in opposition to the framers "intent."

When you read the *United States Constitution*, you will notice there is no mention of a "wall of separation" between church and state. That is because there is no "wall of separation" language in any government document. The "wall" that twentieth century progressives and critics cling to is from a letter Thomas Jefferson wrote to the Danbury Baptist Association in 1802. "*I contemplate with sovereign reverence that act of the whole American people which declared that their legislature should make no law respecting an establishment of religion, or prohibiting the free exercise thereof, thus building a wall of separation between church and state.*" An interesting footnote to the "wall" argument is that critics only recite the "*legislature should make no law respecting an establishment of religion,*" part of Jefferson's letter. They regularly omit the remainder of the sentence: "***or prohibiting the free exercise thereof.***" Supreme Court Chief Justice William Rehnquist has said, "*The 'wall of separation between church and state' is a metaphor based on bad history, a metaphor which has proved useless as a guide to judging. It should be frankly and explicitly abandoned.*"[17]

Even though religion is not a focal point in the Constitution except for the guaranteed freedom of it, make no mistake the Christian religion was the source of our Constitution and the laws that sprang from it. With regard to the Founders, Benjamin F. Morris said, "*They had no state church or state religion, but they constituted the Christian religion, the underlying foundation and the guiding element of their systems of*

---

[17] "Separation Rooted in Jefferson," The *Daily Southtown*, Tuesday, February 13, 2007 [Chicago area newspaper article]

civil, political, and social institutions."[18] Founding Father John Adams, signer of the Declaration of Independence, First Vice President and second President of the United States said, "*...Religion and virtue are the only foundations, not only of republicanism and of all free governments, but of social felicity under all governments and in the combinations of human society. Science, liberty, and religion are the choicest blessings of humanity: without their joint influence no society can be great, flourishing, or happy.*" The words of John Adams as well as all the Founders and our nation's early Supreme Court Justices and Constitutional jurists are among an epic compilation of records and speeches of our Founders and political geniuses from the birth of our nation through the mid-nineteenth century can be found in a book written by Benjamin F. Morris. Morris' book, "**The Christian Life and Character of the Civil Institutions of the United States,**" originally published in 1864 provides clear evidence of the role of Christianity in the lives of our Founding Fathers and its undeniable role in the Constitution and laws of this nation.

Daniel Webster (1782-1852) is known as "the Defender of the Constitution." He was a Constitutional lawyer, U.S. Senator, Secretary of State, and an avid reader with the remarkable ability to memorize and recite what he had read. Webster was also a sincere and outspoken Christian who recognized there was no conflict between the United States government and religion. Freedom of religion is a constitutional liberty and "*God grants liberty only to those who love it, and are always ready to guard and defend it.*" He wanted to be remembered for being a good man, not a good lawyer or politician as evidenced by the words on his tombstone: "*He was a believer in Jesus.*"

Political philosopher, Russell Kirk provides a clear definition of *Constitution*: "*In politics, constitution signifies a system of fundamental institutions and principles, a body of basic laws...a design for permanent political order.*" Mr. Kirk clearly explains the purpose and aims of a constitution this way: "*The aim of a good constitution is to achieve in a society a high degree of political harmony, so that order and justice and*

---

[18] "The Christian Life and Character of the Civil Institutions of the United States," Benjamin F. Morris, 1864, re-published 2008 by American Visions, Inc., Powder Springs, GA

freedom may be maintained. No commonwealth ever has attained perfect order, justice, and freedom for everybody, and the Framers did not expect to achieve perfection of human nature or government. They did expect "to form a more perfect union" and to exceed other nations of their time, and of earlier eras, in establishing a good political order."[19]

To put our American Constitution in a modern perspective, Mr. Kirk noted that most European countries' constitutions that were created after the First World War were destroyed by the end of World War II. The majority of the constitutions created after the Second World War in Europe, Asia and Africa no longer exist or just marginally function. The United States' exceptional Constitution has been upheld for well over two hundred years.

It is interesting to notice that though a Presidential Oath of Office was written into the Constitution (Article II), there was no oath for Congress. In 1862 legislation was passed requiring that everyone elected to office (any office) swear an oath of loyalty to the United States. The oath was revised in 1884 and remains in effect today: ***"I do solemnly swear that I will support and defend the Constitution of the United States against all enemies, foreign and domestic; that I will bear true faith and allegiance to the same; that I take this obligation freely, without any mental reservation or purpose of evasion; and that I will well and faithfully discharge the duties of the office on which I am about to enter: So help me God."***

I find it curious how the meaning of one simple phrase, ***'high crimes and misdemeanors,"*** has changed over time. When we read the phrase we immediately envision serious criminal activity such as treason. The language, "high crimes and misdemeanors" presented in the Constitution was a well-known phrase in English common law meaning misbehavior, misconduct, or transgression. The Founders believed other offenses such as incompetence, neglect, malevolence, and personal bad behavior were reasons for impeachment as well as crimes of treason and bribery. The Office of the President of the United States deserved respect and the president himself was to be held to the highest standard of respectable behavior.

---

[19] "Rights and Duties: Reflections on Our Conservative Constitution," Russell Kirk, Dallas, TX: Spence Publishing Co., 1997

The Constitution of the United States of America should be a reference manual in every home. Many people do not realize the power contained in its pages. It is the "citizen's guide" to the United States and though written over two hundred and twenty years ago is as significant and powerful today as it was when it was written. Copies of the **Constitution of the United States of America** are readily available in book, pamphlet, and on line.

Another essential book on the Constitution, the Founders' intent, and the principles of freedom is, **A Miracle That Changed the World: The 5000 Year Leap – Principles of Freedom 101,** by W. Cleon Skousen, published by the National Center for Constitutional Studies, 1981 (14th Printing 2006). It is an extremely well documented book in which the author clearly explains the Constitution and the principles of freedom that support it with the Founder's own words. The Founders were not trapped inside 18th century ideals; they addressed issues and provided warnings about the very issues we face today including deficit spending, transfer of wealth, overstepping Constitutional power, and abuses of power. Mr. Skousen's book should be read in every school and every home.

I strongly urge you to revisit our early history. You will find there were numerous reasons for discontent in the Colonies prior to the Declaration of Independence. Our military history had humble yet triumphant beginnings and has grown into the finest military force the world has ever seen. The delegates to the Constitutional Conventions had various backgrounds, ideas, and contributions. They researched, debated, and argued before establishing the United States Constitution, a document they knew would change history.

The National Archives in Washington D.C. is a museum of living history. The documents housed there are tangible pieces of our history. Documents and materials spanning the life of the United States can be viewed online at their website: www.archives.gov. The **Smithsonian National Museum of American History**, also in Washington, D.C. compliments the National Archives with a fine collection of American artifacts and documents. The museum's website is http://americanhistory. si.edu. **The Library of Congress** website, http://www.loc.gov houses a wealth of information.

The United States Government Manual, published by the Office of the Federal Register National Archives and records Administration [ISBN 978-0-16-079821-4] is an informative reference manual containing the Declaration of Independence and the Constitution. It plainly explains the branches of government and clarification of how our laws are made.

There are books that focus specifically on the Constitution that are well worth reading. An overlooked book, which I think should be part of every American History curriculum is, **Rights and Duties**, by Russell Kirk. It is an examination of the Constitution and its conservative purpose; "conservative" purpose meaning basic law preserves political order through time and change. "Framers Intent" of Constitutional meaning remains an ongoing debate and the following books are principal sources on Framers Intent, <u>not</u> what some people think the intent should be:

- *The Federalist* is a compilation of 85 newspapers essays written by Alexander Hamilton, James Madison and John Jay in 1787-1788 promoting the then proposed Constitution. It is the most comprehensive political argument for republican government and is key to understanding the Framer's "intent."
- *Blackstone's Commentaries of the Federal Government of the United States*, by St. George Tucker [Professor of law, University of William and Mary], Philadelphia: William Young Birch, and Abraham Small, 1803
- *Commentaries on American Law,* James Kent, New York: O. Halsted, 1826
- *Commentaries on the Constitution of the United States,* Joseph Story [Dane Professor of Law-Harvard University], Boston: Hilliard, Gray and Company, 1833
- *A Familiar Exposition of the Constitution of the United States [1847]* by Joseph Story, General Books, LLC, 2009, [First published 1847]
- *The Christian Life and Character of the Civil Institutions of the United States, Benjamin F. Morris [1864],* Georgia: American Vision, Sixth Printing April 2008

- *What Would the Founders Do?* By Richard Brookhiser, New York: Basic Books, 2007. A great read! Mr. Brookhiser asks currently relevant questions, to which the answers are clearly found in the Constitution itself.
- *A Miracle That Changed the World: The 5000 Year Leap – Principles of Freedom 101*, W. Cleon Skousen, The National Center for Constitutional Studies, Fifteenth Printing, April 2009 [http://www.nccs.net]
- *The Citizen's Constitution,* Seth Lipsky, New York: Basic Books, 2009
- *The Heritage Guide To The Constitution,* **The Heritage Foundation,** Edwin Meese III, David F. Forte, Mathew Spalding, Washington DC: Regnery Publishing, Inc., 2005
- *The U.S. Constitution: A Reader,* Edited by the Hillsdale College Politics Faculty, Hillsdale, Michigan: Hillsdale College Press, 2012
- *The Debate on the Constitution*, Two-volume set: Federalist and Antifederalist speeches, articles and letters from September 1787 to August 1788 for state ratification of the Constitution, The Library of America, Library of Congress catalog number: 92-25449

Some of <u>many</u> thought-provoking books on the Colonial Period and general American History that I recommend include:

- *America The Last Best Hope Volume I: From the Age of Discovery To a World at War* by William J. Bennett, Nashville: Nelson Current, 2006
- *The Unfinished Nation: A Concise History of the American People* by Alan Brinkley, New York: McGraw Hill, 2004
- **What's So Great About America**, by Dinesh D'Souza, New York: Penguin Group, 2003
- *The Politically Incorrect Guide to American History* by Thomas E. Woods, Jr., Ph.D., Washington DC: Regnery Publishing, Inc., 2004

- *The Politically Incorrect Guide to The Founding Fathers,* Brion McClanahan, Ph.D., Washington DC: Regnery Publishing, Inc., 2009
- *To The Best of My Ability: The American Presidents* by James M. McPherson, New York: DK Publishing, 2002
- *Life of Washington,* Anna C. Reed, [Originally published in 1842 by ASSU], AR: Attic Books, First Printing, November 2009
- *1776,* David McCullough, New York: Simon & Schuster, 2005
- *John Adams,* David McCullough, New York: Touchstone, 2001
- *The American Crisis: December 23, 1776,* Thomas Paine, Collection of articles and essays written by Paine during the American Revolution, 1776-1783. (The entire 16-set of pamphlets is available at www.ushistory.org/Paine/crisis/index.htm
- *Tocqueville On American Character: Why Tocqueville's Brilliant Exploration of the American Spirit Is as Vital Today as it was Nearly Two Hundred Years Ago,* Michael A. Ledeen, New York, Truman Talley Books St. Martin's Press, 2000
- *American Courage,* edited by Herbert W. Warden III, New York: William Morrow (An Imprint of HarperCollins Publishers) 2005
- *Presidential Courage: Brave Leaders and how they Changed America 1789-1989,* Michael Beschloss, New York: Simon & Schuster, 2007
- *The Pictorial Life of George Washington*, John Frost, Philadelphia: Leary and Getz, 1859, History of the Seven Years War, The Revolutionary War, The Constitution, and George Washington's presidency. Published: West VA: White Hall Press, Georgia: American Vision Press, 2009
- *Common Sense*, Thomas Paine, 1776, New York: Barnes & Noble edition, 1995
- *Rights of Man*, Thomas Paine, 1791, New York: Dover Publications, 1999
- *Everyday Life in Early America*, David Freeman Hawke, New York: Harper Collins Publishers, 1988

Learn Our History: Take Pride in America's Past is a wonderful and fun DVD set for students and young readers. The series *"Motivates your children to learn U.S. history."* It presents real historical facts without bias proving that American pride is warranted. *Hero Tales from American History*, written by Theodore Roosevelt and Henry Cabot Lodge and published in 1895, is a collection of American hero stories recounted with enthusiasm and patriotism. The book was re-released by White Hall Press in 2002.

Russell Kirk provides us with a great example of why history is important. The American Revolution was nothing like the French or Russian Revolutions. The purpose of the American Revolution was to *recover what was lost*, meaning restoration and improvement of the rights and liberties of Americans, descendants of free Englishmen to govern themselves in their colonies. On the other hand, the French and Russian Revolutions purposely destroyed the fabric of their societies. Entire classes of people were eliminated for the common good. In Russell's own words: *"The history of this slippery word revolution is a case in point...If one is ignorant of those historical origins – if even powerful statesmen are ignorant of them – great errors become possible. It is as if one were to confound the word law as a term of jurisprudence with the word law as a term of natural science. If one assumes that the word revolution signifies always the same phenomenon, regardless of historical background, one may make miscalculation with grave consequences – perhaps fatal consequences."*[20]

"Freedom is not something to be secured in any one moment of time. We must struggle to preserve it every day. And freedom is never more than one generation away from extinction." We would be wise to remember those words spoken by President Ronald Reagan. When you know the history of your country – your home, it is easier to assess current events and make better decisions. I know people who say, "History is boring," "Look to the future, not the past," and "I prefer to focus on the present." All are excuses for not taking the initiative to seek the truth, thus abandoning their responsibility to know what is going on here in America and around the world.

---

[20] *"Rights and Duties: Reflections on Our Conservative Constitution,"* Russell Kirk, Dallas, TX: Spence Publishing Co., 1997

Our history is not hidden away in dark library cellars. **Our history is very much alive!** Our history is not just found in Washington, D.C., Philadelphia, Boston, Jamestown, Plymouth, New York, Charleston, St. Augustine, and the East Coast. It spans this nation from north to south and east to west, and is there for all who care to see. Look about you – our history is in every state, city, and town across America. When you know our "American" history, you can understand why America is exceptional and truly is the greatest nation on earth.

OUR CURRENT
CONSTITUTIONAL CRISIS

"The Constitution is not an instrument for the government to restrain the people. It is an instrument for the people to restrain the government – lest it come to dominate our lives and interests."

-Patrick Henry

Though our Constitution provides for amendments (additions to improve – <u>not</u> diminish the rights established in the document), the core principles of our Constitution also known as "self-evident truths," are permanent. They were established to endure as long as the United States of America exists. Without its basic principles including rights, roles and limits of government, national and personal security, freedom of speech and religion, and the clear requisite that officers of the government protect and defend these principles, the Constitution is meaningless. Our Constitution is not a "cut and paste" document.

Article II of the Constitution clearly defines the role, responsibility and <u>limits of power</u> of the president. The 21st century has seen an unprecedented expansion of executive power in violation of Article II under President George W. Bush and an explosion of comprehensive executive power under President Barack Obama who pledged, more than once, *"If Congress refuses to act; I'll do everything in my power to act without them."* President Obama abuses his "Executive Power" through Executive Actions also known as Executive Orders to institute laws and regulations that only Congress can legally enact. For example, he has decided not to enforce established immigrations laws and has altered Affordable Care Act laws at will. These are violations of his Constitutional authority and though the House challenges him on them, the Senate takes no action (which makes the Senate complicit in the abuse).

Jonathan Turley, law professor and Obama supporter testified at a House Judiciary Committee hearing: *"The problem of what the president is doing is that he is not simply posing a danger to the constitutional system; he is becoming the very danger the Constitution was designed to avoid: that is, the concentration of power in any single branch."*[21] This is a very clear and present danger.

Our Founding Fathers believed that a people's government is a voluntary contract between citizens who elect leaders to make and enforce laws for the common good. **The federal government's responsibility is to secure freedom, administer civil and criminal law, and provide national defense, period**. They also believed that laws not affecting the nation as a whole should be made regionally by locally elected officials who could then be held accountable to the local citizenry. Since all federal laws are not appropriate to all people, under this premise, laws

---

[21] "Obama's end-runs around Congress spark bipartisan criticism," Shannon Bream, Fox News, http://foxnews.com, December 5, 2013

would be written with specific purpose and effectual to the particular people and areas (states, counties, cities) they affect. Enforcement is more effective since it is at a local level with the oversight of the people who are directly affected by it. The Founders understood that in the operation of government, there is a distinct difference between a "federal" and a "national" government. A **federal government** operates by the political bodies and in "their political capacities." A **national government** on the other hand is operated by individual citizens of the nation, "in their individual capacities."[22]

Progressivism's "Irrelevant" Constitution

"Progressivism" flourished over the last century as evidenced by academics, journalists, and political liberals who believe there are no permanent rights and our Constitution should constantly "evolve." They subscribe to the theory of a *living constitution,* signifying that it can, and should be rewritten to meet their philosophical views. The "living constitution" argument is actually an excuse to manipulate the laws of our nation to mold society to fit certain ideologies. They want to redesign our society through distribution of wealth disguised as equality and justice by the expansion of the federal government. They believe the government's role is to regulate our society, economy, political system, and our personal lives. They also believe they know what is best for everyone and so they violate our core principles by amending laws to free their ideology from the limitations of the Constitution.

Progressives dismiss our exceptional principles claiming they are totally inadequate for the modern world. The Heritage Foundation rejects that assertion in an article published July 4, 2011, "Celebrating America's Enduring Principles."

"It is not uncommon to hear that these principles were fine for the 18th century but are woefully inadequate to meet the challenges of today. Since the early 20th century, academics, journalists, and even American Presidents (Woodrow Wilson, for example) have held the view, characterized by Calvin Coolidge, that "we have had new thoughts and

---

[22] "The Federalist 39, *Republicanism, Nationalism, Federalism,*" by James Madison

new experiences which have given us a great advance over the [Founders], and that we may therefore very well discard their conclusions for something more modern."

Once they change our laws, they are free to discard our principles and replace our sacred Constitution with their self-serving enlightened version. Liberal progressives reject the principles that founded our nation. Whereas the Founding Fathers conception of individual freedom for the pursuit of happiness (*opportunity of freedom and choice to make a good life for one's self*), the progressive theory defines freedom as the *guaranteed fulfillment* of individual life as the primary role of government. To the Founders, the main role of government is to protect the people. To the progressives, the government's main role is creating people. The Founders believed the government should protect the private citizen whether that relates to home, industry, science, and yes, religion. Man and his government are based on 'the laws of nature and nature's God." Progressives on the other hand see selfishness and oppression in the private realm and believe it is the government's job to control the private sector. The poor are victims of capitalism and need government protection through redistribution, commerce, production and banking regulations, and price controls. They see spiritualism not in religion, but in the environment and the arts. The Founders believed in individual success, promoted hard work and education, and embraced virtues such as honesty, justice, courage, self-sufficiency, patriotism, and industry.

"Punitive Liberalism" is a natural development in the world of progressives. An article on Roybeaird's Blog, "Words Have Meaning: Punitive Liberalism's Rise," explains the term very well. Liberalism needs to *"punish America for her sins, injustices, and ills going all the way back to our founding... Those who believe they are 'entitled' to redress, reparation should be able to 'punish' all of a particular race or group who do not agree.""*[23] Punitive liberalism's mandatory grievance doctrine demands recompense for the nation's past deeds in order to cleanse the collective conscience of the nation. Facts and laws are irrelevant as social justice condemns all Americans.

---

[23] "Words Have Meaning: Punitive Liberalism's Rise," RoyBeaird's Blog, http://roybeaird.wordpress.com/2013/10/28/punitive-liberalisms-rise/, October 28, 2013

Fabian Socialism gave rise to *Punitive Liberalism* which sees America as a flawed and evil country. Superseding individualism, the Federal Government is seen as the answer to all problems. Punitive liberalism rejects the Constitution as an impediment, not the rule of law that it is and transforming America away from being a Constitutional Republic is their goal. "Transforming America," doesn't that sound familiar?

Then there are the progressives that ascribe to the principles of "collectivism" in general and **"communitarianism"** in particular. The "group" to which individuals belong is of central importance – not individuals themselves. They value "community" not independence. They believe "that the principle task of government is to secure and distribute fairly the liberties and economic resources individuals need..."[24]

David L. Goetsch's 2012 article, "Why Liberals Cling to Socialist Principles In Spite of Evidence Against Socialism," explains the liberal "state-of-god" mentality. *"Liberal secular humanists criticize Christians for having what they describe as "blind faith in God," yet the left clings to its socialist notions – in spite of socialism's consistent record of failure – out of blind faith."*

"Arrogance, false compassion, emotionalism, and blind faith in a system that not only does not work but breeds laziness, sloth, and irresponsibility – these are the characteristics necessary to be a socialist. Until America replaces these characteristics with those of the traditional work ethic – thrift, diligence, self-reliance, self-discipline, responsibility, accountability, and hard work – all the bailouts, handouts, and entitlements in the world will have no more effect than water that is poured into a bottomless bucket..."[25]

David Horowitz is an activist, orator, and prolific author of numerous books on American politics, history, the radical 60's, and Progressivism in the U.S. He is the founder of the "Freedom Center,"

---

[24] "Communitarianism," Stanford Encyclopedia of Philosophy, revised January, 2012

[25] "Why Liberals Cling to Socialist Principles In Spite Of Evidence Against Socialism," David L. Goetsch, Patriot Update, http://www.patriotupdate.com/articles/why-liberals-cling-to-socialist-principles-in-spite-of_evidence-against-socialism, February 13, 2012

which is dedicated *"to the defense of free societies whose moral, cultural and economic foundations are under attack by enemies both secular and religious, at home and abroad."* His significant warnings should not be ignored. His parents were American Communists. Until recently in America, Communists could not openly call themselves Communists or Socialists, so they called themselves Liberals and Progressives and found safe harbor with the ever-increasing Progressives in the Democrat Party. David provides invaluable insight into Progressive mindset and philosophy.

In addition to the facts he presented on the existing state of government during an October 2013 speech, David's radical past provides him a unique view of the Obama administration. Noting that the IRS, the national taxing agency has become a political weapon; the federal government is accumulating financial and health information on all Americans; and the NSA has access to all communications including email, paper mail and telephones David warned, *"...you don't really need a secret police to destroy your political opponents. Once you have silenced them, you can proceed with your plans to remake the world in your image."* [26]

David has authored numerous papers, pamphlets and books. His recently published set *"The Black Book of the American Left Volume I: My Life and Times,"* 2013 and *"The Black Book of the American Left Volume II: Progressives,"* 2014 are absolute must-reads. Volume I chronicles "the years he spent at war with his own country, collaborating with radical figures like Huey Newton, Tom Hayden and Bill Ayers as he made his transition from what writer Paul Berman describes as the American left's 'most important theorist' to its most determined enemy."[27] In Volume II based on his own experiences, he provides honest insight into progressivism and its dangers. Other great books by David include, *"Unholy Alliance"* 2006 and *"The Professors: The 101 Most Dangerous Academics in America,"* 2007.

---

[26] "The Threat We Face," David Horowitz, text of speech at the Kohler Conference of the Bradley Foundation, *Front Page Magazine*, http://frontpagemag.com, October 10, 2013

[27] "The Black Book of the American Left, Volume 1: My Life and Times," David Horowitz, New York: Encounter Books, 2013

Bruce Thornton's October 17, 2013 article, *"Barack Obama and the Bad Idea of Progressivism,"* *Front Page Magazine* substantiates David Horowitz's assessment of Progressivism in America today. Thornton focusses on President Obama's progressive ideals as he presents himself as champion of the people against the wealthy elites. Thornton also highlights The President's total "disregard for the Constitution." He illustrates how Progressivism has been embedded within our government.[28]

Besides appointing czars and panels for everything and editing the White House Presidential Biographies, President Obama loves to create executive orders and issue presidential proclamations. A presidential proclamation issued on December 15, 2013 gained little notice, but was quite telling. The President declared December 15th to be the "Bill of Rights" Day. That sounds nice but as he so often does; Obama cited the Bill of Rights and edited it to include the rights he believes should be included: "dignity, fairness, and a living wage."

In an earlier posted article Bruce Thornton focused on the failed progressive notion that government can "create" economic growth since central-planning experts can manage resources better than the private – free market can. *"But more important is the underlying idea of progressivism that Obama's policies are predicated on: Perfect justice, prosperity, and equality are possible if enlightened elites are given the power to organize and run society according to "scientific" knowledge about human nature and behavior. For two centuries this hubristic idea has led to failure, misery, and murder on a vast scale, yet progressives continue to increase government power in order to create this impossible utopia."*

"Dupes: How America's Adversaries Have Manipulated Progressives for a Century," written by Paul Kengor is a well-researched book exposing Communist – Soviet Intelligence operations right here in the U.S. throughout the twentieth-century that supported progressive academics and intellectuals.[29]

---

[28] "Barack Obama and the Bad Ideas of Progressivism," Bruce Thornton, *Front Page Magazine,* http://frontpagemag.com, October 17, 2013

[29] "Dupes: How America's Adversaries Have Manipulated Progressives for a Century," Paul Kengor, ISI Books, 9/10/2010

David Kupelian, award winning journalist, managing editor of WND, editor of *Whistleblower* magazine, and author of best-selling books, ***The Marketing of Evil*** and ***How Evil Works*** explained why our government "no longer worries about communists," and how "*radically America's attitude toward Marxism and communism has changed during our lifetime.*"[30]

David's father, Vahey S. Kupelian and grandmother survived the early Twentieth century Turkish genocide of Armenians and were able to escape to America, "The Promised Land." Vahey began working at age 13, learned English, did well in school, and graduated from MIT. He was a rocket scientist who became the U.S. Army's chief scientist for ballistic missile defense and later deputy undersecretary of defense for strategic and theater nuclear forces under President Reagan. Vahey was a real American "immeasurably grateful and loyal to his adopted country." He came close to losing everything when the FBI confronted him about an event when his mother innocently accepted a copy of the communist newspaper, *Workers World* at an Armenian Church picnic when he was just a teen-ager. This was at a time when the U.S. government and the FBI were very concerned about the loyalty of federal employees especially the ones with security clearances. He was able to prove neither he nor his mother had any connection to the communist party.

The point of David's story about his father (the complete article is well worth reading) is to highlight the government's current lack of concern about communism in the U.S. Progressives under the flags of "fairness," "economic justice," "redistribution," and "equality," have successfully been able to move the country toward socialism. David Kupelian warns us that, "*The original American spirit – stout, risk-taking, God-fearing, responsible adult – has progressively been displaced by the spirit of dependency and helplessness, of perpetual grievance and victimization, and most of all, of envy and resentment.* All of which cries out for ever bigger government. So the question is: Will we Americans re-embrace the values that made ours the greatest nation in history, or will we continue on our current path toward the godless mirage of

---

[30] "America's Marxist picnic," David Kupelian, *Whistleblower* Magazine, WND (World Net Daily), http://www.wnd.com, Issue: June 2013

"redistributive change" – and the poverty and loss of liberty that always follow?"

Richard L. Cravatts shares recent stories of Progressive students at two of our prestigious universities in his article "The Agony of Moral Defeat."[31] At Harvard University student Sandra Y.L.Korn wrote an op-ed, "The Doctrine of Academic Freedom," in which she states that academic freedom is undeserved by those holding different beliefs than hers. Sandra and like-minded students have determined what is "moral, what is right, and what is acceptable speech" at Harvard and the world beyond. I was shocked to learn that she was majoring in the history of science and studies of women and gender and sexuality. Just kidding – I wasn't at all surprised.

Across the country at UCLA, the undergraduate student government voted down a *Students' for Justice in Palestine* proposed "Resolution to Divest from Companies that Violate Palestinian Human Rights." Mr. Cravatts reported that "The UCLA incident revealed a similar Leftist obsession with obtaining social justice for the Palestinians, even if it necessitates the weakening or destruction of Israel." One distraught student went ballistic at the outcome of the vote. This student went on an "expletive-laden rant" on how disappointed she was and how ashamed she was of the racists who voted against the resolution. Her two minute rant can be viewed on YouTube as another example of educational dollars "well-spent."

Stephen J. Markman, Michigan State Justice delivered a speech in Washington, D.C. February 25, 2010 at an event sponsored by Hillsdale College's Allen P. Kirby, Jr. Center for Constitutional Studies and Citizenship.[32] Justice Markman warns that little public attention is being paid to proponents of a "21st century constitution," or "living constitution," whose aim is to "transform our nation's supreme law…" Justice Markman warns that courts, especially federal courts, will increasingly over turn lower court decisions and the laws enacted by

---

[31] "The Agony of Moral Defeat," Richard L. Cracatts, *Front Page Magazine*, http://www.frontpagemag.com, March 7, 2014

[32] "The Coming Constitutional Debate," Stephen J. Markman, published in *Imprimis*, A Publication of Hillsdale College, April 2010, Volume 39, Number 4

the will of the people. Justice Markman cites six popular concepts of 21st century constitution advocates:

1. **Privileges or Immunities Clause of the Fourteenth Amendment:** Protects a limited number of rights of American citizens. Federal judicial authority over the states has increased considerably through judicial interpretation of the clause. *Living Constitution* proponents demand increasing federal oversight, and a new and unlimited bill of rights covered by the 14th Amendment.

2. **Positive Rights:** Redefining the Privileges or Immunities Clause to transform the Constitution from guaranteeing negative liberties (what the government does not have authority over) into a charter of affirmative government, guaranteeing positive rights, (giving the government more rights over citizens).

3. **State Action:** To achieve fairness and equity, living constitutionalists believe the Constitution must make federal rules and regulations applicable to public **and** private institutions.

4. **Political Questions:** Federal courts are interjecting themselves into matters of national defense and foreign policy (the <u>exclusive</u> responsibility of the elected branches of government). *"If there are no longer any traditional limitations upon the exercise of the judicial power, then every matter coming before every president, every Congress, every governor, every legislature, and every county commission and city council can, with little difficulty, be summarily recast as a justifiable dispute..."*

5. **Ninth Amendment:** The principle purpose of the Ninth Amendment was to prevent the expansion of federal power; not augment judicial power. Living constitutionalist judges feel they have the right to look beyond constitutional text to protect "fundamental" rights not expressed in the amendment. These judges have decided that Ninth Amendment "privacy" rights should include abortion, contraception, and homosexual behavior.

6. **Transnationalism:** *"...international and domestic law are merging into a hybrid body of transnational law...In practice,*

transnationalism would legitimize reliance by American judges upon foreign law in giving meaning to the United States Constitution..." And Transnational (International) law could render American soldiers and elected U.S. leaders subject to the international law for accused actions such as "war crimes" and "violations of the Earth." International law would take precedence over the American legal system.

Many people do not realize the importance of knowing the character of the courts. It would be great if our judges were non-partisan and neutral to political pressure and personal ideology. Unfortunately that is not the case. Progressive judges especially at the federal level and on the Supreme Court are making and changing laws. They justify their decisions by re-wording or intentionally misinterpreting the Constitution. These judges are appointed by people we elect and they are not restrained by term limits.

For instance, during President Obama's first term, he appointed 125 federal judges; 25 of them to appellate courts and 2 to the Supreme Court. That is quite an infusion of liberalism into our judicial system; and the President with a Senate majority backing him has a second term to continue stacking the courts. For instance, the DC Circuit Court hears and rules on challenges to presidential executive orders (President Obama regularly uses this tool to by-pass Congress). The DC Circuit Court will soon have a 7-4 Democrat majority that will guarantee his agenda. Bryan Preston posting on PJ Media wrote: *"...Podesta's appointment shows that Obama is done working with Congress...but there's even more at stake here. Obama recognizes that in Congress his agenda is dying and after the mid-terms will be dead. So he is planning to sideline Congress. Obama is packing the DC Circuit Court in anticipation of losing Congress to the Republicans."* [33]

President Obama continues to issue executive actions (orders) knowing that they will be challenged in court. He also knows that challenges against his "unconstitutional law-making" will fail in court as long as the courts are "packed" with his appointed judges. With his

---

[33] "Obama Is Laying the Groundwork to Move Without, Around, and Outside Congress," Bryan Preston, PJ Media, http://www.pjmedia.com, December 10, 2013

judges deciding law, Congress loses all power to conduct hearings and investigations. Bottom line is that the Legislative branch of government - the only branch empowered to make laws will lose that constitutional guaranteed power to the Executive branch, acting in collusion with the Judicial branch.

These unconstitutional actions on the part of the President and his appointed liberal judges will make elections "irrelevant." When elections become irrelevant like they have become in countries like Venezuela, the people have lost their voice and democratic voting is just a charade.

Supreme Court Justice Ruth Bader Ginsburg demonstrated one of the most disrespectful displays of the judicial progressive corruption of our Constitution and our courts. During an interview with an Egyptian television station, Justice Ginsburg basically told that nation that our United States Constitution was not a good constitutional model to emulate: *"I would not look to the US constitution, if I were drafting a constitution in the year 2012."* She suggested the South African constitution which established an independent judiciary as a model as well as Canada's *Charter of Rights and Freedoms*. Justice Ginsburg continued, *"You would almost certainly look at the European Convention on Human Rights. Yes, why not take advantage of what there is elsewhere in the world?"*

This judge, sworn to "uphold" the very constitution that she obviously thinks is old and irrelevant sits on the highest court of the land. Keep in mind she said this to the Egyptian people after the White House endorsement and support of the "Arab Spring" uprisings. We all know how well that turned out - A Muslim Brotherhood member was elected president. I did not hear Justice Ginsburg comment on that calamity.

Anyone familiar with the television series *Star Trek the Next Generation* will remember the "Borg." The Borg episodes are a great analogy for modern liberalism. Whether you call it socialism, communism, collectivism or communitarianism, the Progressive ideology is the same as the Borg. Individualism is not recognized. Each person is merely an extension of the "whole," working in unison with the "whole," and only for the perceived good of the "whole." All behavior is controlled and the "collective" is entirely dependent upon the Leader. An individual cannot exist alone without group support and certainly not without directives from the leader.

Judges and lawyers for that matter are supposed to be the custodians of our Constitution not editors of it. Progressivism is re-writing our Constitution one fragment at a time and no one is paying attention. We only need to turn to our Founding Fathers for Constitutional clarity and proof that the Constitution is not an "invalid contract."

Alexander Hamilton argued that the judiciary would be the "least dangerous" branch of the new government. No one at the time ever imagined that the judiciary would interpret the Constitution not within its own text but by the whims of progressivism. The Heritage Foundation agrees: "*It seems that there is a right to everything these days: a right to the internet, to free health care, to a good job, and to a free college education. The Supreme Court is famous for finding new rights in the "penumbras" and "emanations" of the Constitution.*"[34]

Dr. Robert Owens, author of "***The Constitution Failed,***" "***The Azusa Street Revival,***" *America Won the Vietnam War*," and "***Never Forget,***" believes that Progressives in the U.S. have turned the best educated, most politically involved and self-reliant citizens in history into an assemblage of indifferent and uninterested Americans eagerly accepting dependence on the government.

Dr. Owens identifies the incremental transformation strategy of progressives. The first step is to control the educational system and "dumb" it down; indoctrinate students to produce ideological clones who then teach more students and so on. Then central planning (the government) targets capitalism to erase "individualism, self-reliance and innovation." With layers and layers of regulations, government policies overwhelm business decisions and investments until private businesses can no longer survive.

The "most insidious aspect" is erasing the objective reality of "truth" and redefining it as whatever is needed to support the efforts and achieve the goals. "*War becomes peace. Inequality becomes equality. Pork becomes*

---

[34] "New Common Sense – Applying First Principles to the Issues of Today," The Heritage Foundation, http://heritage.org, newsletter@heritage.org, December 13, 2011

stimulus. Stonewalling and taking the fifth becomes the most transparent administration in history and the destruction of the greatest health system ever known becomes affordable care." [35]

David Azerrad, The Heritage Foundation summarizes the **progressive detriment** to our country this way: *"Liberalism has in effect redefined democracy along paternalistic lines: enacting, through whatever means necessary, what the people would vote for – if only they were enlightened enough to know what's best for them. This of course, is not democracy. And it's incompatible with what James Madison in The Federalist called "that honorable determination which animates every votary of freedom, to rest all our political experiments on the capacity of mankind for self-government...Simply claiming to be for the people does not make a government democratic..."* [36]

Gary DeMar of *The American Vision* was specifically addressing an inevitable new immigration law but his words ring true for all new laws, when he said, *"What makes any of us think that any new law will be followed or enforced? There are so many legal loopholes and caveats that we will never see any enforcement. We're becoming a third-world country where, quoting Simon Bolivar (1783-1830), 'there is no good faith...Treaties are scraps of paper; constitutions, printed matter; elections, battles; freedom, anarchy; and life a torment."* [37]

Daniel Greenfield posted a thought-provoking article titled, "The American Iron Curtain." Greenfield is not talking about a physical wall but a "wall of words" that is encompassing our country. This wall of words is made up of laws, regulations and mandates. The "Affordable Care Act" alone contains 11 million words of regulations. Clear simple language is lost in the government's wall of millions of words. People need to realize that elections have consequences. *"They need to know*

---

[35] "How Do You Fundamentally Change America? Step by Step, Inch by Inch," Dr. Robert Owens, Freedom Outpost, http://www.freedomoutpost.com, November 16, 2013

[36] "Is Our Government Still Of the People?", David Azerrad, First Principles, The Foundry, The Heritage Foundation, http://www.blog.heritage.org, November 19, 2013

[37] "Immigration: The Constitution is Just a Scrap of Paper," Gary DeMar, The American Vision, http://www.AmericanVision.org, posted on Godfather Politics, http://godfatherpolitics.com, June 25, 2013

that they are not choosing between politicians, but choosing whether they will be able to have the car of their choice, the doctor of their choice, the meal of their choice and the book of their choice."

"The struggle is over whether America will be an open system or a closed system. In an open system, you choose the life you live. In a closed system, life is mandated for you." [38]

Simply stated, individuals are in control in an *open system* whereas individuals are controlled by the state (government) that makes decisions for everyone in a *closed system*. There is no individuality or even independent thinking.

It is more important than ever to heed the warnings. Abraham Lincoln said Americans were the "legal inheritors" of the "fundamental blessings" bequeathed us by the Founders "whose principles, institutions, and very names they had a duty to preserve." [39] Lincoln also warned: *"America will never be destroyed from the outside. If we falter and lose our freedoms, it will be because we destroyed ourselves."*

Constitutionally Guaranteed Freedoms under Assault

The Government Knows What is "Best for Us"

In an attempt to redesign society, a good example of a progressive government intruding into the personal lives of its citizens was prohibition. Ratified in 1919, the Eighteenth Amendment prohibited the manufacture, sale, and transportation of liquor. Prohibition did not stop people from drinking, but it did create a culture of corruption and organized crime that continued long after the amendment was repealed in 1933. The hypocrisy of prohibition is that some of the biggest lawbreakers were government officials sworn to uphold the laws of the United States. The Eighteenth Amendment is a lesson to modern

---

[38] "The American Iron Curtain," Daniel Greenfield, The Daily Mailer, *Front Page Magazine*, http://www.frontpage.com, November 5, 2013

[39] "Darwin's Constitution, Why Progressives took it upon themselves to purify our founding charter of its meaning," Bradley C.S. Watson, *National Review*, May 17, 2010

Americans concerned about individual rights. Progressives make laws for everyone else to abide by, though they have awarded themselves a "selective license" to disregard laws they do not agree with.

Our government today proudly boasts of its *responsibility* to protect citizens from themselves. One case in point is the tobacco industry in which our concerned leaders discovered a "golden calf." Millions of dollars have been made by continually raising sales taxes on cigarette products and suing tobacco manufacturers. So actually where did all the money the government received from litigation that was supposed to finance health care go? No one is talking about it now, even though the taxes on cigarettes keep rising. One of New York City Mayor Michael Bloomberg's last contributions to society before he left office was to ban E-cigarettes in public places to compliment the already illegal activity of smoking real cigarettes in public. E-cigarettes emit "vapor" not smoke or any other harmful residue, but since some people can't tell the difference, and are offended by just looking at anything resembling cigarettes, they had to be banned. Chicago Mayor Emanuel announced in October 2013 his plan to raise taxes on cigarettes another seventy-five cents a pack bringing the total sales taxes (city, county, and state) on cigarettes to the highest in the nation at $7.42 per pack.[40] This is an excessive tax targeting one segment of the population for a "legal" product. There is growing support by politicians to legalize marijuana nationally and to minimize penalties related to illegal use of it. So, cigarettes are bad and the people who smoke them are ostracized, but now marijuana is good and needs to be legalized on a national scale. Second hand smoke from cigarettes can kill you, but second hand smoke from marijuana is just fine – who would have guessed?

Now the politicians' sights are set on obesity and under the lame cover of intense concern for our children, the government is planning to protect us from fatness. An increasing number of cities, and states following suit, are instituting "sugar taxes" also known as "fat taxes" on soft drinks, sweets, fast food, and other consumables. Former New York City Mayor Bloomberg had been on a personal crusade to protect New

---

[40] "Emanuel wants 75 cents a pack cigarette tax increase," *The Chicago Tribune*, October 20, 2013

Yorkers from themselves with a number of other "health" initiatives. One of those initiatives was the soda ban – soda limited to a maximum of 16 ounces. Even though the court found this unconstitutional, Bloomberg vowed to keep fighting for his health initiatives. Just three weeks before he left office as mayor Bloomberg proposed to the City Council to require annual flu shots for all NYC children including Daycare children. Autism advocates are upset over this latest mayoral mandate as well as many parents who have reservations about giving it to their children. Don't worry New Yorkers; Mayor Bloomberg and his Health Department say it is safe and necessary. Bloomberg is a good example of progressivism in action – Relax – he's not a doctor but he still knows what is best for the people of New York.

Newsweek reported in June 2009, the Centers for Disease Control (CDC) launched a new "Lean Works" website to distribute a fountain of information on the health care costs for employers who hire "fat people," and recommendations for citizens on how to control and prevent obesity.[41] Employers can access the website's "obesity cost calculator" that determines added costs of employing persons with a BMI (Body Mass Index) over 30. This is just another ambush in the government's war on fat. In the same publication, Newsweek also cited reports by the CDC's own National Center for Health Statistics finding no evidence that "being overweight or moderately obese as an adult increases the risk of death." Other studies by non-government agencies concur with the National Center for Health Statistics. So, if the CDC cannot establish a unilateral finding on obesity, how can part of their findings influence legislation affecting the rest of us?

In November 2010 the San Francisco Board of Supervisors approved a ban on toys in fast-food restaurant children's meals in another effort to protect children from fatness (though they prefer the term obesity-curbing efforts). Toys would be allowed only if the kid meals meet their "guidelines" with regards to saturated fats, trans-fats, sodium, calories, and if they contained fruits or vegetables. It seems that all parents are not up to the task of feeding their children properly. Well at least now the children will be "healthier" while they're exposed to rampant drug

---

[41] "Who Says Americans Are Too Fat?" Daniel Heimpel, *Newsweek*, August 27, 2009, http://newsweek.com

addiction, STD's, and homeless people urinating on buildings. Maybe the San Francisco Board of Supervisors should take a city tour and see what real health problems look like.

It is a contradiction that the same government obsessed with the health and welfare of its citizens encourages gambling by promoting lotteries and licensed gambling casinos. We see published reports on condom use, obese children, the dangers of drugs, smoking, and drinking, but rarely see anything on the devastating effects gambling has on millions of families. The irony is, gambling is promoted, but sugar is bad. Go figure. Another issue regarding state lotto's is that when they started becoming popular in the 1970's, politicians promoted them as great sources of revenue to among other things fund education without raising taxes. Revenue from gambling was supposed to be a tremendous benefit to the schools. Where did the money go? Our public schools have degraded - not improved.

Unless politicians prove otherwise, they are NOT concerned about your health and welfare, unless of course, it is beneficial to them. If politicians and government officials are concerned about you and your family, they are seeing dollar signs somewhere. Government programs allow and even provide needles and drugs to drug addicts, "medical" marijuana to sick people, and now states are legalizing marijuana use in general, but cigarettes and sugar are bad for you. The federal government's most recent campaign is to ban "trans fats" because they are bad and we are not smart enough to make the decision not to use them. Does any of this make sense? It makes sense to the politicians. The more "services" and "favors" the government provides to the public, the easier it is for politicians to win votes.

Journalist Jonah Goldberg of the *National Review* frames government policies this way: *"Conservatives tend to see government as a necessary evil, and therefore see policymaking with some humility. Liberals tend to see government as a necessary good, and see ordering people to do things 'for their own good' as a source of pride, even hubris.*

From a conservative perspective, telling people how to run their lives when not absolutely necessary is an abuse of power. For liberals, telling people how to run their lives is one of the really fun perks of working for the government."[42]

The First Amendment

> The First Amendment of the Constitution guarantees: ***Congress shall make no law respecting an establishment of religion, or prohibiting the free exercise thereof; or abridging the freedom of speech, or of the press; or the right of the people to peaceably assemble, and to petition the government for a redress of grievances.*** Every one of our "protected" First Amendment freedoms is under attack.

Freedom of Religion[43] (<u>NOT</u> Freedom FROM Religion)

The Establishment Clause: *"Congress shall make no law respecting an establishment of religion,"* was written to guarantee against a single "official" national church. The Anglican Church was Great Britain's national church requiring mandatory membership and supported by taxes. The establishment clause guaranteed no government interference in religion and guaranteed that no one religion would have control over other religions.

The Exercise Clause: *"…or prohibiting the free exercise thereof,"* was written to protect individual religious beliefs and practices, and prevent persecution of religions. This is the clause Progressives do not acknowledge when they go on their erroneous "wall of separation" rants. By eliminating this clause from their war on religion mission statement, they can solely focus on their misguided view that the government is responsible for eliminating all religious references and influence from public view.

---

[42] "Father Fed Knows Best," Jonah Goldberg, *National Review Online*, <u>http://www.nationalreview.com</u>, November 8, 2013

[43] First Amendment: Freedom of religion legal definition, <u>http://legal-dictionary.thefreedictionary.com/Freedom+of+Religion,</u> 2013

The Christian religion has been under attack by Progressives for decades now. Christians are maligned, ridiculed, attacked and intimidated. The words "under God" are pretty much absent in our national "Pledge of Allegiance." Christmas has been denigrated to a generic "holiday," even though every calendar denotes December 25th of every year as "Christmas." School children are not allowed to sing any Christian Christmas songs even though the "holiday" they're celebrating is Christmas – not "holiday." The City of New York's subway system allows anti-religious/anti-God messages on their walls, and our progressive government's crusade to banish Christianity from all public forums marches on.

The commander of this anti-Christian crusade is no other than the President of the United States. What a dismal day for our country. The President has "mentioned" a few times that, *"America is no longer just a Christian nation..."* (2006); *"We do not consider ourselves a Christian Nation..."* (Ankara, Turkey 2009). In a speech at the U.N. in 2012, President Obama said, *"The future does not belong to those who slander the prophet of Islam..."*[44] This is a direct shot at Christians since their core belief is that Jesus is the son of God and our only salvation. It does not recognize Mohammed whatsoever. Since Muslims consider this tenet alone "blasphemy" then the very existence of Christianity is slanderous. So while Christians in the West are demonized for "slandering" Prophet Mohammed; Muslims are murdering Christians throughout the Middle East without any world outrage or condemnation.

Christian churches as well as Jewish Synagogues are targets of vandalism and harassment. In separate instances in California, Catholic Masses have been disrupted by anti-Catholic/anti-Christian groups. A Catholic church in Chicago was set on fire February 9, 2009 and a message of "God is a Lie" was left on the front door, but attacks on Christian churches do not garner much media attention.

- A Christian Evangelical Group, "Child Evangelism Fellowship," that had worked with under-privileged children and sponsored

---

[44] "Anti-Christian: Obama Declare The Future Must Not Belong to Practicing Christians," Eric Erickson, www.redstate.com and www.clashdaily.com, September 25, 2012

a religious-themed summer program for over twenty years was prohibited from conducting Bible study classes in the Tulsa, Oklahoma housing project.

- A Christian food pantry that has operated for thirty-one years in Lake City, Florida was told by the USDA they would no longer receive food from the government unless they removed their "Christian symbols" (pictures of Jesus and a ten-Commandments display) and stopped handing out Bibles. This Christian ministry refused to comply so they no longer receive government food to feed the area's hungry and homeless. They are now totally reliant on private donations.

- In 2010 the city of Mission, Kansas passed a "driveway tax" to supplement property taxes on residences, businesses, and churches. Erik Stanley, an attorney with the Alliance Defense Fund correctly identified the city's program as, "a tax on church attendance. The city of Mission is taxing churches based on the number of people that come in and out of their driveway, the number of people that come to church."[45] The mayor of Mission, KS prefers to call it a "fee."

- In June of 2010 Christian missionaries were arrested by Dearborn, Michigan police at the Arab festival for the crime of discussing Christianity on a public sidewalk – outside of the event.

- President Obama mandated that "sterilization, abortion, and contraception" be covered by all health plans knowing that the Catholic Church as well as most other Christian denominations would not comply with this unparalleled attack on conscience and liberty. Many Catholic hospitals, universities and organizations that millions of people count on have an uncertain future.

- In Colorado, a "Christian" baker was ordered by a judge to bake a wedding cake for a homosexual couple's wedding or be penalized. The baker, a Christian declined to make the cake because of his religious convictions against same-sex marriage.

---

[45] "Taking Liberties: Taxing Church Attendance?" Douglass Kennedy, March 10, 2011, Fox News, www.foxnews.com

This event sounds so like a "set-up." Instead of going to another bakery for their cake, the men went to the ACLU and filed a discrimination suit against the baker. Eric Erickson aptly summarized it this way: Homosexual *"rights activists demand tolerance for their lifestyle, but will not tolerate those who choose to adhere to their religious beliefs."*[46]

- A bakery in Oregon is in the same oven as the Colorado bakery. They were hit with an unlawful discrimination charge based on sexual orientation for refusing to bake a wedding cake for a homosexual couple, even though the Oregon constitution Section 3 of Article 1 guarantees *"freedom of religious opinion. No law shall in any case whatever control the free exercise, and enjoyment of religious opinions, or interfere with the rights of conscience."*[47]

- The ACLU filed another lawsuit against Christianity in Oklahoma City, Oklahoma on behalf of the New York-based Satanic Temple (yes that is correct, a New York based satanic temple in Oklahoma). The offensive issue this time was the "Ten Commandments" monument erected on the Statehouse steps. Instead of suing for the removal of the Ten Commandments, the Satanists decided to sue to erect their own satanic monument next to the Christian Ten Commandments monument.

The Vatican is distressed at the very real erosion of religious freedom in the U.S. and considers it a threat of "unprecedented gravity" to the church's "liberty and moral witness."[48] And the Catholic Church believes that "a brand of secularism is taking hold in America that seeks to exclude the Catholic Church from participating in the debate about issues affecting the future of the nation." Cardinal Raymond Burke,

---

[46] "You Will Be Made To Care," Erick Erickson, http://www.redstate.com, December 9, 2013

[47] "Religious Freedom Voided by Oregon's Bureau of Labor and Industries," Gary DeMar, published by Godfather
Politics, http://www.godfatherpolitics.com, January 22, 2014

[48] "Vatican says religious liberty under attack in America," John Rossomando, Red alert politics, http://www.redalertpolitics.com, August 7, 2012

former archbishop of St. Louis and now head of the *Apostolic Signatura*, the highest court at the Vatican was recently interviewed. *"It is true that the policies of the president of the United States of America have become progressively more hostile toward Christian civilization. He appears to be a totally secularized man who aggressively promotes anti-life and anti-family policies."*[49]

If you are still not sure that there really is a "war" on Christianity in general and the Catholic Church in particular then recent United Nations activities should convince you. As reported in Front Page Magazine[50] the U.N. Committee on the Rights of the Child comprised of 18 independent "experts" released a report in January 2014. These "experts" are described on the Committee's website as, "persons of high moral character and recognized competence in the field of human rights." The absurdity is that some of these "human rights" experts are from Saudi Arabia, Egypt, and Bahrain where human rights do not exist. They are also Muslim states ruled by Sharia Law and have no tolerance whatsoever for Christianity.

Beginning with denouncing the Vatican's handling of sex-abuse cases (which can be understandable) there was no mention of Pope Francis' already implemented initiative to openly address and resolve issues of sexual and alleged-sexual abuse, highlighting the protection of children. The report continued with criticism of the church's ideology on abortion urging the Pope to change the church's view on contraception and homosexuality. Continuing, the committee stated their view of what should be taught in Catholic schools. *"The committee recommends that the Holy See undertake a comprehensive review of its normative framework, in particular Canon Law, with a view to ensuring its full compliance with the Convention."* Joseph Klein, author of the Front Page Magazine article "Hypocritical UN Committee Maligns the Catholic Church," further explained the committee report: *"it proclaimed that in*

---

[49] "Vatican Chief Justice: Obama's Policies 'Progressively More Hostile toward Christian Civilization.'" Originally published in Polonia Christiana (a Polish magazine), translated to English by LifeSite News, published by CNS News, http://www.cnsnews.com, March 24, 2014

[50] "Hypocritical UN Committee Maligns the Catholic Church," Joseph Klein, *Front Page Magazine*, http://www.frontpagemag.com, February 11, 2014

the event of conflict between the provisions of the secular convention and the provisions of the religious Canon Law, the Convention must prevail." Mr. Klein continued: *"In short, the United Nations Committee on the Rights of the Child, with a Vice-Chairperson representing and protecting a country with one of the world's worst human rights records, is in no position to tell the Catholic Church to change or reinterpret Canon Law and Scripture to suit the Committee's biased political agenda."*

Christine Rousselle with Town Hall.com made this statement: *"The U.N. Committee on the Rights of the Child released a new report slamming the Catholic Church and suggesting that it alter its belief system to permit abortion in order to 'protect children.'"*[51] So, since the United Nations as well as the United States federal government decided that somehow killing children (abortion) protects children ... the church should conform to their view regardless of religious doctrine? Tell me again there is no war on Christianity.

Another government sponsored threat to religious freedom is the "Employment Non-Discrimination Act (ENDA)." Since it is already unlawful to discriminate against, race, religion and gender in the workplace, why do we need another "non-discrimination" act? It seems we needed to update the law to specifically include not just homosexuals, but bisexuals, trans-genders, and cross dressers. The new law coerces employers, landlords, private institutions and even churches and religious hospitals and schools from taking any action, valid as it may be to dismiss, or not hire someone in this newly expanded class. Most Christian Churches do not condone any of this behavior and this calculated move by the government is another attack on the liberty and conscience of Christians.

The government now considers sexual preference equal to racism. Dr. Martin Luther King, Jr.'s niece, Alveda King stated that *"...you cannot equate racism with sexual preference – they're two different things entirely. We can as adults decide how we express ourselves sexually, but we cannot reappoint ourselves racially."*[52]

---

[51] "UN Tells Vatican Church to Alter Doctrine to Allow Abortion," Christine Rousselle, Townhall, http://www.townhall.com, February 7, 2013

[52] "Courts Say We No Longer Have Freedom of Conscience," Jerry Newcombe, Godfather Politics, http://www.godfatherpolitics.com, December 12, 2013

Do you realize that the government's crusade to strip us of our "guaranteed" rights like the freedom of religion also strips us of our human right of "conscience?" These laws have been created to purposely cripple Christianity. The government (the entity responsible to uphold and protect our Constitutional liberties) is forcing Christians to obey the government's unconstitutional laws and disregard their religion and conscience. The Christian baker in Colorado forced to accept homosexuality, the Catholic Church along with many other churches, and Hobby Lobby are being mandated to comply with Obamacare demands to support abortions or go out of business. Young school children are forced to learn about homosexuality and sex of all kinds. The parents of these same children have no rights or recourse when their under age children are given condoms and have abortions. The Muslim god is welcomed into government and the public schools but the God of conscience and love is banned. This is just the tip of the iceberg if our government is allowed to continue down its ruinous path.

The Government backed by the judicial geniuses has determined that your religious beliefs do not give you the "right" to follow your conscience. The government will now dictate which of your religious beliefs and convictions you can keep and which ones by law will not be tolerated. Blind "tolerance" is rewriting our laws so we are forced to accept what in our hearts we know or believe is wrong. These new crusaders of humanity know nothing of our God-given and constitutionally protected rights.

Does conscience not matter anymore? Our Founders considered conscience an imperative requirement for political, professional and personal success.

- George Washington ordered his men during the Quebec Campaign not to violate the right of conscience: "As far as lies in your power, you are to protect and support the free exercise of the religion of the country, and the undisturbed enjoyment of the rights of conscience in religious matters, with your utmost influence and authority."
- Washington also wrote: "...any man, conducting himself as a good citizen, and being accountable to God alone for his

religious opinions, ought to be protected in worshipping the Deity according to the dictates of his own conscience."

- Thomas Jefferson (labeled an unreligious man) wrote in 1785: "Our rulers can have no other authority over such natural rights, only as we have submitted to them (in a social compact). **The rights of conscience we never submitted, we could not submit. We are answerable for them to our God...**"

Another disturbing situation is the government's concerted effort to de-Christianize our military by purging it of anything that could be construed as "Christian." Have you noticed that since "Don't ask; don't tell" was cast into the flaming pit of intolerance, many seemingly small insignificant changes have been made to the military by the President and the Department of Defense? I wonder if any of it has to do with the fact that the Pentagon and Department of Defense have consulted with Mikey Weinstein, well known anti-religious activist and founder of the Military Religious Freedom Foundation (though Freedom From Military Religious Foundation) would be a much more appropriate name. Mr. Weinstein regularly compares Evangelical Christians to the Taliban and al-Qaeda.[53]

In May 2009 it was reported that privately owned Bibles of U.S. soldiers serving in Afghanistan were seized and burned because someone feared the soldiers could "proselytize" Afghan citizens. When I heard this, all I could think of was the **false** *Newsweek* article about a Quran being flushed down a toilet at Guantanamo Bay prison sparking worldwide outrage, protest, destruction, and death. So what's the message here? It is acceptable to "import" Islam which must be upheld with the utmost respect while Christianity cannot be "exported," and is even allowed to be denigrated and abused here in America?

The U.S. Air Force has removed the words "so help me God" from their oath of service. David Goetsch wrote about it in a "Patriotupdate. com" article, *"The unceremonious demise of "so help me God" in the*

---

[53] "Sued: Pentagon for Mikey Weinstein documents, Anti-Christian Activist Who Compares Evangelicals with Taliban and al-Qaeda," Judicial Watch, http://www. judicialwatch.org/press-room/press-releases, September 26, 2013

Air Force's oath..."[54] David said an atheist group filed suit representing a single officer candidate who objected to those words. Instead of waiving that part of the oath for a single malcontent, Air Force officials preemptively removed those four words that have been part of the Air Force tradition since its founding.

The *Western Free Press* reported that the Navy SEALS (Navy SEAL Team VI) killed when their helicopter was shot down in Afghanistan in 2011 were denigrated during a ceremony at Bagram Airfield in Afghanistan. Our U.S. military commanders disallowed any mention of "God," but an attending Muslim cleric condemned these heroes as infidels to Allah (in Arabic). *"The shocking words of the Muslim cleric.... yet another example of the abject disrespect of Christians and Christianity endemic to the Muslim world."*[55] The *Press* also cited that during the temporary partial government shutdown, Catholic priests were told they could be arrested for saying Mass with military personnel - here in the United States. They were after all furloughed since Secretary of Defense Chuck Hagel determined that priests do not "contribute to the morale" and "well-being" of military personnel.

Townhall.com published an article on Retired Lieutenant General William G. (Jerry) Boykin who had been invited to speak at a prayer breakfast at West Point Military Academy. General Boykin is truly an American hero. He was with the elite Delta Force group; was wounded in Grenada; was the commanding officer of the Mogadishu, Somalia mission "Black Hawk Down," and he also worked with the CIA and the Pentagon on strategic planning and management. And he is a man of Faith, a committed Christian who speaks at churches across the country. Islamist groups and atheists teamed up to pressure West Point to un-invite Boykin because of his religious beliefs. *"Evidently it's not politically correct to suggest that blowing up children is the devil's work."*[56]

---

[54] "So help me God removed from the Air Force Oath", David L. Goetsch, http://www.patriotupdate.com, November 6, 2013

[55] "Christianity Under Attack in America," Janet Levy, *Western Free Press*, October 28, 2013

[56] "Delta Force Hero Can't Speak at West Point Because of his Christian Beliefs," Ken Blackwell, & Ken Klukowski, Townhall.com, http://www.townhall.com, February 1, 2012

General Boykin chose to excuse himself from the event so not cause controversy for the cadets.

Former NFL player, Craig James was fired from his broadcasting job as a college football analyst for expressing his personal opinion on same-sex marriage <u>before</u> he was employed as a broadcaster at FOX Sports. Craig had the audacity to share his Bible-based opinion about same-sex marriage. *"I said marriage is between a man and a woman. I talked a little bit more about the moral fiber of our country, that we're on a slide and we need people who will stand boldly for their beliefs."*[57]

The assault on Christmas grows larger and louder every year and progressives, secularists, humanists, atheists and their like-minded ilk are committed to permanently secularizing the holiday. Their mission is to erase Christ from Christmas - even though it is a Christian holiday. Sorry but December 25th is not Santa Day or Holiday or "Me" Day. Examples of the annual Christmas "slam" are abundant and 2013 is no exception. Teachers at Brooklet Elementary School in Georgia hung Christmas cards in the hallways by their classrooms. They have been doing this for a very long time but that has now changed. The cards posted this year were ordered taken down so the children would not be exposed to the very word "Christmas" printed on some cards and "Nativity Scenes" on others. The County School Board is cracking down (banning) religious expression in their schools.[58]

Fox4 News, Dallas-Fort Worth, Texas reported in December 2013 that Nichols Elementary School in Frisco, Texas posted "rules" for the school's "winter" party (aka Christmas). The rules are: No reference to Christmas or any other religious holiday; no red or green colors of clothing; and no Christmas trees. These rules are a direct violation of the state's June 14, 2013 "Merry Christmas Bill" guaranteeing that students and staff can discuss "winter" holidays as they please. They can legally say "Merry Christmas" and "Happy Hanukkah," and nativity scenes, Menorahs, Christmas trees and other traditional symbols can be displayed. The school district decided law-or-not, their rules will stay in

---

[57] "Craig James and the Loss of Religious Liberty," David L. Goetsch, Patriot Update.com, http://wwwpatriotupdate.com, November 19, 2013

[58] "Georgia School Confiscates Christmas Cards," Todd Starnes, Townhall.com, http://www.townhall.com, December 3, 2013

place because they do not want to offend anyone. Obviously Christians and Jews aren't included in the "anyone" category.

In an Orange County, California neighborhood, homeowners were ordered by the county to remove their Christmas lights because they were an "obstruction" and they coincidently violated "county code ordinances." Isn't it strange that Christmas lights never violated any codes the past, say, fifty years or so? In Portland, Oregon an 11-year old girl was selling "bags of hand-cut and hand-wrapped Christmas mistletoe at a weekly city market to make money to help pay for the cost of her braces. To me this little girl should be commended for taking the initiative to make money for an important cause. Unfortunately for her she was told that a city ordinance bans this activity in a park without a lease, concession or permit. She would have to move away from the park, and the people or she could just ask for money donations for her braces. "A Portland Parks Bureau spokesman told the station (KATU-TV) that begging is a form of free speech and is protected by the First Amendment."[59]

President George Washington's Farewell Address is a profound warning to us: *"Of all the dispositions and habits which lead to political prosperity, Religion and Morality are indispensable supports. In vain would that men claim the tribute of Patriotism, who should labor to subvert these great pillars of human happiness, these firmest props of the duties of Men and Citizens...Reason and experience both forbid us to expect that nationally morality can prevail in exclusion of religious principle."*

While the government is on mission to neutralize Christianity, it is protecting and promoting Islam which is a theocracy, and was never considered a true religion to our Founders. Why is Islam held to a different standard of tolerance? It is celebrated in some public schools under the guise of "diversity." The children are **mandatory** participants in Islamic teachings, are assigned Muslim names, and even provided Muslim dress. The "progressive" reason is that American children need to learn tolerance of other cultures and religions. "God" is forbidden but Islam's "Allah" is welcome. This is not only hypocritical; it is disgraceful.

---

[59] "Oregon girl told she can't sell mistletoe, but can beg for money," KATU-TV, Portland, published by Fox News, http://www.foxnews.com, December 3, 2013

It would serve us all to remember Louisiana Governor Bobby Jindal's statement:

"America didn't create religious liberty.
Religious liberty created America."

Freedom of speech:

"The right guaranteed by the First Amendment to the United States Constitution, to communicate ideas and opinions without government intervention."[60]

"I may not agree with what you say, but I will
defend to the death your right to say it."

-Voltaire to Helvetius

Definitions of "freedom of speech," may differ slightly but all contain words such as, right, liberty, freedom, ideas, opinions, and clearly state protections such as "without fear of punishment," "without government intervention," and "without hindrance. Freedom of speech is a right we take for granted. Extent of the freedom, subject and contents of speech including offensiveness, and level of perceived offensiveness are all complicated issues that are constantly debated.

For clarification on the subject, we need to know what the Founders meant by freedom of speech. I believe their focus was on preventing government suppression of political and religious speech, whereas eighteenth century American society had established guidelines and limits of acceptable personal expression and speech. These two very different aspects of speech have become foggy over the past century due to government and judicial intervention, and progressive political correctness. The once clear line between political and personal speech has become one-sidedly defined. The government has been steadily restricting and censoring speech whether political or personal already

[60] Definition of "Freedom of Speech," *Webster's New World Law Dictionary*, 2006

to the point that a single careless word or statement can lead to legal prosecution as offensive language; hate speech and racial or gender slurs. Since violations whether real or perceived carry professional and legal penalties, many of us out of fear have stifled our own voices. This is not the freedom of speech our founders envisioned.

The Founders were not concerned about personal comments and language by fellow Americans. They were concerned about the government imposing limits on speech content and the obstruction of criticism and dissent by citizens critical of the government. Once a government has the power to control what its citizens can and cannot say it is no longer a free republican government. Other eighteenth century governments routinely imprisoned and punished citizens for simply disagreeing with the government or its leader. More modern examples would be the USSR and China's imprisonment and even death of dissidents and critics of their regimes. Venezuela's Hugo Chavez did not tolerate criticism or dissent. Our Founders knew it was imperative for the citizens to question their government leaders and be able to freely express their support and dissent without fear of punishment or retribution.

The Supreme Court has passed rulings over the years based on the concept that "all speech is not equal under the First Amendment."[61] The court identified five extents of expression that the government can legally restrict under certain circumstances: *speech that incites illegal activity, subversive speech, fighting words, obscenity and pornography, commercial speech, and symbolic expression.*

Political dissent is the heart of freedom of speech and we are witnessing a new era in government suppression and intimidation that is threatening this basic freedom. Case in point is the Government/Obama Administration attempts to discredit, disparage, demean, and dismiss American citizen protesters such as the TEA Parties (Taxed Enough Already). The Tea Party is not a political party like the Democrat and Republican parties. The "Tea Party" is a consortium of local, county and state citizens who support American Values, lower taxes, smaller government and fiscal responsibility. These citizens representing all

---

[61] First Amendment: Freedom of Speech, http://legal-dictionary.thefreedictionary.com/Freedom+of+Speech

races (though you would not know that from the mainstream media coverage) banded together in the spring of 2009 to protest excessive government spending, taxation, national health care, and unwarranted government intrusion into their lives.

The Tea Party and numerous other "citizen" groups are spreading the message that the government was formed by the Constitution and is bound by the limitations set therein. A tyrannical disengaged government dictating to an over-regulated, over-taxed, and underrepresented citizenry lit the flame for independence resulting in the creation of our Constitution and government of the people - for the people. The Tea Party has hit a nerve with the current government in general and the current administration in particular. The federal government has become accustomed to operating without oversight and does not like over-regulated, over-taxed and underrepresented Americans demanding transparency and accountability, as is required by the Constitution. It is a dangerous step when at the behest of the executive branch of government; the Internal Revenue Service (IRS) manipulates and illegally targets these groups to influence election outcomes. This is a blatant violation of the First Amendment not to mention a politically criminal act. As witnessed the past five years, the Obama administration has to identify and promote some Americans as "threats" to divide the American people. The Tea Party is no more a national threat than the Chicago Cubs are.

Numerous citizen groups participated in "Town Hall" meetings held across America in August 2009. These organized and orderly events were attended by hundreds of thousands of law-abiding, tax-paying citizens of all ages from around the country who are ignored by their own government. They presented legitimate concerns and because they exercised their guaranteed right of free speech, they were and still are labeled "fringe," "mobs," "racists," 'homophobes," and "extremists." The administration with the mainstream media's help has waged a campaign to silence these *real citizens* to keep their message from spreading.

I find it interesting that hundreds of thousands of peaceful, law-abiding American citizens participated in Tea Party and Town Hall events throughout 2009 <u>without</u> riots or vandalism; though there was an incident outside a Town Hall in St. Louis where an innocent citizen was assaulted not by citizen protesters but by members of the SEIU (Service Employees International Union) the very union with close ties to the President. In another incident, a citizen was threatened with arrest for holding a sign critical of Obama outside of a town hall meeting in Virginia.[62] Compare these so-called Tea Party "mobs" to the hundreds of "enlightened" Occupy Wall Street protesters that camped-out in U.S. cities to protest economic inequality, corporate greed and corruption in 2011. The Left and the media loved those *"we are the 99%"* demonstrators portraying them as heroes while ignoring rampant thefts, rapes, vandalism and drug use in their patriotic little villages. Behavioral problems, violence and arrests are common at many liberal protests, though they are not reported accurately if even reported at all by the media. It's like we've shifted to an opposite universe - Peaceful Americans protesting an ever-increasing oppressive government are demonized while unruly and destructive protesters are hailed as heroes.

I believe the so-called "tolerant" left with the media's help has taken demonization of people they do not agree with to an entirely new and "lower" level. A University of Washington political science professor claims that racism is a common element of Tea Party supporters and he compares them to the Ku Klux Klan. So what does the learned professor base his thesis on? *"Similar to the Klan, white middle-class, middle-aged, Protestant men dominate the Tea Party's ranks." "Can we not say that the Tea Party is heavily involved in politics? Further, can we not also say that many Tea Partiers are not educated and accomplished? Finally can we not also say that the Tea Party has an intolerant element?"*[63]

Can we not say that since there is so much wrong with the professor's evaluation of the Tea Party, it needs to be addressed? First of all, no one associated with the Tea Party is alarmed or shocked over a liberal and supposedly enlightened professor's self-aggrandizing assessment of a group he obviously knows little about. And, the "race" card has been so over-played by the Left that it is frivolously thrown around as their go-to, catch-all phrase. For instance, he specifies that the Tea Party

---

[62] "Town-hall clash! Arrest threat over Obama 'Joker' poster," http://www.worldnetdaily.com and Youtube, http://www.youtube.com/watch?v=hIKPKj10-pg
[63] "University sends email equating the tea party with the KKK," Robby Soave, The Daily Caller, http://dailycaller.com, December 6, 2013

is like the KKK of the 1920s as if that decade of KKK members were basically different from the other decades. He also makes a point to identify the KKK as "a national right-wing movement." I find that a strange choice of words considering the KKK and the South in general were dominated and controlled by the Democrat Party – that is a fact! Can we not also say that race-baiting professors rob our children of the truth? Yes, we can.

I have met and talked with many Tea Party members and have witnessed numerous events and never once saw or heard anything racially bigoted. A handful of disparaging signs among hundreds of thousands of signs across the country does not make the organization "racist." Remember when the House was voting on Obamacare and a few African-American members of Congress claimed that Tea Party members shouted racial slurs at them while walking near the Capital and the media made a big deal out of it? Evidence of that unacceptable behavior never materialized even though news cameras, video cameras and smart phones recorded the entire "walk" of those Congressional members. The late Andrew Breitbart (*Big Government.com)* offered $100,000 to anyone who had the alleged racial discrimination recorded. No one did -because the incident did not happen. The media did not cover this development of the story and the Congressmen and women who leveled the accusation suddenly went silent.

Ron Christie (*The Daily Beast*) was present at this event and he did not witness any alleged racial behavior by Tea Party members. Addressing the indiscriminate racial charges, Mr. Christie said: *"Many, many peaceful protesters were out that day. There were synchronized chants of "Kill the Bill," but I did not see anyone saying anything untoward to any of the members of Congress, regardless of their race or gender ... The charge of racism without a shred of proof, much less irrefutable evidence, is doing terrible damage to our cultural fabric. We should be able to agree to disagree respectfully without invoking race at every turn..."*[64]

The truth is there are African-American members of the Tea Party – always were and they are increasing in number. Lloyd Marcus is one man who proudly identifies himself as an "Unhyphenated-American"

---

[64] "Democrats Have Maxed Out the Race Card," Ron Christie, The Daily Beast, http://www.thedailybeast.com/politics.html, December 17, 2013

Tea Party member. He is the author of the book, *"Confessions of a Black Conservative: How the Left has shattered the dreams of Martin Luther King, Jr. and Black America."* He is also a writer, maintains a great website, and is a regular keynote Tea Party speaker. Lloyd penned the Tea Party Anthem and many other songs that he sings beautifully at rallies and events. His signature statement is, *"I am NOT an African-American; I am Lloyd Marcus, AMERICAN."* Liberals including the Washington University political science professor need to meet Niger Innis the Executive Director of the TeaParty.net organization. Aside from being a very effective and respected leader, Mr. Innis is an African-American conservative; a fact that African-Americans in Congress and academics like the Washington University professor do not want to hear and most certainly would never share.

As for the claim that white, middle-class, middle-aged, Protestant men dominate the Tea Party - I did not see that and have never seen that "domination." If the professor knew anything about the Tea Party he would know that women play a huge role in the organization, as well as grandparents, young couples with children, Veterans (God Bless them) – people of all ages, races, economic positions, and professions. The Tea Party is made up of teachers, lawyers, doctors, business owners as well as home makers, retired people and maybe most offensive of all to the Left – young people. It is representative of lower, middle and upper class working, tax-paying American citizens. Surprise - these people are educated, are politically knowledgeable, and what they are "intolerant" of is an out-of-control government that keeps growing, getting more powerful, disregards its own laws, and imposes incessant tax increases to fund excessive welfare programs that are corrupt and fraudulent. These are the people who are bearing the burden to support the government nanny-state.

Other examples of the **"double-standard"** regarding freedom of speech, religion, and the press:

- On one hand there is no problem criticizing Christians and Jews, making fun of them on television and radio, or verbally assaulting them; but no such behavior is tolerated against Muslims. One case in point is the successful censorship of a satirical Muhammad episode on Comedy Central's South Park in 2010 because it was offensive to Muslims. Another 2010 incident was when the Pentagon rescinded their invitation to Christian evangelist Franklin Graham to participate in the National Day of Prayer event because he said Islam was "evil" for how it treats women even though what Graham said was the truth. Islam treats women despicably – there is no way to soften that reality. In Miami, ads were placed on busses supporting religious freedom including how to help Muslims afraid to leave Islam because of the "peaceful" religion's punishment for apostates (those who leave Islam) which is death. The Miami-Dade Transit Authority removed the ads because they were offensive to Islam. Briefly stated, anything Muslims do not like is offensive to Islam – that pretty much covers all other religions and everything we stand for in America.

- First Lady Michelle Obama and her entourage took a trip to China in March 2014. Journalists were banned from accompanying her because the White House said it was a personal trip - not a political trip. (Since it was a "personal" trip, the taxpayers should not have had to pay for it. Oh did we pay)! And, Mrs. Obama did make political speeches about, you guessed it - freedom of speech: "...And that's why it's so important for information and ideas to flow freely over the internet and through the media; because that's how we discover the truth."[65] Article author Michael Hausam summed up the situation this way: "So Michelle Obama lectures a communist police state about freedom of speech standards, while the White House is spying on journalists and restricting access to information in the U.S." Yet another example of the Left's hypocritical double standard.

- Matthew Balan of the Media Research Center interviewed Jonathan Karl whose assessment validated Michael Hausam's though he added: "Unlike Laura Bush and Hillary Clinton, who both pressed human rights on their trips to China, the White

---

[65] "Call the Hypocrisy Police: Michelle Obama Praises Free Speech on China Trip that Banned Journalists," Michael Hausam, the *Independent Journal Review*, http://www.ijreview.com, March 2014

> *House says that Mrs. Obama will shy away from issues that may be controversial with her Chinese host."*[66]

- President Obama who promised to have the most transparent administration ever regularly forbids news media from meetings with foreign visitors and other events. The White House has its own media center and press which distributes Presidential sanctioned photos and descriptions of the events to the media. No freedom of the press here! *The Associated Press* (AP) reported, *"The presidents of the American Society of Newspaper Editors and the Associated Press Media Editors have urged their members to stop using White House handout photos and video, saying they amount to propaganda."*

- Author Pamela Geller writes, *"Not only is Obama shutting out the press, but the Obama White House is rewriting the Freedom of Information Act (FOIA) to suppress the release of politically sensitive documents. Obama rewrote the Freedom of Information Act without telling the rest of America. And AP [Associated Press] also reported that 'in a year of intense public interest over the National Security Agency's surveillance programs, the government cited national security to withhold information a record 8,496 times – a 57 percent increase over a year earlier and more than double Obama's first year, when it cited that reason 3,658 times."*[67]

Freedom of Speech is becoming a freedom reserved only for the Obama administration and their supporters. Anyone critical of the president or his administration is now a target for censorship. This is a huge step into a socialist abyss. Where is the Congress sworn to defend First Amendment freedoms?

---

[66] "ABC, CBS Trumpet Mrs. Obama's 'Ping-Pong Diplomacy' in China; Omit Press Shutout," Matthew Balan, the Media Research Center, http://www.mrc.org, March 21, 2014

[67] "Obama Rewrites FOIA – Doesn't Tell America – Sets Sights on Internet Free Speech," Pamela Geller, published on Freedom Outpost, http://www.freedomoutpost.com, March 24, 2014

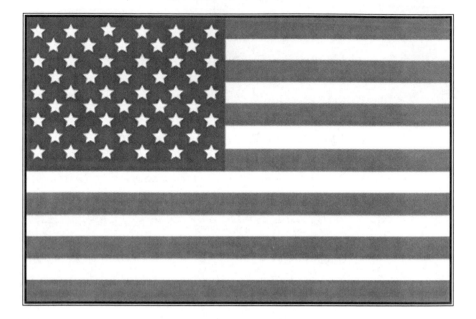

American Symbols Are Offensive?

We are walking in the shadow of our liberties. It is extremely disturbing to me that progressives are gaining ground in their campaign to denigrate America. A glaring example of their mindset is the liberal progressive ambivalence to the desecration of the American flag - the most important symbol of our nation. While they have no problem with the flag being used as a floor mat and being burned in protest, they do have a problem with Americans who respect the flag and what it stands for. For instance:

- A supervisor at a Texas hospital hung an American flag in her office for Memorial Day. The flag was taken down because it "offended" an employee (a woman who had emigrated to the U.S.).[68] This action was not just an assault on the freedom of an American citizen, but an assault on our nation at large.

---

[68] "Texas Woman Told to Remove "Offensive" American Flag From Office," www.foxnews.com, May 29, 2009

- A firefighter in Pennsylvania was suspended without pay because he refused to remove an American flag sticker from the outside of his locker in violation of a policy that banned all personal material on locker doors.[69]

- An apartment complex in Oregon that banned its tenants from flying American flags from the building and from their cars in the parking lot.[70] Violations of this ban would result in eviction.

- A similar incident happened to an Army veteran in Oshkosh, Wisconsin when the management company where he and his wife lived told him that he must take his American flag down or face eviction. The management company instituted the no flag policy because the residents were of diverse backgrounds and, *"By having a blanket policy of neutrality we have found that we are less likely to offend anyone and the aesthetic qualities of our apartment communities are maintained."*[71]

- A thirteen-year old student at a California school flew the American flag on his bicycle to show support for veterans. In November 2010, shortly before Veterans Day, the school decided he could no longer fly the flag citing concern for racial tension with Hispanic students and for his own protection. The school reversed the decision after receiving a flood of complaints, and seeing widespread support for the student.

- Another California school, this one a high school in Morgan Hill sent 5 students home for refusing to take off or turn their tee-shirts with American flag images inside-out. It was May 5, 2010 and the school was afraid there could be violence between the Anglo and Hispanic students (who were free to wear Mexican flag tee-shirts and carry Mexican flags) to celebrate the Mexican non-holiday of "Cinco de Mayo." Parents of the 5 students filed suit against the school district for First Amendment rights

---

[69] *"Pennsylvania Firefighter Suspended for U.S. Flag on Locker,"* www.foxnews.com, October 17, 2009

[70] *"Oregon Apartment Complex Bans Flying the American Flag,"* www.foxnews.com, Wednesday, October 14, 2009

[71] "Wisconsin Veteran Must Remove Flag After Memorial Day, Wife Says," Joshua Rhett Miller, May 26, 2010, www.foxnews.com

violation and discrimination. Turns out a Chief U.S. District Judge ruled against the students, and recently the 9th Circuit Court upheld the ruling siding with the school.

American students and their parents learned some important lessons:

- America's flag and symbol of "liberty" shall be lowered in deference to other country's flags, celebrations and non-holidays. For the record, Cinco de Mayo is not Mexican Independence Day. It is the celebration of a Mexican military victory over the French in the 1862 Battle of Puebla and is not even a big event in Mexico.

- Americans cannot display American symbols in America. "Fear" of violence from those offended by American patriotism takes precedence over American's Constitutional rights.

- Foreign patriotism is welcomed and encouraged in the U.S. but American patriotism is not tolerated.

- American students are "second-class" citizens in their own country while only Hispanic students (whether legal citizens or not) receive Constitutional guarantees. The schools, courts and the government are once again promoting racial tension by pitting one ethnic group against another. Somebody needs to remind California that the state is still located in the United States of America, not in Mexico.

- On Memorial Day weekend 2010 American flags around the country were vandalized including: 25 flags set afire in Wooster, Ohio, a flag in front of a Marine veteran's home was set afire, and a couple in Portland, Oregon found their flag covered in obscenities and burned in front of their home. These were incidents reported by foxnews.com in June 2010.[72] Did you hear much about this from network media and the major newspapers?

- An Arizona man was told by his homeowner's Association to remove his "Gadsden" flag (yellow flag with a coiled snake and

---

[72] "Flag Vandalism Mars memorial Day in Several States," Joshua Rhett Miller, www.foxnews.com, June 01, 2010

the words, *"Don't Tread On Me."*)[73] This flag named after its creator, Christopher Gadsden dates back to 1775 and preceded the American "Stars and Stripes." Benjamin Franklin said the rattlesnake is *an emblem of vigilance – She never begins an attack, nor, when engaged, ever surrenders: She is therefore an emblem of magnanimity and true courage.*[74] Many people automatically associate the Gadsden flag with the Tea Party. The Tea Party did not create the flag but closely associate with its historic significance of patriotism and citizenship. You will probably be seeing more and more Gadsden flags flying along with – not in place of, the U.S. flag.

Images of the "Gadsden Flag" created in 1775

- A 35 foot American Flag mural painted on concrete above I-680 in Sunol, California after 9/11 was ordered painted-over by state

---

[73] "Arizona Man Fights to Keep Gadsden Flag Flying Outside His Home," August 25, 2010, www.foxnews.com
[74] Benjamin Franklin, Pennsylvania Journal, December 27, 1775, (http://www.americanheritage.com/articles/magazine/ah/1988)

officials in 2010. The mural was restored after public outrage convinced the California governor to reverse the decision.[75]

- In 2012 an elderly woman living in public housing in Phillipsburg, NJ was told to remove three small American flags from the balcony of her apartment because all flags are banned so as not to offend anyone. She was threatened with eviction if she did not take the flags down.[76]

Who could have ever imagined that singing the national anthem, the presence of our American flag and the recitation of the "Pledge of Allegiance," would become so controversial and even despised? Sports Journalist and Professor Kevin Blackstone stated that the national anthem which he referred to as a "war anthem' should not be played before sporting events because sports have too much "military symbolism,"

Schools that are supposed to be "educating" our children seem to have a lot of time to spend on "pledge issues." An elementary school in New York State only recites the opening line of the pledge. Besides not reciting the pledge in its entirety (a whopping 31 words), students can "opt-out" of reciting it at all.[77] A public school in Brookline, Massachusetts is allowing the pledge to be recited in school, but parents must sign a permission slip to allow their children to participate in the recital. Aside from the controversy that has created, it is further complicated by the fact that some other parents feel permission slips will compel children to recite the pledge only because their parents are imposing their own beliefs on their children.[78] *Those dastardly parents!*

On an encouraging note, when the debate moderator at a congressional candidate debate in Grayslake, Illinois in October 2010

---

[75] "Covered-Up Flag Mural near Calif. Freeway Restored," *Associated Press*, July 06, 2010

[76] "Elderly Woman Told She Can't Fly American Flag," Todd Starnes, Fox News, May 29, 2012

[77] "Partial Pledge Has Some Seeing Stars at New York School," Todd Starnes, foxnews.com, November 09, 2010

[78] "US Mass. School Requires Permission Slips to Recite Pledge of Allegiance," Jonathan M. Seidl, Patriot Action Network, December 22, 2010, www.patriotactionnetwork.com

told the audience the Pledge of Allegiance would not be recited, the crowd began to shout, "why not?" Since the debate moderator would not allow the pledge to be recited, the audience stood and said the pledge themselves. The miffed moderator scolded the audience and called the crowd recital "phony patriotism." The video of this event was posted and can be viewed on YouTube ["Pledge of Allegiance BANNED at Melissa Bean Debate"].[79]

These are not isolated instances; they are becoming daily occurrences. Those who wish to see America reduced to just another global country have become empowered and if we do not stand up for our country now, we will see more and more of our constitutionally guaranteed rights diminish.

Like a breath of fresh air, the Supreme Court upheld the cornerstone principles of free speech in their decision on the case of *Citizens United v. FEC* in January 2010. The justices' affirmed the right to engage in free speech, political speech in particular, and the right to freely assemble specifically in regard to corporate and union political donations and political ads. In response to this Supreme Court ruling, President Obama said that he couldn't "think of anything more devastating to the public interest."[80] Senator Chuck Schumer of New York declared the decision was "un-American,"[81] It is obvious the elected officials in Washington need a refresher course on the Constitution. Maybe someone can explain the First Amendment to them.

The Second Amendment

Guarantees *"...the right of the people to keep and bear arms, shall not be infringed,"* is under monumental assault by progressives who want the citizenry disarmed.

---

[79] "No Pledge at Debate? Watch Crowd say otherwise: Audience drowns out moderator's objections that recital of allegiance to flag 'disrespectful,'" Drew Zahn, World Net Daily, October 23, 2010, www.worldnetdaily.com

[80] "Obama blasts campaign finance ruling", The Associated Press – msnbc.com, January 23, 2010. http://www.msnbc.com

[81] "Chuck Schumer (D-NY): Free speech is un-American," Moe Lane, Red State. com. http://www.redstate.com

> *"Arms discourage and keep the invader and plunderer is awe, and preserve order in the world as well as property…Horrid mischief would ensue were the law-abiding deprived of the use of them."*
>
> —Thomas Paine

Progressives promote the argument that crime is exacerbated by the fact U.S. citizens are guaranteed the right to bear arms - though facts prove otherwise. They are committed to their war against guns which is an extremely dangerous attack on our Constitutional right to bear arms. History has proven that once a government successfully disarms it citizenry, the door to tyranny opens wide. Many people especially those who do not own guns do not pay much attention to the political battle over gun laws and bans. This is a mistake. None of our Constitutional rights are negotiable and we must stand together to defend all of them.

Law abiding gun owning citizens are not the problem; criminals and gang members are. If all guns were banned, criminals and gang members would still have guns. NRA-ILA Executive Director, Chris W. Cox, in an April 2010 article said: *"While a ban would harm the law-abiding, it obviously wouldn't affect violent criminals. After all, government studies have found that at least 40 percent of felons acquire their firearms from 'street/illegal sources' – ranging up to 97 percent for criminals who attack law enforcement officers. And an attacker determined to commit mayhem can always use multiple magazines, multiple guns or a more powerful gun that holds less ammunition."*[82] It's idiocy to think these thugs would adhere to gun laws. We have the right to protect ourselves and our properties from criminals who have everything to gain from gun bans.

To the dismay of gun-control proponents, Washington D.C., known as one of the highest-crime cities in the nation, saw a 10% decrease in the murder rate in 2010 – AFTER the Supreme Court ruling (*District of Columbia v. Heller*) that the second amendment guarantees the right to keep and bear arms for protection in one's home.[83] On the other hand, The City of Chicago with some of the most stringent gun control

---

[82] "Tragedy in Arizona," Chris W. Cox, *America's 1st Freedom*, April 2007
[83] "D.C. Violence Plummets! Heller's Lesson," *America's First Freedom*, NRA News, www.NRAnews.com, March 2011

laws in the nation is the 2013 national "murder capital." The Chicago Tribune reported that from January 1st to October 8th, 2013 there were 1,771 shooting victims in Chicago.[84] Here are just some of the 2013 media headlines: "Eight Shot, One Killed in Chicago in a Single Hour Overnight," DNAinfo.comChicago, March 31, 2013; "Four Dead, At Least 22 Wounded in Weekend Shootings," *DNAinfo.comChicago Neighborhood News* April 15, 2013; "10-year-old boy among victims as more than 20 shot on one Chicago day," *NBC News*, May 2, 2013; "Violence reverberates through the city, even with decline in shootings, homicides," (More than 40 people had been shot over a single weekend in Chicago), *The Chicago Tribune*, July 7, 2013; "Boy,3, among 13 injured in Chicago park shooting," *MSN News*, September 19, 2013.

The City of Chicago's handgun ban is a great illustration of how the city operates. Chicago required that all firearms in the city be registered and then refused ALL registrations when a citywide handgun ban was passed in 1982 preventing any Chicagoan from legally owning a handgun. That ban was overturned in 2010 when the Supreme Court decided that the Second Amendment right to keep and bear arms is incorporated by the Due Process Clause of the Fourteenth Amendment. Mr. Otis McDonald, an exceptional man, deserves tremendous credit for this significant change of events. A 2012 story in the *Examiner* summed up Mr. McDonald's challenge this way: *"McDonald took on the most oppressive citizen disarmament laws in the country, which Chicago's mayor at the time defended with millions of Chicago taxpayer's dollars – and won. This quiet man could no longer stay quiet in the face of the denial of his constitutionally guaranteed, fundamental human right of the individual to keep and bear arms. He could no longer meekly submit to laws that denied his right to defend his life and loved ones."*[85]

Otis McDonald's biography, *"An Act of Bravery: Otis McDonald and the Second Amendment"* by Sue Brown, was published on 9/21/2012 and is a great "American" story. Follow his life from poverty in the cotton fields in Louisiana to being the first person in his family to earn a

---

[84] "Chicago Shooting Victims," Chicago Tribune – Crime in Chicago, http://crime.chicagotribune.com/chicago/shootings, October 8. 2013

[85] "An Act of Bravery: Otis McDonald," *The Examiner*, http://www.examiner.com/article/an-act-of-bravery-otis-mcdonald-biography, September 26,2012

college degree. Once secure in the middle class of Chicago, he witnessed the rise of gang and drug activity which threatened his family and his home. Even with burglaries, vandalism and personal threats Mr. McDonald persevered to stand up for his rights guaranteed under the U.S. Constitution. See, one man can make a difference!

Chicago citizens may now have a "legally registered" gun but only inside their own home. City Residents and workers must still rely on the Chicago Police Department for their safety and protection. I've worked in Chicago so believe me that is not a comforting thought. I have the utmost respect for police officers; theirs is a difficult, dangerous and thankless profession. The officers on the front lines do not formulate policy so I am in no way criticizing them. I imagine many Chicago police officers are just as frustrated with the city's rampant crime and feckless political policies as the rest of us. The reality is there are not enough police officers in the city to adequately protect the people. I have sat through safety meetings where we (law abiding citizens) were taught how to be good victims; to comply with attackers in order to survive an assault, rape, or robbery. Unfortunately there was little talk about the city getting tough and prosecuting criminals. I don't know about you, but I do not want to be a "good little victim" while criminals run free with no fear of the police or the justice system. If police departments are not capable of protecting their citizens, then let the citizens protect themselves, as is, a fundamental right.

The Chicago Police Department implemented a novel anti-crime tactic in July 2013. They had identified a network (known to the rest of us as gangs) of 400 people responsible for over 70% of the murders in the city and put them on a "heat list." "Warning" letters not to commit violent crimes or they would be charged with the "most serious crime possible," were then delivered to those people on the list.[86] Did anyone seriously think this could work? I hope no one was shocked by the results - These hard core killers and drug-dealers just kept on shooting and killing. How about jail sentences as a deterrent to violent crime?

Cap Black, Coordinator of the Home Defense Foundation is an

---

[86] "Chicago's new war on guns: Letters," Tal Kopan, Politico, http://dyn.politico.com, July 19, 2013, and the *Chicago Sun Times* newspaper

insightful man who posts regularly on Face Book and Twitter.[87] His September 14, 2013 post, "The Hood Needs More Protection Not Social Programs," should be read by every politician and urban police force (especially the Chicago PD). *"The Hood needs more protection (armed citizens united with supportive police, prosecutors, judges & legislators), not more social programs benefitting a distant politburo using thugs as political leverage!"* .... *"Unlike the Obamas, other Black elected officials and celebrities, the average Hood hostage can't afford private guards or off duty police protection."*

Just as gun-control folks cannot bear the thought of American citizens legally owning guns, they have no tolerance for toy guns either. As the trend to abolish guns and anything that resembles or "may" depict a gun continues, we really need to pay attention. An NRA Political Report from 2010 illustrates the lunacy of "no-gun" proponents:[88]

- Providence, Rhode Island city leaders held their seventh annual "Toy Gun Bash" on December 18, 2010. Children who brought a toy gun to school to be destroyed received *"a Christmas present that reflects a more peaceful way to play and have fun."*
- A 9-year old Stanton Island, New York student was targeted for suspension after bringing a 2 inch toy gun to school
- A 6-year old kindergartner in Ionia, Michigan was suspended for pointing his fingers in the shape of a gun
- Marian Wright Edelman, head of the "anti-gun" Children's Defense Fund testified at a Congressional hearing: *"The terrible Taliban terrorist threat to American child and citizen safety is rivaled by the terrible NRA threat which terrorizes our political leaders from protecting our children ..."*
- A Maryland boy in Kindergarten was interrogated for over two hours and then suspended from school for ten days because he

---

[87] "The Hood Needs More Protection Not Social Programs," Cap Black, Home Defense Foundation, September 14, 2013, http://www.hdfnola.org, Home Defense Foundation Nola on Face Book, @HomeDefenseNola on Twitter
[88] "On The Front Lines Of The Culture War," Chris W. Cox, NRA Political Report, America's 1st Freedom, September 2010

showed a friend his plastic orange tipped cap gun on a school bus on the way to school.[89]

- A second-grade boy in Florida was suspended from school because he was playing cops and robbers with another child using his finger and thumb to represent a gun. He had nothing in his hand![90]

- A high school senior in Georgia was arrested on a felony weapons charge when police found his "fish cleaning knife" inside his tackle box which was inside his car parked in the school parking lot.[91]

- A sticker of a gun with a red line through it is now required by law to be displayed in public schools to signify a "gun-free" zone made some school officials at a suburban Chicago High School very angry. Why, were they angry, you ask? They were angry because it was a "picture of a gun." Keep in mind, these people are teaching our children.

Schools have embraced across-the-board "zero tolerance" policies since some teachers and school officials are obviously unable to determine that a slice of bread and a pop-tart chewed into the shape of a gun are not "real" gun threats just as plastic toy guns are not "real" guns which will make children grow up to be murderous thugs. Adult ignorance is creating unnecessary stress and punishment for children, even young kindergarteners who are made to feel like little criminals and are subjected to suspension and ridicule. Since this is unacceptable to sensible people, a Florida lawmaker introduced a bill to protect children from serious consequences for playing with harmless imaginary guns like their fingers, pastries and even Lego blocks.

A few more examples of out-of-control liberal logic forced upon us:

---

[89] "Kindergartener interrogated over cap gun until he pees his pants, then suspended 10 days," www.dailycaller.com, May 31, 2013

[90] "Second Grader Suspended for Carrying Invisible Gun …. No Really," Tim Brown, Freedom Outpost, http://freedom outpost.com, October 5, 2013

[91] "Student Faces Felony Weapons Charge For Fishing Gear in Car," Dave Jolly, Godfather Politics, http://godfatherpolitics.com, October 7, 2013

- The Brady Campaign denounced the NBA, Nike, and star Kobe Bryant for an advertisement in which Bryant said, *"I don't leave anything in the chamber."*

- On July 7, 2012 Washington DC police – thirty officers in full tactical gear with guns drawn entered a man's home with a search warrant for "firearms and ammunition..." His 14-year old daughter was terrified, his 16-year old son was dragged naked out of the shower, and his house was totally ransacked. Turns out, there were no guns but the man was arrested because they found one inoperable shotgun shell and one spent brass casing. *"This man and his children committed no crime, yet they were treated worse than murderers and child molesters. The madness has to stop."*[92]

- The *New York Post* reported on May 2, 2013 that the owner of a Midtown New York tourist shop was hit with a $60,000 fine ($5,000 each) for 12 bronze-and-silver colored 3 inch butane lighters shaped like a gun. The *Post* also reported that New York City officials have seized over 7,200 illegal toy guns from stores and fined those stores 2.4 million dollars. [93]

- A federal judge ruled the New York City "Stop and Frisk" successful crime fighting tactic used by the NYC Police Department is unconstitutional. Former New York Governor, George Pataki has evidence to the contrary. He said, *"The effect of the policy is thousands of lives that are saved, largely low-income, minority lives, because we have much lower rates of violent crime."*[94]

- In Augusta, Georgia Army veteran Tanya Perry-Mount received a "no trespassing order" from her daughter's elementary school. Tanya is banned from the school because the principal decided

---

[92] "DC cops raid home, drag 16-year-old naked from the shower, arrest father for 2 EMPTY shell casings," The *Washington Times*, published on Poor Richards News, http://poorrichardsnews.com, October 23, 2013

[93] "Smoking gun nets 60G fine," Julia Marsh, The New York Post, http://www.nypost.com, May 2, 2013

[94] "Pataki: Stop and Frisk Saved Thousands of Lives," Newsmax, http://www.newsmax.com, August 13, 2013

that she is a potential risk for having served in the U.S. Army, and has a conceal carry gun permit.[95]

These are just some of the results of ridiculous laws and regulations that have been established because of pressure from liberal groups to exert "control." Does anyone know of a law to provide psychiatric therapy to the children traumatized by liberal policies? There should be one since incidents like these will be increasing.

It seems that the state of Maryland does not allow you to defend your own home. Air Force Sergeant Matt Pinkerton was charged with second degree murder after he fatally shot an intruder who broke down the door of his home and would not stop approaching him. The District Attorney who charged Matt with murder claimed that Matt exhibited "bizarre behavior" by getting his gun when there was someone unexpectedly at his door at 2AM and then by not calling 9-1-1 after the intruder kicked in the door and rushed Matt.[96]

IN 2013 the State of New York passed a gun law with the innocuous name of the S.A.F.E. Act. With this law in their holsters, the New York City Police Department notified gun owners of certain shotguns and rifles also known as "long guns" having a five-round or more capacity, that the guns must be turned in (surrendered), altered, or taken out of the city. So far three gun companies and a growing number of gun owners have left the state.

The Citizens Committee for the Right to Keep and Bear Arms (CCRKBA) reported on March 12, 2011 that the State of Illinois Attorney General, Lisa Madigan demanded the Illinois State Police "Release the name of every person in Illinois who holds a firearm owner's identification card (FOID)."[97] That would mean more than 1.3 million legal gun owner's names would be made public and criminals would

---

[95] "Legal Gun Owners Banned From Schools, Arrested and Will Be Shot," Dave Jolly, Godfather Politics, http://www.godfatherpolitics.com, November 13, 2013
[96] "Air Force Sgt. Mark Pinkerton Fires 2 Fatal Shots at Home Intruder – Now Faces 2nd Degree Murder Charge," Mac Salvo, Freedom Outpost, http://freedomoutpost.com, September 13, 2013
[97] "Illinois 'Outs' Gun Owners," Citizens Committee For the Right to Keep and Bear Arms, March 12, 2011, www.ccrkba.org

easily know who has a gun in their home, and just as important, who does not have gun to protect his home. Legal gun owners could become targets of harassment, anti-gun fanatics, and criminals looking to pick up some quick guns. Illinois Representative Ron Stephens made it clear that, *"You can own a handgun, and information about whether you do or don't is private information. There is no reason for anyone or any government agency to make available to you or anyone else whether I have a FOID card."* This is another example of the government interfering into the lives of legal, tax-paying, American citizens.

Seems to me the only thing these groups are advocating is victimization. I wonder what they would say if their vision of a " no gun or anything that resembles one" society came to fruition. I know one thing for sure – we would have no choice but to be victims living in fear at the mercy and whim of criminals with guns. That is a society I want no part of.

A very serious problem that we don't hear enough about is that drug cartels are engaged in an all-out war with the Mexican government. Thousands of people have been murdered and the Mexican government has not been able to stop the slaughter or put a dent in the over 30 billion dollar a year illegal drug trade into the United States. The drug cartels operating out of Mexico are better armed than many small countries. Their arsenals include automatic machine guns, grenade launchers, fragmentation grenades, ships, planes, and even private armies. In addition to the drug trade, Mexico is a major player in international arms trafficking. Russian mobsters, Eastern European countries, the Chinese government, and global black market syndicates operate without fear.[98]

The Mexico-US border is a bustling area of drug related crime. So what does that have to do with the Second Amendment and the right to bear arms? Some of our political leaders and their news network cronies who yearn for gun control legislation to disarm Americans loudly proclaim that firearms including shotguns and semi-automatic pistols must be banned because of the unstoppable bloodshed at the border. Senator Dianne Feinstein of California said the Mexican drug/crime problem is our fault because our gun laws don't keep Mexican criminals from getting guns. Anti-gun proponents claimed that 90%

---

[98] NRA (National Rifle Association), August 24, 2009

of firearms in the possession of Mexican drug criminals are from the United States. That makes for dramatic reading but it is not true. Only a fraction of the guns came from the U.S. For tracing purposes the Mexican government gives the U.S. government a small percentage of the firearms they confiscate. As it turns out many of the guns that did indeed originate in the U.S. were legally sold to the Mexican Army. Truth be told, 150,000 Mexican army members have deserted the military along with their weapons to join the drug cartels. Other deserters just sell their weapons to the cartels.

It is an insult that our own public officials like Senator Dianne Feinstein, Secretary of State Hillary Clinton, Attorney General Eric Holder, and Secretary of Homeland Security, Janet Napolitano have accused their own countrymen (gun owners and dealers, not drug buyers and users who purchase the illegal drugs) as contributing to the Mexican drug wars. Since the Mexican government cannot control its border and our law enforcement organizations are not given adequate resources to defend our border, Americans have the right to protect themselves and their property from criminals coming across the border and criminal gangs fanning out across our country.

The National Rifle Association (NRA) has been demonized by progressives as a barrier to a safe society. Nothing is further from the truth. The NRA works diligently to protect our Second Amendment right to bear arms from liberal government attacks. The NRA is a bastion of information and resources. You can access the NRA website at: http://www.nra.org. Another responsible organization protecting our Second Amendment right to bear arms is the Citizens Committee For The Right To Keep And Bear Arms (CCRKBA). The CCRKBA keeps readers updated on current news, proposed legislation and provides portals to contact our legislators. It is well worth your while to visit their website at http://www.ccrkba.org or call 800-486-6963 for information. The National Association for Gun Rights (NAGR) is a fast-growing grass-roots association that is committed to gun ownership education and championing federal and local gun rights issues. NAGR's website is http://www.nationalgunrights.org.

Two separate reports were released in May 2013 citing the same statistical data. The government Bureau of Justice Statistics Report and the PEW Research Center both published data that gun killings dropped 39% between 1993 and 2011. They also both report that only 12% of the population thinks the number of gun crimes is lower.[99] The conundrum for gun ban enthusiasts now is explaining how gun crime could decrease as gun ownership has increased exponentially.

The current progressive administration is committed to gun control. Since the President did not successfully garner enough congressional support to institute his gun bans legally, he went around Congress and issued executive actions giving his agencies legal regulatory power to institute and enforce his vision of disarmament. The NSA is spying on American citizens for no legal reason. The DHHS with its Obamacare powers along with the support of the American Psychiatric Association (APA) can determine who has <u>any</u> of variety of mental disorders (even a simple occasional anxiety attack is considered a "mental disorder") and declare those persons mentally unfit to own a firearm and the government can then legally confiscate your gun(s).

The administration began its disarmament campaign against the very people who sacrificed selflessly to defend our constitutional freedoms – our veterans. Since Obama took office, over 100,000 veterans and their families have been stripped of their Second Amendment right.[100] It's outrageous that bureaucrats working for the Veteran's Administration have the power to suspend constitutional rights. Now a veteran can lose his gun ownership right on the whim of a department administrator deciding who is and who is not a possible threat. You can be considered a threat even if you have mild anxiety; and if your spouse handles your family finances you can be deemed incompetent, without even a medical evaluation. Why is the government so afraid of armed (and militarily trained) veterans when most Americans feel a sense of security knowing these veterans are in the civilian population? Scary – isn't it?

---

[99] "Gun crime has plunged, but Americans think it's up, says study," *The LA Times*, http://www.latimes.com/news, May 7, 2013

"Two new reports show gun homicides down since 1990s," *Associated Press*, published by foxnews.com, www.foxnews.com, May 7, 2013

[100] "Feds Take Away Veterans Second Amendment Rights!" Joe Otto, Conservative Daily, http://www.conservativedaily.com, January 13, 2014

Who would have guessed that healthcare and psychiatry would coalesce into a political weapon? Actually and for the record, political dissenters in Germany and also in the Soviet Union under Stalin were labeled "mentally ill" and subjected to incarceration, abuse and even death. "Psychiatry for political purposes" has correspondingly been used in countries like Romania, Hungary, Czechoslovakia and Yugoslavia. Political abuse of psychiatry also takes place in China.[101] I am not saying we are headed for physical and mental abuse from our government like in those countries. That might be misconstrued as "paranoid" which would immediately put me on the federal "mental disorders" list. Think of it this way: If charges that the New Jersey governor shut down lanes on the George Washington Bridge causing incredible traffic jams, inconvenience and at least one death because the EMS could not get across the bridge in time as retribution against an uncooperative mayor of one of the cities in his state – just think what the federal government can do.

Disarming people does not stop crime but it does enable the government to better control its citizens. It would serve us well to remember former United States Governor and Senator, Zell Miller's warning, *"Time and time again history has shown the first step toward tyranny is to disarm the subjects. Under Kofi Annan, the UN has become the most powerful advocate of civilian disarmament in history."*[102] The United Nations continues its campaign to ban weapons, even here in the United States.

The UN approved The Arms Trade Treaty on April 2, 2013. This treaty which regulates global trade in conventional weapons was signed by our Secretary of State, John Kerry on September 25, 2013. This treaty would give the administration the green light to establish a national gun registry and a slew of gun restrictions in violation of the Second Amendment. Our rights are not just being compromised – they are being stolen by the very government sworn to protect them. Remember

---

[101] "How the Feds Plan to Use the APA, NSA and Obamacare to Get Your Guns," Jim White, Freedom Outpost, http://freedomoutpost.com, January 8, 2014
[102] "A Deficit of Decency," Zell Miller, GA: Stroud & Hall Publishers, 2005

this important fact: <u>The Constitution is our law and no foreign treaty has legal power over it</u>.[103]

Katie Worthman has a very important message for us and you can watch her video on YouTube at *www.youtube.com/watch?v=TvLdRz5pF7s*. Katie was born in Austria. She lived under Hitler's Regime for seven years and then lived another three years under Soviet occupation after WWII. Hitler's government established gun registration, which was followed by the order to turn in all weapons to the police station (to cut down on crime). Katie said *"...it took 5 years, gradually, little by little, to escalate to a dictatorship."* The citizens feared the government. *"When the people fear the government, that's tyranny, but when the government fears the people, that's liberty."* Katie, a Nazi survivor warns us: "Keep your guns, keep your guns and buy more guns."[104]

Another important warning comes from an eyewitness to Castro's communist regime in Cuba who fled to the safety and security of the United States. Manuel Martinez spoke before the Oregon Senate Judiciary Committee objecting to Senate Bill 1551 which is intended to mandate strict background checks for gun purchases whether public or private. The Bill in question does not seem so out of line – that is, until you read Mr. Martinez's testimony. He said that the U.S. government is doing "exactly" what he watched happen under the rule of Fidel Castro in Cuba.[105] *"Marxism is HERE. Marxism has been in this country for quite a while, and the politicians allow that, because they are ignorant, or they are part of the plot...Don't sell me this. A very powerful man tried to sell me this 50-something years ago. I didn't buy it."* Mr. Martinez explained how the Castro government claimed they were protecting the people while in fact they enslaved them and destroyed the country. He warns us not to let the U.S. government destroy our country the same

---

[103] "Treaties Don't Trump the Constitution," Congressman Steve Stockman, American Thinker,
http://www.american thinker.com, November 5, 2013

[104] "Hitler Survivor Katie Worthman: 'Keep your guns. Buy more guns,'" Christopher Cook, *Western Free Press*, http://www.westernfreepress.com, January 5, 2014

[105] "Castro Eyewitness to Oregon Senate: 'Marxism in Not Coming, Marxism is HERE,'" Kim Paxton, Freedom Outpost, http://www.freedomoutpost.com, February 9, 2014

way. Gun-control politicians are not selling protection; they are selling subjugation.

There is a little good news out of Detroit. The city has witnessed a decrease of nearly 13% in murders and 7% in violent crime under the direction of new Police Chief James Craig. Chief Craig believes that legal gun owners actually stop violent crime. Craig, the former head of the Portland, Maine Police Department said, *"Good Americans with CPLs (Concealed Pistol License) translates into crime reduction, too. I learned that very quickly in the state of Maine. A lot of CPL holders...Maine is one of the safest places in America. Clearly, **suspects knew that good Americans were armed.**"*[106]

Molon Labe

"A militia, when properly formed, are in fact the people themselves... and include all men capable of bearing arms...To preserve liberty, it is essential that the whole body of the people always possess arms and be taught alike, especially when young, how to use them."

—Richard Henry Lee

Citizens across the nation need to be aware of the situation gun owners in Connecticut are facing. The state's new gun law requires all gun owners to register assault weapons and high-capacity magazines. This really is a constitutional violation, and 90% of gun owners refuse to obey. The Connecticut State Police sent out "warning letters" to hundreds of thousands of gun owners they claim are "defying" the law. The outcome of this situation will affect the Second Amendment rights of all Americans. If Connecticut successfully enforces this unlawful law, other states will follow suit. Americans need to stand with Connecticut gun-owners and say, *"I will not comply."*

We need to carefully listen to and decipher what our politicians are really saying. We need to read between the lines to find the truth.

---

[106] "Police Chief James Craig Says What Detroit needs Is More Guns," Ashley Woods, The Huffington Post, http:www.huffingtonpost.com, January 6, 2014

Politicians are adept at telling people what they want to hear. They are great at promising the world – before an election. We need to contact our officials and tell them what we think. We need to be aware of issues, laws, and resolutions even if they do not directly affect us. Citizens need to band together, collect petitions, and speak in a collective voice against things that are unjust or questionable. We need to stop just accepting what our leaders tell us. While they do not know what is best for us; they do know what is best for them personally and politically.

The Declaration of Independence clearly states that we are endowed with inalienable rights, including "all men are created equal," and "governments derive their just powers from the consent of the governed." These are clear and applicable principles that apply to all people for all time. Matt Spalding addresses this issue in a July 3, 2009 article for the Heritage Foundation. *"We don't need to remake America, or discover new and untested principles. The change we need is not the rejection of America's principles but a great renewal of these permanent truths about man, politics, and liberty – the foundational principles and constitutional wisdom that are the true roots of our country's greatness."*[107]

James Madison, one of our Founding Fathers and the fourth President of the United States was a principle author of the Constitution. He clearly knew the collective intent of the Founders which was that the Constitution is a static document whose principles are not editable. We need to take his warning to heart: *"Do not separate text from historical background. If you do, you will have perverted and subverted the Constitution, which can only end in a distorted...form of illegitimate government."*

Daniel Webster unambiguously defines our mission, *"The contest for ages has been to rescue liberty from the grasp of executive power."*

---

[107] "*The Left's Assault on the Declaration of Independence*," Morning Bell, The Heritage Foundation, http://blog.heritage.org/2009/07/03

Our Founder's Warnings Are Relevant Today

Our Founding Fathers created the Constitution not just for people of the 18th century, but for Americans of all centuries. They left us warnings which some in government, academia, and the media have buried in the archives of "irrelevant" history. W. Cleon Skousen's book, *The 5000 Year Leap: The 28 Great Ideas That Changed the World* is an excellent and easy to understand look at the Constitution; the principles that support it, and the Founders unequivocal intent. It leaves no doubt as to the Constitution's content, meaning, government responsibilities, powers and limits, as well as citizen rights and responsibilities.[108] The Founders clearly and purposely explained how to sustain the Constitution for national growth and prosperity. And, through their documented writings, they clearly warned us of the things that would threaten the Constitution and therefore the rights of the people.

A January 14, 2011 study by the Intercollegiate Studies Institute (ISI)[109] revealed disturbing results. ISI quizzed more than 2,500 adults on civics (many questions taken from the U.S. Citizenship Exam) and on the U.S. Constitution. 164 of the quiz participants were elected officials (Federal, state, and local) and their results were abysmal:

- Only 15% knew that the "wall of separation" phrase was not in the Constitution (it was in Thomas Jefferson's letter)
- Only 57% knew the purpose of the Electoral College (20% actually thought the Electoral College was a school for training those aspiring for higher political office)
- Only 49% could name all three branches of government
- Only 46% knew that Congress, not the president, has the power to declare war
- 74% of officeholders failed the exam

---

[108] "A Miracle That Changed The World: The 5000 Year Leap – The 28 Great Ideas That Changed the World," W. Cleon Skousen, The National Center for Constitutional Studies, 1981, 14th printing 2006

[109] The Intercollegiate Studies Institute, (non-profit, non-partisan, tax-exempt educational institution) founded in 1953. The purpose of ISI is "to further successive generations of college students a better understanding of the values and institutions that sustain a free and humane society." http://www.isi.org

> Based on the overall results of the quiz, the co-chairman of the intercollegiate Studies Institute's National Civic Literacy Board said, *"The fact that our elected representatives know even less about America's history and institutions than the typical citizen (who doesn't know much either) is troubling indeed, but perhaps helps explain the lack of constitutional discipline often displayed by our political class at every level of our system…Given this dismal performance, it would seem that last week's House reading of the Constitution shouldn't be described 'presumptuous and self-righteous' (as described by the New York Times) but as a necessary national tutorial for all elected officials."*

Since many of our leaders in Washington either have not read the Constitution, or studied our history, or both, we, the citizens of America need to know the Constitution to arm ourselves with knowledge to "firewall" their violations of our Constitutional rights.

The Constitution Institute was founded with just that educational purpose in mind. The Constitution Institute's mission is to: *Preserve the blessings of liberty for ourselves and our posterity by promoting a greater understanding of the United States Constitution and providing an education in the practical application of Constitutional principles thereby producing citizen-statesmen.* The Constitution Institute's website is a valuable resource for Constitutional knowledge and application. On-line and sponsored seminars are available for all citizens to participate. The website is: http://www.constitutioninstitute.org.

Constitutional Organization of Liberty is a Project of the Alexander Hamilton Institute For Constitutional Studies. The Constitutional Organization of Liberty is based on Alexander Hamilton's plan for a "Constitutional Society" established to support the Constitution and (close your eyes Liberals) to support the Christian religion. The diffusion of information and the election of "fit men" were important goals. The Institute on the Constitution is a course that thoroughly examines the religious, philosophical and legal concepts that comprise the Constitution including a detailed look at the Articles and Amendments. The organization's website, http://reclaimliberty.com offers a treasure trove of Constitutional information.

Hillsdale College in Michigan was founded in 1844 and has adhered to its charter of academic excellence and institutional independence ever since. Hillsdale College receives no federal taxpayer subsidies so it truly has academic freedom without government intervention. As a shining example of educational honesty, Hillsdale offers numerous no-expense courses, lectures, and publications to anyone interested in the Constitution, U.S. Government, American heritage, and the rights and responsibilities of American citizens.

I encourage everyone to visit the Hillsdale College website http://www.hillsdale.edu and explore the courses and lectures presented by Hillsdale professors, experts in various fields and subject matter. The president and instructors at Hillsdale College are committed to educating all people who wish to learn regardless of educational background, economic, and social status. I commend President Larry P. Arnn and the Hillsdale team on their most noble mission to educate the masses and preserve liberty. They have embraced Thomas Jefferson's warning, *"Educate and inform the whole mass of the people...They are the only sure reliance for the preservation of our liberty."* Check it out. Time is your only investment though donations are greatly appreciated to help defray costs and I guarantee you will be impressed.

There are many more organizations that can provide us with factual knowledge and guidance on constitutional and political issues. **The Heritage Foundation**, www.heritage.org headquartered in Washington, DC is a research and educational institution promoting public policies based on the principles of free enterprise, limited government, individual freedom, traditional American values, and a strong national defense. **The CATO Institute**, www.cato.org studies and provides guidance on public policy based on individual freedom, limited government, and free markets. **Judicial Watch**, www.judicialwatch.org is a non-partisan organization that promotes accountability and integrity in government and politics and advocates high standards of ethics and morality in our political and judicial officials.

Freedom University www.connect.freedomworks.org/university sponsored by the Freedom Works organization, www.freedomworks.org offers a great course on the Constitution. HIST101: Judge Napolitano's "Founding the American Republic" examines why the founders created the Constitution as they did to protect individual rights and limit the power of government. The judge also discusses how and why Constitutional protections have eroded resulting in a larger, more powerful federal government. Freedom University offers other courses including political and economic policy.

Like him, or hate him, Newt Gingrich is an extremely knowledgeable and experienced "Constitutional citizen." He has made a career of learning, participating and teaching the true principles of our Constitution and government. Newt was a Congressman for twenty years and Speaker of the House for four years during which time he designed the very successful "Contract with America" holding politicians responsible to the people of the nation. He is also an expert on American history, world history, military issues and international affairs. Newt has published nineteen books including *To Renew America, Real Change, Winning the Future: A 21ˢᵗ Century Contract with America,* and *Rediscovering God in America.*

Aside from Constitutional rights, citizens have **constitutional responsibilities**. It is our responsibility to know our government structure and its limits of power. We are responsible to know our elected officials, observe them to make sure they comply with their Constitutional obligations, and we need to take action when they ignore, disallow, or blatantly violate those responsibilities. Our Founders warned us of the importance of an educated electorate. Too many people today vote for candidates based on appearance, oratory skills, political ads, recommendations by others, or by the direction of their union or employer – not based on the candidate's platform, record and performance. How can you intelligently elect a person to represent you if you do not know what that person stands for?

Free Market Economics and Debt

Free market economics and the burden of debt are two serious issues we face today. A free market economy with a minimum of government intrusion produces the highest level of prosperity while government intervention into private business (selective bank and auto company bailouts, controlling wages, prices and distribution, subsidies, etc.) is the greatest threat to economic prosperity. This is especially troubling since the government is making greater and greater intrusions into our free market society putting our economic freedom (the fundamental right for people to control their own property and their own labor) at perilous risk.

Free enterprise NOT government produces and maintains wealth. The fact is independent small businesses create over 80% of all new jobs, but that will change soon as more and more small businesses are forced to close. Uninformed people are being told that free enterprise is nothing but greed, selfishness and evil. Even our students are being taught that Free Enterprise only creates rich people who abuse the less fortunate. They are learning that "fairness" must conquer the free enterprise system to spread the wealth equitability to benefit society. This is nothing but economic redistribution which is fatal to a healthy economy.

President Obama is trying to "legitimize" economic redistribution to remedy his perception of "income inequality." During a speech in December 2013 the President declared to the country that **income inequality is the "defining challenge of our time."** Sorry Mr. President that is not the defining challenge of our time. The defining challenges of our time are an excessively bloated government with corrupt leaders, a "new order" health care system that is a disaster, over-regulation of industry, unemployment and under-employment, out of control taxes, and disastrous foreign policies, all of which are detrimental to every American. While millions of people are still without jobs, millions more are losing their health insurance and doctors cannot afford new mandated premiums. Our economy is barely treading water, illegal aliens continue to stream across the border and the very real threat of terrorism grows daily.

Keep in mind this President is a man who does not like and does not adhere to our Constitution because it does not "guarantee economic rights." He also said the Constitution imposes "essential constraints" that we must be liberated from. To President Obama the Constitution is an outdated mistake. To most Americans it guarantees liberty and economic "opportunity" to create wealth and own property; the very principles that made our nation prosperous and successful.

The absolute truth is free enterprise made the U.S. the most prosperous and successful country in the history of the world. William Hall writing for *AMAC Advantage Magazine* summed up the free enterprise system, from its founding implementation in the U.S. in the Eighteenth century: *"Free Enterprise allowed people to take charge of their own economic destiny, profession or business without interference from the government, a concept that did not exist in Europe at the time."*[110]

President Thomas Jefferson warned us in his First Inaugural Address on March 4, 1801: *"A wise and frugal government which shall restrain men from injuring one another shall leave them otherwise free to regulate their own pursuits of industry and improvement."*

President Coolidge warned us when he said: *"A government which lays taxes on the people not required by urgent public necessity and sound policy is not a protector of liberty, but an instrument of tyranny. It condemns the citizen to servitude."*

President Ronald Reagan warned us in his Farewell Address to the Nation on January 11, 1989: *"Common sense told us that when you put a big tax on something, the people will produce less of it. So, we cut the people's tax rates, and the people produced more than ever before...Our economic program brought about the longest peacetime expansion in our history: real family income up, the poverty rate down, entrepreneurship blooming, and an explosion in research and new technology. We're exporting more than ever because American industry became more competitive and at the same time, we summoned the national will to knock down protectionist walls abroad instead of erecting them at home."*

The Heritage Foundation publication, *The Link Between Economic Opportunity & Prosperity: The 2010 Index of Economic Freedom,*[111]

---

[110] "Understanding Free Enterprise and How It Generates Wealth for the United States," William Hall, AMAC Advantage Magazine of the Association of Mature American Citizens, Vol. 7, Issue 3, 2013

[111] "*The Link Between Economic Opportunity & Prosperity: The 2010 Index of Economic Freedom,*" The Heritage Foundation, http://www.heritage.org/Index [Report that covers 183 countries across 10 specific freedoms including trade freedom business freedom, investment freedom, and property rights]

illustrates the importance of economic freedom for a prosperous economy. Economic freedom improves quality of life and promotes political and social progress. Increased government interference into the economic arena is harmful to the country's economic health and they have evidence that increased government spending by the Obama administration did not improve economic performance. A sobering fact is that the United States ranked 9th place on the 2011 Index of Economic Freedom World Rankings.[112] Hong Kong, Singapore, Australia, New Zealand, Ireland, Switzerland, and Canada ranked higher than America. If it's any comfort, the U.S. is still ahead of most of Europe and all the third world countries, but if current financial policies continue it's a good bet we will continue to drop in world rankings which seems to be a "progressive" goal. Heritage Foundation's Center for International Trade and Economics explained the continued decline:

"The U.S. economy faces enormous challenges. The government's recent spending spree has led to fragile business confidence and crushing public debt. Interventionist responses to the economic slowdown have eroded economic freedom and long-term competitiveness. Drastic legislative changes in health care and financial regulations have stunted job creation and injected substantial uncertainty into business investment planning.

The 2013 Economic Freedom of the World Report[113] published by the CATO Institute[114] highlights the critical decline of United States economic freedom and subsequent overall decline. In 2000 the U.S. ranked 2nd in the world. In 2005 we ranked 8th. From a 9th place rating in 2011 we are free-falling rapidly toward 3rd world rankings. The U.S. fell to 16th place in 2012, and then another drop to 17th place in 2013. The data for these annual reports are a compilation of measurement of

---

[112] "America Falls to Ninth in Economic Freedom," Nathaniel Ward, *The Heritage Foundation* Member Briefing, January 14, 2011

[113] "Economic Freedom of the World," The Fraser Institute, published annually in September, http:www.economicfreedom.org

[114] "The Continuing U.S. Decline in Economic Freedom of the World Index," Ian Vasquez, CATO at LIBERTY, The CATO Institute, http://www.cato.org, September 18, 2013

the: Size of government, the legal system, the security of property rights, sound money, freedom to trade, and regulations.

The Heritage Foundation's 2014 Index of Economic Freedom rates the U.S. as only the 12th freest economy in 2014. This rating was based on: deteriorations in property rights, fiscal and business freedom, substantial expansion in the size and scope of government including new and costly finance and healthcare regulations. *"The growth of government has been accompanied by increasing cronyism that has undermined the rule of law and perceptions of fairness."*[115]

"Increased spending, a weakening of rule of law, worse monetary policy, greater trade barriers, and more regulations are to blame." Other factors affected by Economic Freedom include political and civil liberties, standard of living including longer life spans, and poverty. Authors of the 2013 Economic Freedom Report concluded that, *"unless policies undermining economic freedom are reversed, the future annual growth of the U.S. economy will be half its historic average of 3%."*[116]

Liberal claims that the economy is good and well on the way to recovery are just not true. *"Despite years of promises to the contrary… All of the important economic markers that indicate recovery are still down. The recession "ended" in 2009 and yet we still see unacceptably high unemployment, record debt and very weak economic growth."*[117]

- 1.4 million Jobs were "created" in 2013 but most were part-time jobs. As a matter of fact over the past five years there are 12.6% more part-time jobs while there are 4.6% <u>fewer full-time jobs.</u>[118] That is not a good thing.

---

[115] " America's Economic Freedom Declines for Seventh Straight Year," The Heritage Foundation 2014 Index of Economic Freedom, http://myheritage.org, January 14, 2014

[116] "Economic Freedom of the World 2013 Annual Report," James Gwartney, Robert Lawson, Josh Hall, The Fraser Institute, http://www.fraserinstitute.org, September 2013

[117] "What has Obamanomics brought us?" Bruce McQuain, HotAir.com, July 28, 2013

[118] "5 Years Later: 16 Stats That Put Any Liberal's Claim That Our Economy Is Healthy to Shame," Emily Hulsey, *Independent Journal Review*, September 19, 2013

- The White House website published a very condescending and snarky piece, "Quick Update on the Economy" on November 13, 2013 stating: We know that Washington hijacked our economy last month: THE GOVERNMENT SHUTDOWN AND THREATS TO DEFAULT ON OUR DEBT CAUSED UNNECESSARY DAMAGE. BUT THE AMERICAN PEOPLE AND BUSINESSES WERE RESILIENT and the economy still added 204,000 jobs in the month of October."

  - First of all, isn't the White House part of Washington; and the president part of the government? So why is the President and White House staff promoting the misconception that somehow they are not part of all this?
  - Second, on the very same day, the Bureau of Labor Statistics (BLS) reported that 932,000 more people dropped out of the labor force in October bringing us to a high of 91,541,000 Americans <u>not</u> participating in the work force.
  - In reality, adding 204,000 jobs in October 2013, but loosing 932,000 more people from the workforce during the very same period – is NOT GOOD.
  - November 2013 saw a decrease in the unemployment rate, but while the national unemployment rate dropped to 7.0%, government workers unemployment rate registered at 3.2%. As private sector employment stagnates, the government is growing ever larger.
  - The Bureau of Labor Statics (BLS) released statistical data that the 2013 average annual labor force participation rate hit a 35-year low at 63.2%,. Ali Meyer of CNS News observed, *"The last time the average annual labor force participation rate was that low was in 1978, when it was also 63.2 %. Jimmy Carter was president."*[119] That's not a surprise.
  - The Bureau of Labor Statistics reported that in January 2014, 92,535,000 people were not in the American labor

---

[119] "Labor Force Participation in 2013 Lowest in 35 years," Ali Meyer, CNS News, http://www.cnsnews.com, March 3, 2014

force. That would mean a million more people dropped off the labor force during the last 2 months of 2013.

- You are not imagining higher prices at the super market and gas station. The average price of regular unleaded gas in November 2008 (pre-Obama) was $1.61 per gallon. In November 2013, the average price of regular unleaded gasoline was $3.27. And that was down from over $4.00 per gallon. Funny I haven't heard any complaints about gas prices since Obama has been president. If the official rate of inflation calculations had not been changed a number of times since 1978, the official rate in 1978 terms would actually be between 8 and 10 percent.

- The 2014 Social Security cost of living increase will only be 1.5% because according to the government's calculation, inflation is not high.

- The President boasts about major increases in alternative (clean) energy while our gas prices continue to rise and the coal industry has been annihilated leaving thousands of hard working people without jobs.

- Median household income fell 5% since 2009.

- The *Independent Journal* published a chart compiled by the Senate Budget Committee with data from the Social Security Administration, the Department of Health and Human Services and the Department of Agriculture demonstrating how between 2008 and 2012 our ever increasing "welfare state" is overwhelming the workforce. While Disability Enrollment rose 17.6%, and Medicaid Enrollment grew by 19.3%, and Food Stamp Enrollment increased a stunning 65.2%, the Total Number of People Employed is still in negative territory at -0.7%.[120]

The once thriving city of Detroit, Michigan which has deteriorated to the point of bankruptcy is a pragmatic warning. Financial mismanagement including the inability to repay debt, deferral of public pension contributions and an unsustainable welfare system

---

[120] "Why the Welfare State is Increasing Burdens on the U.S. Workforce in This Simple Chart," Kyle Becker, *Independent Journal Review*, http:www.ijreview.com, December 6, 2013

have reduced this wealthy industrial city to a wasteland of poverty and despair. Detroit is just the tip of the iceberg. Other large American cities are on the same rutted road to financial collapse; and the federal government in Washington DC has jumped on the express train to economic disaster.

While on the subject of Detroit, when the Treasury Department sold its final shares of General Motors stock acquired during the 2008-2009 auto industry bailout, president Obama touted that GM had repaid all the taxpayer funded money. That sounds like a successful investment but in reality the government lost around $10.5 billion on the $49.5 billion received in GM stock as part of the bailout.[121] Add that to the other bailout losses and the fact is the taxpayers lost about $15 billion. So, why is the government celebrating a 15 billion dollar loss?

Our Founders perceived debt as a destructive force against freedom and were adamant that debt be paid as quickly as possible – whether it is public or private debt. They considered national debt a "temporary" situation resulting from an emergency or a war. They felt that the least amount of money should be borrowed and it should be repaid promptly. They also felt all debts incurred by one generation should be reconciled by that generation and never handed down to the next generation. The Founders would be aghast at the current economic situation in the U.S.

Americans are drowning in debt – personal and public debt. The 111th Congress (January 2009 – December 2010) accumulated more "new" debt ($3.22 trillion) than the first 100 Congresses combined.[122] Ironically, the Speaker of the House, Nancy Pelosi (110th and 111th Congress), vowed in 2007 that Congress would incur no new deficit spending: *"After years of historic deficits, this 110th Congress will commit itself to a higher standard: Pay as you go, no new deficit spending...Our new America will provide unlimited opportunity for future generations, not burden them with mountains of debt."* The legacy of the 112th Congress mirrored the 111th Congress with little positive progress.

Nancy Pelosi, though no longer Speaker continued to support

---

[121] "Billion loss for taxpayers," Dave Boyer, *The Washington Times*, http://www.washingtontimes.com, December 10, 2013

[122] Official debt figures published by the U.S. Treasury reported by Terence P. Jeffrey, CNSNEWS.com, December 27, 2010

and promote government spending in the 113ᵗʰ Congress totally contradicting her not-so-long-ago promise of no new deficit spending. It seems clear that deficit spending was not allowed when the president was a conservative; but now that the president is a liberal, deficit spending is a good thing for America.

For a quick look at the makeup of the 113ᵗʰ Congress (January 2013 – December 2014) and to see how your representatives have voted, visit http://www.fas.org/sgp/crs/misc/R42964.pdf

Many retired seniors who once were able to look forward to retirement with confidence have actually gone back to work. Uncertainties over the recession and it's painfully slow recovery, and the Affordable Care Act (Obamacare) have made retirement impossible. Dan Weber, president of the Association of Mature American Citizens (AMAC) describes the gloomy situation this way: *"Two recent Gallup surveys show that there are more post-retirement job seekers out there than ever before, mainly because they've lost confidence in the economy. The historically destructive recession that started as the president took office and his inability to speed up the recovery have seniors scrambling for ways to salvage what's left of their retirement. Bear in mind that while the net worth of all Americans has declined sharply during this period, seniors have been hardest hit."*[123]

Housing market and stock market plunges, unemployment, business closures, bankruptcy, welfare, bailouts, stimulus programs, Obamacare, illegal immigration, government waste, Medicare and Medicaid fraud cost all of us dearly. Unbelievably the government is contributing to and promoting debt instead of reducing it. A November 2010 *New York Post* article[124] notes the nervousness around the globe over the United States current financial state. The U.S. *"is on a spending spree of historic proportions."*

The housing market didn't just collapse overnight – it was years in the making. It started back in the 90s when the Clinton administration turned home ownership into an affirmative action program. The government forced banks and mortgage lenders to lower the set standards

---

[123] "Seniors Going Back To Work to Salvage Their Retirement Nest Eggs," AMAC, October 25, 2013

[124] "Obamanomics leaving world nervous," Daniel J. Mitchell, *New York Post*, November 14, 2010

of qualification for home mortgages so more and more unqualified people could buy homes. These bad loans triggered massive defaults and the financial crisis we have come to know. The banks began "bundling" mortgages to buy and sell like any other asset. By 2007 Fannie Mae and Freddie Mac owned or guaranteed nearly half of the $12 trillion mortgage market. The massive failure of Fannie Mae and Freddie Mac sparked the taxpayer bailout and initiated the "too big to fail" financial excuse. Make no mistake, Wall Street and the big banks have thrived since the "bailout." The Feds saved Wall Street by abandoning Main Street.

Regarding entitlement spending, Walter Williams, Economist, Commentator, Professor of Economics at George Mason University, and syndicated columnist wrote, *"The Office of Management and Budget calculates that total entitlement spending comes to about 62% of federal spending. Military spending totals 19% of federal spending .... Putting those two figures into historical perspective demonstrates the success we've had becoming a handout nation. In 1962, military expenditures were almost 50% of the federal budget, and entitlement spending was a mere 31%."*[125]

Mr. Williams reminds us that Congress has NO resources of its own. The government can only give people money by taking money away from others – redistribution. The confiscation of earned money is acquired through taxes.

We have heard for five years now that the rich must pay "their fair share" of taxes. So, who defines "rich" and what is a "fair share?" I do not think that the President of the United States was authorized by the Constitution to define what "fair" taxes are and unilaterally decide who should pay more, who should pay less, and who should pay nothing. The Congressional Budget Office (CBO) reported that in 2010 the top 40% of American households paid more than 100% of the nation's net income taxes. The report further stated that the bottom 40% of households received an average of $18,950 in "government transfers."[126] The bottom

---

[125] "Entitlement Madness: Is There a Way Out?" Walter Williams, *Front Page Magazine*, http://frontpagemag.com, October 29, 2013

[126] "United States of Unfair Taxation," Onan Coca, Liberty Alliance, http://www.libertyalliance.com, December 19, 2013

40% got over $18,000 from the top 40%. So that means the President's oath to spread the wealth is real and it's called "government transfers."

Countries including Germany, Brazil, South Africa and China worried when the Federal Reserve planned to "pump $600 billion into the economy" as it would distort trade and cause other nations to devalue their currency. Daniel J. Mitchell of *The New York Post* has good advice for the federal government: *"We all tell our kids that their friends' misbehavior is no excuse for them to do the wrong thing as well. If China is keeping its currency artificially weak, that doesn't mean we should do the same thing. If European nations have bigger governments and more debt, that doesn't mean we should copy their mistakes."*

The U.S. debt continues to rise to frightening and unsustainable levels. When the U.S. debt topped $16 trillion on September 04, 2012,[127] Veronique De Rugy of the Mercatus Center of George Mason University said of the government's FY 2012 debt, *"The unfunded liabilities of Social Security, Medicare, and Medicaid are often omitted from discussions about the large size of US public debt. Once these are taken into consideration it becomes clear that the US government is clearly on an unsustainable path."[128]*

By October 18, 2013 the national debt grew to over $17 trillion ($17,000,000,000,000). That number docs not bother the administration and progressives across the country like it does those silly Conservatives and Tea Party people who wanted to grow jobs not debt. To put our $17 trillion debt into perspective: It is higher than the total U.S. gross domestic product (GDP) which is the measure of everything produced in our economy. That is a 60% increase since 2009.[129]

Adding insult to injury, Chinese rating agency Dagong downgraded its U.S. credit rating in October 2013 – AFTER Congress passed another

---

[127] "US Debt tops $16 million: So who de we owe most of that money to?" Greg Wilson, published September 04, 2012, Fox News.com, http://www.foxnews.com
[128] "The US Debt in Perspective," Veronique De Rugy, Mercatus Center, George Mason University
[129] "$17,000,000,000,000," The Heritage Foundation Morning Bell, October 21, 2013
"U.S. debt jumps a record $328 billion – tops $17 trillion for first time," Stephen Dinan, *The Washington Times*, http://www.washington times.com/news, October 18, 2013

debt ceiling increase and the government was shut down (partially shut down) for two weeks.[130] Since we are indebted to China to the tune of $1.28 trillion in U.S. Treasuries, and an estimated $54 billion more in private U.S. investments and our government is obviously dysfunctional, we now must endure lectures and mocking from Communist China.

NBC News published an article, *"China state media blasts US shutdown, calls for a 'de-Americanized' world,"* that conveys the Chinese government's position in the world economy. Chinese state news agency, *Xinhua* declared that it is, *"...perhaps a good time for the befuddled world to start considering building a de-Americanized world...Days when the destinies of others are in the hands of a hypocritical nation have to be terminated, and a new world order should be put in place, according to which all nations, big or small, poor or rich, can have their key interests respected and protected on an equal footing."[131]*

Understanding the difference between the **national debt** (the sum of all money owed by the federal government), and the **federal deficit** (the amount of money lost by the federal government during each fiscal year – expenditures exceed revenue) is vital and should not be confused. For example, as the Obama administration was trumpeting the Treasury Department report that the federal deficit for fiscal year 2013 was $680 billion, down from the 2009 high of $1.4 trillion, but they did not mention a few pertinent facts. First, there was no comment that the congressionally-mandated sequester spending cuts, as well as a slightly improving economy and the President's tax increases deserve most of the credit for the drop. There was also no acknowledgment that the national debt continues to rise at unprecedented rates.

The truth is as Brendan Bordelon of *The Daily Caller* describes: *"The better-than-expected deficit reduction is certainly good news, but economic analysts are more concerned with long-term deficit and debt projections. As unsustainable entitlement programs like Social Security*

---

[130] "Chinese agency downgrades US credit rating," reported by France 24, http://france24.com, October 17, 2013

[131] "China state media blasts US shutdown, calls for a 'de-Americanized' world," Ed Flanagan, Producer, NBC News, http://behind thewall.nbcnews.com, October 14, 2013

and Medicare consume a greater share of federal spending in coming decades, both the deficit and debt will grow at increasingly faster rates."[132]

Has anyone wondered how the President, the driving force of national debt could be so contradictory since he assumed the Presidency in 2009? On March 16, 2006 then Senator Obama was a very vocal opponent of raising the debt ceiling. *"The fact that we are here today to debate raising America's debt limit is a sign of leadership failure. It is a sign that the U.S. Government can't pay its own bills. It is a sign that we now depend on ongoing financial assistance from foreign countries to finance our Government's reckless fiscal policies."*

On the same day, March 16, 2006 and at the same debate Senator Harry Reid supported Senator Obama's opposition to raising the debt ceiling. Since 2009 Senator Reid had completely reversed his position and became wholeheartedly supportive of national debt ceiling increases – very large increases.

In October 2013 Senator Chuck Schumer said he will propose legislation to transfer the power to raise the debt ceiling from Congress to the Executive Branch which would give the president unilateral power to borrow money. This would violate the rigid separation of powers established by the Constitution. Congress is the only branch of government with the power to raise revenue (impose taxes to pay debts). Senator Schumer, another politician with a Harvard Law degree either does not know the Constitution or is a willing conspirator to undermine the Constitution. His proposition is an assault on the "checks and balances" protection the founders built into the Constitution to safeguard us from one branch of government becoming more powerful than the other two.

We, the people who are paying dearly for these unsustainable government spending increases must hold our elected representatives responsible and their spending must have merit and reasonable limits. We should be challenging them to justify their positions and their votes on crucial financial matters. I for one am weary of hearing politicians say one thing and then do a complete turn-around and validate the

---

[132] "Obama and media trumpet deficit decline, ignore ever-growing debt," Posted by: Brendan Bordelon, The Daily Caller, http://dailycaller.com, October 28, 2013

opposite position. It is sad that politicians can unequivocally lie to their constituents and still be re-elected.

An honest financial house cleaning across the board in Washington DC would reveal the extent to which federal officials and employees whether elected or appointed use our (taxpayer) money for their personal benefit. I am in no way suggesting all federal workers are wasteful or corrupt, but an alarming number are. A couple of examples of waste and fraud in government follows and it is important to note that this is NOT exclusive to the current administration - this has been and continues to be a major problem in Washington DC.

- In April 2010 *The Washington Post* reported that 92 Washington DC city workers were suspended pending an investigation that they received hundreds of thousands of dollars in unemployment benefits while they worked for the city.
- In April 2012 Fox News Boston reported that Internal Revenue Service documents showed that 98,000 federal employees owed a total of $1 billion in back taxes. Senate members and employees alone owed over $2 million. These figures are only for 2010.
- *FoxNews.com* reported on May 16, 2012 that the amount the government paid out for 2011 salaries of federal workers was $105 billion. An additional $439 million was paid out in bonuses. Tax payers are not getting cost of living raises and many are forced to take pay cuts. Private sector employees are losing their jobs and income while federal employees get bonuses? That is beyond insulting.
- Federal employees who were furloughed during the temporary partial government shutdown for two weeks in October 2013 received back pay for that period. So while private sector citizens continued to be laid off from their jobs, furloughed federal employees got an additional two-week PAID vacation.
- Did you know that we the taxpayers are funding Congressional oil painting portraits that can exceed $50,000 each? *FoxNews. com* reported on December 13, 2013 that a Senate bill was to be introduced to limit the taxpayer portion of these portraits to $20,000. ABC News reported in 2013 that the Obama

Administration spent almost $400,000 on official paintings over a two-year period. *The Washington Post* reported in 2008 that the portraits can exceed $40,000. Hmm, I would think in this super-digital age of photography that a large photograph at say even $50.00 each would look just as good as an oil painting costing up to $50,000.

The Administration publicized the government shutdown in October 2013 in "catastrophic" terms with dire warnings of doom. Actually it was a partial-government shutdown. Both the Congressional Budget Office and the Office of Management and Budget estimated that only 17% of government operations were affected. With only a partial shutdown, average Americans and private industry did not feel the "pain" the administration wanted them to. David Freddoso explained that situation as reported by the *Washington Examiner*: "*Most people - even in the poor in state-run safety net programs - don't have that many interactions with the federal government agencies affected now by the shutdown...So it's a challenge to make people notice that your agency is vital to the survival of the Republic. The feds have to apply a lot of force and behave in unsubtle ways to make you angry with Congress.*"[133]

The same Washington Examiner article identified the 6 groups targeted "to make the shutdown look worse."

1. **Veterans**: House Democrats voted against bills to restore funding to veterans programs; only 4% of Veterans Affairs employees were furloughed; Memorials such as the World War II Memorial, the Normandy Cemetery, the Vietnam Veterans Memorial Wall, and the Iwo Jima Memorial were closed.
2. **Property Owners on Federal Land**: Lake Mead, Nevada cabin owners were evicted from their homes until the government "re-opened." Privately run - privately funded parks and businesses across the country (that received NO government money) were ordered closed by the White House.

---

[133] "6 groups targeted to make the shutdown look worse," Ashe Schow, *The Washington Examiner*, http://www.washingtonexaminer.com, October 7, 2013

3. **Cancer Patients**: House Democrats selectively voted against a bill to restore funding to the National Institutes of Health (NIH) a federal agency that funds medical research. 49% of its employees were furloughed.

4. **National Guard and Reserve Units**: House Democrats voted against funding for National Guard and Reserve units to work during the shutdown.

5. **Tourists**: Besides closing the Washington DC monuments, the government shut down all the National Parks including the Grand Canyon. That is one very large area to "close." The state of Arizona offered to fund the operation of the canyon including paying the 2,200 people who work there during the shutdown, but their offer was declined by Washington. Mount Rushmore in South Dakota was even closed. To show just how serious the White House took these closures, overlooks NOT on federal land where you can see the monument were barricaded to prevent even a drive-by glimpse of the "Fab-Four." The feds could not shut down George Washington's Mount Vernon estate because it is private property but they did close off the parking lot so no visitors could access it anyway.

6. **Taxpayers**: Ironically, the IRS was not shutdown. The agency continued to accept tax payments but they weren't able to issue any tax refunds. No surprise there.

Unbelievably, underwater national parks and preserves were also closed. 1,100 square miles of the ocean (Florida Bay and Biscayne Bay) were closed to boating, fishing and recreation, though the federal government was able to pay personnel to police those areas to keep people out.

I noticed something strange during the shutdown. The National Parks and Monuments were closed as indicated by the countless "detailed" signs. These signs were very specific. The National Park Service and the U.S. Department of the Interior were clearly identified and the message was: *"Because of the Federal Government SHUTDOWN, All National Parks Are CLOSED."* Since printing all these signs had to have been done in advance, unless the government planned it, how did the federal government KNOW that the October 1, 2013 shutdown would be definite? And, how much did the federal government spend on those meticulously detailed signs?

It was reported by a number of federal employees that the message from the White House was to "make it hurt;" make sure people are affected negatively by the shutdown, and make sure to pound the drum that the Republicans are responsible for the people's pain. It is noteworthy that the President and the Congress were paid during the shutdown which reinforces the observation that different rules apply for government leaders and American taxpayers.

These are just a few examples of the billions of dollars the government wastes that we as taxpayers cannot afford. Now compare this Washington environment with the reality of ordinary unappreciated American taxpayer life. The very same people who are working hard to support their families with decreasing resources and have no voice about out-of-control Washington spending, are volunteering their own limited time and resources to keep their local communities alive and operating. I guarantee these Americans do not have oil painting portraits of themselves to record their contributions to society.

Citizens in some communities hit hard by budget cuts are answering their civic call to duty by volunteering in many different capacities to keep their communities running with less revenue. Volunteers do everything from preparing and serving food to building and repairing low income housing. Senior and community centers have been able to remain open. Churches organize and provide labor for volunteer services including clean-up of municipal parks and public areas. This is a wonderful example of how Americans have always pulled together to take care of each other without government help. Fox News reported that a 2011 study stated 63 million Americans volunteered more than 8 billion hours of their time saving local governments 173 billion dollars.[134] Who could possibly have a problem with this commendable volunteer effort? Unfortunately some labor unions do. They feel volunteers are taking away work (salary and benefits) from their union members, which in turn reduces union revenue, and so they are causing grief

---

[134] "Volunteers save cities billions, but unions cry foul," Dan Springer, Fox News, http://foxnews .com, February 24, 2012

for some of these cities. I guess union logic dictates that when there is economic strife, it's not better to have some union members laid off rather than all members laid off when municipalities cannot afford their services.

On a final note, *The Independent Journal Review* reported that the federal debt jumped $409 billion in October 2013 (figures from the US Treasury Dept.). ***"Turns out raising the debt ceiling does mean we're adding more debt;*** *another legalistic falsehood from the president."*[135] President Obama had said: "Now this debt ceiling – I just want to remind people in case you haven't been keeping up – raising the debt ceiling, which has been done over a hundred times, <u>does not increase our debt</u>; it does not somehow promote profligacy. All it does is it says you got to pay the bills that you've already racked up, Congress. It's a basic function of making sure that the full faith and credit of the United States is preserved."

Thomas Jefferson warned:

"We must not let our rulers load us with perpetual debt."

Equal Rights – Not Equal Things

"In the nature of things, those who have not property, and see their neighbors possess much more than they think them need, cannot be favorable to laws made for the protection of property. When this class becomes numerous, it grows clamorous. It looks on property as its prey and plunder, and is naturally ready, at all times, for violence and revolution."

—Daniel Webster

---

[135] "2nd Largest One-Month debt Jump in History: So, Raising the Debt Ceiling DOES Mean Adding More Debt!" Minute Men News, <u>http://minutemennews.com</u>, November 6, 2013 - reprint of article by the *Independent Journal Review*, <u>http:www.ijreview.com,</u>

The Founders spoke and wrote a lot about unalienable and equal rights. It is a self-evident truth that all men are created equal, but no two human beings are exactly alike. People are different with regard to physical and mental abilities and talents, inherited social and economic standing, motivation, and opportunities for self-fulfillment, so how can they be equal? The Constitution guarantees them equality before the law and equality in protection of their rights. It does not guarantee that everyone is equal in every way and everyone should have what others have. By guaranteeing equal protection of all people's rights, the Constitution provides freedom to prosper based on individual effort, independence and self-reliance.

The Government's responsibility is to protect equal rights – not provide equal things.

It is a violation of the Constitution for the government to "take" property, including money from one group and give it to another to make them more equal. Sound familiar? John Adams said it best: *"That all men are born to equal rights is true. Every being has a right to his own, as clear, as moral, as sacred, as any other being has....But to teach that all men are born with equal powers and faculties, to equal influence in society, to equal property and advantages through life, is a gross fraud...."[136]*

Dr. Martin Luther King, Jr. was an exceptional American. Dr. King knew equality (natural rights) is the foundation of the Declaration and Constitution. All Americans (all people) must be equal under the rule of law, and must have the opportunity to pursue economic and personal freedom (happiness). He, like the founders wanted equality of rights and equality before the law – not equality of outcomes. Dr. King defined justice as when people are judged by their character, not the color of their skin. ***"Actual equality is achieved when arbitrary standards are replaced by meaningful criteria such as talent and virtue."[137]*** Martin Luther King could have stood shoulder to shoulder with the Founders

---

[136] *John Adams quoted in A Miracle That Changed the World: The 5000 Year Leap*, W. Cleon Skousen, Published by the Center for Constitutional Studies, 1981, 14th printing 2006 (quoted in The American Enlightenment, Adrienne Koch, George Braziller Publisher, 1965)

[137] "Martin Luther King, Jr. Held These Truths. Do You?", Julia Shaw, *In First Principles*, The Heritage Foundation, *Morning Bell*, January 18, 2010

in word and deed. Dr. King made a profound statement in June 1963 when he said: *"If a man hasn't discovered something that he will die for, he isn't fit to live."*

John Adams warned us in 1787 when he said: *"Property is surely a right of mankind as really as liberty...but the time would not be long before courage and enterprise would come, and pretexts be invented by degrees...in sharing it equally with its present possessors. Debts would be abolished first; taxes laid heavy on the rich, and not at all on the others; and at last a downright equal division of everything be demanded, and voted. What would be the consequence of this? The idle, the vicious, the intemperate, would...sell and spend all their share, and then demand a new division of those who purchased from them...anarchy and tyranny commence.*[138]

Poverty and the Welfare State

CAPITALISM is the proven economic system that has lifted millions of people from poverty and has continually raised our standard of living. The well-being of millions of people has been secured. Property is a God-given right not a government-given right. The federal government exists to protect our rights not to create legislation to relieve us of those rights and our property. Personal property includes so much more than tangible possessions. "Property" also includes our thoughts, actions, education, ideas, spirituality and our very lives. Government protection of these rights is what made this country so successful. Ideas, inventions, innovations, and man-made technology all produced by individuals not government and financed by capitalism has resulted in prosperity, self-reliance, and financial security. Progressivism, communism and socialism eliminate the individual and thus his freedom as well as his property.

Aside from warnings that the government not be allowed to impart equal distribution of things (including money and other property) and not to accept national debt as a normal operating expense, the Founders

---

[138] *"What John Adams Foretold Has Come True,"* W.A. Beatty, *American Thinker*, http://www.americanthinker.com, September 18, 2013

also warned against a "welfare state" where the government takes care of everyone, and against collectivism, socialism, and communism. These ideas are destructive to a free society, as Samuel Adams so clearly stated: *"The Utopian schemes of leveling [re-distribution of wealth] and a community of goods [central ownership of production and distribution], areas visionary and impractical as those which vest all property in the Crown. [These ideas] are arbitrary, despotic, and in our government, unconstitutional."*[139]

The Welfare State Adams warned us about is here. Social Security started the "entitlement culture" when it was introduced in 1935. Medicare, and welfare programs seemed like good ideas when created, but they were promises the government can no longer afford. Andrew Biggs of the American Enterprise Institute states Social Security and Medicare deficits together are approximately $75 trillion and Social Security, Medicare and Medicaid make up about half of the budget.[140] Medicare was created to take care of the elderly and Medicaid was created to take care of the poor. Yes, there are people that legitimately need these programs to exist, but both programs have expanded exponentially and both programs are laden with fraud and abuse thereby robbing the very people they were intended to help.

I realize the need, and I support assistance for the truly poor, whether that is food, health care, or housing. I also realize that our "welfare state" supports countless people who are not truly needy. Temporary assistance programs have become lifestyles providing cradle to grave support. Where is the incentive to finish school, get a job, and support yourself and family when the government will provide for you your entire life? There is no incentive and there doesn't seem to be any motivation by politicians and government officials to clean up the corruption - so it's deeper into debt we go.

A 2012 Poverty Policy Analysis report published by the CATO Institute noted that over 46 million Americans live in poverty. President George W. Bush increased welfare spending considerably and

---

[139] *"A Miracle That Changed the World: The 5000 Year Leap,"* W. Cleon Skousen, Published by the Center for Constitutional Studies, 1981, 14th printing 2006
[140] "Entitlement Evolution Poses Threat to America's Finances," http://www. FoxNews.com, February 18, 2011

then President Barack Obama increased it another 41%. The federal government has spent nearly $15 trillion for welfare programs since 1964 and *"the poverty rate is perilously close to where we began more than 40 years ago."*[141] Federal and state governments combined spent $20.7 trillion[142] on welfare programs since the "War on Poverty" was declared, and liberals continue to argue that more money needs to be spent on a program that is obviously flawed.

The CATO Institute report provides a detailed appendix of the 126 government funded anti-poverty programs managed by 7 different cabinet agencies and 6 independent agencies including:

- 33 Housing programs run by 4 different cabinet departments
- 21 Food programs administered by 3 different federal departments and 1 independent agency
- 8 Health care programs administered by 5 separate agencies within the Department of Health and Human Services (DHHS)
- 27 Cash or general assistance programs

Regulations keep expanding as oversight diminishes. Is it any wonder there is so much chaos, theft and fraud in the welfare system? Here are just a few examples of regulations and fraud that are costing working taxpayers dearly. "Free" is not free - someone has to pay for it. The government's Universal Service Fund mandates free cell phones to people living below a designated income level are entitled to "free" cell phones. The "Lifeline" program furnished "free" cell phones (Obama Phones) and 250 free minutes each month. These phones are available to anyone on food stamps, WIC, Medicaid, Head Start, and more – even if you have a cell phone already. This is yet another program paid for by the taxpayers through extra taxes on your phone bill (Universal Service Charge) and higher prices you must pay for your phones and service.

Since that has been working out so well, politicians like Chicago's

---

[141] "The American Welfare State; How We Spend Nearly $1 Trillion a Year Fighting Poverty – and Fail," Michael Tanner, Policy Analysis No.694, CATO Institute, April 11, 2012

[142] "The War on Poverty's Biggest Casualties," Matthew Vadum, Front Page Magazine, http://www.frontpage.com, January 10, 2014

Mayor Rahm Emanuel have decided that the Universal Service Fund should include providing "free" internet service, laptop computers and net-books to poor Chicago public school children. Who's paying for all this? Not the cable company – Working taxpayers are paying. What's next?

Are you aware that the federal government gave $2 billion to Puerto Rico (an unincorporated U.S. territory) in food assistance programs? Thanks to our government, over one-third of Puerto Rico's population receives food stamps. And just like all government programs, money goes "missing." The U.S. Department of Agriculture reports that up to 25% of the $2 billion dollars going to Puerto Rico is "unaccounted for," and there is no way to verify that money was spent for food.[143]

Rampant welfare fraud (theft of taxpayer's money) is everywhere. For instance a Massachusetts state audit discovered that 1,160 "dead" people received $18 million in benefits. The audit also revealed up to $15 million in suspicious electronic benefit card (EBT) transactions, and 5 regional offices lost documentation for over 30,000 EBT cards.[144] This is just one of 50 states!

The *New York Post* reported that New Yorkers' receiving taxpayer-funded EBT cards for food to feed their families do purchase food but then ship it to relatives living in Jamaica, Haiti, and the Dominican Republic. Michael Tanner with the CATO Institute said, *"I don't want food-stamp police to see what people do with their rice and beans, but it's wrong. The purpose of this program is to help Americans who don't have enough to eat. This is not intended as a form of foreign aid."*[145]

Welfare fraud and abuse are happening from coast to coast. In California a 29-year old healthy avid surfer who chooses not to work receives food stamps. He boastfully told his story to John Roberts of *Fox News* and showed the reporter what kind of food he purchases including

---

[143] "1/3 Population of Puerto Rico Gets Food Stamps from U.S. Gov't." CNS News. com post, published by Vision to America, http://www.visiontoamerica.com, May 13, 2013

[144] "Mass. Audit finds dead welfare recipients collecting millions of dollars," Fox News, http://www.foxnews.com, May 29, 2013

[145] "NY food stamp recipients are shipping welfare-funded groceries to relatives in Jamaica, Dominican Republic and Haiti," Kate Briquelet and Isabel Vincent, *New York Post*, July 21,2013

sushi and lobster. Michael Miller, *Independent Journal Review* concludes: *"As I've said in the past, we as a moral country have an obligation to help those who cannot help themselves – for however long they are unable to do so. But, "doing" for those who will not help themselves – absolutely, not.*[146]

CBS News (www.cbsnews.com) reported in October 2013 that half of all disability claims are fraudulent. Yes, disability is considered a welfare benefit. Another media source, cnsnews.com stated that over 10 million people in the U.S. are receiving disability benefits and so are nearly 2 million children of disabled workers.[147]

Andrew C. McCarthy's article published by *National Review Online*, December 5, 2013 highlights the extent of welfare fraud. The Justice Department and the F.B.I. charged 49 current and former Russian diplomats and their spouses for defrauding Medicaid. About $1.5 million in benefits were given to these individuals due to fraudulent documents and applications.[148]

The Heritage Foundation reported in August 2013 that 1,000 prisoners collected weekly unemployment benefits over a four-month period, costing taxpayers $7 million.[149] I guess liberal logic rationalizes that since incarcerated inmates cannot go out to work, they are entitled to unemployment compensation.

A report published by *The Weekly Standard* on October 23, 2013 states that the "U.S. has spent $3.7 trillion on welfare over the past 5 years."[150] That astronomical amount dwarfs the $797.4 billion spent on NASA, Education, and Transportation <u>combined</u> for the same period.

"At what point is the welfare state a bit too big for our own good as a

---

[146] "Food Stamp Nation: Surfer Dude Buys Sushi, Lobster, Avoids Work," Michael Miller, *Independent Journal Review*, August 12, 2013

[147] "Record 10, 978,040 Now on Disability," *CNS News*, http://www.cnsnews.com, May 29, 2013

[148] "Wow! U.S. Charges Dozens of Russian Diplomats in Medicaid Fraud Scheme," Andrew C. McCarthy, National Review Online, http:www.nationalreview.com, December 5, 2013

[149] "Morning Bell: 15 Pictures of Ridiculous Government Spending Guaranteed to Make You Mad," Kelsey Harris, The Foundry-The Heritage Foundation, http://www.blog.heritage.org, August 20, 2013

[150] "Report: U.S. Spent $3.7 Trillion on Welfare Over Last 5 Years," Daniel Halper, The Weekly Standard, http://weeklystandard.com, October 23, 2013

nation?" asked Silvio Canto, Jr., in an *American Thinker* article. *"Where is the line between helping people and creating dependency? I'm all for helping people who've been laid off or uprooted by economic dislocations. There are also charities and churches who are willing to help people in need."*[151]

Canto provided startling statistics based on George Washington University (GWU) School of Public Health research. Medicaid was responsible to pay for 48% of the 3.8 million births in the U.S. in 2010. That was an 8% increase since 2008.

Backgrounder, a periodical published by the Heritage Foundation published an in-depth report on poverty in the U.S. authored by Robert Rector and Rachel Sheffield.[152] The authors clearly show how the U.S. Census Bureau statistic citing that more than 30 million Americans live in poverty is questionable. The Bureau's definition of "poverty" is not what the generally accepted definition of poverty is. *"In fact, other government surveys show that most of the persons whom the government defines as "in poverty" are not poor in any ordinary sense of the term. The overwhelming majority of the poor have air conditioning, cable TV, and a host of other modern amenities. They are well housed, have an adequate and reasonably steady supply of food, and have met their other basic needs, including medical care. Some poor Americans do experience significant hardships, including temporary food shortages or inadequate housing, but these individuals are a minority within the overall poverty population."*

Poverty is a serious social concern and accurate and timely information is necessary to address the issue and form beneficial public policy. Misinformation about such a serious problem leads to ineffective programs and fraud. The "living standards" of poor people are not always as the media and activists portray it. Aside from feeding their families, many of the poor are also struggling to pay for cable TV and air conditioning.

The Merriam-Webster Dictionary defines **"Poor"** as having little

---

[151] "The welfare state is way too big when I pay for your baby's birth," Silvio Canto, Jr., The American Thinker, http://americanthinker.com, September 14, 2013

[152] "Air Conditioning, Cable TV, and an Xbox: What is Poverty in the United States Today?" Robert Rector and Rachel Sheffield, Background, Published by the Heritage Foundation, No. 2575, July 18, 2011

money or few possessions; <u>not having enough</u> money for the basic things that people need to live properly. **"Poverty"** is defined as the state of one who <u>lacks</u> a usual or socially acceptable amount of money or material possessions.

Since living in poverty means you do not have the amount of things society in general determines you "should" have does not necessarily mean you are poor. If you were poor, you would not have the basic necessities to live.

Star Parker, founder and president of CURE (Center for Urban Renewal and Education), author, and syndicated columnist tackles the issue of poverty and the government's failed War on Poverty, in her book, **"Uncle Sam's Plantation: How Big Government Enslaves America's Poor and What We Can Do About It."**[153]

Star provides examples of poverty and how poverty has been and is currently addressed. Star's family is from the South. Her grandfather died leaving her grandmother with 6 boys to raise on her own. *"It must not have occurred to my grandma that she needed anyone to alleviate her condition as she struggled to raise her boys without a husband and without complaint. Grandma pressed on without a dime from welfare. She grew her own food, trained her own kids, and paid her own way. All six grew to become professional and accomplished men."* Star explains that most people associate poverty with the images fed to us by the media: *"Images of downtown LA with dirty, smelly homeless men milling around the Union Rescue Mission, toddlers in filthy diapers roaming around filthy 'hour-rated' motels and the mailmen who "fear for their lives to deliver welfare checks."*

The "War on Poverty" executed by the government was supposed to eradicate poverty, but it has failed miserably. It did succeed in creating and maintaining <u>generational poverty</u>. Star states that Conservatives on one hand contend that liberal social engineering created the entitlement culture for illegitimacy and poverty to skyrocket. *"A burgeoning lower class of people dependent on the government will likely vote for the party that keeps the handouts coming..."* On the other hand, liberals and Democrats continue to claim that *"racism, sexism, and capitalism are responsible for the problems of the poor."*

---

[153] "Uncle Sam's Plantation: How Big Government Enslaves America's Poor and What We Can Do About It," Star Parker, Nashville: Thomas Nelson, 2003, 2010

The CATO Institute provides some unquestionable facts about poverty:

- High school dropouts are more than three times more likely to end up in poverty and any jobs will most likely be low-wage
- Children in single parent-homes are four times more likely to be poor than children in two-parent homes. Approximately 63% of all poor children live in single-parent homes[154]

"Yet with the exception of some education programs such as Pell grants and some job training programs, little of our current welfare state encourages – and much discourages – the behavior and skills that would help them stay in school, avoid unmarried pregnancies, find a job, and save money."

The results of a Harvard University study on the "ability of low-income children to achieve social mobility" concluded that the biggest factor for lack of success is "being raised by a single parent."[155] The study also determined that "[children] of married parents also have higher rates of upward mobility if they live in communities with fewer single parents...Income inequality was not a statistically significant predictor of social mobility."

A 2013 study, *"Trends in Poverty with an Anchored Supplemental Poverty Measure,"* claims that government welfare policies and programs have made a "significant" difference for poor Americans by reducing the poverty level from 26% in 1967 to 16% in 2012. Sounds good, but unfortunately it is not true. Based on facts, the Washington Post and the CATO Institute state there has <u>not</u> been a decline in the rate of Americans living in poverty. "In other words, the statistics have been manipulated to reach the desired result."[156] While the media promotes

---

[154] "The American Welfare State; How We Spend Nearly $1 Trillion a Year Fighting Poverty – and Fail," Michael Tanner, Policy Analysis No.694, CATO Institute, April 11, 2012

[155] "Harvard study: Single parents a hindrance to social mobility," Ashe Schow, *The Washington Examiner*, http://www.washingtonexaminer.com, January 26, 2014

[156] "The Government's War on Poverty Reduction," Arnold Ahlert, Front Page Magazine, http://www.frontpagemag.com, December 11, 2013

the poverty success story to show how well the President's welfare funding increases are working; the Obama Administration quietly utilizes their "own new measurement" which rates poverty at a never-changing level. Why would the administration tout a decrease in the poverty rate and then institute a "new" way to measure it that would guarantee a static poverty rate?

Robert Rector explains this poverty measurement in a 2010 *National Review* article: "Obama's New Poverty Measurement." The old measure was based on **absolute purchasing power** – which determines how much of something you can buy. The new measure will count **comparative purchasing power** - how much of something you can buy relative to what other people can buy.[157] <u>Now the poverty rate rises in direct proportion with income levels.</u> *"For example, if the real income of every single American were to magically triple overnight, the new poverty measure would show there had been no drop in "poverty," because the poverty income threshold would also triple. Under the Obama system, poverty can be reduced only if the incomes of the "poor" are rising faster than the incomes of everyone else."* This guarantees perpetual poverty and perpetual government expansion.

"The welfare state has done to black Americans what slavery couldn't do, what Jim Crow couldn't do, what the harshest racism couldn't do, and that is to destroy the black family," says economics professor Walter E. Williams of George Mason University, a black man who rose from poverty."[158]

There is absolutely no doubt government welfare programs need to be reformed. The first reform needs to eliminate the Obama Administration's deceitful "poverty measure." Then the government must motivate the poor to become self-reliant and financially solvent, not reward dependency and failure. For this monumental undertaking the Heritage Foundation is a great place to start. The Heritage Foundation's "principles of welfare reform" establish a solid base for true and effective reform. *"If we want to avoid becoming a European-style welfare state, we*

---

[157] "Obama's 'New Poverty' Measurement," Robert Rector, National Review Online, http://nationalreview.com, march 8, 2010

[158] "The War on Poverty's Biggest Casualties," Matthew Vadum, Front Page Magazine, http://www.frontpage.com, January 10, 2014

must abandon President Obama's War on Poverty surge and return to the type of common-sense welfare reform that proved so successful in the '90s."[159]

Many of The Heritage Foundation's principles of welfare reform were incorporated into a bill introduced by Representative Jim Jordan in March 2011including:

- Requirement of disclosure of total means-tested welfare spending
- An aggregate cap on welfare spending
- Extended work requirements to the Food Stamp program.

The "War on Poverty" is an abject failure considering that poverty rates rise right along with the continually increasing welfare programs. The CATO Institution suggests a shift from government anti-poverty programs that only give out money, goods, and services to government programs providing environments and incentives to help people lift themselves out of poverty. *"Indeed, throughout most of human history, man has existed in the most meager of conditions. Prosperity on the other hand, is something that is created. And we know that the best way to create wealth is not through government action, but through the power of the free market."*[160]

- End government policies of high taxes and regulatory excess that inhibit growth and job creation
- Protect capital investment and help people have an opportunity to start new businesses
- Reform our failed government school system to encourage competition and choice
- Encourage the poor to save and invest

---

[159] "Representative Jim Jordan Introduces Heritage-Inspired Welfare Reform," Bethany S. Murphy, The Heritage Foundation Member Briefing, March 18, 2011
[160] "The American Welfare State; How We Spend Nearly $1 Trillion a Year Fighting Poverty – and Fail", Michael Tanner, Policy Analysis No.694, CATO Institute, April 11, 2012

The "Farm Bill" is a perfect example of what needs to be included in welfare reform. Nearly 80% of the Farm Bill provisions are for food stamps and nutrition assistance programs; only 20% goes to "farm" related issues like conservation, insurance, and commodity programs. Food stamps aka welfare has no place in a federal farm bill.

Another item that needs to be addressed to successfully reform welfare is the fact the welfare system "pays" more than minimum wage jobs in 35 states. A CATO Institute publication notes that "even after accounting for the Earned Income Tax Credit, and in 13 states it [welfare] pays more than $15 per hour."[161] So, just what would be the incentive to get a job? Welfare reform will not be an easy task but it is an imperative step in the restoration of America.

The Founders worried that the federal government would grow so large and powerful that it would subjugate the states' and the people's rights. Even with the separation of powers and the checks and balances mandated by the Constitution, their fears were with merit as evidenced by the size and power of the federal government today. James Madison explained the Founder's intent of powers delegated by the Constitution in "The Federalist Papers," No. 45: *"The powers delegated by the proposed Constitution to the federal government are few and defined. Those which are to remain in the State governments are numerous and indefinite....The powers reserved to the several States will extend to all the objects which, in the ordinary course of affairs, concern the lives, liberties, and properties of the people, and internal order, improvement, and prosperity of the State."*

The Founders feared a "gradual" erosion of the Constitution and the honesty and integrity of the nation's leaders. James Madison warned: *"I believe there are more instances of the abridgement of the people by gradual and silent encroachments of those in power, than by violent and sudden usurpations....This danger ought to be wisely guarded against."*

---

[161] "The Work versus Welfare Trade-Off: 2013," Michael D. Tanner and Charles Hughes, CATO Institute, http://www.cato.org, August 19, 2013

LIBERTY IS WORTH FIGHTING FOR

"War is a political act, a method for continuing political commerce after diplomacy fails; the political view is the object; war is the means, and the means must always include the object in our conception."

—Carl von Clausewitz, 1832

The Human Cost of Freedom

The United States of America was a country born on the move and it has never slowed down. Americans explored and developed the nation from coast to coast building cities and developing industries. Americans invented and developed technologies, transportation systems, and one of the world's most productive agricultural structures. America welcomed immigrants from around the globe. Diversity, hard work, self-improvement, self-sufficiency, and making a better life for one's family were "American values." America grew in strength and wealth because of the free-market system – capitalism; not socialism, communism, fascism, theocratic government, or monarchy. America was successful because it was designed as a "democratic republic."

The United States has fought a civil war, two world wars, and regional wars, in which America emerged from each experience a stronger nation. Of course there have been mistakes along the way. History has recorded the successes and the mistakes though recently it seems some academics like to focus on the errors of America to the exclusion of her honorable deeds. They like to portray America as just another ordinary country whose people and leaders are nothing extraordinary. Critics attack our heroes by only addressing their "human shortcomings" and excluding their merits and contributions to our nation and the world. A handful of scoundrels whose deeds are inexcusable are highlighted to purposely tarnish the valor and honor of the majority. A case in point is Abu Ghraib prison in Iraq: Seven U.S. soldiers were convicted of prisoner abuse in that 2004 event. Detractors indicted the U.S. military as a whole for the actions of seven people. Seven soldiers are not representative of the United States military forces.

I do not ignore or reject America's mistakes. They are part of our history and should not be forgotten. They are lessons to all of us lest we make the same mistakes again. There seems to be no shortage of people who like to highlight the errors of our nation, so we need to focus on the nobleness of America and her people whose dauntless valor has indeed built the greatest nation on earth. America is also THE nation that has saved countless millions of lives worldwide. America's greatness far outweighs her faults. **America is exceptional**.

Our Founders created this nation, our citizens built it, our leaders have guided it, and our military has defended it. As a matter of fact the United States military has fought for and defended freedom all over the world. From the Revolutionary War through the 1991 Gulf War over 41.5 million men and women have served in our Armed forces. Over

627,000 American military personnel died on battlefields in the name of liberty.[162] Nearly 345,000 of those brave patriots died fighting during the two world wars of the twentieth century, most on foreign soil.

Defense of America during the **War of 1812** reaffirmed our American commitment to liberty. Our young nation once again stood up to Great Britain who was at odds with France and was blockading American ships and seizing American sailors. There also was an ongoing dispute over the US-Canada border since the Revolution that was never resolved. British soldiers were able to raid and burn government buildings in Washington, DC, including the White House, but were stopped in Baltimore. Fort McHenry overlooking Baltimore Harbor sustained a substantial bombardment of British fire and survived with the American flag still flying. This is the event that Frances Scott Key witnessed which inspired him to compose the "Star Spangled Banner." In Louisiana, General Andrew Jackson decisively defeated the British during the Battle of New Orleans. The War of 1812 ended and has been overshadowed by history. Events, battles and colorful American heroes – military and civilian, including the heroic deeds of the First Lady, Dolly Madison are highlighted in numerous books on the war.

Fort McHenry in Baltimore, Maryland is open to visitors and is a great way to experience interactive history. Baltimore is also home to the **USS Constellation**, the last "all-sail" US Navy warship. The Constellation is permanently docked in the Inner Harbor, and its mission now is to serve as a walk-through hands-on museum to educate visitors. Another historic ship also serving as an educational center is the **USS Constitution**, anchored in Boston Harbor, Massachusetts. The USS Constitution is the oldest commissioned warship afloat in the world. It has been in service for America for over 200 years. Walking the decks of these ships is like stepping through time. I guarantee your kids will love it. These remarkable wooden warships are historic treasures that should not be missed.

The Civil War is the most traumatic war the country has ever

---

[162] U.S. military service, deaths, wounded, 1775-1991:
Http//www.americanfamilytraditions.com/war_cas
Defense Manpower Data Center, Statistical Information Analysis Division: http://siadapp.dmdc.osd.mil/personal/CASUALITY/WPRINCIPAL.pdf

experienced. It was not a war of unified Americans fighting a foreign force, but fighting each other. The "causes" for the war were issues like slavery, states' rights, expansionism, and commerce that were unresolved since the Revolution. The Civil War tested the very tenets of our Constitution and the wills of men. The industrial revolution produced devastating weapons that inflicted unimaginable death and destruction. To complicate matters many of the commanding officers on both sides knew each other. They had been classmates at West Point and they fought together during the Mexican-American War. They all had the same training and they knew how each other strategized. It was like a chess match where both opponents had the same teacher.

President Abraham Lincoln was devoted to preserving the Union. He knew that when the issues of division were finally resolved, the nation, ever stronger, would move forward. The assassination of Lincoln was not just the death of one of our greatest leaders; it was also the death of his re-unification plan to heal the wounded country. The flawed "Reconstruction Plan" that was instituted in its place has left scars on the nation to this day.

The Civil War is not a war Americans are proud of, but it is an integral part of our history. Hundreds of thousands of men died for a principal – freedom; the freedom of an entire group of people, and the freedom of states to determine their own rights. Approximately 618,009 people died during the Civil War. That was 2% of the population. For reference, 2% of today's population would be a loss of 6 million Americans.[163] Though the war was fought mainly in the South, it did reach into the North during a very important battle at Gettysburg, Pennsylvania. Gettysburg National Military Park documents the intense 3-day battle that claimed the lives of tens of thousands of Americans. It covers a very large area that you traverse along the self-guided auto tour. By visiting the battlefield museum and following the auto tour, you can grasp the magnitude of that horrific and history changing event. It is a remarkable chapter in the history of the Civil War. The war was also fought west of and along the Mississippi River. As a matter of fact, General Grant was

---

[163] Civil War Casualties – *The Right Words: Great Republican Speeches That Shaped History*, Wynton C. Hall, Hoboken, NJ: John Wiley & Sons, Inc. 2007

engaged in a massive battle at Vicksburg, Mississippi at the same time the Gettysburg, Pennsylvania battle raged.

Civil War memorials, monuments, museums, and battlefields dot the Eastern half of the country providing exceptional centers of education on the war and people of the war. The monuments and memorials are not to glorify war, but to educate Americans about the cost of freedom and to honor the sacrifice of so many Americans. Tragically it took sixteen Presidents and the deaths of over a half million people to finally recognize the equality of all men by the abolishment of the despicable institution of slavery in the United States.

The world wars of the twentieth century produced civilian aggression on a massive scale. Aggressor nations like Germany and Japan viewed civilians and personal property as legitimate targets while the United States viewed civilian casualties and destruction of property as unavoidable collateral damage in a total war. There is NO comparison between civilian casualties purposely inflicted by aggressor nations and casualties inflicted by the United States military. German Governor, Field Marshall Baron von der Goltz explained Germany's lack of concern for civilians this way, *"It is the stern necessity of war that the punishment for hostile acts falls not only on the guilty, but on the innocent as well."*[164] During World War I, German military atrocities against civilians were recorded as early as 1914. Later in the war Germans sent French and Belgian men and women to labor camps in Germany.

The world was ablaze in 1917 when the United States finally entered the **First World War**. President Wilson addressed the nation: *"It is a fearful thing to lead this great peaceful people into war, into the most terrible and disastrous of all wars, civilization itself seeming to be in the balance. But the right is more precious than peace, and we shall fight for the things we have always carried in our hearts – for democracy, for the right of those who submit to authority to have a voice in their own governments, for the rights and liberties of small nations, for a universal dominion of right by such a concert of free peoples as shall bring peace and safety to all nations and make the world itself at last free. To such a task we can dedicate our lives and our fortunes, everything that we are and*

---

[164] "German military leaders viewed civilians as targets of war." *The First World War: A Complete History*, Martin Gilbert, New York: Holt and Company, 1994

everything that we have, with the pride of those who know that America is privileged to spend her blood and her might for the principles that gave her birth and happiness and the peace which she has treasured..."

World War I ended on November 11, 1918. Over 320,000 Americans had given their lives during U.S. participation in the war. Overall approximately 9 million military personnel died during WWI and an estimated 8.5 million civilians died from mass murder, military operations, disease, and starvation. It is astonishing to realize that nearly as many civilians died as military personnel. World War I was supposed to be the war to end all wars. Unfortunately world nations including the United States learned nothing from that horrific war and only 23 years later were facing off again with massive armies and much deadlier weapons on the bloodied battlefields of World War II.

Appeasement does not work is one of the most important lessons NOT learned from World War II. To appease Germany and protect themselves, Great Britain and France sacrificed the defenseless country of Czechoslovakia on Hitler's altar with the Munich Agreement in 1938. Political appeasement only bought them a little time. Treaties, agreements and promises are meaningless to aggressor nations and it didn't take long for Hitler to go after all of Europe. In 1940 Great Britain stood alone against Germany. Too many people today still don't understand that appeasement only temporarily placates conflict and never averts an inevitable war. **Appeasement does not work!**

While Germany was planning the invasions of Europe and the Soviet Union, Japan in the 1930s pillaged China slaughtering at least 50,000 Chinese during their invasion of Nanking. They established a bacteriological weapons testing facility in Manchuria (Detachment 731) and killed thousands of Chinese, Koreans and Americans during brutal experiments. Indiscriminate brutality and killing by the Japanese continued until the end of the war.

After the Japanese bombing of Pearl Harbor in December 1941 the United States entered the war on two fronts – Atlantic (Europe and Northern Africa) and the Pacific. **World War II** lasted 6 years, encompassed 56 countries and was the most destructive war in human history. In a letter to his wife, Mamie in June 1943, General Dwight D. Eisenhower said: "*More than any other war in history, this war has* *been an array of the forces of evil against those of righteousness. It had to have its leaders and it had to be won-but no matter what the sacrifice, no matter what the suffering of populations, no matter what the cost, the war had to be won."*

The war in Europe was won in May 1945 and the horrors of the Holocaust and the utter devastation of Europe were revealed to the world. Japan finally surrendered in August 1945, only after the U.S. dropped atomic bombs on the cities of Hiroshima and Nagasaki. The decision to drop the bombs was made with great deliberation. The Japanese military would not stop fighting and killing; and Japanese civilians were ordered to fight an Allied military invasion force. The planned invasion of Japan would have cost millions more lives – American, Allies, and Japanese. Aside from the casualties prevented by not invading Japan, the end of the war liberated hundreds of thousands of people including 200,000 Dutch, and 400,000 Indonesians in Japanese concentration camps. It also ended the atrocities against millions of Chinese, and saved the lives of over 100,000 Allied POWs since the Japanese War Ministry issued an order on August 1, 1945 to execute all POWs in the event of an invasion.[165]

Talk to American civilians who lived through World War II. What was it like? What did they do during the war? They supported our military members as they banded together to make sure the soldiers were equipped and the country was safe. Mothers, wives, and widows went to work in industrial centers to manufacture war supplies. Citizens willingly gave up purchasing new cars, and products containing rubber and nylon as manufacturing facilities and resources focused on the war effort. Gasoline, meat, butter, sugar and even shoes were rationed. Americans endured blackouts as civilian pilots and sailors used their own planes and boats to patrol the coasts for possible enemy attacks. They did what they could and what was needed for America to win this horrendous war. I wonder how that would work today. Are there enough American civilians who would willingly "sacrifice" for their country, their soldiers or for the freedom of those oppressed?

The National WWII Museum in New Orleans, Louisiana is an

---

[165] *"Hiroshima During World War II,"* http://en.wikipedia.org/wiki/ Atomic_bombings_of_Hiroshima_and_Nagasaki (June 2005)

exceptional resource for World War II history and an interactive adventure of the "American experience in the war that changed the world." Check it out at http://www.nationalww2museum.org.

It is interesting to note how many celebrities served in the Armed Forces during World War II. The list of "celebrity" veterans is impressive and includes: Henry Fonda (Navy), Humphrey Bogart (Navy), Eddie Albert (Navy), Walter Matthau (Army Air Force), Lee Marvin (Marines), James Arness (Army), Don Adams (Marines), Ernest Borgnine (Navy), Ronald Reagan (Army Reserves), Gene Autry (Army Air Force), Clark Gable (Army Air Force), Johnny Carson (Navy), Glenn Ford (Marines), Audie Murphy (Army), Tony Bennett (Army), Charles Bronson (Army Air Force), Charlton Heston (Army Air Force).

Numerous websites provide biographies and military information about these WWII veterans and celebrity veterans of other wars. A few of these websites are:

- www.homeof heroes.com
- www.militarytimes.com
- http://www.freerepublic.com/tag/vetscor-vetscor/index

The Korean War has been labeled an "international conflict," a "limited war," a "police action," a "proxy war," and a "substitute for World War III." It was not a conventional war with large-scale battles. It was a combination of conventional weapons and guerilla warfare. Soviet and Chinese documents have conclusively proven that North Korea and the Soviet Union were responsible for the planning and execution of the invasion into South Korea in 1950 prompting the U.S. and United Nations offensive into North Korea. That offensive led to China's involvement in the war – as planned by the Communist Soviet Union. The "puppet master" behind the Korean War was Joseph Stalin. Both the USSR and China viewed the United States as weak at this time, and Stalin seized the opportunity that a limited war in Korea would provide to keep the United States distracted from his plans for European expansion.

Now the United States was appeasing an aggressor nation – the U.S.S.R. Since U.S. policy was to avoid war with the Soviet Union and

China, and China could not sustain a war with America without Soviet help, the stalemate began. America was focused on European and Japanese reconstruction as well as rearmament in Europe to contain Soviet aggression. The war was not managed well. Sporadic escalations followed by indecisive action wasted opportunity and lives. A decision should have been made at the beginning to either commit to fight a "total war" to win, or find a diplomatic means to deal with the problem. The war fumbled along until it ended in 1953 right where it began. Nothing gained; nothing lost, except the lives of 33,000 Americans[166] and up to 4 million Koreans.[167]

Do you think the U.S. government learned its lesson in Korea? Think again. When the United States inherited the scourge **of Vietnam** from France, our government's failure to learn from the mistakes of Korea led to a protracted war in Vietnam costing thousands of additional American lives and millions of South Vietnamese and Cambodian lives. The war was ineptly micro-managed from the White House by President Johnson and his advisors. Johnson told an advisor, *"I don't think it's worth it…and I don't think we can get out."*[168] Thus began Johnson's "limited war," and years of mismanagement resulting in the deaths of 58,000 Americans. The way the war was executed was clearly in violation of the objective of the U.S. Army Field Manual: *"Every military operation must be directed toward a clearly defined, decisive and attainable objective. The ultimate military objective of war is the destruction of the enemy's armed forces and his will to fight. The objective of each operation must contribute to this ultimate objective. Each intermediate objective must be such that its attainment will most directly, quickly, and economically contribute to the purpose of the operation. The selection of an objective is based upon consideration of the means available, the enemy, and the*

---

[166] *The United States in Korea* (U.S. military casualties) http://www.korean-war-com/USUnits.html (May 2005)

[167] *The Korean War*, Steven Lee, New York: Pearson Education, Ltd., 2001 [Over 1 million ROK soldiers and civilians, 2 million DPRK civilians, and a half million DPRK soldiers died during the war

[168] *The U.S. Gets Involved: Scholastic Encyclopedia of the United States at War*, June A., English and Thomas D. Jones, New York: Scholastic, Inc., 1998 [Johnson did not want to fight the war, but he did not know how to break the support agreement with the South Vietnamese]

area of operations. Every commander must understand and clearly define his objective and consider each contemplated action in light thereof."[169]

In 1965, a civilian, Secretary of Defense Robert McNamara decided the war was militarily "unwinnable." McNamara and his "defense intellectuals" comprised of academics not military minds determined the course of the war resulting in seriously flawed strategies. The "Tet Offensive" launched by North Vietnam in January 1968 was a North Vietnamese military failure. Even though U.S. troops successfully defeated the North Vietnamese, the media decided the war was "lost." Media images of the horrors of war were viewed in living rooms across America daily. The Tet Offensive was a propaganda success resulting in growing anti-war protests across the U.S. Richard Nixon was elected president on the promise of ending the war. He initiated troop withdrawal in 1971.

To summarize the Vietnam War: Overwhelming superior U.S. forces with technologically advanced weapons and equipment were sent to Vietnam, but were <u>not</u> allowed to fight the war to win. It was designed to be a doomed operation. The tragedy of Vietnam is that so many Americans died fighting a war that was "winnable."

After the humiliating experience in Vietnam, the disgraceful treatment of our returning veterans was inexcusable. They were virtually ignored by the government that sent them into war and the vitriol of the not so peaceful "peace protesters," was chilling. These valiant warriors were shunned and mistreated. The U.S. military was at an all-time low. Through the 1980s the military underwent dramatic changes with a renewed interest in Special Forces for rapid deployment and mobility, and began taking counter-terrorism seriously. There had been significant advances in weapons systems. "Stealth" technology would be introduced to the world in January 1991 during The Gulf War.

When Saddam Hussein's Iraqi Army invaded Kuwait and then ignored the United Nations mandate to withdraw, the United States led a coalition of 690,000 troops (541,000 Americans) to remove them. **Operation Desert Storm** was a brilliant military operation and a great example of the modern "total war" strategy. A massive assault was launched utilizing air, sea, and land forces. Immediate overwhelming air superiority with precision bombing destroyed Iraq's capability to

---

[169] Field Service Regulations; 1962 edition of Field Manual 100-5

supply its front lines by 90% within the first 2 weeks of the operation. The operation began on January17, 2001 and ended on February 28, 2001. The war was over; mission objectives had been accomplished. A new era in military technology had arrived including stealth aircraft, global positioning systems (GPS), laser guided "smart bombs," computer guided mechanized systems and precision weapons. Unfortunately, peace in the region was not to be.

It is not arrogance to say the United States of America saved the free world during the twentieth century. America liberated Europe – twice, rebuilt Japan into a successful industrial nation even after Japan attacked the U.S. America stepped up to defend South Korea and South Vietnam. America led a coalition force to liberate Kuwait. With the invasion of Afghanistan in 2001, and the invasion of Iraq in 2003, America took the lead in the Global War on Terror. **Yes, there really is a global war on terror**, even though early in 2009 our president and some of our leaders decided to call it "Overseas Contingency Operations" so as not to offend our enemies. An undeniable fact that is extremely inconvenient to critics is that the United States has never taken over any country, oppressed any peoples, or stolen their resources (oil for example) during these military actions. In 1984 President Ronald Reagan said, *"We are not the cause of all the ills in the world. We're a patient and generous people. But for the sake of our freedom and that of others, we cannot permit our reserve to be confused with a lack of resolve."* We need to remember Reagan's words.

War is a terrible thing. We don't live on planet "Utopia" so unfortunately in this human world, war is inevitable. History has proven the continual existence of "aggressor nations" driven by greed, power, and fanaticism without regard for human life. The United States is not an "aggressor" nation. It is a "defender" nation. With regard to recent events, the Unites States invaded Afghanistan in response to the actions of terrorist organizations. The war in Iraq was highly criticized and debated, but the fact remains - the United States reacted to the world intelligence communities' consensus that Saddam Hussein's Iraq possessed weapons of mass destruction and was a threat to the Middle East and the West. The actual Iraq War was a success and only lasted two months (March – May, 2003). Military strategy and implementation were spectacular. The problem with Iraq was post-war mismanagement.

Unfortunately, politicians and analysts did not have a solid plan for rebuilding and securing the peace which indirectly led to civil strife and an influx of terrorists resulting in continued instability in Iraq.

The "Give Peace a Chance" contingent likes to criticize America as an imperialistic, war-mongering nation. I don't understand their logic. Facts, also known as real history totally contradict their thesis. They do not even mention the real aggressors, nations that are a threat to the world around us; nations that abuse and massacre their own citizens; nations that enable terrorist groups with financing and weapons including weapons of mass destruction; nations like North Korea, Iran, Syria and Somalia.

Our military personnel need our support and deserve our honor and respect. We need to pressure our legislators to ensure our military gets the equipment, weapons and medical care they need to do their jobs. We need to pressure our Government to sustain a healthy military/defense budget. As was proven during the 1990's, military budget cuts are a detriment to the safety of our soldiers and our nation. Unfortunately, the current administration seems to be ignoring history and recklessly imposes defense budget cuts which are devastating to our military and our national security. The administration also seems to be forgetting that a primary duty of government is to protect its citizens. The U.S. should be increasing its defense budget especially now that we are facing unstable regimes in possession of nuclear weapons and terrorist organizations in the process of acquiring them.

The president and his minions are hostile toward our military and they do not even try to hide it. Intentional budget cuts, dismissals of competent officers, lies, and the reduction of service member rights and privileges are detrimental to morale. The current administration takes dishonor for our warriors to a new level. Some of the unfortunate, disrespectful events that have occurred are:

- A disabled Purple Heart Veteran was told to leave an American establishment because he had the word "Kafir" tattooed in Arabic on his leg. This was offensive to Qatar Muslims who saw it because Kafir translates to "infidel," and "unbeliever." But that is what he was called for over two years while serving in the Middle East and <u>his</u> tattoo was <u>his</u> expression that he was not a Muslim.[170]

- A group of Vietnam Veterans joined by Iraqi, Afghanistan, and even WWII vets were arrested at the Vietnam War Memorial in New York City for violating a 10PM curfew. They were a peaceful group there to honor the fallen.

- President Obama declined attendance at the 150th Gettysburg anniversary ceremony on November 19, 2013. As an avid admirer of President Lincoln and considering the significance of the event the President seems disrespectful to the memory of Lincoln, the memory of those who died there, and the very ideals of freedom and liberty.[171]

- Samantha Power, our U.S. Ambassador to the United Nations praised Jane Fonda at the United Nations Association of the USA 2013 Global Leadership Awards in New York: *"There is no greater embodiment of being outspoken on behalf of what you believe in – and being 'all in' in every way – than Jane Fonda. And it's a huge honor just to even briefly have shared the stage with her."[172]* That would be the same Jane Fonda who went to North Vietnam in 1972 (where over 50,000 Americans had already been killed during the war) to aid the North Vietnamese (the enemy) with propaganda events.

- Death benefits to families of soldiers killed during the temporary government shutdown were not paid even though the President could easily have signed an emergency executive action. He had no problem previously signing trivial executive orders. Congress passed an emergency bill for the families to receive payments.[173]

---

[170] "Iraq war veteran says skydiving business kicked him out over Arabic tattoo," *The Examiner,* http://www.examiner.com, April 5, 2013

[171] "Obama dis: President snubs historic Gettysburg 150th anniversary ceremony," Ben Wolfgang, *The Washington Times,* http://www.washingtontimes.com, October 31, 2013

[172] "Oh Great: UN Ambassador Praises 'Hanoi Jane,'" Leah Barkoukis, Town Hall. com, http:www.townhall.com, November 10, 2013

[173] "Rumsfeld: Denial of Benefits to Fallen Soldiers' Families 'Inexcusable'" Lisa Furgison, Cathy Burke, Todd Beamon, Newsmax, http://www.newsmax.com, October 8, 2013

- Also during the shutdown the President closed all our National Parks and Monuments including the "open air" monuments and parks that are normally accessible 24 hours a day in Washington DC. This action was especially disparaging to our veterans. World War II veterans in Washington to visit the WWII National Memorial sponsored by national "Honor Flight" programs were threatened with arrest for visiting their memorial. The National Park Service put barricades around the memorial expressly to keep the veterans out. In a unified action demonstrating what Americans used to be, veterans present from all wars removed the barriers so the valiant WWII veterans could experience their memorial.

  □ The Heritage Foundation thought this government action shameful. *"Americans are justifiably angry over the political game being played by the Obama administration.* **Under federal law, there is no justifiable reason for closing the memorial.**[174]

  □ Likewise, police ordered visitors to leave the Vietnam Veterans Memorial (an outdoor wall). The *Weekly Standard* reported, *"The Vietnam Veterans Memorial Wall is a black granite outdoor wall on which the names of the 58,272 service members who died or were unaccounted for during the Vietnam War are inscribed. It takes more manpower and costs the government more money to close down an outdoor wall than to let people walk by and pay their respects."*[175]

  □ Even the Flight 93 National Memorial in Shanksville, Pennsylvania was closed and barricaded.

  □ In reaction to the Obama Administration's closing the monuments, WWII veteran Merwin Cowles made a profound statement that I believe is supported by most

---

[174] "Storming the Barricades in Washington," Morning Bell – The Heritage Foundation, October 3, 2013

[175] "Police Force Veterans from Vietnam Memorial," (Weekly Standard report) posted by Tim Brown, Freedom Outpost, http://www.freedomoutpost.com, October 5, 2013

Americans. *"I think it's the most dishonorable thing they ever could do for us. Without us veterans working like that there would be no America."*[176] Mr. Cowles, Sir, you are a patriot and have the respect and honor you deserve from Americans across the country!

- The Obama Administration very quietly filed a new Veteran's Administration policy directive on October 31, 2013 (*38 CFR Parts 3.19 and 3.20 Standard Claims and Appeals Forms*) in contempt of a 2013 Circuit Court Order (*Harris v. Secretary of Veteran's Affairs et al Eric Shinseki*). This policy would reduce veteran's rights, increase disability claim denials, and make it extremely difficult for veterans to challenge administration disability decisions. This is the administration's solution to reduce the incredible number of backlogged claims. Read the complete story published by *Freedom Outpost* and prepare to get angry.[177] Keep in mind this was before the VA scandal and the deaths of veterans due to VA neglect came to light.

- The Two-Year budget deal, signed, sealed and delivered by the December 31, 2013 deadline cut military pensions by $6 billion over 10 years. Senate Democrats blocked a vote on the Republican amendment to restore veteran's pensions. The amendment targeted closing a child tax credit "loophole" that allows illegal aliens to "illegally" obtain welfare benefits at a cost to taxpayers of over $4 billion per year.[178] Bottom line – the administration chooses to give our money to illegal aliens and make our military veterans suffer …. So wrong!

Former Secretary of Defense Robert Gates, who by the way has worked for both Democrat and Republican administrations during

---

[176] "Is the Obama Administration worthy of American veterans?" Dennis Jamison, The Washington Times, http://washingtontimes.com, November 11, 2013

[177] "Obama Administration Violates another Court Order and More Veterans will Die," John DeMayo, http://freedomoutpost.com, December 17, 2013

[178] "Senate Dems block amendment to restore veteran benefits by closing illegal immigrant welfare loophole," Caroline May, The Daily Caller, http://dailycaller.com, December 18, 2013

wartime, wrote a book, *"Duty: Memoirs of a Secretary at War,"* in which he exposes President's Obama's lack of respect and responsibility for our military. Mr. Gates' disappointment with the President's spineless foreign policy is evident. Bob Woodward at the *Washington Post* wrote: "...*former defense secretary Robert Gates unleashes harsh judgments about President Obama's leadership and his commitment to the Afghanistan war, writing that by early 2010 he had concluded the president 'doesn't believe in his own strategy, and doesn't consider the war to be his. For him, it's all about getting out.'"*[179]

So it would seem that our President was more concerned about his own political career than the Americans he sent into battle since taking office, the Afghan people, and all the blood and sacrifice of our military in Afghanistan since 2001. Current events in Afghanistan and Iraq validate Mr. Gates assessment of the President's attitude. As I write this, Iraq has reverted back to a near pre-civilization state with al-Qaeda and other terrorist groups including ISIS which is growing and strengthening daily vying for power. All they had to do was wait until the Americans left, and they had plenty of notice to prepare since the administration heralded to the world the date of withdrawal. Afghanistan will follow suit.

Defense Secretary Gates was criticized by the left and the media for publishing a "tell-all" book about a sitting president. As proof of the President's dishonor to the men and women who fight for America, the administration will feverishly spend time and unlimited resources trying to defame Mr. Gates but will spend no time addressing the abject failure of the Obama administration's foreign policy. There will also be no remorse for the fact that this President has thrown away <u>everything</u> our military had accomplished in those countries. What, Mr. President did our men and women die for? How did you so callously send them on virtual suicide missions knowing you had no intention of supporting them or of attaining success? That sir is despicable. It is no longer hard to understand how the President and then Secretary of State Hillary Clinton could so easily have let four Americans in Benghazi, Libya be slaughtered and then lie to cover it up and deflect blame.

---

[179] "Former Secretary of Defense Gates Soundly Criticizes Obama's Leadership," Tami Jackson, Liberty Alliance, http://libertyalliance.com, January 10, 2014

Since our current administration has obviously lost all respect for honor and valor, and does not do enough for our wounded and disabled soldiers, we need to step up to support and defend our courageous military personnel. An effortless smile and a simple "Thank You" to military people that you may encounter are important gestures of acknowledgement and appreciation of their service to our country.

Now you ask, is there anything you can do for our injured heroes whether in hospitals, veterans facilities or at their homes readjusting to civilian life? Why yes, we need to actively interact with organizations committed to supporting our troops, and we can help in a number of ways. Whether contributing financially or through donations of material or time, or attending events, or providing moral support – we all can help. The U.S. Department of Defense Community Relations hosts an official website encouraging support of our troops. "**Operation Troop Support U.S.**" is a non-profit organization with an extensive index to organizations and websites committed to help and support our troops and their families. The "**Wounded Warrior Project**" is a superb organization that supports wounded soldiers and their families. **"Honor and Remember"** is a non-profit organization dedicated to the memory of our Fallen Heroes. The "Honor and Remember" flag symbolizes selfless sacrifice and as the organization becomes nationally known, expect to see these beautiful flags everywhere. There is no shortage of people and organizations dedicated to our troops. Here is a sampling of government and privately funded non-profit organizations that <u>really need our help</u>.

Organization	Website
U.S. Department of Defense Community Relations: Index to organizations and Veteran services, benefits and resources	www.defense.gov
U.S. Department of Veterans Affairs: Benefits and resources information for veterans and their families	www.va.gov

Give 2 The Troops: Organization of U.S. citizens whose mission is to ensure that every deployed soldier feels remembered, appreciated, and loved. The site offers numerous ways to get involved volunteering time, money, and resources.	www.give2thetroops.org
Operation Care and Comfort: Non-profit organization for troop support - California	Occ-usa.org
Support Our Troops: Entire website is devoted to troop support and provides links to an extensive list of organizations providing resources to our military personnel.	www.troopsupport.com
Relief for U.S. Soldiers: Emergency financial and other assistance to wounded veterans and military families.	www.OperationHomefront.net
The USO: Worldwide private organization that supports U.S. troops by providing support and recreation services to military personnel and their families.	www.uso.org
Military Support Groups of America: A federation of national organizations providing financial and emotional support for our service members, veterans and their families.	www.militarysupportgroups.org
The Navy League of the United States: Citizen organization founded in 1902 to serve and support the U.S. Navy, Marine Corps, Coast Guard, and U.S. – flag Merchant Marine Corps	www.NavyLeague.org
Operation Gratitude: Non-profit, volunteer organizations that provides care packages for active duty and wounded personnel and veterans as well as their care-givers.	www.opgradititude.com

Wounded Warrior Project: Supports wounded troops and advocates public help to meet the needs of injured service members	www.woundedWarriorProject.org
Boot Campaign: Assistance for military and families. *Walk in their Boots*	www.bootcampaign.com
Microsoft Corporate Citizenship: Elevate America Program: Technology, training, employment resources, and support services including child care, transportation, and housing for veterans and their families Supports the USO, The Wounded Warrior Project, The American Legion, Iraq & Afghanistan Veterans of America, and Paralyzed Veterans of America	www.microsoft.com/about/ corporatecitizenship/en-us/
The Independence Fund TRACK CHAIRS – All Terrain Wheelchairs *Collective of nonprofit organizations led by the Independence Fund to provide track chairs for double, triple & quadruple amputees	www.independencefund.org
Homes for Our Troops: National Organization - Builds handicap accessible homes for severely injured veterans at no cost to the vet. State-sponsored programs also available.	www.hfotusa.org
***American Bible Society:** *God Understands* – "Veterans struggle with the spiritual, physical and emotional wounds of war, even after returning home. *God Understands* is a scripture-based series that helps veterans experience healing through the Word of God." *True stories of soldiers' emotional issues.*	www.Veterans.AmericanBible.org www.AmericanBible.org

Military Order of the Purple Heart Service Foundation: Raises money to provide assistance for veterans and their families. Donations of clothing and household items fund foundation services.	www.PHDonation.com
Vietnam Veterans of America: Provides funding for local, state and national service programs by raising funds through wholesale of donated items – clothing, shoes, household items...	www.VVADonation.com
Disabled American Veterans: Excellent national organization of veterans helping veterans and their families by providing free services. Assistance is provided to secure medical care, housing, jobs, transportation, VA benefits and much more through numerous programs.	www.dav.org
Operation Support Our Troops: Provides comfort and care to active duty military, veterans and their families. Actor Gary Sinise is extremely committed to this organization. Sinise and the "Lt. Dan Band" provide entertainment at numerous OSOT fund raisers.	www.osotamerica.org
Honor and Remember: "Perpetually Recognizing the Sacrifice of our Military Fallen Heroes and Their Families"	www.honorandremember.org

Our children need <u>real</u> action heroes and what better models of valor, strength, and loyalty are there than our patriotic men and woman who put their lives on the line for us. We need to celebrate our heroes, and a true patriot who merits special mention is Tim James, a former NBA player who became a U.S. Army soldier to serve in Iraq. Tim's professional basketball career included playing for the Miami Heat, the Charlotte Hornets, and the Philadelphia 76ers. Tim enlisted in the Army in September 2008 turning away from a comfortable safe life to go into harm's way to serve his country. In Tim's own words: *"I got my degree, lived the life I was able, have my freedom and became a professional athlete. I am the example of the American Dream."* This young man, a retired professional basketball player and United States Army veteran is an inspiration. Tim now is the head coach of the Vance-Granville Community College basketball team.

Another true American hero is Than Naing. Than was a 25 year-old immigrant from Burma. He was living in New York City when our country was changed forever by the attacks on 9/11. He spent the next two years studying English and in 2004 enlisted in the U.S. Marine Corps. Than was wounded in Iraq during his second tour of duty in 2006. During his recovery he became a U. S. citizen and underwent extensive physical therapy to pass the "fitness test" to return to combat. He was in Afghanistan when in June of 2010 he was shot in the chest by a Taliban fighter. Recovering again in the States, Than was determined to return to active duty with the Marine Corps – for a fourth tour.

Many "native-born Americans" do not understand why an immigrant would be so dedicated to the U.S. as to put his life on the line by fighting for America even after being shot in combat twice. Than said, *"Many people in America don't appreciate democracy..."* He then explained that in Burma, where he is from there is no freedom of speech. He further explained why he joined the Marine Corps. *"I was so happy to have the chance to live in a democracy, and I wanted to defend it. I saw the people dying in the Twin Towers. I felt like I had to give something back, because America gave me such a good life."*

To Tim James, Than Naing, and all the brave men and women who have put their lives in harms-way to serve a higher purpose, "Thank You!"

Dover Air Force Base in Dover, Delaware is an extraordinary military installation in the sense that in addition to its military function, it is the base that receives our fallen heroes from overseas. Solemn respect embraces the returning members of the military family. Don't ever think our military takes the death of any service branch member lightly. If you have any doubts, just observe the military honor guard at any active-duty member or veteran's funeral. It is a sincere and heart-warming sight.

We need to honor our fallen soldiers, who sacrificed their lives for liberty whether here in America or on foreign soil. Arlington National Cemetery near Washington D.C. is a remarkable resting place. An honor guard is on duty protecting the "Tomb of the Unknowns" (Resting place of unidentified soldiers from WWI, WWII, Korean War, and Vietnam War) 24-hours a day, 365 days a year. It is never unattended. As a matter of fact, even during the East Coast hurricane, the sentinels refused to take shelter. We **need** to pay our respects and **remember** that they sacrificed their lives for OUR freedom.

The Tomb of the Unknowns

Arlington National Cemetery

The Sentinels Creed

My dedication to this sacred duty is total and wholehearted. In the responsibility bestowed upon me never will I falter. And with dignity and perseverance my standard will remain perfection. Through the years of diligence and praise and the discomfort of the elements, I will walk my tour in humble reverence to the best of my ability. It is he who commands the respect I protect, His bravery that made us so proud. Surrounded by well-meaning crowds by day, alone in the thoughtful peace of night, this soldier will in honored glory rest under my eternal vigilance.

—Third United States Infantry Regiment ("The Old Guard")

The United States Armed Forces are a part of our collective history – a history that is very much alive. It is worth noting that American history is not composed of static events on a time line focusing on "major" events even though that is how it is presented in basic social studies classes. Wars do not "just" happen. There are reasons for them. Unless we understand *why* a war occurred we cannot fully comprehend the event itself. It is important to know the causes and the people involved leading up to a war. When you know why and how it happened you acquire a more comprehensive understanding of the event, the people involved, and how it affects the country as a whole.

We are surrounded by history. It is in Washington DC. It is in Boston, Philadelphia, New York, Savannah, Atlanta, Charleston, New Orleans, St. Louis, San Francisco, Denver, Anchorage, and Honolulu. It can be found at Gettysburg, Valley Forge, Yorktown, Vicksburg, Chattanooga, Ft. Laramie, Salt Lake City and many, many other places across America. You can find it along the Oregon Trail, the Mississippi River, Death Valley, and the National Road. There are large, small, urban and rural museums, government buildings, memorials, National Parks, and monuments just waiting to be discovered. They offer glimpses into history, our history and teach us so many things we did not know.

America is an open book of living history. We can learn so much just by "visiting" our own country. There are Americans who spend more vacation time in foreign countries and know more about those countries than their own country. We owe it to our children to show them the real America – not the America they only see on television or learn about in "selective" history courses in school. Instead of spending repeated vacations at *Disney World*, how about taking the kids to see their nation? They will enjoy, learn and remember historical destinations like Washington, DC, Jamestown, Williamsburg, Plymouth, the cities and towns of the Appalachians, the Great Lakes, the South, and the West. America is blessed with natural wonders. Our National Parks are unsurpassed. Yellowstone, Rocky Mountain, and the Grand Canyon are awe-inspiring. When you see the majesty and bounty of our nation, you understand why we say **"God Bless America."**

Countless books have been written on the military history of America. We need to know our ancestors and our heroes. There are movies, biographies and autobiographies of remarkable people you have never heard of. Their stories teach and inspire. Listed below are just a few books on special Americans and American history well worth reading. There are <u>many</u> more great books.

- *American Courage*, edited by Herbert W. Warden III, William Morrow Publishers, 2005 [Stories of real people who have made significant contributions to America - from the Pilgrim's to the Flight 93 passengers]
- *1776* by David McCullough, New York: Simon & Schuster, 2005
- *Hearts In Conflict: A One-Volume History of the Civil War* by Curt Anders, New York: Barnes & Noble, 1999
- *America's Armed Forces: A History,* by James M. Morris, New Jersey: Prentice Hall, 1996
- *Don't Tread on Me: A 400-Year History of America at War, from Indian Fighting to Terrorist Hunting,* by H.W. Crocker III, New York: Crown Forum, 2006
- *America's Victories: Why the U.S. Wins Wars and Will Win the War on Terror,* Larry Schweikart, New York: Sentinel - Penguin Group USA, 2006
- *Union 1812: The Americans Who Fought the Second War of Independence,* A.J. Langguth, New York: Simon & Schuster, 2006
- *"Decision at Sea: Five Naval Battles That Shaped American History,* Craig L. Symonds, New York: Oxford University Press, 2005

The news media is an information source, but do not rely on them to give you a full account. They are selective in their reporting and do not give a complete picture of events, and just as importantly – the causes leading up to the events. You need to research things on your own. This is where the internet is invaluable. Multiple information sources woven together clarify an incident resulting in a more thorough awareness of events based on multiple accounts and perspectives.

Great sources for military news and views:

- **Stars & Stripes News:** www.stripes.com
  Independent military news and information that has been in continuous publication since World War II
- **American Military News:** www.americanmilitarynews.com
  Publishes news and current events issues that affect all branches of our military
  *Volunteer bloggers are most welcome: www.info@ americanmilitarynews.com

Aside from veterans and the victims of the 9/11 attacks most modern native-born Americans have never experienced war. These same Americans have also never experienced political oppression or genocide, both of which are present in our 21st century "civilized" world. From our "safe" world it is easy to criticize the actions of others. It is wise to remember these words of General George S. Patton: *"Wars may be fought with weapons, but they are won by men. It is the spirit of the men who follow and of the man who leads that gains the victory."*

"A soldier above all others prays for peace, for it is the soldier who must suffer and bear the deepest wounds and scars of war."

-General Douglas McArthur

OUR ELECTED LEADERS

The United States Capital, Washington, D.C.

"God give us men! A time like this demands strong minds, great hearts, true faith, and ready hands. Men whom the lust of office does not kill; Men whom the spoils of office cannot buy; Men who possess opinions and a will; Men who have honor; Men who will not lie."[180]

—Josiah Gilbert Holland 1872

[180] *Wanted, 1872, American Quotations* by Gorton Carruth and Eugene Ehrlich, New York: Gramercy Books, 1988

George Washington and Abraham Lincoln immediately come to mind as great American leaders. Both risked their lives for America and consistently put America first. I am not insinuating that personal risk is what makes a great leader. I am saying that their personal actions proved love and commitment to their country. It is easy to criticize the faults and mistakes of past presidents. I know of no American President, or leader of any country for that matter that did not make mistakes. I am not aware of any American President that had 100 percent support of the American people. The point is, Presidents should be judged on their leadership, words, and actions in support and defense the United States of America. Presidents who sincerely lived up to their oath of office should be celebrated. Any person who does not put America first does not deserve the title of The President of the United States of America.

Aside from the job of guiding our new nation, George Washington, as the First President, set the tone for all future Presidents. He understood the solemnity and the responsibility of the position. He was well aware of the power of the presidency and he knew that men are susceptible to greed and corruption. When he said, *"I hope I shall possess firmness and virtue enough to maintain what I consider the most enviable of all titles, the character of an honest man,"* he expected himself to be honest and also expected all future presidents to be virtuous and honest. Washington provided the following advice: *"Labor to keep alive in your breast that little spark of celestial fire, called conscience."*[181] One additional facet regarding the character of George Washington that will make secularists grimace is the fact that Washington felt God was an undeniable part of his life and the life of America. There are numerous documented references to God by Washington including his Inaugural Address in 1789 when he said, *"It would be peculiarly improper to omit in this first official act my fervent supplications to that Almighty Being who rules over the universe, who presides in the councils of nations, and whose providential aids can supply every human defect, that His benediction may consecrate to the liberties and happiness of the people of the United States a government instituted by themselves for these essential purposes, and enable every instrument employed in its administration to*

---

[181] *American Presidents' Wit and Wisdom*, Edited by Josyln Pine, New York: Dover Publications, Inc., 2002

execute with success the functions allotted to his charge…No people can be bound to acknowledge and adore the Invisible Hand which conducts the affairs of men more than those of the United States." The book, **"General Washington's Christmas Farewell - A Mount Vernon Homecoming 1783,"** by Stanley Weintraub, 2003 is a wonderful heart-warming look at the honorable man who would become our first president.

Abraham Lincoln's steadfast allegiance to the preservation of the Union gave him the strength to endure the Civil War. Can you imagine the stress he was under? He was loved and hated, respected and mocked, supported and undermined; yet he persevered because he believed in the United States of America. During his inauguration in 1861 Lincoln said, *"You have not oath registered in heaven to destroy the government, while I shall have the most solemn one to preserve, protect, and defend it."* He had the courage to say, *"If slavery is not wrong, nothing is wrong,"* at a time in history when it would have been "easier" to let the Southern States secede from the Union. A fantastic collection of Abraham Lincoln speeches, commentaries, correspondences, and witticisms has been compiled by H. Jack Lang in his book, **"The Original Wit & Wisdom of Abraham Lincoln as Reflected in His Letters and Speeches,"** 2006 (Originally published in 1941 by Greenberg Publishers).

Franklin D. Roosevelt was the only American president to have been elected four times. His presidency spanned a tumultuous era in world history; the Great Depression and World War II. FDR's economic stimulus policies to help the country recover from the "Great Depression" actually prolonged the depression, but, this was uncharted territory and he sincerely believed he was doing the right thing to help America – not hurt America. FDR's decisive and strong leadership guided America through the years of World War II. Roosevelt said, *"The ultimate failures of dictatorship cost humanity far more than any temporary failures of democracy."*[182] Those are words we need to remember and take to heart.

Ronald Reagan was The Man to fit The Time. Reagan recognized the character of the American people and the goodness of America long before he took office. He embodies the "American Character." In 1976, Reagan said: **"We're Americans and we have a rendezvous with destiny.**

---

[182] *American Presidents' Wit and Wisdom*, Edited by Joselyn Pine, New York: Dover Publications, Inc., 2002

No people who ever lived have fought harder, paid a higher price for freedom or done more to advance the dignity of man than Americans." Reagan took office as America was still bleeding from the open wounds of the Vietnam War, Watergate, economic crisis, and our initiation into the arena of world terrorism. Reagan loved his country and gave Americans what they needed most – patriotism. Reagan helped America stand up straight and proud. He identified the problems and stood up to the threats. When many in Congress preferred to continue the stalemate of appeasement President Reagan had the audacity to identify evil and call it by name – Communism.

President Reagan reinvigorated our nation and helped us reclaim our honor. He is responsible for winning the Cold War without firing a shot for which he still is not given enough credit. He and a small circle of unlikely cohorts including, then British Prime Minister Margaret Thatcher, Polish trade union-human rights activist, Lech Walesa, and Roman Catholic Pope John Paul II literally brought down the Soviet Union. Speaking in Gdansk, Poland on December 7, 1980 Lech Walesa accurately defined Reagan's presidency by saying, *"...Reagan will do it better. He will settle things in a more efficient way. He will make the U.S. strong and make it stand up."*[183] The story of this "fearsome foursome" comes to life in John O'Sullivan's 2006 book, **The President, the Pope, and the Prime Minister.**

When the Congressional Democrats were trying very hard to take President Reagan down a few notches during the "Iran Contra crisis" in 1986, Prime Minister Margaret Thatcher's support of Reagan never wavered as evidenced in a letter she sent him, *"The message I give to everyone is that anything that weakens you weakens America; and anything that weakens America weakens the world."*[184]

I greatly admire Ronald Reagan as a President and as an honest man. He truly loved America and respected the American people. His words of warning should not be ignored: ***"We will always remember.***

---

[183] *The Crusader; Ronald Reagan and the Fall of Communism,* Paul Kengor, New York: Regan, 2006

[184] *The President, the Pope and the Prime Minister,* John O'Sullivan, Washington DC: Regnery, 2006

We will always be proud. We will always be prepared so we may always be free."

Since every elected official "freely" takes the oath of office and swears to support and defend the Constitution, I find it especially disturbing when any of our elected leaders' words or actions violates that sacred oath.

> **"...There is no nation on earth powerful enough to accomplish our overthrow...Our destruction, should it come at all, will be from another quarter. From the inattention of the people to the concerns of their government, from their carelessness and negligence, I must confess that I do apprehend some danger. I fear that they may place too implicit a confidence in their public servants, and fail properly to scrutinize their conduct; that in this way they may be made the dupes of designing men, and become the instruments of their own undoing."**
>
> —Daniel Webster 1837

Senator Ted Kennedy is a sterling example of a leader violating his Constitutional Oath. Kennedy, fondly referred to as the Lion of the Senate was a United States Senator from 1962 until his death in 2009. Did the "Lion of the Senate" not know what the Constitution specified? Did he not know that an oath is a sworn promise? Is not offering assistance to an enemy country of our nation a violation of the oath to support and defend our Constitution? Does the word "treason" have more than one definition? After the fall of the Soviet Union, many KGB documents providing evidence that Senator Kennedy contacted the KGB offering his support became available. A 1978 KGB report stating Kennedy requested KGB assistance was published in a Moscow newspaper in June 1992. Kennedy offered the KGB assistance to establish an association with a U.S. firm owned by former U.S. Senator John Tunney from California.

This KGB document published in the Moscow newspaper, *Izvestia* in June 1992 states: In 1978, American Senator Edward Kennedy appealed to the KGB to assist in establishing cooperation between

Soviet organizations and the California firm Agritech, headed by former Senator John J. Tunney. This firm in turn was connected to a French-American company, Finatech S.A. which was run by a competent KGB source, the prominent Western financier D. Karr, through whom opinions had been confidentially exchanged for several years between General Secretary of the Communist Party and Sen. Kennedy. D. Karr provided the KGB with technical information on conditions in the U.S. and other capitalist countries which were regularly reported to the Central Committee.[185]

Another KGB report stated that former Senator John Tunney met with the KGB on behalf of Kennedy in Moscow in March 1980. This time Kennedy offered to speak out against then President Jimmy Carter's policy on Afghanistan - and he did make speeches opposing Carter.

Then in 1983 he yet again sent John Tunney to Moscow to meet with the KGB. This time he had a message for Yuri Andropov, the General Secretary of the Soviet Communist Party. It seems Kennedy was "concerned" over President Reagan's anti-Soviet activities and offered to help the Soviets launch a propaganda campaign aimed at the American people to counter Reagan's militaristic policies. He seemed to believe that the problem between the U.S. and USSR was the American President. He went so far as to offer to help get Soviet views on major U.S. media networks and suggested that Soviets invite the ABC Network chairman of the board, and reporters, Walter Cronkite and Barbara Walters to Moscow. He seemed to feel so strongly about this that he was willing to go to Moscow himself.

Ted Kennedy paid a visit to Michail Gorbachev in Moscow in February 1986. Vadim Zagladin met with Kennedy after the Gorbachev meeting and felt that Kennedy was sympathetic to the Soviet position that opposed President Reagan and his Foreign and Soviet Policies. Author John O'Sullivan recounts what Vadim Zagladin said about Sen. Kennedy in his book, *The President, The Pope, and The Prime Minister.* Zagladin said Senator Kennedy was of the opinion to pressure the Reagan

---

[185] *The State Within a State: The KGB and Its Hold on Russia-Past, Present, and Future,*,by Yevgenia Albats was published in June 1992 in Moscow newspaper [*The Venona Secrets: Exposing Soviet Espionage and America's Traitors,* Herbert Romerstein and Eric Briendel, Washington, DC: Regnery Publishing, Inc., 2000]

administration both in the U.S. and abroad. Zaglidin, summarizing Kennedy said, *"The present complacency of the Americans, their almost Christmas mood, must be broken. You should put more pressure, and firmer pressure, on Reagan...And of course, I shall think over what can be done on my side, on the Senate's side. At the Congress session, I shall report on my meeting with Gorbachov...Gorbachev is right; we should not miss this opportunity."*[186]

I had a flashback of Ted Kennedy when I heard the tape of President Obama talking to Russian President Dmitry Medvedev near an open microphone while at a nuclear summit in South Korea in 2012. President Obama was assuring President Medvedev that he will have flexibility on missile defense issues after the 2012 election. *"This is my last election. After my election I will have more flexibility."*[187] I was disgusted to hear that exchange, and appalled at the media shielding Obama by calling the comment a "misstep," his "candor," his "unintended remark."

The Crusader: Ronald Reagan and the Fall of Communism, by Paul Kengor, 2006; ***The President, the Pope, and the Prime Minister*** by John O'Sullivan, 2006, and ***The Venona Secrets***, by Herbert Romerstein and Eric Breindel, 2000 are very well-researched books that extensively address this subject.

Why was there no outrage over these actions of a sitting U.S. Senator? I don't understand it. If not an outright traitor, Kennedy was an enemy "collaborator." Either way, he violated his Constitutional Oath. To be specific, Amendment XIV, Section 3 clearly states: ***No person shall be a Senator or Representative in Congress, or elector of President and Vice President, or hold any office, civil or military, under the United States, or under any state, who, having previously taken an oath, as a member of Congress, or as an officer of the United States, or as a member of any state legislature, or as an executive or judicial officer of any state, to support the Constitution of the United States, shall have engaged in insurrection or rebellion against the same, or given aid or comfort to***

---

[186] The President, The Pope, and The Prime Minister, John O'Sullivan, Washington DC: Regnery Publishing, Inc., 2006

[187] President Obama and Open Mic, http://youtu.be/XsFR8DbSRQE, http://www.cbsnews.com/video/watch/?id=7403332n

the enemies thereof. But Congress may by a vote of two-thirds of each House, remove such disability.

Besides collaborating with the KGB, Kennedy was also a key player in the 1970s to restrict CIA and FBI surveillance to protect the country. The Foreign Intelligence Surveillance Act (FISA) was passed in 1978 and made wiretapping for "national security purposes" extremely difficult. This was "step one" in the concerted effort to tie the hands of our intelligence agencies and thereby exposing Americans to great danger – as was proven on 9/11/2001.

President Bill Clinton is an interesting case. I grow weary of hearing that it was "just about sex." I don't care about his sex life. I do care that he committed perjury, the willful lying under oath. I was always under the impression that perjury is a serious offense in our judicial system. There is no doubt that he lied under oath to a federal grand jury and obstructed justice in his attempt to cover up his affair with Monica Lewinski.

Perjury was just the tip of the iceberg. President Clinton disregarded his sacred oath of office repeatedly exposing our country to foreign and domestic threats. His actions are definitely examples of dishonesty and misconduct that President Washington warned of.

- Clinton continued sending millions of dollars in aid to North Korea, and ignored North Korea's role in nuclear activities in China, Pakistan, Iran, Iraq, and Libya.
- Clinton allowed security to lapse at our national laboratories resulting in espionage and theft of national defense secrets. China was the recipient of highly classified secrets on advanced thermonuclear warheads.
- Clinton sold a $9 million national security mission configured supercomputer to China for the generous price of $30,000.[188]
- Clinton's 1996 re-election campaign funding activities were excessive and illegal. Both President Clinton and Vice President Al Gore made fund raising phone calls from the White House (illegal). They auctioned off meetings and photo ops. They

---

[188] *Dereliction of Duty: The Eyewitness Account of How Bill Clinton Compromised America's National Security*, Lt, Col. Robert Patterson, Washington, DC: Regnery Publishing Inc., 2003

rewarded large-scale donors with overnights in the White House Lincoln Bedroom. Clinton received millions of illegal dollars from among others, the People's Republic of China made through "straw donor," companies. Do the names: Charlie Trie, Johnny Chung, John Huang and James Riady, Maria Hsia, and Ted Sioeng ring a bell? There were key players in the 1996 election campaign donation scandal. Twenty-two people were convicted of fraud for funneling money into the election campaigns.

- Clinton successfully hampered our intelligence agencies' ability to track and apprehend terrorists which contributed to the 1993 World Trade Center bombing and the 2001 devastating World Trade Center and Pentagon attacks. Our porous borders and politically correct restriction on "profiling" made it easy for terrorists to enter the country.

- Clinton's lack of response to terrorist attacks on American military personnel and installations overseas emboldened terrorist groups like al Qaeda. One thing is clear. President Clinton was well aware of the terror threat and did nothing about it. He took no action against countries providing sanctuary to terrorists. He did not attack terror training camps. He did nothing to topple Saddam Hussein's regime. He certainly did not seriously try to capture or kill Osama bin Laden, a known threat. Clinton viewed terrorists as criminals, not as soldiers of terror networks, which is what they really are.

- Eighteen Americans were killed and seventy-eight wounded during the now infamous "Black Hawk Down" incident in Somalia in 1993. Clinton's response to the deaths of the men he sent to Somalia was to withdraw giving terrorists a real morale boost. But then, he did not have a problem with supporting the United Nations withdrawal from Rwanda even though over 800,000 people had been slaughtered.

- Attacks including the 1996 bombing of the Khobar Towers in Saudi Arabia prompted no action.

- The U.S. Embassy bombings in Africa in 1998 did incur a hand-slap as evidenced by the cursory bombing of an aspirin factory in Sudan.
- Even the attack on the US Battleship Cole in October 2000 which killed seventeen sailors didn't illicit a response. Is it any wonder the terrorists felt America was an easy target?

These are not the actions of a president who took his Presidential Oath seriously. I think the Founders of our Nation would be horrified by the indiscriminate disregard and total rejection of his sacred oath to protect and defend the nation that he was chosen to lead.

Retired USAF Lt. Colonel Robert Anderson's 2003 book, **Dereliction of Duty** is an extremely insightful look into the Clinton Administration. Patterson was a presidential military aide who witnessed first-hand how President Clinton and his administration jeopardized the security of America. Another book that takes a sobering look at the Clinton Administration is **Legacy: Paying the Price for the Clinton Years**, by Rich Lowery published in 2003.

The following are examples of *"not-so-minor"* misdeeds and indiscretions of members of Congress (the very people who make laws for us) and Cabinet appointees.

Speaker Nancy Pelosi: Speaker of the House from January 2007 until January 2011.
- Pelosi blatantly lied to the American people about "enhanced interrogations." in April 2009 she accused the Bush Administration of interrogation torture at Guantanamo Bay and pushed for investigations and action against Bush Administration personnel. On April 23, 2009 Pelosi said, *"We were not-I repeat-were not told that water boarding or any of these other enhanced interrogation methods were used."* The facts state otherwise. Pelosi and 64 other lawmakers received 40 briefings about interrogations, and between 2002 and 2006 the House voted 13 times to authorize intelligence funding with no objection to any intelligence programs.

The Speaker was well aware of what was going on at GITMO.

- In 2007 Pelosi traveled to Syria to meet Syrian President Bashar Assad despite a Pentagon warning against it because it would complicate U.S. efforts to dissuade Syria from allowing al-Qaeda to pass through Syria into Iraq to kill American soldiers. Syria, also connected to terrorist groups has been receiving nuclear program aid from Iran. President Bush's successful "Iraq Surge" started in January 2007 and not surprisingly, Pelosi was very vocally against it. The Pentagon memo warned: *"We ask that you support our efforts by not further rewarding the Syrian government."*[189] This is not responsible behavior of an elected official. Her actions were strictly self-serving. She did not have the best interests of the American people and especially American soldiers in mind.

- Speaker Pelosi repeatedly "demanded" the use of Air Force Planes for travel across the country, not just for herself but for her family and friends as well. This is not responsible behavior befitting her office and it certainly is not responsible use of taxpayer money.

- Pelosi's March 9, 2009 comment on the Affordable Care Act (ObamaCare), *"We have to pass the bill so that you can see what is in it."* Oh did we find out what was in it, and we'll be finding out more and more over the next few years.

- Pelosi's lasting legacy will be that the national debt increased $5.2 trillion, a 60% increase during her four years as Speaker.[190]

---

[189] *"Pentagon Warned Pelosi Not to Travel to Syria,"* Rowan (National Security writer), Scarbough, *Human Events*, Week of March 30, 2009

[190] "National debt increased 60% under Speaker Pelosi," Dan Spencer, January 3, 2011, http://www.redstate.com

Senator Dianne Feinstein:

- Feinstein resigned her position as Chairperson of the Military Construction Appropriations Subcommittee in 2007 due to a conflict of interest issue - her husband's ownership in two major defense contractors who were awarded billions of dollars for construction projects she approved.[191]

  - Besides military construction, the Military Construction Appropriations Subcommittee is responsible for military veterans "quality of life" issues including housing, hospitals and medical clinics for wounded veterans. She was well aware of the inadequate medical care Iraqi vets were receiving but it seems she did not have time to get involved with that aspect of her committee. Making sure her husband was financially taken care of was of much greater importance.

- In 2009 this senator leaked classified information confirming that CIA Predator aircraft were based inside Pakistan. Maybe I could accept this "slip" of information from a novice legislator, but she is a veteran Senator and more importantly, the Chairperson of the Senate Intelligence Committee. Feinstein's irresponsible "slip" complicated the counterterrorism collaboration between the United States and Pakistan.

- Feinstein had been informed of abuses and corruption at the ATF (Bureau of Alcohol, Tobacco, Firearms and Explosives) before we ever heard of "gun walking" and learned about the Fast and Furious fiasco and subsequent cover-up. ATF Special Agent Vince Cefalu contacted Feinstein for help to investigate ATF abuses, "*I listed a series of corrupt acts, gross mismanagement and abuse of employees, etc.*" The senator never responded and certainly took no action to investigate. Cefalu was

---

[191] "*Feinstein Resigns,*" Peter Byrne, *Metroactive News*, March 21, 2007, www://metroactive.com/metro/03.21.07/Dianne Feinstein resigns

terminated by the ATF in 2012 and other ATF agents report widespread retaliation against whistleblowers.[192]

Senator Barbara Boxer:
- During a Senate hearing in 2009, Boxer arrogantly chastised Brigadier General Michael Walsh for addressing her as "ma'am" instead of "Senator."
- At a news conference in November 2010, Boxer expressed her distaste for the military's "don't ask don't tell" policy by comparing our United States military to countries like Iran, North Korea and Pakistan: *"We now stand – with this rule – with countries like Iran, North Korea and Pakistan in banning [homosexuals] from military service."* What an astonishingly illiterate comment from one of our leaders.
- A little known fact is Boxer's close ties with the radical leftist group "Code Pink." Code Pink hates our soldiers and labels them terrorists and assassins; but supports terror groups like the Muslim Brotherhood, Hamas, and the Taliban because they are freedom fighters.
  - Senator Boxer provided Code Pink a diplomatic courtesy letter for a trip to Fallujah, Iraq where they gave $600,000 in money and supplies to the insurgents who had just killed 51 Americans and wounded 560. It seems to me, the Senator is aiding the enemy.[193] Why is that not treason?

Senator Christopher Dodd: Five-term Connecticut Senator. With all that experience you would think he would know the meaning of the Oath of Office he freely swore to uphold. As the

---

[192] "Veteran agent: Feinstein did not act on ATF abuse, corruption evidence," *The Examiner*, March 15, 2012
ATF Retaliation against Whistleblowers rampant, Anthony Martin, The Examiner, October 25, 2012, http://www.examiner.com
[193] "Media Won't Cover Boxer's Scandals," Tim Ziegler, American Thinker, November 1, 2010

chairman of the banking committee he downplayed Fannie Mae and Freddie Mac's financial problems. It is worth noting that Dodd was the biggest recipient of donations from Fannie Mae and Freddie Mac employees and political action committees. As Americans were losing their homes at unprecedented rates, Dodd received preferential treatment on his personal home mortgages. He was very vocal in support of assistance for mortgage lender "Countywide Financial," but I am sure it is just a coincidence that Countrywide had given him two below market rate loans to refinance his personal properties. To add salt to the financial wound, Dodd played a role in the legislation that allowed AIG employees to receive $400 million in bonuses after AIG received $173 billion of taxpayer bailout money. In 2009 it was found that Dodd undervalued property he owns in Ireland on his Senate Financial Disclosure form.

Congressman Charles Rangel House Representative of New York was named in an ethics report in 2008 that he, as Chair of House Ways and Means Committee sought money from companies that had business dealings with that committee. Rangel reportedly rented four apartments in a prestigious Harlem apartment building at reduced rates. One of the apartments was used for his campaign office, which violates a city regulation that "rent-controlled" apartments be used for primary residences. He took tax breaks for his homes in New York and Washington and failed to report over $75,000 in income from a vacation rental. Rangel failed to report up to $1.3 million in outside income, and also failed to reveal $3 million in various business transactions between 2002 and 2006.

- Representative Rangel also "arranged" tax breaks for donors who contributed money for a school named after him. Like many others in Washington, Rangel seems to need a course on U.S. tax law. Shouldn't the Chairman of the House Ways and Means Committee at least know the basics of the U.S. Tax Code? Whether he doesn't understand tax codes and regulations or is blatantly breaking the law, he is not responsible enough to be a U.S. Representative.

- Judicial Watch reported that since the ethics probe began on Rangel, he has made campaign donations to 119 members of Congress including 3 of the 5 Democrats on his House Ethics Committee. That doesn't seem "ethical."

- Rangel was found guilty of 11 of 13 ethics charges in November 2010.

Representative Rangel is still a House member, making decisions for people of New York.

Representative Barney Frank: spent his time in office condemning the Bush Administration for the lack of regulation resulting in the Fannie Mae and Freddie Mac meltdown even though he spent the 1990s deregulating Fannie Mae. He spent a lot of time and effort blocking Republican lawmakers from imposing stricter regulations. Frank urged that $12 million in TARP money be given to One United Bank in Massachusetts. The problem is that TARP money was only supposed to go to "healthy" banks to open lending; and One United was in known financial trouble.

Governor Bill Richardson: (New Mexico) was nominated by Barack Obama as the Secretary of Commerce. He withdrew his nomination when a grand jury investigation questioned whether he exchanged government contracts for contributions to his political committees. Why didn't questions surface when he was campaigning for the Democratic presidential nomination? Richardson was the Energy Secretary when classified nuclear secrets disappeared from our nuclear laboratories in 1999 and 2000. In May 1999 Richardson said, *"Americans can be reassured our nation's nuclear secrets are today safe and secure."*[194] That was not the case since two computer hard drives "disappeared" from

---

[194] *"Will Senators Recall Bill Richardson's Scandalous Cabinet Record?"* By Timothy P. Carney, *Human Events* week of December 15, 2008

Los Alamos National Laboratory early in 2000. Even after that he refused to support a bill to put an independent officer in charge of nuclear laboratory security.

- Notra Trulock – former Director of Intelligence at the Department of Energy and whistleblower on the espionage at Los Alamos Laboratory published a book in 2004 exposing the spying scandal that the government tried to keep quiet. *"Code Name Kindred Spirit: Inside the Chinese Nuclear Espionage Scandal,"* is extremely informative and sheds light on the government's shoddy commitment to our national security. For example, *"How did that piece of paper make it from the intelligence vault in Los Alamos all the way to China,"* was Mr. Trulock's question referring to a copy of a US intelligence agenda from Los Alamos laboratory that was shown to a Stanford professor during a visit to China.

Samuel "Sandy" Berger: Presidential appointee with access to classified information. Berger served as President Clinton's National Security Advisor from 1997 to 2001. He was also the chairman of an international advisory firm and an international advisory board, served on the Advisory Board of the National Security Network, was an informal foreign policy advisor to Senator John Kerry during his presidential campaign, and was Hillary Clinton's foreign policy advisor during her 2008 presidential campaign. I mention all this to illustrate that this is a man who knows the law. That is why it was extremely disturbing when he stole classified documents from the National Archives in 2003. Some people tried to minimize his actions by saying he only stole copies – the originals are still there. Why would he do that? As the story unfolded, he purposely stole the documents with Clinton administration notes on them relating to the administration's handling of the 2000 Millennium attack plots. Those specific documents could have had an adverse effect on President Clinton during his testimony before the

9/11 Commission. So what happened to this man who stole and intentionally destroyed classified documents? He was fined $50,000, sentenced to 100 hours of community service, and put on probation. Not a bad sentence for a premeditated crime. I wonder how the Clinton's repaid his loyalty.

The Washington Post reported on October 30, 2009 that "Nearly half the members of a House panel in control of Pentagon spending are under scrutiny by ethics investigators in Congress."[195]

Unfortunately there are many, many more examples of the deeds of elected and appointed officials who disregard or blatantly violate their sworn oaths of office. I have purposely omitted personal bad behavior that includes extra-marital affairs like South Carolina Governor, Mark Sanford and Nevada Senator, John Ensign in May 2009. An affair is not a violation of the oath of office, but it is an indication of character. I don't put a lot of faith in a public official who claims to be committed to my welfare and security when that person can't even uphold his personal sworn oath of commitment and responsibility to his spouse and family. A person who is not respectful of his own family certainly is not going to be respectful of mine. Herbert Hoover may not be a notably memorable president, but these words of his are worth remembering: *"When there is lack of honor in government, the morals of the whole people are poisoned."*[196] A more current comment by retired Senator Zel Miller is equally pertinent. *"Principles are not situational."*[197]

---

[195] "Report: Dozens in Congress Under Ethics Scrutiny," Published by the *Washington Post*, October 30, 2009, reported by FoxNews.com, http://www.foxnews.com/politics/2009/10/30

[196] President Herbert Hoover, American Presidents' Wit and Wisdom, Edited by Joslyn Pine, New York: Dover Publications, Inc., 2002

[197] *A Deficit of Decency*, Zel Miller, Macon GA: Stroud & Hall Publishers, 2005

President Barack Obama and the Obama Administration

It's a lot easier Running for President than being one

The more I learned about Barack Obama it became evident to me that while he may be a great guy on a personal level, he is blinded by his allegiance to the progressive agenda. The President has no aptitude for leadership, no economic or business experience, and no respect for our constitutional rule of law. He is not a friend of the middle class or small business - the very people that built and maintain the economic health of this country. I originally had no intention of being negative about the President, but the negative effect he has had on the country and the world, has made it impossible to ignore his governance. The following assessment of President Obama is based on facts not on the color of his skin.

The past five years have been very worrisome for many Americans, and the actions of the Obama Administration and Congress fueled those worries. First and foremost, the Obama Administration has not taken responsibility for anything. They assign blame on everything from the economy, unemployment, foreign policy, and even the attempted bombing of a US air carrier on Christmas Day on the previous administration. I am in no way dismissing the Bush Administration for some of the problems, but claiming "inheritance" of all the country's problems is just an excuse. Senator Obama knew exactly what he was getting into and even supported some of the problems he would "inherit." The housing bust and subsequent bailouts are two of the most annoying claims of "inheritance." The subprime mortgage fiasco began in the mid-nineties under Democratic president Clinton when the government forced mortgage companies and banks to provide risky sub-prime mortgages to people who could not afford them. Increased lower income and minority home ownership was strictly a political move that we are all paying for now. Prior to the 2008 election, then Senator Obama was well aware of the mortgage crisis along with the catastrophe on Wall Street resulting in bailouts BEFORE he became president. He was one of our Congressional leaders who supported and voted for it. The federal deficit has tripled since 2008, as government spending rose to $3.52 trillion (an 18.2% increase from 2008). Then there was the $700 billion bailout and the $787 billion economic stimulus program, all pushed through Congress by Obama during 2009.[198]

While campaigning for the office of President, Senator Barack Obama promised "change" for America and to the surprise of many voters that elected him; it's not exactly the change they had hoped for. Obama took the oath of office and swore to "preserve, protect, and defend" the Constitution of the United States. Even though he said, *"We the people have remained faithful to the ideals of our forbearers and true to our founding documents,"* back in 2001 Obama criticized the Supreme Court for not doing more to redistribute wealth in the U.S. addressing his basic issues of political and economic justice. Obama's problem with the U.S. Constitution in 2001 was *"that generally the Constitution is a charter of negative liberties. Says what the states can't do to you. Says what the federal government can't do to you, but doesn't say what the federal government or state government must do on your behalf."*[199] Constraints placed by the Founding Fathers? Negative liberties? This man is the "face of America" representing our Constitution, laws, and ideals to the rest of the world. During the very first year of his presidency he discarded the ideals of our forbearers and our founding documents.

Whether you support or oppose President Obama, everyone should be skeptical about what he says. Obama's "Changing America" failed promises and actions include:

- Promised to close Guantanamo Bay by December 31, 2009. It is still open though he did release 5 of the worst terrorists.
- Promised to create millions of jobs. The jobs "created" were in expanding government; part-time jobs are counted as full time jobs; for all of the jobs created, more have been lost
- Promised to win the war in Afghanistan (took months to make a decision on troop increases requested by military advisers.

---

[198] "Federal Deficit Triples From Year Ago: Recession, cost of financial bailout leads to record $1.42 trillion imbalance," AP on MSNBC.com, http://www.msnbc.com, October 16, 2009

[199] "Obama: Get Free From Founders' Restraints," *Human Events*, Week of May 11, 2009

How many American soldiers died during the extended period he took to make a simple decision?)

- Promised "Cap and Trade" to reduce global warming. Since global warming has been proven to be highly-exaggerated it has been down-graded to "climate change." Guess what? The climate has always been changing and will continue to do so.

- Promised a comprehensive immigration bill during his first year in office. Since the majority of Americans do not want amnesty for illegals, which is the crux of his comprehensive immigration plan it has not moved forward. He swears he will do it by executive action. I guess it's his way or the highway.

- Promised tougher rules on lobbyists working for the administration. Still there.

- Promised not to let the unemployment rate go over 8% (it exceeded 10% nationally, and over 15% in Detroit, Michigan – late 2009).

- Promised the public would have 5 days to look at every bill on his desk. Never happened - not once.

- Promised to be the most "transparent" president in history but conspired with political allies "behind closed doors" and made under the table deals/bribes to get his proposed legislation passed (i.e., Health Care Bill)
    - Promised a public option for the uninsured (then said it wouldn't be required for passage),
    - Will not release the real figures on paid and insured Obamacare participants. The simple reason is that - Obamacare is a failure.

- Promised he would not impose "**any form of tax increase**" on families making less than $250,000 annually. *Politifact.com* noted that "provisions in the Affordable Healthcare Act would raise taxes in a more broad way such as the indoor tanning tax, medical device tax (not good for technology research and development),and the fact that there is a fine, brokered through income taxes, on those who don't purchase mandatory health insurance."[200]

---

[200] "Obamameter," Politifact, www.politifact.com, December 8, 2010

- □ **Taxes rose by nearly 3 trillion dollars in less than 5 years into his Presidency.** *"President Obama has already raised taxes substantially twice – first as part of Obamacare and then as part of the "fiscal cliff" deals earlier this year. Together those increases raised taxes by more than $1.3 trillion over 10 years. Including the payroll tax increase that was also part of the fiscal cliff deal, taxes have risen by almost $3 trillion during President Obama's tenure."*[201]

- Claims the "Privacy Act" does not apply to the White House. I guess that it must only apply to everyone else.

- Repeatedly stalls to comply with Freedom of Information Act requests. It would seem that so many scandals (not phony) and cover-ups get really complicated.

- Promised to put all legislation on the internet for at least 5 days before he signs it into law so the citizens can read and examine it. Nope, didn't do that either.

- Promised to end no-bid contracts above $250,000. How many millions did it cost to design the Obamacare website and then how many more millions did it cost to do an emergency fix?

- Promised to double the Peace Corps. I haven't heard a word about the Peace Corps in years.

- Promised to veto pork-barrel bills:
  - □ Obama did not veto anything during first year in office.
  - □ Obama made first "veto threat" in January 2010 warning Congress not to pass a resolution blocking release of the second half of the financial bailout, or he will veto it.
  - □ Obama did not veto the $636 billion dollar 2010 Defense Appropriations Bill which contained $4.2 billion dollars of earmarks for 1,720 "pet projects" including $5 million for a visitor center in San Francisco, $23 million for indigent health care in Hawaii, $18 million for the Edward Kennedy Policy Institute in Massachusetts, $5

---

[201] "3 Trillion Reasons Not to Raise Taxes Again," Curtis Dubay, The Heritage Foundation Morning Bell, http://www.morning bell@heritage.org, October 30, 2013

billion for 2 destroyers and 10 C-17 cargo planes the Pentagon does not need or want, and many more.[202]

- Said TARP (Troubled Asset Relief Program) $830 billion stimulus aka financial bailout would create shovel-ready jobs. Can you say f-a-i-l-u-r-e?
- Said he would end politics that "breeds division, conflict and cynicism" and would restore trust in Government. On what planet would that be?
- Said, "You didn't build that," thereby insulting every working American and business owner.
- Said he knew nothing about the "Fast and Furious" gunrunning operation. Not true.
- Said the IRS wasn't targeting anyone and then said he knew nothing about the IRS targeting conservatives. Though facts proved otherwise, he still said there wasn't a "smidgeon" of evidence of IRS wrong doing.
- Said Benghazi was a "spontaneous" riot over a movie. Four Americans were murdered and the best the president of the United States could repeatedly tell the world was a lie that a stupid video was the cause?
- Said he knew nothing about what happened in Benghazi even as evidence proved that he did. Exactly, where were you Mr. President as Americans were dying in repeated attacks?
- Said **he** is not spying on American citizens. He could be telling the truth on this one since the NSA, the IRS, the EPA and the DHS are doing the actual spying.
- Draws "red lines" challenging the actions of foreign leaders and then when he looks foolish he says *"It's not my red line – it's the world's red line."* (Why didn't anyone tell him that is not a good way to conduct foreign policy?)
- **Repeatedly promised that under his "Affordable Care Act" health care costs would go down, you can keep your health care plan, and you can keep your doctor.** Too bad so many

---

[202] "Tracking Your Taxes: Defense Bill Pays for Prostate Screenings, Sprinkler System," William LaJeunesse and Laura Prabucki, FOXNews.com, December 30, 2009

people didn't question his Obamacare plan BEFORE his re-election which guaranteed it would go into effect.

If the citizens of the United States can't believe what their President says, how are international leaders going to believe anything he says and be confident in his word? They are not. He looks "weak" in the world's eye and that makes America look weak also.

Elizabeth MacDonald, *Fox Business* wrote an interesting article on fact-checking the President after President Obama gave a speech at Carnegie Mellon University criticizing the Republicans for America's problems: *"This is the same crowd who took the record $237 billion surplus that President Clinton left them and turned it into a record $1.3 trillion deficit."*[203] Ms. MacDonald cites Brian Riedl of the Heritage Foundation who compared actual financial facts between President Bush and President Obama. For instance, while President Bush enlarged the federal budget by $700 billion in eight years; President Obama added trillions of dollars to the federal budget in just four years. As President Bush increased the public debt over $2.5 trillion in eight years; President Obama will have added $4.9 trillion to the public debt during his eight year tenure. President Obama is an oratory genius able to present manipulated data as believable fact.

The current administration exhibits an attitude of indifference towards its tax-paying, law-abiding citizens. A Rasmussen Report at the end of December 2009 showed that 52% of Americans "disapproved" of President Obama's job performance. A Gallup poll showed that 69% of Americans disapproved of Congress' job performance.[204] After the disastrous launch of the ObamaCare website, healthcare.gov on October 1, 2013, NBC News and Wall Street Journal poll results showed Obama job approval down to 42%. Those poll results also identified that almost two-thirds of the poll respondents say America is in a "state of decline." Those numbers were bad, but they got even worse. A CBS News poll in November 2013 showed the President's approval rating drop to 37% and only 7% of those polled said his health care law is working.

---

[203] "Fact-checking the President," Elizabeth MacDonald, www.foxbusiness.com, June 02, 2010

[204] Real Clear Politics Polls, http://www.realclearpolitics.com, December 30, 2009

These are grim statistics that affirm our President and Democrat controlled Senate are enforcing their own agenda against the will of the citizenry by blatantly violating the Constitution. The President's abuse of Presidential (Executive) Orders to create and change laws by circumventing Congress gives President Obama virtually unlimited power to institute and enforce his agenda – against the will of the majority of the people. The President issued 165 executive orders (not be confused with his executive actions, edicts and proclamations) during his first five years in office.

- One serious example is the executive order issued May 1, 2013 ("Promoting International Regulatory Cooperation") which gives a White House appointed "policy panel" the power to consider changing U.S. trade regulations that the panel or regulated businesses deem "inconvenient" to make "our" laws equal to foreign laws. Our president just handed bureaucrats the power to make, set terms and change laws which only Congress is legally empowered to do.

- Congressman Allen West very clearly explained the President's proposed "Fast Track" Trade authority virtually giving himself the authority to negotiate and sign commerce treatise with other nations: *"Article One, Section 8 of the Constitution assigns Congress the exclusive responsibility to set the terms of "commerce with foreign nations – trade."* The Founders established this clear check and balance to prevent the president from unilaterally negotiating deals that reward his supporters while harming opponents or the nation as a whole. Under Fast Track, Obama would be able to sign commercial trade agreements before Congress votes on them. Congress would not even be able to amend the agreements in any way – it would only have an up-or-down vote when the president says so, before members could even read it.[205]

---

[205] "Are House Republicans inexplicably ready to grant Obama a Fast Track Promotion?" Allen West, Allen West Republic, http://www.allenwestrepublic. com, October 15,2013

- President Obama's signature legislation, the Affordable Care Act aka Obamacare was pushed through Congress with no Republican input or support (and yes, the Republications did have alternate health care plans). Once the "law" went into effect, President Obama changed parts of his law as he deemed necessary by granting waivers and exceptions. The problem here is that the president does not have the power to alter and disregard laws at will.

- The Democrat controlled Senate led by Harry Reid changed Senate protocol to give the majority party (and the President) unconstitutional power to pass laws and appoint judges (stack the court with liberal judges) without any oversight or debate.

- President Obama and his cabinet promised to focus on "executive actions that don't require legislation." Obama said, *"I've got a pen and I've got a phone and I can use that pen to sign executive orders and take executive actions...and I've a phone that allows me to convene Americans from every walk of life."* In other words, he will continue illegally making laws without the Legislature. And, his agency secretaries (unelected bureaucrats) have his blessing to correspondingly make laws which is also unconstitutional.

- In February 2014, President Obama once again unilaterally changed a mandate in the Affordable Care Act to allow more time for businesses to comply. Again, this is illegal. Why doesn't anyone care?

- Coincidently, or not, around the same time he "tweaked" the Obamacare law, he was heard to say, *"That's the good thing as a president; I can do whatever I want."* Even if said in jest, what a contemptible remark; though it is obviously true since no one in Washington will stop him from blatantly violating the law.

How does the President keep getting away with this? The Senate has the power to call out a rogue president, but since Harry Reid and Democrats control the Senate they will not raise an objection. To me that makes Senator Reid complicit in the destruction of our Constitution.

Kevin Williamson's article, "Presidential Lawlessness: It's So Cool," presents a telling aspect of the President's disregard for our laws. *"He has spent five years methodically testing the limits of what he can get away with, like one of those crafty velociraptors testing the electric fence in Jurassic Park. With a compliant Congress in his first two years, and a divided, gridlocked Congress thereafter, Mr. Obama has been able to "get away with" an awful lot. One of the ways the president flouts the law is by not enforcing it ... Where does the president get off thinking he has the authority to refuse to enforce a law?"*[206]

Numerous books have been written about President Obama but one stands out for accurately telling the story of Barack Obama before the White House. Investigative reporter David Freddoso's 2008 book, **"The Case Against Barack Obama: The Unlikely Rise and Unexamined Agenda of the Media's Favorite Candidate,"** clearly delineates the man we have come to know. The 2012 documentary, **"2016: Obama's America,"** by author and commentator Dinesh D'Souza is based on D'Souza's 2010 book, **"The Roots of Obama's Rage."** D'Souza explores Obama's early years and the tie to his father's family in Kenya. Through interviews with Obama relatives, documentation and history, D'Souza carefully presents what drives the man who is president. Seeing current events playing out just as described in the documentary is unnerving. What's even scarier is what America will look like at the end of Obama's presidency in 2016 if D'Souza's predictions continue to be true.

The administration seems to have successfully destroyed the "checks and balances" built into our Constitution to prevent the Executive branch from becoming "more" powerful than the other branches. When a President has the unfettered power to fill the federal courts with his judges, as will happen, then the Executive Branch controls the Judicial Branch and the Legislative Branch becomes powerless. This is a very serious situation and another step into the socialist twilight zone governed exclusively by one like-minded cabal. It is calamitous for the country when the President of the United States publicly states that the House of Representatives (Republican majority) is the *"biggest barrier and impediment"* to his idea of progress. He calls his political opponents the *"enemy"* and calls young supporters *"The White House Youth."*

---

[206] "Presidential Lawlessness: It's So Cool," Jon N. Hall, American Thinker, http://www.americanthinker.com, August 14, 2013

Unchecked government spending including bailouts, stimulus programs, "cap and trade" legislation, threats and bribes to pass a disastrous mandatory healthcare program, and easily getting the Congress to raise the national debt ceiling time and time again is a chronic pattern. We are now a nation in debt to China; a nation that has saddled our children and grandchildren with an insurmountable debt. We are on the precipice of massive wealth distribution which is not a Constitutional ideal any more than traveling the globe "apologizing" for America. Don't think for one minute our taxes will not continue to rise, though now they will be disguised as fees, fines, and increases.

The federal government in Washington DC is a giant maze of agencies, departments, sub-departments, divisions, units, sub-units, and so on. Most of these government bodies are too large, over-staffed, and wasteful. They make countless regulations for Americans, yet they are under-regulated themselves resulting in corruption and fraud. For instance, our president and politicians passed the "Affordable Care Act" for all of us - but they are exempt. They are safe from the effects of this very law that will destroy the health and finances of millions of Americans. Since they make the laws for everyone, they should also be bound by the laws they make. This is a fundamentally corrupt situation and unfortunately the Affordable Care Act (Obamacare) Law is not the only example.

Wouldn't it be nice if public service employees were required by law to adhere to their own "Code of Ethics?" What is the point of an official "Principles of Ethical Conduct for Government Officers and Employees" when it is not enforced? You can read the government code of ethics at http://oge.gov/Laws-and-Regulations/Executive-Orders/Executive-Order-12731-%28Oct--17,-1990%29---Principles-of-Ethical-Conduct-for-Government-Officers-and-Employees/, or, just Google – Executive Order 12731 (updated in 1990 to revise EO 12674)

Wouldn't it also be nice if there was Presidential Code of Ethics, not just a *President's Executive Order for the "other" government officers?* Then maybe the president would be able to act more dignified than these "Presidential" incidents:

- President Obama lied about his health care plan and the IRS and the NSA and Benghazi and then proclaimed that, his enemies the Republicans were promoting "phony scandals" to distract the American people from the real issues.

- President Obama acknowledged in his commencement address to the graduating class of Ohio State University in 2013 that commencement addresses are no place for partisanship...But then went on to the tell the graduates to "*ignore antigovernment movements that 'gum up the works...Unfortunately you've grown up hearing voices that incessantly warn of government as nothing more than some separate, sinister entity that's at the root of all our problems...They'll warn that tyranny is always lurking just around the corner. You should reject these voices.*"[207] If I had been a graduate listening to that administration pep rally speech, I would be very suspicious about a government that has to continually promote itself as a good thing for me!

- I find the White House photos of President Obama in numerous casual poses with his feet on the Oval Office Desk, well, disrespectful. Our allies in England may agree since that very desk was a gift from Queen Victoria in 1880 that was built with wood from the HMS Resolute (Her Majesty's Ship). The Israeli newspaper *Ha'aretz* wrote: "*A photo released by the White House, which shows Obama talking on the phone with [Prime Minister Benjamin] Netanyahu on Monday speaks volumes. The president is seen with his legs up on the table, his face stern and his fist clenched, as though he were dictating to Netanyahu...As an enthusiast of Muslim culture, Obama surely knows there is no greater insult in the Middle East than pointing the soles of one's shoes at another person...*"[208]

- It seems that President Obama might feel a little insecure, or maybe he forgot that we are guaranteed the right of free speech

---

[207] "Obama urges graduates not to fear government," Jackie Calmes, *The Boston Globe*, May 6, 2013

[208] "Obama's foot on Oval Office desk sends shockwaves around the world," Cheryl K. Chumley, *The Washington Times*, http://www.washingtontimes.com, September 4, 2013

by the Constitution. He has a history of encouraging people to snitch, tattle, and report on other people who do not support him or his policies.[209]

- 2008 Team Obama set up a website called *"Fight the Smears"* so supporters could report others that might be saying negative things about candidate Obama.
- 2009 President Obama launched flag@whitehouse.gov for supporters to email the president about citizens that oppose him and his policies
- 2011 Another new website, *"AttackWatch"* was created to report ungrateful citizens critical of his presidency and so supporters could get the "cold hard facts."
- 2012 *"The Truth Team"* website became operational for the same purpose but with extra zeal since it was an election year. Now supporters could receive updates and information – their own talking points directly from the White House and all that the President requested in return was at least a $5 donation for the privilege.
- 2013 *"The Truth Team"* was updated to mirror Obama's "Organizing for Action" campaign and contains all the information tools offered by White House supporters.
  - So you never know who is watching, listening, recording, or stalking you. Big Brother Barack is here.
- The Obama administration updated the other Presidential Biographies on the White House website taking impertinence to an entirely new level. Team Obama has defiled every Presidential biography back to President Calvin Coolidge by inserting Barack Obama into their biographies to show how he advanced or improved previous presidential actions.[210] For example:

---

[209] "Obama's Organizing for Action Launches 'Truth Team' Again," Warner Todd, Breitbart-Big Government, http://www.breitbart.com, August 2, 2013
[210] "Obama vandalizes WH presidential biographies," *Washington Times*, May 15, 2012; "White House under fire for adding Obama policy plugs to past presidential bios," Fox News, May 16, 2012; "All about me: Obama 'stealing Reagan glory'," Bob Unruh, WND, May 2012

- □ Under Ronald Reagan's original 1985 speech calling for a fairer tax code, one where a multimillionaire did not have a lower tax rate than his secretary now has an additional line: *"Today, President Obama is calling for the same with the Buffett Rule."* Actually the Buffett rule had nothing to do with what Regan was talking about.
- □ Under Calvin Coolidge the first president to make a radio address to the American people, the entry read: President Coolidge later helped create the Federal Radio Commission which has now evolved to become the Federal Communications Commission (FCC). Now the entry has an additional sentence: *"President Obama became the first president to hold virtual gatherings and town halls using Twitter, Facebook, Google, LinkedIn, etc."*
- There are numerous examples. It would be funny if it was not so shameful. Just "Google" the above topics for complete information and pictures.

Examples of unacceptable behavior are numerous and we can endlessly debate the severity of the violations of law and personal indiscretions of our elected officials. Many people excuse bad behavior in government, based upon the person/people involved, party affiliation, role in government, and position of power. Cover-ups and excuses are rampant. In too many cases a feigned public apology for misbehavior is all it takes for the indiscretion to fade away. It's like putting a band aid on a severed limb – the moral wound still hemorrhages, but the band aid prevents political death.

Our Founding Fathers were not naïve. They were well aware of the shortcomings of men and strove to weave honesty into our government. They feared the "folly of men" and the damage dishonest officials could do to our nation. John Adams understood that when he said, *"It is weakness rather than wickedness which renders men unfit to be trusted with unlimited power."* The Founders <u>expected</u> honesty, commitment, and responsibility of themselves and of future elected officials. Adams was of the same sentiment on honesty as Washington: *"The first of qualities of a great statesman is to be honest..."* They would be extremely disappointed now.

The bottom line is bad behavior should be unacceptable. If politicians cannot put their constituents ahead of themselves, they have no place in government. Political corruption should be the exception, not the norm and we have become accustomed to accepting political corruption as a cost of doing business When public office is viewed as a vehicle to wealth or power, then our system has been corrupted. I for one want and expect honesty in government and we need to seek out honest and sincere people as our representatives. We citizens of America need to demand honesty and accountability from our elected officials. I am sick and tired of being lied to by government officials.

It is imperative that we know who we are voting for. Since this is a "Representative Government" these people make the decisions for us. I reject the notion of "block voting." WE must vote based on the person, not staunch party lines, race, affiliation, or recommendation. We need to take responsibility to find out as much as we can about the people running for office. We need to do a little research into their political records and biographical data. We cannot rely on the honesty of their campaign promises. We cannot rely on promotional ads and commercials that support specific politicians. The ads in support of a candidate will always be positive, and the ads against a candidate will always be negative. We need to know the "honest" truth about the people we put into office since once they have been elected – it's too late to ask for a do-over!

Where are the honest men and women we so urgently need? If more of our presidents, politicians, officials, and government employees in leadership positions were honest, the government would function as it should - efficiently, and we would not have this insidious pandemic of financial, educational, societal and moral decay. We need to recruit knowledgeable, honest, and sincere candidates. We need to research and fact-check potential candidates since honestly vetting candidates is not a priority with the government.

Government Agencies - Created by the Government for the Government

Professor and legal scholar Jonathan Turley addressed the threat of ever-expanding government agencies amassing unconstitutional powers as if they were a "fourth branch" of government in a Washington Post article: *"The growing dominance of the federal government over the states has obscured more fundamental changes within the federal government itself: It is not just bigger, it is dangerously off kilter. Our carefully constructed system of checks and balances is being negated by the rise of a fourth branch, an administrative state of sprawling departments and agencies that govern with increasing autonomy and decreasing transparency... Today we have 2,840,000 federal workers in 15 departments, 69 agencies and 383 non-military sub-agencies..."*[211]

California Representative Darrell Issa issued a chilling statement regarding the current government environment when he said we are in a time to, *"love my country, and fear my government...Right now, there's a reason to fear the IRS and other agencies, including the EPA, who are loaded with people who feel empowered to bend the rules against those they disagree with."*[212]

These agencies and departments are amassing great power and control with little to no oversight or transparency. So, exactly what is the purpose of these agencies endowed with powers to regulate, fine and prosecute citizens? How it that these agencies can make, and enforce laws (called "regulations" since the Constitution sanctions only Congress with the power to make laws)? The answer quite simply is that President Obama has unilaterally created an army of executive agencies who will advance his agenda with nothing to hinder their actions. He said he would go around Congress, and he is charging ahead with a vengeance.

Congress authorizes the agencies that are then run by bureaucrats who decide what we do. It is unconstitutional for unelected officials to

---

[211] "The rise of the fourth branch of government," Jonathan Turley, *The Washington Post*, http://washingtonpost.com, May 24, 2013

[212] "Issa: 'There's a reason to fear' Obama agencies," Darrell Issa, The Daily Caller. com, posted on http://www.conservativebyte.com, October 8, 2013

make and have authority to enforce laws, aka regulations. **Congress is responsible for these out-of-control agencies**. Congressional members, no matter the political party need to stand up for the American people and abide by their oath of office to protect and defend the Constitution of the United States.

Internal Revenue Service (IRS):   www.irs.gov

The IRS was created in 1862 by President Lincoln and Congress when an "income tax" was enacted to pay for war expenses. In 1872 the "income tax" was repealed, but Congress reinstated it in 1894. The Supreme Court ruled the "income tax" unconstitutional in 1895. The "income tax" was made law by the 16th Amendment in 1913. The income tax rate soared in 1918 to pay for the First World War. The rate dropped sharply after the war until the Great Depression when it increased again. Congress presented "payroll withholding" and "quarterly tax payments" during WWII.

During the 1930s President Franklin Roosevelt used the IRS as his personal weapon against political enemies. Corruption and bribery were rampant within the IRS through the 1940s and 1950s. "In the 50s, the agency was reorganized to replace a patronage system with career, professional employees. The Bureau of Internal Revenue name was changed to the Internal Revenue Service."[213] That obviously didn't work out very well considering IRS political abuse continues to this day. FBI Director, J. Edgar Hoover had unlimited access to IRS files throughout the 1950s and 1960s.

In the early 1960s the IRS generated the "Ideological Organizations Audit Project" that investigated conservative groups and challenged their tax-exempt status. The Nixon administration created the "Special Services Staff" within the IRS to target activists and political dissidents. The "IRS was restructured once again in 1998 with the "IRS Restructuring and Reform Act," that focused on tax-payer rights and

---

[213] "Brief History of IRS," IRS, http://www.irs.gov

abusive IRS power. It seems that suspicious audits and IRS abuses are inherent agency functions as evidenced by the recent IRS scandals.

The latest example of the IRS being used as a political weapon is the targeting of conservative groups applying for 501(c)4 tax exempt status. Beginning in 2010, the IRS separated conservative groups based on the names in their titles such as "Tea Party" or "Patriot," for investigation. Early in 2012, and coincidently another election year, the protocol was then enlarged to include organizations associated with: Government spending, limited government, debt, taxes, the Constitution, and social economic reform. Intimidation and burdensome documentation requests including personal information and were used to delay status approval of these organizations, coincidentally until after the elections. The IRS asked these groups to produce membership lists, donor and contributor names, roles and responsibilities of members, transcripts or copies of any press releases, media interviews, op-ed articles, and income and expenses from the current year and estimates for future years. They wanted emails, social media entries and contacts.

The organizations under investigation were required to document rallies, educational events, meetings, discussion groups and any other event they had already and those they were "planning" to have. The IRS wanted to know the date, location, and nature of the event. They also needed copies of all materials distributed at the event and relating to the event. Event lists of revenues and expenses were also required. And the IRS needed to know what issues are important to the organization and personal position of the applicant on those issues.

The IRS then expanded its inquisition to include Pro-Life Organizations and religious groups. In another "coincidence," groups opposing the President and his administration's views and policies were spotlighted for investigation and audits. Both of Rev. Billy Graham's organizations were audited (for the first time) shortly after ads supporting traditional marriage ran. As coincidences kept piling up, the Southern Baptist official news journal, *"The Biblical Recorder"* was audited too. The *Recorder* has been in existence for 181 years since its founding in 1833 and has never had an IRS audit. A reporter from St. Louis stated he started being harassed by the IRS right after he did an interview with President Obama and Obama did not like the interview. Since <u>no</u>

Constitutional authority is given to government officials to snoop into the political activities of any individual or organization, how is it that the IRS can operate independently outside of Constitutional limits?

In still yet another unusual coincidence, the President claims he knew nothing about any of this even though IRS officials met with him at the White house over one hundred times during this period. President Obama actually denied an IRS scandal saying the media just sensationalized it. While conservative organizations were under siege, labor groups and liberal organizations did not merit the same scrutiny. Organizations with "progressive," "progress," or "Obama" in their names had no trouble securing tax-exempt status. Charles C. Johnson of the *Daily Caller* wrote, *"Lois Lerner, the senior IRS official at the center of the decision to target tea party groups for burdensome tax scrutiny, signed paperwork granting tax-exempt status to the Barack H. Obama Foundation, a shady charity headed by the president's half-brother that operated illegally for years."*[214] Malik Obama's organization received tax-exempt status within one month of filing and retroactive tax-exempt status.

When the liberal investigative website, "ProPublica" asked the IRS for information on conservative, liberal and centrist organizations, the IRS gave them only conservative documents. The Agency released "confidential" information on nine conservative organizations that were still under review even though releasing unapproved applicant information is against IRS rules. Confidential tax payer information was also shared with senior White House officials in 2012 as proven by emails – and the President didn't know anything!

The President tasked his supposedly "non-biased and non-partisan" Department of Justice to investigate. The lead DOJ investigator was an Obama supporter and campaign contributor. Investigators (no surprise here) did not find "political bias" or "enemy hunting" that violates law so the FBI does not plan to file charges. That was an interesting conclusion considering the IRS admitted to wrongdoing for targeting "Tea Party" or "Patriot" named groups. An article by Arnold Ahlert for *Front Page Magazine* cites unnamed law enforcement officials questioning the

---

[214] "IRS official Lerner speedily approved exemption for Obama brother's charity," Charles C. Johnson, The Daily Caller, www.dailycaller.com, May 14, 2013

legitimacy of the investigations and noted that the investigation should have been by The Public Integrity Unit of the Department's Criminal Division. They also question how the FBI could release its findings when only 10 of the victims had been interviewed. Attorney Cleta Mitchell said, *"As far as I can tell, nobody has actually done an investigation. This has been a big, bureaucratic former Soviet-Union-type investigation, which means that there was no investigation…This is a deplorable abuse of public trust, but I am not surprised."*[215]

If there had been an investigation we would have learned sooner that IRS official Lois Lerner, *"conspired to draft new 501(c)(4) regulations to restrict the activity of conservative groups in a way that would not be disclosed publicly according to the House Committee on Ways and Means."*[216] The Treasury Department and the IRS (Lois Lerner) "devised new rules" off-plan so no documentation of this debauchery would be available on public record. Seriously? Now add to the fact that 292 conservative organizations and only 6 liberal groups were targeted between the 2010 mid-term elections and the 2012 Presidential election, and email and other evidence keeps mounting even though Ms. Lerner's computer crashed and here's that word again – "coincidentally" lost all the emails during the period subpoenaed by Congress. How can the Justice Department investigation conclude no wrong-doing? Maybe the DOJ is coincidentally just as corrupt as the IRS.

While the IRS **was** investing so much time and resources investigating conservative groups and perceived political enemies of the President, the agency lost $4 billion to identity thieves. For example, 343 tax refunds were sent to one address in Shanghai, China and another 655 tax refunds to a single address in Lithuania. Over a million tax returns were filed *"with clearly fabricated social security numbers that the IRS could have detected, costing taxpayers $3.6 billion in 2011."*[217]

---

[215] "Obama IRS' Crimes Against Americans to go Unpunished," Arnold Ahlert, Front Page Magazine, http://frontpage.com, January 16, 2014

[216] "Email: IRS' Lerner, Treasury Department secretly drafted new rules to restrict nonprofits," Patrick Howley, The Daily Caller, http://dailycaller.com, February 5, 2014

[217] "IRS lost $4 BILLION to identity thieves in 2012 as it targeted the tea party," Katie McHugh, The Daily Caller, http://dailycaller.com, November 10, 2013

The Treasury Inspector General for Tax Administration reported that over 5,000 active IRS credit cards charged $103 million in purchases during the 2010-2011 fiscal-year. Five agency credit cards had been stolen. Numerous unallowable charges were noted including $140 per person dinners, $100 per person lunches, wine, decorations, give-away items, pornography, and personal purchases. I would like to know why 5,000 IRS employees have credit cards and what is the protocol for employee use? Obviously oversight is not a priority.

The IRS spent $235 million during 2011 just on computer software and could not keep track of software license records since they have no software to track and manage the enormous file of licenses used daily. On October 8, 2013 Conservative Daily highlighted a report that the IRS *"accidently misplaced $67 million dollars."*[218] No one can account for it and the IRS has no interest in "finding" it.

The "Earned Income Tax Credit" intended to help low income families lower their tax liability has evolved into just another entitlement. *"The size of the credit depends on their income and number of dependents. If the credit is larger than what they owe, or they didn't owe any taxes, they get the appropriate credit in a check payment."*[219] Knowing that, it is no surprise to learn that the IRS pays out over $11 billion each year to people who do not even qualify for this program.

Like other federal agencies, the IRS doesn't seem to have a problem squandering billions of dollars of taxpayer money - every year. As proof of the agency's callous disregard for hard working, tax-paying Americans, in 2010 alone the IRS spent $4.1 million on a conference in California for 2,609 of its employees. Some conference expenses included: $50,000 for line-dancing and videos, $135,350 for speakers, and $64,000 for employee baubles. This is above the cost for meals, cocktails, and hotel suite upgrades. Where is the outrage over this deliberate theft of our hard-earned money?

The IRS is blatantly defrauding legal taxpayers out of billions of dollars through theft, mismanagement, fraud, incompetence and

---

[218] "Taxpayers Are Not An Open Wallet," Joe Otto, Conservative Daily, http://conservativedaily.com, October 8, 2013

[219] "Taxpayers Are Not An Open Wallet," Joe Otto, Conservative Daily, http://conservativedaily.com, October 25, 2013

politics, and we have absolutely no recourse. Now the agency has been empowered with expanded authority to manage and enforce the "Affordable Care Act" (Obamacare). This is an outrage since the IRS cannot even manage its own agency. Obamacare is a time bomb laden with fraud, deceit, and financial hardship on tax paying Americans already burdened with the responsibility to pay for the agency's habitual negligence and abuse.

The IRS priority of auditing political opponents, administration critics and successful small businesses while turning a blind eye to 312,000 (2011) federal employees and retirees who failed to pay income taxes in the combined amount of $3.5 billion and millions of dollars handed out to illegal aliens is appalling. The seriousness of a dishonestly run government and a malicious government agency cannot be overstated. Mr. Bill Elliot has cancer. He lost his insurance coverage because of Obamacare. He was interviewed on national television and an insurance broker who saw the interview stepped in to help. C. Steven Tucker convinced Mr. Elliot's insurance company to let him keep his existing insurance because the cancer was a pre-existing condition (prior to Obamacare). This story garnered a lot of negative attention for the President and his Affordable Care Act. Now and not-so-coincidently, cancer patient Bill Elliot is being audited by the IRS for year 2009. The Good Samaritan, C. Steven Tucker is also being audited – back to 2003.

The IRS is getting a new tax power weapon to use against groups and organizations who oppose President Obama. Ernest Istook of the *Washington Times* wrote: "*The power to tax is the power to destroy. Its new powers will let the IRS destroy certain groups, especially those connected to the Tea Party, by imposing a tax on their work and messages during campaign seasons. Even the value of volunteer work could be taxed.*"[220] It's another Obama plan that can be traced appropriately to the "Roosevelt Room" White House meeting with IRS Chief Lawyer William Wilkins on April 23, 2012 which was coincidentally just two days before the IRS issued its directives to target Tea Party and other conservative groups. The new IRS/Obama weapon "*will deliver a death penalty to many of almost 100,000 grass-roots non-profits known as 501(c)*

---

[220] "IRS to get 'license to kill' groups that oppose Obama agenda," Ernest Istook, *The Washington Times*, http://washingtontimes.com, January 8, 2014

(4) groups." These are groups that inform and educate the public about political issues to "benefit social welfare."

The IRS will change the law by redefining current common voter information activities as "candidate-related political activity." It's like Representative Sheila Jackson Lee's suggestion to replace the word "welfare" with the term "transitional living fund," except it will be detrimental to millions of people. This move effectively violates citizen voters' freedom of speech but that principle has never stopped this administration anyway. Mr. Istook also noted that new IRS speech restrictions did not apply to labor unions, trade organizations or political parties. He made it clear that Tea Party groups were absolutely targeted by the IRS.

Journalist Onan Coca summarized the IRS situation in a December 2013 article. *"There is no WAY the IRS would target people who have made things harder for President Obama and the Democrats. There is no way that the IRS could be used as political tool against law abiding citizens. Oh wait..."* Mr. Conan reminded the reader about the definite IRS targeting of conservative groups especially the Tea Party and then the lies and cover-up. *"This is the same IRS that hasn't yet been punished for any of the malfeasance they've committed over the last five years."*[221] I wonder if Mr. Coca has received an audit notification from the IRS yet. I wonder if I'll get one now.

Department of Justice (DOJ):   *www.doj.gov*

Mission Statement: *To enforce the law and defend the interests of the United States according to the law; to ensure public safety against threats foreign and domestic; to provide federal leadership in preventing and controlling crime; to seek just punishment for those guilty of unlawful behavior; and to **ensure fair and impartial administration of justice for all Americans**.*

Wow, that sounds great - except I don't believe it's true. The

---

[221] "Cancer Patient Who Lost Insurance Now Being Audited by IRS," Onan Coca, Eagle Rising, http://www.eaglerising.com, December 2, 2013

Department of Justice under the leadership of Attorney General Eric Holder "selectively" defends U.S. interests. The DOJ does not ensure public safety from foreign and domestic threats as evidenced by the flood of illegal immigrants flowing across the southern border. The DOJ ensures "fair and impartial administration of justice for all Americans?" No, not even close.

Attorney General Eric Holder's professional biography clearly highlights why Americans do not trust the Department of Justice. And when the President tasks the Attorney General with investigating his own department, you know we're over the cliff.

Eric Holder: Appointed by President Obama had a very questionable ethics history under the **Clinton Administration**:
- Holder obstructed an FBI investigation into the theft of nuclear secrets from the Los Alamos Nuclear Laboratory
- Holder rejected requests for an independent investigation of alleged fundraising abuses by Vice President Al Gore
- Holder undermined the criminal investigation of Clinton during the Lewinsky investigation
- Holder had a part in planning the armed raid of a private home to take Elian Gonzalez and return him to Cuba
- Holder bypassed Justice Department policies to push through Clinton's presidential pardons which included 16 FALN organization members

Attorney General Eric Holder - The Obama Administration:
- Holder refused to investigate charges that the Obama Administration traded access to the White House for campaign contributions
- Holder dropped charges against members of the New Black Panther Party for threatening voters at a Philadelphia polling station in 2008 even though there was video evidence. This is the same New Black Panther Party that issued a ten thousand dollar "dead or alive" reward for George Zimmerman (Trayvon Martin

shooter) and that regularly launches hateful anti-white tirades.

- Holder failed to investigate ACORN (which does have close ties to Obama) for corruption even with video evidence of wrong-doing.

- Holder strongly supported the closing of GITMO and civil trials for terrorists (enemy combatants). As a final slap in the face – Holder's old law firm provides pro bono legal representation to terrorists at Guantanamo Bay. So much for "objectivity" in an Attorney General.

- Holder claims that "Voter-ID" laws place "an unfair burden on non-whites." He attacked responsible states that have voter-ID laws in place and commanded the state of Florida to stop "purging" illegal foreigners and dead people on the state's registered voter list.

  □ Holder has no problem with fact that ID's are required to confirm names on tickets for Obama events. Photo ID's and social security numbers were required to attend Michelle Obama's book signing.[222]

  □ Holder also had no problem with the NAACP requiring all members attending a march present a photo ID. The hypocrisy is that the purpose of the march was to protest Voter ID laws.[223]

  □ Photo ID's are required to board planes, cash checks, verify credit cards, and have documents notarized. Since even most employers now require employees to display photo ID's how is it discriminatory to require photo identification to vote?

---

[222] "Michelle Obama requires photo ID and SS number for book signing," Joel McDurmon, American Vision News, http://www.americanvisionnews.com
[223] "NAACP Holding Rally to Protest Voter ID Laws; Photo ID's Required to Attend," published by The Pundit Press, http://www.thepunditpress.com, February 8, 2014

- Holder failed to indict an Ohio woman who gleefully admitted on national television that she alone voted 6 times for Obama in the 2012 presidential election. Attorney General Holder should know that it is a "felony" to vote more than once. Per law, those 5 extra votes should have gotten her like 15-20 years in federal prison. Melowese Richardson was charged in Ohio with state voter fraud and sentenced to 5 years in prison. She was released after serving only 8 months. There was a rally in Cincinnati, Ohio to celebrate her release and she was welcomed home and praised by non-other than Al Sharpton. The message here is that criminal behavior is acceptable when it benefits certain "above-the-law" government officials.

- Holder's office was warned that known bomb maker Jean Baptiste Kingery was exporting hand grenades (it was estimated that he produced 2,000 explosives) and machine guns converted from AK-47s to Mexico. The Justice Department did not prosecute Kingery when they had him in custody. They set him free. He was caught by Mexican police in 2011 and is currently in jail on terrorism charges.[224]

- Holder did not accept responsibility for the Department of Justice's botched gun trafficking investigation "**Fast and Furious**" responsible for the deaths of Mexican officials, U.S. Border Officer Brian Terry, and Jaime Zapata, Immigration and Customs Special Agent with DHS. Documents prove Holder received briefings on the investigation as early as July 2010 even though he lied and testified before a congressional hearing in May 2011 that he knew about the gun-walking for only a few weeks. Holder and his department then had no problem leaking U.S. Department of Justice information to the

---

[224] "Fast and Furious Grenades – Another Obama ATF Smuggling Operation," Tim Brown, Freedom Outpost, http://www.freedomoutpost.com, November 16, 2013

media in an attempt to discredit whistleblower John Dodson's testimony.

- In October 2013 a federal judge ordered a retrial for five New Orleans police officers convicted for a shooting in 2005 because of "grotesque" misconduct by federal prosecutors and a subsequent DOJ cover-up. The judge had 10 pages listing rules violated by the Department of Justice attorneys in the original trial. For example, 2 senior prosecutors made numerous anonymous postings mocking the defendants and their attorneys, as well as saying the defendants were guilty and revealed jury deliberations.
- Ironically, Holder doesn't tolerate anyone else releasing information. His department took phone records of Associated Press reporters and then cited the Espionage Act for a warrant to seize email records of a Fox News reporter.
- To quiet widespread voices of concern over the government targeting reporters, President Obama ordered Attorney General Eric Holder to investigate himself and his Justice Department's probe of reporters (who are protected by the first amendment, by the way). I don't believe Eric Holder found any wrong-doing by himself and his department. How is that for government arrogance?
- The Department of Justice made a Florida school district cancel a meeting with parents who planned to protest the implementation of a history book required under the administration's "Common Core" education curriculum that included 36 pages and a major chapter on Islam and NO chapters on any other religion. This is scary - the Justice Department enforcing government selected education!
- Eric Holder was sent by President Obama to "personally reassure Muslims" that the Department of Justice is dedicated to protecting them. Holder said, "Muslims

and Arab Americans have helped build and strengthen our nation," and is grateful to have Muslim partners in promoting tolerance, ensuring public safety, and protecting civil rights. Holder has warned the rest of us that criticism of Muslims on social media may violate Muslim civil rights.

- □ Not coincidentally, a man in Palm Beach Florida is being investigated after a complaint from the Council on American Islamic Relations (CAIR - Hamas) for his Facebook post about Islam on 9/112013. The man's criminal post was a reminder to not forget 9/11. He also posted: *"There is no such thing as radical Islam. All Islam is radical. There may be Muslims who don't practice their religion, much like others. The Quran is a book that preaches hate."* So now "truth" is criminal.

- The Justice Dept. filed a civil lawsuit against the Tuscany Hotel and Casino in Las Vegas for treating non-citizen employment applicants "differently" than citizen applicants. The hotel's crime - requiring additional information to comply with the Federal I-9 E-Verify law. Yes, the Dept. of Justice is complicit in helping illegal aliens break the law.

- It seems that since the department is so busy "selectively" enforcing laws that they didn't think taxpayers would mind paying for their entertainment. The department spent nearly $500,000 on food and beverages at 10 conferences. This was <u>after</u> the DOJ implemented a new conference policy in 2008 because of extravagant spending.

- The DOJ is spending over $500,000 to "enhance" its company profile on the professional media site *"LinkedIn"* to increase its "brand awareness." They claim they will better be able to seek out potential employees.[225] Or, maybe it has more to do with surveillance and information mining of LinkedIn members because the NSA is too busy watching everyone else!

- The Attorney General quietly chose a lawyer in the Justice Department's civil rights division who just so happens to be a major President Obama political campaign contributor to investigate the IRS' targeting of groups who oppose President Obama's policies.

- Not to be outdone – President Obama nominated radical civil rights lawyer, Debo Adegbile to be the country's "top civil rights enforcer." Debo Adegbile is described by Front Page Magazine as the "race-obsessed lawyer who tried to permanently free unrepentant cop-killer Mumia Abu-Jamal."

  - He was a previous head of the NAACP Legal Defense and Education Fund
  - Just like Attorney General Holder, he's *"a staunch affirmative action supporter and doesn't appear to believe that white Americans are entitled to civil rights protection."*[226]

- The Fraternal Order of Police (FOP) quite understandably objected to the nomination. Former police detective Henry Melmann said this is proof that the president is determined to "radicalize" the Justice Department. He cites that Attorney General Eric Holder's "priority is prosecuting businessmen and corporations rather than organized crime, radical groups and terrorists."

- There's just no end to the Attorney General's involvement with Obama conspiracies to silence opponents and critics. Breitbart News reported that the Obama

---

[225] "Justice Department Spending $544,338 for 'Enhanced Company Profile' on LinkedIn," Elizabeth Harrington, The *Washington Free Beacon*, http://www.freebeacon.com, January 2, 2014

[226] Mumia Abu-Jamal's Lawyer to Obama's Justice Department," Matthew Vadum, Front Page Magazine, http://www.frontpage.com, January 7, 2013

administration launched another missile to disrupt the business world. This weapon's name is "Operation Choke Point," and the delivery source is the Department of Justice with backup from the FDIC and the shiny new CFPB (Consumer Financial Protection Bureau). *"It appears to be the latest example of the Obama administration's successful efforts to weaponize the apparatus of the federal government against people and industries it opposes ideologically."*[227] In this case it is the "third party payment processors, payday lenders, and online lenders segment of the private lending industry.

Eric Holder is the man at the helm of our "Justice" Department; A man who has sworn an oath to uphold and defend our Constitution and our laws. Instead, he blatantly disregards the Constitution and makes decisions not based upon the law but upon his personal and the President's personal ideologies. "Injustice Department" is a much more fitting name.

John Fund, National *Review* and Hans Von Spakovsky, the *Heritage Foundation* authored the 2014 book **Obama's Enforcer: Eric Holder's Justice Department**. One of the book's subjects is the revelation of the Environment and Natural Resources Division (ENRD) of the Department of Justice that takes taxpayer money collected by fines from successful DOJ prosecutions (more accurately described as extortion like what happened to Gibson Guitar). The millions of dollars collected each year are then "redistributed" to political allies. The Department of Justice uses its muscle to orchestrate litigated settlements mandating defendants to "provide benefits to a private group that was not involved in the lawsuit and was not injured by the defendant's actions." The Attorney General, "Top Cop" of the country needs to be indicted. But then again it is unlikely he will indict himself. There is something seriously wrong here and Congress must have a mechanism to stop rogue, criminally out-of-control government officials.

---

[227] "Obama's Operation Choke Point Seeks To Destroy Sectors of Private Lending Industry," Breitbart News Big Government, http://www.breitbart.com, January 8, 2014

Speaking of injustice, are you aware of a silent scheme to eliminate the office of sheriff nationwide? County sheriffs are elected by the people of the county that they serve. They are <u>not appointed</u> by anyone in government. The office of sheriff was established over a century before the United States was founded. For example, the first sheriff in Delaware was elected in 1669 and the Delaware constitution states: *"The Sheriffs shall be conservators of the peace within the counties...in which they reside."*[228]

Federal and state governments have been cutting budgets and stripping power from elected sheriffs and their departments who have traditionally been the highest ranking law enforcement officers in their respective counties. To use Delaware again as an example, Sheriff Jeff Christopher of Sussex County, Delaware was elected sheriff in 2010. The state Attorney General sent mandates to the commissioners that sheriffs no longer have power to make arrests. As a matter of fact they cannot even make a traffic stop. Again, once the government takes away the power of elected officials, the checks and balances safety net is shredded. All law enforcement members will be under the umbrella of political policy control - no more voter supported independent people of law to protect them.

U.S. Department of State (State Department):   www.state.gov

Mission Statement: *Create a more secure, democratic, and prosperous world for the benefit of the American people and the international community.*

2013 Key priorities of the State Department's *Strategic Plan;* "many of which represent Presidential initiatives." (*My unsolicited comments are in italics*).

- *Arab-Israeli Peace*: "The United States is committed to achieving the vision of two states, Israel and Palestine living side-by-side in peace, security, and dignity..."

---

[228] "Sheriffs Bushwacked," Pat Shannon, *American Free Press*, http://www.americanfreepress.com, April 8, 2012

- □ *There will never be "peace, security and dignity" since the Palestinians do want peace, security and dignity - They ONLY want Israel eradicated.*
- **A Stable and Democratic Iraq**: "...the United States will work side-by-side with the Iraqi people to build a free, democratic, and stable Iraq that does not threaten its people or neighbors..."
  - □ *That dream died when the U.S. announced the date of our military withdrawal. The war was a success but the post-war administration and politics was disastrous and Iraq is sliding right back to what it was. So what exactly did our soldiers die for?*
- **Democracy and Economic Freedom, in the Muslim World**: "... The department will take the lead in working with countries in the Muslim world to advance economic reform, increase educational opportunity, and boost political participation especially for women..."
  - □ *Why is appeasing the Muslim world so important while at the same time we are turning our backs on time-tested allies?*
- **A Stable and Democratic Afghanistan:** "Helping Afghanistan to achieve peace and stability will require a continued commitment by the Department, USAID, and international donors..."
  - □ *Like Iraq, Afghanistan has evolved into a fatal political game. A corrupt Afghan president is taking his country back to the dark ages and again, my outrage is the deaths of so many Americans for nothing.*
- **Reduction of the North Korean Threat to the Region and World**: The Department will continue to work with friends and allies, particularly South Korea, Japan, and China, to meet North Korea's challenge to peace and security..."
  - □ *North Korea knows the U.S. is NO threat so how can there be a successful dialog? Also, does the government consider China a "friend" or an "ally?" I don't think China considers the U.S. as either.*
- **Reduction of Tensions between India and Pakistan**: "Both countries are key partners in the war on terrorism...We seek

broad-based bilateral partnerships with both India and Pakistan spanning a range of security, political, economic, social and cultural issues..."

- *Our Pakistan partner receives billions of dollars from us and then harbors terrorists like Osama bin Laden.*

- **Drug eradication and Democracy in the Andean Region:** "The narcotics trade in the Andean Region, especially in Columbia, imposes a very high cost on its ordinary citizens in addition to being a major source of such drugs trafficked to the United States..."

- *So how long now have we been fighting the War against Drugs? Maybe they should consider a new strategy.*

- **Strengthened Alliances and Partnerships: Within the North Atlantic Treaty Organization (NATO):** "We will integrate new members into the alliance and develop capabilities to fight terrorism and respond to 21st century dangers. We will work with the European Union on transnational threats and challenges... Our new relationship with Russia is yielding positive results for both countries...We encourage the emergence of a peaceful and prosperous China, whose citizens enjoy the blessings of liberty..."

- *This is scary. Our new relationship with Russia is a disaster. They are building their military while we are reducing ours. They make demands - We comply. We recently handed Putin the "keys" to the Middle East. Putin also knows that no one is going to stop him from seizing Ukraine. A peaceful China? They are also building their military and buying their way in to strategic global locations.*

- **A More Effective and Accountable United Nations:** "...We engage countries in the UN system to ensure that our priorities are taken seriously and our resources used wisely. The UN can only be truly effective if its member states willingly meet their responsibilities and adhere to the principles for which the organization was founded..."

□ *If this was not so serious, it would be funny. The UN organization principles have long been desecrated. The United Nations was founded for "democratic" countries.* The purpose of the United Nations was: **"to maintain international peace and security, and to that end: to take effective collective measures for the prevention or removal of threats to the peace and for the suppression of acts of aggression or other breaches of peace."** -United Nations Charter; Chapter One

□ *The UN is so corrupt - mismanagement, theft, fraud, nepotism, and selective humanitarianism to say the least. Tyrannical dictatorial regimes are welcomed regardless of their human rights records and foreign policies. You rarely hear about atrocities committed by the UN Peacekeepers. In Africa alone over the past decades there are countless accounts of rape, theft, and even murder, not by rogue groups, but by UN Peacekeepers.*

□ A few very good books that address the fraudulent cabal known as the UN which we, the U.S., contributes the most financially are:

  ▪ **"The U.N. Exposed: How the United Nations Sabotages America's Security,"** *by investigative reporter Eric Shawn, New York: Sentinel, Penguin Books, 2006*

  ▪ **"Tower of Babble: How the United Nations Has Fueled Global Chaos,"** *by former UN Ambassador, Dore Gold, New York: Crown Forum, 2004*

  ▪ **"Surrender Is Not An Option: Defending America at the United Nations and Abroad,"** *by another former US Ambassador, John Bolton, New York: Threshold Editions, division of Simon and Schuster, 2007*

▪ **HIV/AIDS Prevention, Treatment and Care:** "...AIDS relief that will focus on prevention, treatment, and care in 14 severely affected countries in Africa and the Caribbean..."

- **Reduced Threat of Famine**: "...Famine is a preventable tragedy with the right economic and governance policies and institutions to prevent the conditions that lead to famine..."
- **Accountable Development Assistance**: "...The goal is to increase U.S. development assistance by 50 percent over the next 3 years for countries that take responsibility for their own development by ruling justly, investing wisely in their people, and encouraging economic freedom..." *There is never accountability to U.S. taxpayers who pay for it all.*
- **Aligning Diplomacy and Development Assistance**: "In pursuing our shared mission and goals in the international arena, U.S. development assistance must be fully aligned with U.S. foreign policy..."
  - *The last two goals relating to INCREASING foreign development assistance (taxpayer money) for countries with "just" rulers who concur with U.S. foreign policy is troubling. What countries are they talking about? We give a lot of money to countries like, Pakistan, Afghanistan and Iraq and not one of them is ruled justly or supports U.S. foreign policy.*

The complete list can be found on the Department of State website, www.state.gov. I noticed that a few extremely important and relevant issues were absent from the list. There is no mention of Iran, Libya, and Syria. Iran is on the verge of nuclear weapons and what is the U.S. doing about that? The President is negotiating with that hostile nation that openly supports terrorism. The Libyan revolt and subsequent assassination of its president, unrest in Egypt, Syria and Northern Africa have resulted in a very dangerous Middle East. Why are these countries not on the State Department Priority List? There is also **no mention of Islamic terrorism** or any hint of concern for Middle Eastern Christians who are being slaughtered by Islamic terrorists.

Prince Turki al-Faisal, former head of Saudi Arabia intelligence isn't very impressed with President Obama's State Department foreign policy. *"We've seen several red lines put forward by the president, which went along and became pinkish as time grew, and eventually ended up completely white. When that kind of assurance comes from a leader of a country like the United States, we expect him to stand by it. There is an issue of confidence"...With allies," you should be able to give them the assurance that what you say is going to be what you do."*[229]

Secretary of State Hillary Clinton (Jan. 2009- Jan. 2013):

Once elected, President Obama boasted that his administration would improve America's world image and restore global respect. I'm not sure what globe he was referencing, but our image and respect on this globe, "Earth" has never been worse. Our allies can't believe or trust us and our enemies have no fear of or respect for us. The State Department under the direction of Hillary Clinton and the Obama Administration could not have done greater damage tarnishing the reputation of the United States and destroying relationships around the world.

Hillary Clinton has worn many hats while playing different roles throughout her career. Unproductive tenures and questionable practices have always shadowed her. The perceived "Clinton image" far exceeds the "Clinton reality." There are countless examples of the "real" Hillary that clearly demonstrate her unethical character and natural ability to lie and then cover-up the truth to sustain her political life.

Dan Calabrese published an article in January 2013 titled: "Watergate-era Judiciary chief of staff: Hillary Clinton fired for lies, unethical behavior," is a reminder that Secretary of State Hillary Clinton was no different than lawyer Hillary Clinton during Watergate. In the article Dan expresses former counsel and chief of staff of the House Judiciary Committee Jerry Zeifman's opinion of Hillary Clinton. Keep in mind that Mr. Zeifman, a lifelong Democrat supervised attorney Hillary Clinton's work on the Watergate investigation and he fired her from the committee staff once the investigation was completed. Jerry Zeifman said, *"Hillary's history of lies and unethical behavior goes back farther – and goes much deeper – than anyone realizes...she was a liar...*

---

[229] "Saudi Prince to Obama: You've made a mess of the Mideast," Cherly K. Chumley, *The Washington Times*, Saudi Prince quotes from *The New York Times*, http://washingtontimes.com, December 16, 2013

she was an unethical, dishonest lawyer. She conspired to violate the rules of the House, rules of the committee and the rules of confidentiality.'"[230]"

In 2005 when Hillary Clinton was still a Senator from New York, Edward Klein's book, "*The Truth about Hillary,*" was published. Based on evidence, Klein's account of Hillary's character concurs with Jerry Zeifman's account of Hillary's character. Klein illustrates how easy it is for Hillary to, "*lie, bully, cheat, and manipulate people in her quest for power.*" Decades of bad behavior have culminated in her tenure as Secretary of State. No matter how it is spun, Hillary and the President are responsible for the deaths of four Americans and an unhinged world.

There are numerous examples of foreign policy inexperience and outright bad policy by the State Department in general and Hillary Clinton in particular but one scandal stands heads above the rest. What happened in **Benghazi, Libya on September 11, 2012** and the massive coordinated cover-up that followed are criminal. Secretary of State Clinton easily lied, deceived, and hid information about State Department roles and responsibilities. She then was able to walk away from the State Department with no responsibility for the deaths of four Americans.

The accounts, stories, investigations and questions continue nearly two years after the attack. A single suspect was finally taken into custody in 2014. The State Department scapegoats suspended by Secretary Clinton have been reinstated by Secretary Kerry. No one in the government has yet to be held responsible for any aspect of this scandalous event.

Undisputable Facts about the Benghazi Attack and Subsequent Cover-up:

- Libya was (and still is) a very unstable country with numerous terrorists groups.
- For months prior to the 9/11/2012 attack, several reports were sent to the State Department about deteriorating security conditions. Numerous requests for additional security were also made - all requests for additional security were denied and the

---

[230] "Watergate-era Judiciary chief of staff: Hillary Clinton fired for lies, unethical behavior," Dan Calabrese, http://www.eohistory.info/2013/hillaryHistory.htm, January 23, 2013

State Department reduced existing security assets including protective security for Ambassador Stevens even after al Qaeda forces held open rallies in Benghazi and al Qaeda leader Ayman Al-Zawahri called on Libyans to avenge the death of Abu Yahya al-Libi.

- Less than a month before the attack, the Regional Security Officer (RSO) emailed Secretary Clinton's office with dire warnings of insufficient security. On the very day of the attack Ambassador Stevens cabled the State Department about deteriorating security in Benghazi.

- September 11, 2012, on the 11th anniversary of the horrific attacks on the U.S. the United States Consulate in Benghazi was attacked. U.S. Ambassador Chris Stevens and Sean Smith were killed at the Consulate. Two other Americans, Tyrone Woods and Glen Doherty, ex-Navy Seals working as independent military security contractors went directly into the attack on the annex and were killed. There were 31 survivors thanks to the quick thinking non-hesitant actions of these heroes.

- The Department of Defense ordered a drone over the mission complex for surveillance. The State Department notified the White House and Pentagon of the attack; followed by a meeting of President Obama, Vice President Biden and Defense Secretary Leon Panetta.

- State Department email identified Ansar al-Sharia as claiming responsibility for the attack - YET Secretary of State *Clinton officially blamed a "YouTube" internet video for inciting mob violence responsible for the attack.*

- **Already Knowing** this was a planned and organized terrorist attack NOT an impromptu violent response to a video:
  - 09/13: White House Press Secretary Jay Carney publicly blamed the internet video for the violence and attack and said there was no advance warning.
  - 09/14: Jay Carney stated the attack was not pre-planned and there was no advance warning.
  - 09/15: President Obama blamed the violence on the video

- 09/16: Susan Rice, U.S. Ambassador to the United Nations stated on numerous television shows that the video was to blame for the violence. That was the same day the Libyan President said it was a planned terror attack.
- 09/17: State Department supported Susan Rice's statements.
- 09/18: Press Secretary Jay Carney again claimed the video was the cause for the violence and the next day repeated his earlier statement that there was no evidence of a pre-planned attack.
- 09/20: Again - both Jay Carney and President Obama blamed the video for the violence.
- 09/21: Ten days after the attack, Secretary of State Clinton finally said it was a terrorist attack.
- 09/24: President Obama appeared on the television show "The View" stating that the investigation was ongoing.
- 09/25: In a speech at the United Nations President Obama still claimed the internet video was to blame for the attack.
- **09/27**: Secretary of Defense Leon Panetta admitted Benghazi was a terrorist attack.
- 10/02: Press Secretary Jay Carney now blamed the intelligence organizations for the "misinformation."
- 10/03: Clinton promised to be cooperative with the House investigation.
- 10/06: Echoing Press Secretary Carney, Susan Rice now blamed the intelligence community for misinformation.
- 10/18: General Ham was relieved of his Africom command.
- 10/26: President Obama claimed he was unaware of the requests for additional security in Libya.
- 10/27: Rear Admiral Gaouette was relieved of his Mideast Command.

It took months and a congressional hearing to extract the facts surrounding the Benghazi attack from the State Department. It was evident very early on that the State Department, the CIA, and the White House were hiding pertinent information and threatening witnesses to not to testify before Congress.

- The FBI did not enter Libya to investigate this tragedy until October 4th, nearly 3 weeks after the attacks. It is important to note that media reporters were walking through the debris looking at evidence and reporting long before our investigative professionals ever saw it. Was this delay a deliberate attempt by our government to ensure evidence was destroyed, stolen and compromised?
- "The February 17th Martyrs Brigade," was the Libyan militia group hired by our government to provide security at the U.S. mission. No one noticed that group's Facebook page prominently displayed the Al-Qaeda flag for months before the attack? This same terrorist group coincidently disbanded right after the attacks.
- During the attack, Special Operations called multiple times for all available military and other assets to help. The State Department and the White House did not give permission for them to go into Libya.
- Secretary of State Clinton convened an "Accountability Review Board" to investigate the department's responses and actions, though key witnesses and personnel were not interviewed. (I guess if the Dept. of Justice can <u>investigate itself</u>, so can the State Dept.) Coincidently enough, Hillary's Review Board found that "systemic failures and leadership and management deficiencies at senior levels" but well below Clinton were to blame for "inadequate" security in Benghazi. Ironically some media outlets were doing a better job investigating the tragedy than the State Department.
- Lack of credible information and lack of witnesses as well as bogus comments and actions by the government led many citizens and Congress to recognize this as a shoddy cover up.

- Against the wishes of the President and the State Department, a Congressional House Oversight Committee Hearing convened in May 2013. President Obama called the congressional investigation a political sideshow. Sideshows don't kill people Mr. President.
- We learned (even without much coverage from CNN, ABC, CBS and NBC News) that:
    - The administration's "talking points" about the attack were "deliberately false." There were no video protests in Benghazi. The White House talking points were revised twelve times and references of terror and terrorism were removed.
    - The body of Ambassador Stevens was missing for hours after the attack. His body ended up at a Benghazi hospital operated by Ansar al-Sharia - the same terror organization that attacked the consulate and killed him.
    - Gregory Hicks, former Deputy Chief of Mission in Libya testified before the committee. He spoke with the Ambassador as the first attack commenced, and his testimony, supported by other witnesses, contradicted the administration and State Department accounts. He and other whistleblowers testified they were threatened not to testify.
    - Evidence was presented that the State Dept. and White House did indeed refuse at least twice to give Special Forces permission to leave Tripoli and go to Benghazi after the initial attack.
    - President Obama called Secretary of State Clinton at 10pm on 9/11/12 - six hours after the attacks began and before Tyrone Woods and Glen Doherty were killed saving countless lives because they would not "stand-down."

After a congressional hearing in late May 2013, more whistleblowers came forward providing exceptional testimony of a White House and State Department cover up. Upon learning that the groups receiving weapons from the State Department were al-Qaida linked, Ambassador

Stevens was sent to Benghazi to buy-back stinger missiles that the State Department never should have given out in the first place. Former diplomats said that Ambassador Stevens was in Benghazi to buy back Stinger missiles from an al Qaeda group that the State Department (not the CIA) gave to them after learning the group actually was al Qaeda. Other whistleblowers added that the Ambassador and the Benghazi annex were involved in arms distribution. The Benghazi mission was to supply Syrian rebels with missiles from Libyan armories until it was discovered that these Syrian rebels were actually al Qaeda and other "professional jihadists."

There is so much more to this story that the administration does not want known. The complete story will eventually be unraveled but it won't change what has already been done. The U.S. government let four Americans die without doing anything to try to save them. Secretary of State, Hillary Clinton deliberately lied about the cause of the attack. Her internal investigation was a fraud. She was well aware of the lack of security in Benghazi and she knew military help was available in the region that could have easily made it to Benghazi during the attack. Witnesses and whistleblowers were threatened and kept from testifying. So what did Hillary Clinton get for all the lies, deception, and callous disregard for life? She got to walk away from the State Department to concentrate on her potential upcoming presidential run and she received the "Liberty Medal" one day before the first anniversary of the Benghazi terror attacks. Of note, the Liberty Medal is presented to people who have "*furthered the ideals of freedom, democracy, and equality.*"

I will never forget Hillary Clinton's theatrical response to Congress when pressed about the administration's insistence that the Benghazi attack was a spontaneous protest. ***"With all due respect, the fact is we have four dead Americans. Whether it was because of a protest or because guys outside for a walk one night decided to go kill some Americans. What difference at this point does it make?"***

What difference does it make? To the families of those killed, it makes all the difference in the world. They deserve to know the truth. Patricia Smith, mother of Sean Smith who was murdered in the attack responded to President Obama's comment that Benghazi was one of the "phony scandals," by saying, "*President Obama has never revealed what, if anything, he was doing while workers at the Benghazi Embassy were urgently requesting support, nor has the administration explained why no forces were sent to protect the embassy...I don't believe him anymore. My son is dead. How could that be phony?"*[231] All Americans deserve to know the truth about why our government turned its back on the very men who gave so much.

It also proved to the world and terrorists everywhere that the United States is weak and not serious about fighting terrorism.

Though our government wants to forget Benghazi, we Americans must not forget! The organization *SOS - Special Operations Speaks* will not forget. In July 2013 a 60 foot long scroll with the signatures of over 1,000 Special Operations veterans was unrolled near the Capital calling for the end of the "Benghazi cover-up," and demanding Congress hold those in the administration accountable. In August 2013 the SOS submitted a petition to Congress demanding a "Watergate-style select committee to investigate Benghazi."

The U.S. Senate Select Committee Intelligence report on the Terrorist Attacks was released on January 15, 2014 stating that the "Attack was Preventable."[232] Some of the report citations noted:

- Intelligence provided ample warning about the deteriorating security situation in Libya
- The State Department should have increased security
- There were no military resources able to intervene on short notice
- The State Department Bureau of Intelligence and Research did not disseminate any independent analysis in the year following the attacks
- The DNI Office of Analytic Integrity and Standards failed to provide complete and accurate information to Congress during its review of the Benghazi attacks
- The terrorists responsible for the attacks still have not been brought to justice

---

[231] "Mother of slain Benghazi victim Sean Smith: 'My son is dead. How could that be phony?'" Jeff Poor, The Daily Caller, http://dailycaller.com, July 25, 2013
[232] "The Terrorist Attacks on U.S. Facilities in Benghazi, Libya, September 11-12, 2012," The U.S. Senate Select Committee on Intelligence, January 15, 2014

The President and Secretary of State knew immediately it was a terrorist attack, yet they both intentionally lied. The White House then intentionally directed U.N. Secretary Susan Rice to repeat the "video caused the mob action protest that went out of control" talking points on numerous news shows and at the United Nations. President Obama and Secretary of State Hillary Clinton covered-up the truth because of the upcoming November 2012 election. Don't forget that prior to the attack President Obama had announced to the world that he killed Osama bin Laden, al-Qaeda was on the run and the war on terror was effectively won. The truth would not have played so well at the polls!

Special Operations Speaks concisely summed up Benghazi: *"Four American citizens were brutally murdered on September 11, 2012 - including two courageous special operations soldiers who fought for their lives against scores of heavily armed Islamic terrorists so that others could escape the carnage. They were abandoned; left to die by their president, despite repeated pleas for backup. Barack Obama refused to provide cover for those American citizens, and they paid with their lives."*[233] This could be a problem for Hillary's 2016 White House bid, but the most important thing is that <u>Obama won his re-election in 2012.</u>

The Department of State now under the direction of John Kerry is still floundering. In a press release on August 12, 2013 after a suicide bombing in Baghdad, Iraq, according to the State Department, *"The terrorists who committed these acts are enemies of Islam and a shared enemy of the United States, Iraq, and the international community."* It states that the U.S. government is offering a $10 million reward for information for the capture or death of the terrorists responsible for the attack. The amount of this reward is second only to the reward issued for al-Qaeda leader Ayman al-Zawahiri. A post on the Independent Journal Review website asks a very pertinent question: *"Where were all the 'Wanted' posters for the killing of Christians in such idyllic Middle Eastern nations as Egypt and Syria over the past few years? What about strongly condemning the terrorists who carried out Benghazi and putting*

---

[233] "Special Ops Billboards Target Boehner: 'Justice for Benghazi,'" Special Operations Speaks, B. Adams posted on Revive America website, http://www.reviveamericausa.com, August 8, 2013

a huge bounty on their heads? Oh, but they just slandered and killed some Christians, right?"[234]

John Kerry's self-heralded great nuclear deal with Iran will be another State Department disaster. While Kerry was patting himself on the back, the Iranians were celebrating the "surrender of America." We are in a "world-of-hurt."

Department of Health and Human Services (DHHS or HHS): www.hhs.gov

"The mission of the Department of Health and Human Services is to help provide the building blocks that Americans need to live healthy, successful lives. We fulfill that mission every day by providing millions of children, families, and seniors with access to high-quality health care, by helping people find jobs and parents find affordable child care, by keeping the food on Americans' shelves safe and infectious diseases at bay, and by pushing the boundaries of how we diagnose and treat disease.

The Department of Health and Human Services (HHS) is the United States government's principal agency for protecting the health of all Americans and providing essential human services, especially for those who are least able to help themselves. HHS is headed by the Secretary who is the chief managing officer for our family of agencies, including 11 operating divisions, 10 regional offices, as well as the Office of the Secretary."

Former HHS Secretary Kathleen Sebelius and other Obama administration officials liked to refer to the new *sensitive and caring government* as our *"federal family."* Would this be because the federal government is genuinely concerned about us, our health, and our welfare? Or, could it be that government officials think we're too stupid to know how to take care of ourselves and we need them to direct our lives? I know for sure I do not want the government as part of my family.

The HHS website displays a list of "Priorities." Some of them make sense, others, not so much. For instance links to the *Health Insurance*

---

[234] "State Dep.t Offers $10 Million Reward For Kill or Capture of 'Enemies of Islam,'" post by Soopermexican, The *Independent Journal Review,* http://www. independentjournalreview.com, August 12, 2013

Marketplace, HealthCare.gov website, the *Affordable Care Act* (aka Obamacare) are numerous and redundant. The *Raise Healthier Kids* link illustrates Michelle Obama's initiative's to eat healthy, drink more water, and increase physical activity to combat obesity in children. It's sad that the government is compelled to show parents how to raise healthy children.

Another link on the HHS website is *Open Government* which touts the goodness of HHS. The Open Government priority claims *"significant" strides* with the "Open Government" Initiative started in 2009 for HHS transparency, collaboration and participation... Seriously? How did HHS fail to report $800 billion in spending on time on the government spending website, www.USASpending.gov.

Bullying is a national issue especially in schools. The HHS priority *Stop Bullying* clarifies that the agency does not use the label "bully" for children. More sensitive labels used are *"the child who bullied,"* and *"the child who was bullied."* I guess they don't want to hurt any child's feelings even if the child is a mean little menace. I didn't see any initiatives for teaching children things like respect and responsibility for one's self and one's actions.

The *Be Tobacco Free* priority makes sense, but why are there no priorities to be "drug free," "gang free," "domestic violence free," "illiteracy free," "STD free," "alcohol abuse free," and so on...?

The *Stop Medicare Fraud* priority also makes sense, but what about Medicaid fraud, welfare fraud, and agency fraud? The HHS 2013 financial report identified that $65.3 billion were "improperly spent." Erroneous administrative and documentation errors resulting in payments by Medicare alone cost taxpayers $44.3 billion in 2013.[235]

Since HHS is projecting a "family" image, why do they as well as the IRS need armed investigators? The *Daily Mail* reported in August 2013: *"More than 1,600 new employees hired by the U.S. Department of Health and Human Services in the aftermath of ObamaCare's passage include just two described as 'consumer safety' officers, but 86 tasked with 'criminal investigating' - indicating that the agency is building an army*

---

[235] "HHS: $60 Billion in Medicare and Medicaid Overpayments in 2013," Edwin Mora, http://www.breitbart.com, January 2, 2014

of detectives to sleuth out violations of a law that many in Congress who supported it still find confusing." [236]

Tom Fitton, president of Judicial Watch confirmed that the President indeed received authority to hire over 1,800 federal employees under an emergency *Direct Hiring Authority Order*. It seems that the predicted "ObamaCare police force" is quite real.

On the day President Obama signed the Affordable Care Act into law in 2010, HHS received authority from the Office of Personnel Management (OPM) to make as many as 1,814 new hires under an emergency 'Direct Hiring Authority' order...Judicial Watch, a nonprofit that has told MailOnline it files 'hundreds' of FOIA requests, first published evidence in July of the HHS hiring binge. 'Sounds like we now have the Obamacare police,' said the group's president, Tom Fitton, after MailOnline showed him the new data."

As the federal government "family" is creating a federal civilian police force to enforce its questionable laws, they are just as feverishly working to disarm American citizens. This is serious folks. Our current government is walking in the footsteps of fascist regimes in Europe prior to World War Two. I can't stress too much how dangerous this is.

United States Environmental Protection Agency (EPA):   *www.epa.gov*

The Environmental Protection Agency is the *"Jabba the Hut"* of federal agencies. It is huge, gluttonous and ceaselessly utters mandates and regulations that make no sense. It's a "Bully" agency." I found this statement on their website interesting: *"One of EPA's top priorities is to expand the conversation on work for* **environmental justice (EJ)**. *EPA is integrating EJ into enforcement and compliance planning and program implementation..."* I wonder if that is like the EPA representing a protected species of frog that you accidently killed while trying to save your home from a devastating flood that could have been prevented but you weren't allowed to touch/alter the frog habitat land to prevent the

---

[236] "Obama's HHS: Now Hiring for the Obamacare Police Force," published on freedomoutpost.com from a Daily Mail report, www.dailymail.com, August 2013

flooding that just destroyed all of your property. Circumstances do not matter - what the EPA dictates is all that matters. You will be fined, and, or jailed for killing that frog.

To be fair, in 1970 the concept of an environmental protection agency was a good thing. The EPA was responsible for cleaning up industrial waste offenders, cleaning up our rivers and lakes, and educating the public on the importance of environmental protection of our health. But as the environmental movement turned into a sacred religion garnering ultra-liberal support, excessive and burdensome regulations were created that are damaging to our industry and economy and have even become dangerous.

Charles Monnett is the scientist who reported that polar bears were dying trying to swim long distances of open water because the ice was melting which then became the rallying cry for the global warming crowd. The dead bears were big news but the suspension of Monnett in 2011 by U.S. Bureau of Ocean Energy Management, Regulation and Enforcement did not make the news.

It seems **Monnett released government records and he and another scientist intentionally omitted and used false data in an article on polar bears.**

- The federal government told the city of Tombstone, Arizona that crews could not use machinery to rebuild pipelines and water collection systems that were badly damaged after forest fires and devastating flooding. Everyone knows how abundant water is in the arid Southwest!

- Arizona as well as Utah, Montana, Colorado, and New Mexico were told "federal water rights" supersede any state water rights legislation. The federal government is deliberately keeping water from the city of Tombstone. But in the larger picture, the government took another step in stripping states of their sovereignty. Don't forget that the Obama administration has a vendetta against Arizona for boldly contradicting the President regarding illegal immigration. It seems the federal government may have found the Achilles Heel of the West and can hold the states resistant to his illegal immigration, healthcare, and unionization policies hostage over water. It sounds a lot like Russia holding Europe hostage over oil.

- In 2012 farmers in Greeley, Colorado faced one of the worst droughts in Colorado history but were forbidden to pump well water to water their crops. It was the Colorado Supreme Court that decided to shut down the wells because the farmers were considered "junior right holders." Growing cities like Boulder, Centennial, Sterling, and Highlands Ranch needed the water and they were the "senior right holders" of state water rights.

- The *Alaska Dispatch* reported that in 2013 an *Alaska Environmental Crimes Task Force* (the Force is made up of agents from the EPA, FBI, Coast Guard, Department of Defense, and the Alaska Department of Public Safety) dressed in full body armor descended on the little Alaskan placer mining town of Chicken. The task force dressed like storm troopers was there to check for violations of the "Clean Water Act."[237] Though terrified, no miners were arrested during the raid.

- The states of Texas and Wyoming along with the National Mining Association, Peabody Energy Corp, and two other

---

[237] "Gold miners near Chicken cry foul over 'heavy-handed' EPA raids," Sean Doogan, *Alaska Dispatch*, http://www.alaskadispatch.com, September 3, 2013

power companies lost a challenge against the EPA to stop superseding the state's greenhouse gas and carbon emissions regulations. Texas Representative Pete Olson said, *"The fact remains that overly strict carbon regulations have the potential to ripple through the economy, costing jobs and impacting almost every facet of life in America."*[238]

- The House Science Committee accused the EPA of "muzzling" independent scientists on EPA's science advisory board who disagreed with the EPA consensus that carbon-capture technology is adequate enough to proceed with the implementation of their new regulations. It is not. New EPA power plant regulations will make electricity even more expensive and will cause job losses.

- Many farmers and ranchers in Nebraska, Iowa, Kansas and Missouri are unaware that they reside in the EPA's "Section 7" of the Midwest and are regularly under aerial surveillance to monitor livestock and farm or ranch operations.

- EPA Region 6 Administrator Al Armendariz gave a speech in 2010 explaining how the EPA keeps oil and gas companies under control. *"I was in a meeting once and I gave an analogy to my staff about my philosophy of enforcement...It was kind of like how the Romans used to conquer little villages in the Mediterranean. They'd go into a little Turkish town somewhere, they'd find the first five guys they saw and they'd crucify them...And then you know that town was really easy to manage for the next few years. And so you make examples out of people who are in this case not compliant with the law. Find people who are not compliant with the law and you hit them as hard as you can and you make examples out of them, and there is a deterrent effect there."*[239]

- The EPA is proposing that its regulatory powers be extended to include wetlands and waterways. This little "change" to the existing *Clean Water Act* would redefine the "waters of the

---

[238] "Guess what happened when two states tried to stop the EPA's greenhouse gas rules," Michael Bastasch, The Daily Caller, http://www.dailycaller.com, July 26, 2013

[239] "EPA official apologizes for "crucify" the oil and gas producers comments," Caroline May, The Daily Caller, http://www.dailycaller.com, April 25, 2012

United States" to include all tributaries - regardless of size and water flow, all lakes, ponds and wetlands within a floodplain." That covers all of the nation's water since most bodies of water are within a floodplain. It also includes all water on private land including seasonal ponds, natural run-offs, and irrigation water. The EPA will have the power to control privately-owned land and can, and will regulate your use of your water on your land. This is nothing more than a government sanctioned land grab.

- In another EPA move championing President Obama's policies, the agency shut down the last lead smelting plant in the U.S. that smelts lead from ore to make bullets. See, the government will punish gun owners one way or another for being so inflexible with their Second Amendment right to bear arms.

The epitome of EPA theft is what the agency is doing in Wyoming. The EPA has actually changed the geographical composition – unilaterally changing the state's border including the removal of an entire city out of the state and onto federally controlled and now larger tribal reservation land. The town of Riverton is no longer in the state of Wyoming. Michael Bastasch of the *Daily Caller News Foundation* reported: " *...One day they were Wyomingans, the next they were members of the Wind River tribes – after the Environmental Protection Agency declared the town part of the Wind River Indian Reservation, undoing a 1905 law passed by Congress...*"[240] The citizens of Riverton and Fremont County are no longer under local jurisdiction, "*Among other things, because the ruling makes the area part of the Wind River Indian Reservation, the city and its surrounding areas are subject now, not to local laws, but to federal law, including law enforcement (police) and other laws.*"

Wyoming Governor Matt Mead said he will not honor the EPA boundary. Governor Mead stated, "*I understand that the Northern Arapaho and Eastern Shoshone Tribes have a different opinion about the Wind River Reservation boundary. My deep concern is about an administrative agency of the federal government altering a state's boundary and going against over 100 years of history and law. This*

---

[240] "EPA Steals Land From Wyoming, Changes State Boundary, Gives It To Indian Tribes?" Michael Bastasch, Daily Caller News Foundation, January 8, 2014

should be a concern to all citizens because, if the EPA can unilaterally take land away from a state, where will it stop...?" Utterly incredible! Wake up folks, agencies like the EPA and IRS have the power to destroy everything you have.

Social Security Administration (SSA):   www.ssa.gov

A single example of how the SSA is robbing taxpayers summarizes how that department operates. In July 2009, The Social Security Administration sponsored a "Retreat" for hundreds of staffers at a resort in Las Vegas. They justified spending an excessive amount of tax payer money this way because the employees were "stressed." Excuse me! Stress is not having a job and trying to feed your family and keep your home. This is another over-inflated agency with over 1,400 offices worldwide. Maybe if the department spent more time w-o-r-k-i-n-g instead of relaxing 117,000 "double-dipping" people in 2010 alone would not have received $850 million in disability and federal unemployment insurance cash benefits they were not entitled to.

U.S. Department of the Treasury: www.treasury.gov

The Treasury Department is the agency responsible for "promoting economic prosperity and ensuring the financial security of the United States." Its mission is *to "Maintain a strong economy and create economic and job opportunities by promoting the conditions that enable economic growth and stability at home and abroad, strengthen national security by combating threats and protecting the integrity of the financial system, and manage the U.S. Government's finances and resources effectively."* Repeatedly printing money seems to be the only function the department is really good at.

Back in 2009 the federal government bailed out the auto industry/ Detroit and literally took control of General Motors. We were told that the *Presidential Task Force on the Auto Industry (AUTO TEAM)* and the *Treasury Department* would not be involved in day-to-day decision making at GM. It was no surprise to learn that was not true. The 2009 deal between "government controlled" GM and Delphi, a major industry supplier included the unethical action of GM (Obama Motors) to cut the pensions of non-union personnel while preserving full pension benefits for the union employees. This is just one example of the Administration's self-authorization to bestow expanded power to an Executive Agency, the Treasury Department in this case, to inject the government into private business. The government distorted normal business function knowing that failure and potential bankruptcy of a company are private business concerns, not government concerns, AND guaranteed that the outcome was advantageous to the administration.

U.S. Department of Housing and Urban Development (HUD):   www.hud.gov

From the Hud.gov website, *HUD's mission is to create strong, sustainable, inclusive communities and quality affordable homes for all. HUD is working to strengthen the housing market to bolster the economy and protect consumers; meet the need for quality affordable rental homes; utilize housing as a platform for improving quality of life; build inclusive and sustainable communities free from discrimination, and transform the way HUD does business.*

I thought HUD's purpose was to subsidize housing and ensure safety and quality of such. I had no idea that the government was endowed with the power to **"create" communities**. Creating communities is "social engineering." Creating communities is what governments in countries like China, North Korea, and Russia do. A new policy was added to HUD's arsenal in 2013. HUD now has the power to gather data on segregation and discrimination in every single neighborhood and has the authority to "rectify" what they perceive as violations under the *"Affirmitively Furthering Fair Housing"* policy. There will be a federal discrimination database which from which HUD can determine zoning laws, home financing policy, infrastructure code and even transportation planning to "alleviate alleged discrimination and segregation." So now this federal agency will dictate who lives where and with what neighbors; make and change zoning laws at will; and determine financial policy for the housing sector.

This is wrong on so many levels. Economics and culture, not race, dictates the majority of homeownership and locations defining the makeup of most neighborhoods. Quite simply, middle class salaries support middle class neighborhoods. Upper class money lives in upper scale areas. Unfortunately there is an economically less fortunate class that makes up the majority of poor and inner-city neighborhoods. The focus should be on incentives and assistance to upgrade one's poor status with education, skill training, and jobs to be able to move into another level of economic standing. In other words, strive for success no matter the race. Injecting lower income persons into middle class and upper class areas does no one any good. How does "material have nots" and "material haves" forced to live together work out? It Doesn't - as proven by past social equity experiments enforced by the government. Though some incidents involve race, cultural misunderstandings, entitlement and envy, the majority of the resulting problems are economic. HUD's original purpose was commendable. It was and still should exist to represent and protect persons who are discriminated against based on race, religion and sexual orientation, NOT exaggerate and even invent discrimination to control people and neighborhoods. HUD and all agencies are not allowed to make laws; only the Congress can do that. So to avoid any adherence to the Constitution of the United States, and with the blessing of the president they make *"regulations"* which are enforced as law. Coming to a city or town near you - watch for an explosion of discrimination lawsuits initiated by this member of the "federal family" agency.

There are so many government agencies and departments, all having one thing in common, disregard for the law and misuse of taxpayer money. Many federal employees seem to feel entitled to free perks, squandering taxpayer money, bonuses, and promotions. Upper level employees influence laws and regulations to protect this behavior. Honest employees risk their jobs and careers to report misdeeds. Even with "whistle blower" laws that guarantee employee protection, there is no protection when dealing with dishonest supervisors and corrupt departments. This is one more reason not to support expanding the government.

Since most of us who "pay the government freight" work for a living and are busy raising families, getting kids through school, and getting through life, we don't have a lot of time to "watch the Government." Fortunately there are organizations and people who do just that. They can inform and educate us about politicians and problems. We need to get involved with them and work together to ensure our Government is working as it should. Some of these organizations are:

- **The Heritage Foundation**: (http://www.heritage.org) a research policy organization truly concerned with the welfare and security of America. The Heritage Foundation is committed to conserving the principles and ideas of the American Founding: Free enterprise, limited government, individual freedom, American values, and a strong national defense. The Heritage Foundation has numerous "policy centers" staffed by experts in all fields as well as programs, resources, and internships.

- **The American Enterprise Institute for Public Policy Research**: (http://www.aei.org) a private, nonpartisan, not-for-profit institution dedicated to research and education on issues of government, politics, economics, and social welfare. Founded in 1943, AEI is home to some of America's most accomplished public policy experts--from economics, law, political science, defense and foreign policy studies, ethics, theology, health care, and other fields. The Institute sponsors research and conferences and publishes books, monographs, and periodicals. Its website, http://www.aei.org, posts its publications, videos and transcripts of its conferences, biographies of its scholars and fellows, and schedules of upcoming events.

- **Judicial Watch** (http://www.judicialwatch.org) **a** non-profit, conservative and non-partisan educational foundation promoting transparency, accountability, and integrity in government. Judicial Watch advocates high standards of ethics and morality in our nation's public life and seeks to ensure that political and judicial officials do not abuse their powers. Litigation, investigation, public outreach, and education are at the core of the Judicial Watch foundation.

- **Freedom Watch**: (http://www.freedomwatchusa.org) **a** political advocacy organization dedicated to preserving our freedom, protecting our constitutional rights and our national sovereignty. Freedom Watch is dedicated to American values at home and around the world and is devoted to preserving freedom for our children and grandchildren. Freedom, which was "given to us by our Creator, with certain unalienable rights."

- **Citizens United:** (http:www.citizensunited.org) an organization "dedicated to restoring our government to citizens' control." Citizens United goal is to *"restore the founding fathers vision of a free nation, guided by honesty, common sense, and good will of its citizens."* They are committed to the traditional American values of limited government, free enterprise, strong families, national security, and national sovereignty.

- **Our Country Deserves Better PAC:** (http://www.ourcountrydeservesbetter.com) an organization that champions the "Reaganesque" conservatism of lower taxes, smaller government, a strong national defense, and respect for the strength of the family as the core of a strong America.

- **Fact Check:** (http://www.factcheck.org) Annenberg Political Fact Checker - A nonpartisan, nonprofit consumer advocate organization for voters. Fact Check monitors the factual accuracy of what U.S. politicians say in TV ads, debates, speeches, interviews and news releases. Their goal is to apply the best practices of both journalism and scholarship, and to increase public knowledge and understanding.

All of our Government Officials, from the President to the Senators, Congressional Representatives, and agency and department managers and directors have websites. The websites have contact information listed (phone, mail, email). When you hear or notice something wrong or questionable, immediately contact your State Senator and Representative, and, or federal, state, local government agencies. You may feel that your one little email won't matter, but hundreds and hundreds of thousands of them will. It is more important than ever to hold our politicians responsible for their actions supposedly on our behalf, and question our elected officials on all levels. Shining a spotlight on dishonest people and agencies and departments must become standard practice. The very last thing any politician or corrupt official wants is attention directed to their often times illegal misdeeds.

Speak up – Speak out. We can no longer afford to remain silent!

U.S. Senate	http://www.senate.gov
The White House	http://www.whitehouse.gov/
U.S. House of Representatives	http://www.house.gov/
US Government Official Portal	http://www.usa.gov/
A-Z Index of U.S. Government Departments and Agencies	http://www.usa.gov/Agencies/Federal/All_Agencies/index.shtml
US Gov't Official Web Search	http://usasearch.gov/
Fed World – Government Information	http://www.fedworld.gov/
Newspaper & Current Periodical Reading Room – Government Publications	http://www.loc.gov/rr/news/fedgov.html
State and Local Government on the Net	http://www.statelocalgov.net/
Official Business Link to the U.S. Government	http://www.business.gov/
Official U.S. Government Site for People With Medicare	http://www.medicare.gov/
U.S. Government Blog	http://blog.usa.gov/roller/
Ben's Guide to U.S. Government for Kids	http://bensguide.gpo.gov/
Official Kids Portal for the U.S. Government	http://www.kids.gov/
e-CFR: Electronic Code of Federal Regulations	http://ecfr.gpoaccess.gov
Information on the legislative process, committees, procedures, agencies and resources	http://www.gpoaccess.gov/legislative.html
Current information on legislation and testimony	http://www.whitehouse.gov/omb/legislative_testimony_default

America

PART 2
DOMESTIC TRANQUILITY

View of the Potomac River from the grounds of Mt. Vernon

National Security and Defense

"Of the four wars in my lifetime none came about because the United States was too strong."

-Ronald Reagan

Article 1 Section 8 of the United States Constitution clearly states that our government is responsible for the safety and protection of its citizens. *"The Congress shall have power to...provide for the common defense and general welfare of the United States...*

To provide for calling forth the militia to execute the laws of the union, suppress insurrections and repel invasions...." To that end we have the formal military and also civilian security agencies such as the Federal Bureau of Investigation (FBI), Central Intelligence Agency (CIA), National Security Agency (NSA), and the Department of Homeland Security (DHS).

The United States Military: Finest Fighting Force in the World

The Constitution gives Congress the authority and power to protect American citizens from domestic and foreign threats. Deployed worldwide, the superb United States Military is our ultimate bastion of defense and is the reason we have enjoyed freedom and safety in the U.S. So why are the Commander-in-Chief and the federal government on a campaign to decimate it through leadership purges, insane regulations, discrimination, and unrealistic and deadly rules of engagement?

The actions of President Obama, our "Commander-in-Chief" are evidence of his disdain for our military. It seems that he prefers a weak, splintered and disenfranchised military organization led by political leaders loyal to him, not to the citizens they swore to protect. Huge military budget cuts are just the tip of the iceberg. Slashing personnel, equipment, technology, and support resources is a knife in the back of every serviceman and woman. With the world in crisis and instability and terrorism on the rise, we need a strong – NO, <u>we need the strongest military on Earth.</u>

The New Obama Military: A Politically Correct Social Experiment

Are you aware of the fact that President Obama has never used the word "victory" regarding any military operation? It is understandable considering he is on a mission to destroy military preparedness, ability and morale. I don't know about you, but I get nervous when an American president refers to the U.S. military as *"his military,"* and that they are *"fighting on my behalf."* Those are phrases you'd expect to hear from the late Hugo Chavez of Venezuela, and the soon to be late Fidel Castro of Cuba. What is even more frightening is the fact that the U.S. President is re-tooling our military machine right before our very eyes and the Pentagon is leading our fighting forces like sheep to the slaughter.

In the past five years President Obama has fired (forced resignations) of nearly 200 generals and senior officers. We as a nation have lost a century of military knowledge, experience, and above all, leadership. Many retired officers and war heroes have characterized Obama's actions as an all-out attack on our Armed Forces. Senior battle hardened officers are being replaced with those who fit a diversity model and who will tow the new enlightened military line. Retired Navy Capt. and many times decorated war hero, Joseph John summed it up. *"The truly sad story is that many of the brightest graduates of the three major service academies witnessing what the social experiment on diversity is doing to the US military are leaving the service after five years. We are being left with an officer corps that can be made to be more compliant, that is, exactly what Obama needs to affect his long-range goals for the U.S. military."*[241]

Retired Army Lt. General William G. "Jerry" Boykin said that an unprecedented number of four-star generals have been relieved of duty, *"and not necessarily relived for cause. I believe there is a purging of the military. The problem is worse than we have ever seen."*

Retired Marine Corps Lt. Col. Oliver North (a model officer and an honest man) echoes Retired Navy Captain Joseph John's military assessment. *"The military is being turned into a laboratory for radical social engineering experiments. They're wrecking the finest military force the world has ever known – brighter, better educated, trained, led, and the most combat-experienced military force in the history of the world."*[242]

Lt. Col. North has worthy advice for generals and admirals who *"feel strongly that something has gone wrong and something isn't being done right, you have a moral obligation to know, first of all, your career*

---

[241] "The New Face of Obama's Military," The Common Constitutionalist, posted on Freedom Outpost, http://www.freedomoutpost.com, March 7, 2014

[242] "Purging and Transforming Our Military," Matthew Vadum, *Front Page Magazine*, http://www.frontpagemag.com, November 8, 2013. Retired Army Lt. Gen. William G. "Jerry" Boykin, Retired Marine Corps. Lt. Col Oliver North

is probably over anyway, **so have the courage to stand up at a podium, take off your stars, throw 'em down [on] the podium, and tell the truth to the American people on your way out the door."**

Three noteworthy "political" terminations are directly connected to the White House and State Department Benghazi scandal.[243]

1. U.S. Army General Carter Ham, head of the US African Command when the Benghazi Consulate was attacked on September 11, 2012 was highly critical of the Obama Administration's decision not to send reinforcements to Benghazi. Even though he told a House Committee member that he was not given a "stand down" order, military sources cited by the *Washington Times* said he indeed was given a "stand down" order and was relieved of duty for "defying" it.

2. U.S. Navy Rear Admiral Charles Gaouette, Commander of Carrier Strike Group Three was in charge of Air Craft Carriers in the Mediterranean Sea at the time of the Benghazi attack. After telling Congress that he could have sent planes to Benghazi, he was relieved of duty. He was accused of using profanity and making "racially insensitive remarks." He was subsequently cleared of the criminal violations, but still was relieved of duty.

3. Major General Baker was commander of the Joint Task Force-Horn at Camp Lamar in Djibouti, Africa during the Benghazi attack. Military officials confirmed that counter-terror operations were run out of Djibouti and the General was involved with Benghazi. He was coincidently fired on alcohol and sexual misconduct charges.

The President's "Purge List" is extensive. I am not saying all the purged officers were angels. I am saying that most of them have impressive service records and the charges against them are bogus. Google "Obama's Purge" for numerous sources of information including the list of officers found on: *Front Page Magazine, Investment Watch, and Clash Daily.*

---

[243] "Obama's Military Purge," Arnold Ahlert, *Front Page Magazine,* http://www.frontpagemag.com, October 28, 2013

Retired U.S. Army Major General Paul Vallely said, *"The White house fails to take action or investigate its own, but finds it easy to fire military commanders who have given their lives for their country. Obama will not purge a civilian or political appointee because they have bought into Obama's ideology...He's intentionally weakening and gutting our military, Pentagon and reducing us as a superpower, and anyone in the ranks who disagrees or speaks out is being purged."*[244]

This Commander-in-Chief dishonors the very group of Americans who sacrifice the most for America. What President Obama is doing to our military is deplorable. Where are the voices of American citizens to support these brave patriots and to protest the neutering of our military forces? Purging officers is just one step in the President's multi-step plan to systematically suck the life out of our defenders of freedom.

Other presidential steps taken to remake the United States military into a 21st Century third-world fighting force:

- Radical changes in U.S. "Rules of Engagement" that are resulting in higher casualties. One example is the mandate *"no suppression fire at landing zones,"* where troops are most vulnerable thus making them easier enemy targets.
- Deplorable neglect of the Veterans Healthcare system. Free health care (a government promise) will no longer be free. Co-pays will be required.
- Slashing military pensions, services, and programs insuring a higher cost of living that these service men and women can no longer afford.
- 1% salary increase limit for fiscal year 2015 as well as cuts in housing allowances and reduction of available commissaries.
- Downgraded physical fitness qualifications even for infantry and elite units like the SEALS and Rangers just so women can participate on the battlefield.
- Diversity over security: *"As CMR's (Center for Military Readiness) report rightly notes, this turns the entire purpose of what the military is supposed to be about on its head... As a result, the*

---

[244] "Why are so many generals getting the axe?" Michele Hickford, author posting on Allan West.com. http://www.allanwest.com, October 31, 2013

military is prepared to embrace the circular reasoning of "diversity metrics" designed to obscure the genuine differences that exist between men and women, in order to reach predetermined outcomes that allow more women to be assigned to combat units. Thus we get the essence of radical feminism, the idea that men and women are equal in every respect, even if it means 'fudging' some realities to get there. As the CMR's report reveals, that's exactly what the Pentagon has done, noting that physical capability tests measuring common skills have been scaled back from six to three and adjusted to reduce physical demands and improve women's achievement scores."[245]

- Military dress regulations altered for Muslims to include prayer beads, beards, and hijabs, while the majority of servicemen will soon be sporting the "unisex" hat – yep, it's quite "girly." Who needs dignity and cohesion when Muslim appeasement takes priority?

- While catering to Muslims in the military, Christian servicemen and women are being discriminated against and harassed for their faith. The speech and actions of Christian military chaplains are censored, and they "must" accept same-sex marriages. Are the Muslim military clerics forced to do the same? I guarantee they are not.

- Troops in the Middle East are forbidden to have any visible religious symbolism. This rule applies to Christians and Jews, not Muslims.

- Open homosexuality resulting in increased tension, anxiety and male-on-male sexual assaults. 53% of the 26,000 sexual assaults in 2012 were men on men.[246]
  - Increased sexual misconduct and inappropriate behavior.

[245] "The Diversity Cult's Attack on the Military," Arnold Ahlert, *Front Page Magazine*, http://www.frontpagemag.com, January 25, 2013

[246] "UNREAL: Military Sexual Assaults At An All-Time High, Most Are Male On Male," *New York Times* article posted on Clash Daily, http://www.clashdaily.com, March 18, 2014

- Endorsed homosexual entertainment like the fundraiser at the U.S. air base in Okinawa, Japan where homosexual service members dressed as "drag queens" to entertain the troops. I'm sure more of this type of entertainment for the new sacred minority will be forthcoming - though not in the Middle East.

- A final nail in the coffin of morale is the ban on Navy SEALS wearing historic Navy Jack "Don't Tread on Me" patches. On May 31, 2002 this centuries old symbol revered by the US Navy was ordered **to be flown on all U.S. Naval ships through the duration of the War on Terror.** Since the war on Terror is nowhere near over, why is the government banning this time-honored military symbol? It seems the government (from pressure disguised as advice on Islamic tolerance) deems this flag is too similar to the Gadsden "Don't Tread on me Flag" embraced by Conservatives and the Tea Party even though BOTH versions of the "Don't Tread on Me" flag are representative of American independence and freedom since the time of the American revolution.

DONT TREAD ON ME

U.S. Navy Jack (flag)

- The Department of Defense (DOD) Opportunity Management Institute (diversity training center) penned the Pentagon's 637 page *Equal Opportunity* officers training manual. This indoctrination manual includes propaganda and instructions on a host of social justice issues:

    □ Warns of domestic "extremists," Conservatives and liberty supporting Americans who talk about "individual liberties," "states rights," and "constitutional rights." Nowhere is there mention of Communists, Socialists or Marxists, the triumvirate of hate.

    □ Teaches that healthy, white, heterosexual, Christian men hold an unfair advantage over other races.

    □ Presents issues of rampant racism, religious diversity, cultural awareness, and domestic extremism.

    □ Relies on the faulty and unreliable *Southern Poverty Law Center* for information on "extremist" and "hate" groups. Keep in mind that the Southern Poverty Law Center is totally liberal, is funded by George Soros, and systemically labels conservative groups including the Tea Party as hate groups. SPLC identifies the American Family Association and Concerned Women for America as hate groups also because they are "pro-life." The SPLC basically labels any group it disagrees with, a hate group. It also claims that large numbers of neo-Nazi skin heads and other white supremacists are in the military acquiring training for a domestic war. So technically, the organization that defines "extremism" and "hate" for the government is itself a hate group. No surprise there.

    □ Falsely labels Evangelical Christians, Catholics and a number of high-profile Christian ministries as domestic hate groups.

    □ Is obsessed with racism, social advantage, racism, equitable distribution, racism, social justice, racism (repeatedly printing "racism" was intentional). Attorney General Eric Holder could have authored the book.

Judicial Watch Organization (www.judicialwatch.com) obtained the "education materials" through a Freedom of Information Act request.[247] One section states, *"Nowadays, instead of dressing in sheets or publically espousing hate messages, many extremists will talk of individual liberties, states' rights, and how to make the world a better place."* Colonists (who fought and died for the freedom we enjoy today) are called extremists with "extremist ideologies." As if that isn't insulting enough, the 9/11 *terrorist attack is listed as an "historical event."* Judicial Watch President Tom Fitton said the *"Obama administration has a nasty habit of equating basic conservative values with terrorism…And it is striking that some of the language in this new document echoes the IRS targeting language of conservative and Tea Party investigations. After reviewing this document, one can't help worry for the future and morale of our nation's armed forces."*

Todd Starnes reporting for Fox News said Former Congressman and Lt. Col. Allen West (ret.) thought a congressional investigation into this military manual was in order. *"This is the Obama administration's outreach of social justice into the United States military. Equal Opportunity in the Army that I grew up in did not have anything to do with white privilege. When the president talked about fundamentally transforming the United States of America, I believe he had a dedicated agenda of going after the United States military. The priorities of this administration are totally whacked."*[248]

David L. Goetsch posted an interesting article on patriotupdate. com regarding a recent study on the character problems of the U.S. Army resulting from moral relativism. The army is a mirror of society and our progressive society has created this disgrace. *"Secretary of Defense Hagel and others in the Obama administration are expressing concern over a recent study showing that the U.S. Army is experiencing the highest rate of ethical lapses, moral breaches, and character problems in its history. Apparently instances of cheating, lying, stealing, sexual*

---

[247] "Defense Department Documents: "Extremists" Speak About Individual Liberties, States' Rights & How to Make the World a Better Place," Tim Brown, published by Freedom Outpost, http://www.freedomoutpost.com, August 25, 2013

[248] "Pentagon training manual: white males have unfair advantages," Todd Starnes, Fox News, http://foxnews.com, October 31, 2013

harassment, extra-marital affairs, drug use, and other character-related issues are on the rise in today's politically-correct, culturally-tolerant, gender-neutral, homosexual-friendly Army. It is hardly surprising that the Army is experiencing these problems. What is surprising is that Secretary of Defense Hagel and liberals in Congress don't understand why such problems are on the rise."[249]

The day after the 2008 presidential election a Russian immigrant colleague of mine was extremely upset and fearful. She was afraid that President Obama was going to take over the military and use it to police citizens like they did in Russia. I promised her that our military has sworn an oath to defend the Constitution against domestic enemies as well as foreign enemies. The United States military would never stand against the citizenry just as surely as they would never blindly follow illegal orders of any president - ever. Now that those ethical military members have been purged, how will the new Obama military react to illegal orders? Wow, I owe her an apology.

Dr. Jim Garrow posted an unnerving statement on Facebook: *"I have just been informed by a former senior military leader that Obama is using a new 'litmus test' in determining who will stay and who must go in his military leaders...'The new litmus test of leadership in the military is if they will fire on US citizens or not.' Those who will not are being removed."* Dr. Garrow said the source of that information was "one of America's foremost military heroes."[250]

Dr. Garrow is not a paranoid extremist that the Pentagon's Equal Opportunity manual warns of. He is a respected author and humanitarian. His book, *The Pink Pagoda: One Man's Quest to End Gendercide in China* chronicles his multi-million dollar rescue of about 40,000 baby girls from China. Dr. Garrow is also the founder and

---

[249] "Army Experiencing Character Problems: Imagine That!" David L. Goetsch, http://patriotupdate.com, March 1, 2014

[250] "Obama Tailoring Military Leadership to Only Those Who Will Shoot Fellow Americans," published by Godfather Politics, http://www.godfatherpolitics.com, January 24, 2013 and "Shock claim: Obama only wants military leaders who 'will fire on U.S. citizens," Dave Gibson, Examiner.com, http://www.examiner.com, January 21, 2013

director of the Bethune Institute's 168 Pink Pagoda schools that teach Chinese girls in an English environment.

20th century history alone provides vitally important warnings. One such warning comes from the actions of Josef Stalin of the Soviet Union on the eve of World War II. The Soviet military was included in Stalin's "Great Purge" from 1934-1939 resulting in the deaths of over a million Russians. By 1939 Stalin decimated the Soviet military by purging senior army and navy officers. 3 of a total of 5 Marshalls of the Soviet Army were executed. 13 of 18 army commanders, 8 of 9 admirals, 50 of 57 army corps commanders, and 154 out of 186 division commanders were removed.[251] The lesson here is that *"the most-experienced and proficient military officers in the Soviet Army and Navy were lost during the madness…More often than not these able commanders and leaders were replaced by ideologically-reliable but militarily-incompetent Communist party hacks."* During WWII, the Russian people paid a horrific price for Stalin's folly.

Please note that I am not comparing President Obama with the brutality of Soviet dictator Stalin. I am comparing their irrational and ideological decisions to destroy their own country's military machines. Peter Farmer's November 12, 2013 article, "The Great Purge (Of the US Military)" puts Obama's "purge" in perspective. *"Stalin's purge of the Red Army is historically-significant for many reasons, but perhaps none more important than that the episode illustrates the folly of allowing ideology to trump military necessity, practicality and pragmatism. Stalin's evil and feckless acts left his nation and people all-but-defenseless in the face of the Nazi onslaught …."*

Peter Farmer fears that the U.S. military is being "gutted" to comply with an ideology, just like the Soviet army was before World War Two. Corruption and ideological social experimentation are driving Obama's actions; and leadership purges were necessary to silence the truth about his Benghazi failure.

In October, 2013 News.investors.com quoted Gen. Ray Odierno, *"Right now we have in the Army two brigades that are trained. That's it. Two."* The general also confirmed that during the last six months of the

---

[251] "The Great Purge (Of the US Military)" Peter Farmer, The Free Republic, http://www.freerepublic .com, November 11, 2013

fiscal year ending September 30, 2013, the U.S. Army didn't conduct any training. Maybe there aren't enough qualified officers to lead the training – just a thought. No matter what the government's reasoning is – between leadership and budget decimation, we are in deep trouble here in the land of the free and the home of the brave.

Pentagon defense cuts will result in shrinking the US Army to its smallest number since <u>before</u> World War Two (1940). The cuts will also eliminate the entire fleet of Air Force A-10 attack aircraft and the U-2 spy plane. The federal government in general and the sitting President in particular have a problem accepting real lessons of history. For instance, because Japan knew the U.S. was not prepared for a war it confidently attacked Pearl Harbor. The U.S. surprised Japan and the world with how quickly Americans reacted and engaged in the war. Unfortunately we were so ill-prepared for it that our early combat soldiers in Africa did not have adequate equipment, training, or leadership. What the United States did have was a capitalist (free market) industrial and manufacturing system that immediately swung into war production, and a population willing to sacrifice.

President Truman deeply cut the military after WWII resulting in China's assessment that the U.S. was weakened, ill-prepared for war, and the Americans would not get militarily involved in Korea. They were correct about the not-prepared part, just as adversaries today are correct that America is weak. It's quite unnerving to see how easy it has been for just one man to undermine the power of a strong country and reduce it to ashes.

Dr. Earl Tilford, military historian and Middle East and terrorism fellow at the *Center for Vision and Values* at Grove City College published a very sobering article on the deterioration of the Department of Defense. Dr. Tilford has a Ph.D. in American and European History. He has served as an Air Force intelligence officer, Director of Research at the U.S. Army's Strategic Studies Institute, and was a professor at Grove City College where he taught courses in military history, national security, and international and domestic terrorism and counter-terrorism. I can confidently say that Dr. Tilford is a military expert and when he is concerned that the *"American armed forces are in a death spiral,"*[252] we need to listen.

"After eight years of military cuts overseen by President Clinton, whose concept of defense had more to do with lawyers and juries than military strength, President George W. Bush found himself in the unfortunate position of having to respond to the worst attack on U.S. soil since Pearl Harbor..."

Dr. Tilford added that if the U.S. had followed its <u>original plan</u>, forces would have been out of Afghanistan in a short period of time with al Qaeda decimated, and Osama bin Laden captured or killed. Then with a clearly defined strategic objective going into Iraq, the war would have ended after securing Baghdad. Unfortunately, the decision was made to bring democracy to these two countries, neither of which had any experience with democracy, freedom or liberty.

U.S. military leaders successfully executed operations but there never was a strategy for victory. Lawyers and politicians weighing policies watched over the commander's shoulders influencing decisions as the officers were actively fighting dangerous enemies. *"Moreover, because President Barack Obama has been unwilling to make the critical financial investment needed to keep the U.S. a top military power, the American defense establishment entered its current death spiral...The military weakness admired by the extreme left invites aggression from terrorists and possible hegemons in Teheran, Beijing, and Moscow."* Dr. Tilford concluded that **the cost of weakness far exceeds the cost of strength**.

We need to take seriously what is happening to the U.S. military and listen to experts like Dr. Tilford and the officers who have been warning us about this travesty. As usual, the media is silent on this issue and sadly, so is Congress. We, the recipients of liberty and security paid for by these brave men must support them now and make sure their messages are heard by enough patriotic Americans to demand acknowledgment and action by the U.S. Congress. Americans need to know that Major General Patrick H. Brady said, *"There is no doubt he [Obama] is intent on emasculating the military and will fire anyone*

---

[252] "Department of Defense's Death Spiral," Dr. Earl Tilford, The Center for Vision & Values, November 15, 2013

who disagrees with him over such issues as "homosexuals, women in foxholes..." And, retired U.S. Navy Captain Joseph John's warning *"the bigger picture...the U.S. Armed Forces have been under relentless attack by the occupant of the Oval Office for five years."*[253]

We also need to support organizations such as Oath Keepers, SOS Special Operations Speaks and The United West.org.

Oath Keepers: (www.oathkeepers.org) Guardians of the Republic, an organization founded by military veterans and peace officers who continue to live by their sworn oath to defend the Constitution. Oath Keepers is apolitical, sworn to uphold the Constitution without allegiance to any political party. They are loyal to the American people and the Constitution under which we live.

> *Oath Keepers is a non-partisan association of current and formerly serving military, reserves, National Guard, veterans, Peace Officers, and Fire Fighters who will fulfill the Oath we swore, with the support of likeminded citizens who take an Oath to stand with us, to support and defend the Constitution against all enemies, foreign and domestic, so help us God. Our oath is to the Constitution. Our motto is "Not on our watch"*

Oath Keepers published a "Declaration of Orders We Will Not Obey" clearly stating that they will uphold the Constitution and the rights of American citizens. Oath Keepers will not obey:

- Orders to disarm the American people.
- Orders to conduct warrantless searches.
- Orders to detain Americans as "unlawful enemy combatants."
- Orders to impose martial law or a "state of emergency" on any state.
- Orders to invade any state that asserts its sovereignty.
- Orders to blockade American cities.

---

[253] "The Great Purge (Of the US Military)," Peter Farmer, Free Republic, http://www.freerepublic.com, November 11, 2013

- Orders to force Americans into any detention camps, under any pretext.
- Orders to assist or support any foreign troops on U.S. soil against Americans under any pretext including to "keep the peace" or to "maintain control" during an emergency. I believe they are referring to the United Nations who would love to have UN forces active in America.
- Orders to confiscate any property of the American people.
- Orders to interfere with the right of Americans to free speech, to peaceably assemble, and to petition their government for a redress of grievances.

"And for the support of this Declaration, with a firm reliance on the protection of Divine Providence, we mutually affirm our oath and pledge to each other our Lives, our Fortunes, and our Sacred Honor

—Oath Keepers

Special Operations Speaks (SOS): Veterans and supporters of the Special Operations communities committed to identifying and combatting internal and external threats to the sovereignty of the United States of America. The founders of SOS are all distinguished retired Special Operations veterans who served our nation bravely and proudly. Lt. Gen. William G. (Jerry) Boykin is the SOS Chairman. SOS advocates for and speaks for active military who cannot speak for themselves. They are dedicated to uncovering the truth about the Benghazi, Libya carnage and subsequent government cover-up.

You can learn more about SOS on their website: www. specialoperationsspeaks.com and on Facebook and YouTube.

Special Operations Speaks (SOS) mission goals: **Remember Benghazi**

- Uncover the truth with regard to the Benghazi massacre, to include failed security preparations, intentional abandonment of our citizens in distress and the blatant cover-up surrounding this national tragedy.

- Protect the rights, benefits and privileges earned by active duty personnel and veterans for their honorable service to and sacrifice for our nation.
- Support qualified congressional candidates or serving members who support and defend our Constitution.
- Restore credibility, integrity and honor to the office of the Commander-in-Chief of the United States of America.

"Betrayed"

Betrayed: The Shocking True Story of Extortion 17 as Told by a Navy SEAL's Father, is the book written by Billy Vaughn, father of Special Operations Chief (SEAL) Aaron Vaughn who was killed on August 6, 2011 along with 29 other of America's best. It is a remarkable book about amazing warriors who were betrayed by our own government; the same government that is still working hard to bury the incident, the deaths, the terrorist component and the unforgivable cover-up of the tragic event. www.forourson.us and www.unitedwest.org

www.forourson.org: Aaron Vaughn's parents Billy and Karen Vaughn are committed to the truth and the prevention of another such incident. *"As we began searching for answers, our eyes were opened to the vile atrocities being played out on America's military. We quickly came face-to-face with our worst nightmare…our boys shouldn't have died that night. The downing of Extortion 17 was at best unnecessary and at worst negligent, reckless loss of life."*[254]

Extortion 17 was the moniker for the CH-47 Chinook helicopter that was shot down by the Taliban during "Operation Lefty Grove" on August 6, 2011 in Afghanistan killing all on board including U.S. Special Operations Forces and seven "unidentified" Afghan commandos. There was no standard helicopter escort, mission directions were unclear, and "pre-assault" fire to cover the Chinook's landing was never ordered. Three of the Special Forces members were part of the SEAL Team Six

---

[254] "Betrayed: The Shocking Story of Extortion 17 as Told by a Navy SEAL's Father," Billy Vaughn, and contributors Monica Morrill and Cari Blake, CreateSpace Independent Publishing Platform, October 29, 2013

operation that got Osama bin Laden just three months earlier. SEAL Team Six was identified by the administration for that successful operation and Vice President Biden went further and acknowledged the commander by name effectively informing our terrorist enemies who the men responsible for the death of their "terrorist treasure," Osama bin Laden were.

It might have ended there except for what the parents of the SEALs uncovered since that heartbreaking event. The "rules of engagement" were changed by the White House which prevented the U.S. military from being successful. They no longer were fighting to "win" as evidenced by casualty numbers. **In a war that started in 2001, 80% of the military men and women have been killed in the past 5 years, coinciding with the Administration's new Rules of Engagement.**

Billy and Karen Vaughn spoke at the Freedom Center's West Coast Retreat in Palos Verdes, California in March 2014. The video and transcript of their talks are compelling and available for viewing on Freedom Center's website, www.freedomcenter.org and on *Front Page Magazine* at www.frontpagemag.com.[255] Billy Vaughn related that the U.S. military is now controlled by the operational coordination group of Afghanistan, *"They [untrustworthy Afghans] have eyes on every special operations mission. They're in on the intel, they're in the pre-op, the post-op, the flight routes, everything about it. And in fact, they have the authority to squash special ops missions. In theory we have lent our special contractors out to the Islamic Republic Sharia-compliant government of Afghanistan."*

Christian clergy were not allowed to be present at the Grimera Air Base from where the dead are flown back to the U.S from Afghanistan. As a final insult and the epitome of disrespect, a Muslim Imam was allowed to "pray" over the bodies and he took the opportunity to blatantly condemn our heroes *as infidels.* Karen Vaughn related that eight of the bodies were returned to the U.S. draped by Islamic Republic of Afghanistan flags. Who in the administration and military is responsible for allowing such contemptible disregard for our fallen heroes?

---

[255] "The War on Our Warriors," *Front Page Magazine*, http://www.frontpagemag.com, April 10, 2014

This is a story every American should read about. The United West Organization (www.unitedwest.org) was established by the Vaughns to continue the fight for truth and to protect our military members from a vile enemy and from their own government. United West.org is a national grass roots organization and a leader in our civilian war on terror. Contributions to the organization finance efforts to "investigate and analyze the Islamic threat that attempts to infiltrate our society." The "Islamic threat" mentioned is very real and extremely dangerous.

Civilian Security Agencies: The Power to Protect and Destroy

There are numerous civilian agencies and organizations working abroad and within our borders tasked with the mission of ensuring national safety and security. The main security organizations are the Central Intelligence Agency (CIA), the Federal Bureau of Investigation (FBI), the Department of Homeland Security (DHS) and the National Security Agency (NSA). Since most Americans are familiar with the FBI and its function I will take a look at others.

One agency that many of us have never heard of is the National Nuclear Security Administration (NNSA). The NNSA is the agency responsible for securing the nation's nuclear weapons and the facilities where they are stored. That includes nuclear weapons, all their components, and even the weapons laboratories where critical research is conducted and weapons are designed. Again, I gave the government too much credit thinking it would strictly enforce security and oversight with something as important and dangerous as our nation's nuclear weapons. I was wrong, again. The Department of Energy (DOE) Inspector General audit confirmed that NNSA agency negligence is detrimental to national security - which affects all of us.

In Part One I referenced security breaches and espionage at the Los Alamos National Laboratory in New Mexico exposed by Notra Trulock, former Director of Intelligence at the Department of Energy in his book, "*Code Name Kindred Spirit: Inside the Chinese Nuclear Espionage Scandal.*" An April 2014 article by *Judicial Watch* substantiates Mr. Trulock's findings and confirms that security at our nuclear facilities has not improved. *"For instance, the Los Alamos National Laboratory in New Mexico, long embroiled in major security breach scandals, granted unauthorized access in violation of DOE rules. This includes access to nuclear weapons drawings to entire organizations or functional groups. This is the sort of stuff that's supposed to be top secret. The lab also used parts for a specific type of bomb that did not conform to design specifications and it failed to ensure that the problem was corrected."*[256]

Inexcusable security disasters are not unique to Los Alamos. At the Sandia National Laboratory also located in New Mexico, *Judicial Watch* noted that investigators discovered "repeated" instances of *"ineffective management of classified nuclear weapons drawings, a situation that could lead to unauthorized changes to the drawings."* Investigators at the Pantex nuclear weapons assembly plant in Texas revealed that officials at the plant could not find a nuclear weapons part for testing. These are examples from just three of the nation's "<u>maximum security</u>" <u>nuclear weapons facilities</u> that we know about. It is a fact that our nuclear weapons technology has been stolen and given away. Theoretically, our nuclear technology in the hands of our enemies just might be used to kill us. I find it reprehensible that our government is so lax with our security.

The Central Intelligence Agency (CIA): www.cia.gov

The Central Intelligence Agency (CIA) operates globally and is responsible for collecting information on adversaries, analyzing threats, providing warnings, interrogating terrorists and conducting world-wide covert action (at the direction of the President) to <u>preempt</u> threats and achieve United States policy objectives. You can read about the CIA's vision, mission and "values" on their website: <u>https://www.cia.gov/about-cia/strategic-intent.html</u>.

Under the CIA's "The Strategic Intent 2007-2011" section, "<u>The Strategic Environment</u>" clearly states the global threats against our nation. These perilous threats are very real. *"We operate in an unstable and dangerous world where international terrorism, the rise of new*

---

[256] "U.S. Has Long Failed to Protect Nuclear Weapon Stockpile," Judicial Watch Organization, <u>http://www.judicialwatch.org</u>, April 4, 2014

powers, and the accelerating pace of economic and technological change will place enormous strains on the ability of states to govern and will sharply increase the potential for strategic surprises." [257] "Potential strategic surprises" include:

- Terrorist enemies around the world are committed to the murder of Americans
- Propagation of weapons of mass destruction threatens international and homeland safety
- The global geopolitical and economic landscape is changing and the economic rise of China and India will have an impact
- Regional crisis' will emerge due to weak governments, economic recessions, and the availability of resources

As evidenced above, the CIA openly publishes general threats to our nation, so why do the President and members of Congress disregard the warnings? Why do they identify captured terrorists as common criminals deserving of civil trials complete with U.S. citizenship rights? And above all, why do they act surprised when incidents such as the attempted bombing of a domestic airliner on Christmas Day 2009 and the deadly 2013 Boston Marathon bombings happen? The simple answer is that "politics" has now officially trumped our "common defense and general welfare."

We don't hear much about CIA achievements. We only hear about CIA errors and intelligence lapses. We don't get to know the brave men and women who risk their lives daily in defense of our nation. They work, live, and die in obscurity. I would think that an organization that shoulders so much of the responsibility for our country's safety would be strongly supported by the government and given all the resources necessary to successfully fulfill their missions. This does not seem to be the case under the current administration. The government is purposely hampering the successful operation of the CIA. Case in point is the Justice Department decision with the approval of the White House to open investigations with possible "criminal" charges of CIA personnel

---

[257] "Strategic Intent 2007-2011," Central Intelligence Agency, https://www.cia.gov/about-cia/strategic-intent-2007-2011.html

involved in the interrogations of terrorists and enemy combatants. Security agencies should never be political pawns, but since 2009 there has been a concerted attack on CIA personnel portraying them as human rights violators for successfully obtaining important information from terrorist prisoners. It seems this administration prioritizes pampered treatment of incarcerated terrorists over the safety and security of Americans.

The disastrous reality that our government has returned to a "pre 9/11" mentality by treating terrorists not as the ruthless murderers that they are, but as common criminals, and the fact that the administration has implausibly removed the word "terrorist" from its vocabulary is extremely disturbing. They call terrorist actions "man-made events," and want captured terrorists (who have "declared war on America" and who are committed to killing us) tried in civil court instead of military court where they belong. Our military, law enforcement and intelligence agencies work diligently to protect us and our nation. Instead of supporting them with all resources possible, the very government whose "purpose" is to protect us is erecting obstacles at every turn to hamper their efforts. The U.S. government is putting every American world-wide at risk.

The April 2014 revelation that a huge Al Qaeda gathering in Yemen was never noticed by U.S. intelligence is an inexcusable example of the government's complicity in hampering intelligence-gathering and national security. I cannot accept allegations that the CIA was asleep at the wheel. I believe the CIA has been so hampered by stringent administrative regulations and rules of engagement that it is unable to operate at a level of excellence as "on the ground" agents are not allowed to do their jobs. The CIA has been demoralized much like the U.S. military has.

Onan Coca reported: *"Al Qaeda recently took an opportunity to poke our intelligence community in the eye. They did by conducting a mass get together i.e. party, in Yemen. Somehow our intelligence missed the biggest gathering of Al Qaeda bigwigs in the history of the war on terror."*[258] Al Qaeda leader Nasir al-Wuhayshi was the keynote speaker. He wants

---

[258] "Al Qaeda Has a Party and Makes the USA Look Foolish," Onan Coca, Eagle Rising, http://www.eaglerising.com, April 17,2014

to attack the United States, *"We're coming for you."* It was a terrorist party to show the world that Al Qaeda is not weak, it's not going away, it's stronger than ever and it is ready for action.

To illustrate, I assumed that the director of the Central Intelligence Agency would know that "classified" information was "top secret" and shhh - you do not talk about it in public. I was wrong. Former Obama appointed CIA director Leon Panetta gave a speech in June 2011 in which he revealed classified information. The Hollywood filmmaker of the movie, *"Zero Dark Thirty,"* who does not have security clearance, was an attendee at the event and a recipient of classified information. The Judicial Watch organization confirmed that Panetta *"specifically recognized the unit that conducted the [Osama bin Laden] raid and identified the ground commander by name."*[259] Unbelievably, the CIA's own director "out-ed" the Seal Team and their commander making them and their families' targets for terrorist revenge. It must be difficult at times for CIA field agents serious about American security to remain steadfastly dedicated to their mission when careless bureaucrats do not take the "mission" seriously.

Seemingly as if not to be up-staged by the CIA Director, our own Vice President Biden did the exact same thing. Two days after the Bin Laden raid, V.P. Biden was speaking at a gathering in DC and he told the audience: *"Let me briefly acknowledge tonight's distinguished honorees: Adm. Jim Stavridis is the real deal; he could tell you more about and understands the incredible, the phenomenal, the just almost unbelievable capacity of his Navy SEALS and what they did last – last Saturday."*[260] Talk about unbelievable, the vice president of the United States knowingly released classified information and identified the people responsible for the May 1, 2011 death of Osama bin Laden.

After the identity leaks by the Vice President and CIA Director, SEAL Team 6 members, very worried about the safety of their families, contacted them urging extreme caution and instructing them to "wipe

[259] "CIA Internal Review Confirms that Leon Panetta Revealed 'Top Secret' Information to Hollywood Filmmaker at bin Laden Assault Awards Ceremony," Judicial Watch, http://www.judicialwatch.org, December 13, 2013
[260] "Extortion 17 is a Bigger Scandal and Betrayal than Benghazi," Tim Brown, Freedom Outpost, http://www.freedomoutpost.com, August 15, 2013

clean" their social media accounts. They knew they were now targets carelessly out-ed by their own government. Their fear was merited. On August 6, 2011 three months after the bin Laden raid a Chinook CH47 helicopter, *"Extortion 17"* carrying SEAL Team 6 members was on another covert raid, this one in Afghanistan (The tragic *Betrayed* incident – page 146). As the helicopter approached the drop-zone it was hit with a rocket propelled grenade fired by the Taliban killing all 38 people on board. 25 of those killed were Special Operations forces and 3 were part of the SEAL Team 6 that participated in the bin laden raid.

The government officially concluded that the helicopter was taken down by a "lucky shot" from Taliban fighters - case closed. Many others including SEAL members, Special Operations veterans and family members of those killed believe otherwise. They believe the Taliban was tipped-off about this Special Forces mission and the specific "secret" landing location. Taliban forces knew U.S. Special Forces were coming. Billy Vaughn father of Aaron Vaughn, one of the SEALs killed on that helicopter said, *"They [Taliban] knew who was on that chopper that night. By 2009, our ambassador had made a statement that the American government believed that at least 25 percent of the Afghan national Army was infiltrated by the Taliban."*[261] Of note, two of the Afghans on that helicopter were last minute add-ons and so were not on the manifest meaning they were not vetted.

"Sadly, President Barak Obama and his administration failed to acknowledge the deaths of these warriors and in fact have set up roadblocks to prevent full disclosure of the Taliban ambush, according to several special operations individuals and organizations."[262] We will likely never know the government's unconscionable complicity in this tragedy, but one thing is for certain, Vice President Joe Biden and CIA Director Leon Panetta are responsible for their own reckless actions leading to the deaths of brave and heroic Americans. It is disgraceful!

---

[261] "Did SEAL Team 6 die in Afghanistan to give Obama good publicity?" Grace Stafford, The Daily Caller, http://www.dailycaller.com, March 9, 2014

[262] "Anniversary of Massacre of Navy SEALs Ignored by President," Clash Daily, http://www.clashdaily.com, August 7, 2013

Department of Homeland Security (DHS):   www.dhs.gov

Does the term "Big Brother" make you uneasy and apprehensive? It should. The Department of Homeland Security is Big Brother controlling our fleet of domestic security and law enforcement organizations and is known by many as the *Department of Homeland Insecurity.*

The Department of Homeland Security was created after 9/11 based on the theory that all agencies, departments, and organizations must work in concert to effectively and efficiently protect the nation. It was a great theory – until bureaucracy turned it into a chaotic quagmire. Established in 2002, The Department of Homeland Security was created by combining 22 separate federal departments and agencies. The missions of DHS include: Preventing terrorism, enhancing security, managing the borders, administering immigration laws, securing cyberspace, responding to natural disasters and other emergencies.

I suppose we should feel safe knowing our government is taking *"Our founding principle and highest priority...to protect the American people from terrorist threats,"*[263] but the current administration won't even call terrorists "terrorists." Another aspect of the DHS mission statement is to secure our borders, but our borders are wide open and there is no serious effort to safeguard them as evidenced by well over 12 million illegal aliens freely roaming the U.S. and thousands more are arriving daily. How can we feel secure knowing that our government is more concerned with the "rights" of illegal aliens in our country than the lives of American citizens including murdered border agent, Brian Terry? The "Fast and Furious" scandal identified Terry's murder weapon as one of the government's many guns left untracked during the botched operation. Also, according to its own mission statement DHS is responsible for *"facilitating legal immigration and enforcing laws,* but they are not enforcing existing immigration laws when it comes to illegal aliens. The government does not even recognize the word "illegal." With the president's blessing and the Justice Department's support, DHS is instructing other agencies NOT to enforce immigration laws, specifically laws relating to *illegal* immigrants.

---

[263] Mission," Homeland Security, Official website of the Department of Homeland Security, http://www.dhs.gov

How can the Department of Homeland Security operate legitimately and without oversight when many of its own employees do not accept existing laws? A December 2013 article in the *Independent Sentinel* reported, the President is filling DHS positions with *"radical open borders attorneys they don't need."*[264] Article author Sara Noble explained that these new Department of Homeland Security employees are from radical left organizations like the Mexican American Legal Defense and Educational Fund, The Advancement Project, and the Tides Foundation (Funded by George Soros, socialist corporatist). These people are hostile to immigration laws and have the power to protect illegals as well as have the power to influence the White House.

Embracing the administration's bizarre mission to change policies for the protection of adversaries, armed illegals and drug dealers at the expense of American servicemen and civil service employees, the DHS has changed its *rules of engagement* for border patrol officers. Border officers have been ordered to "retreat" when illegals throw rocks at them and not to get in the way of drug smuggler vehicles heading north. Neil Munro reporting for The *Daily Caller* shares some of the new rules: *"Agents shall not discharge firearms in response to thrown or hurled projectiles...agents should obtain a tactical advantage in these situations, such as seeking cover or distancing themselves...agents shall not discharge their firearms at a moving vehicle merely fleeing from agents..."*[265]

Even though 3 U.S. border guards have been killed (1 killed during a shoot-out with drug smugglers armed with AK47's) and 6,000 have been attacked since 2007; the deaths of 10 drug-smugglers and armed criminals seems more of a tragedy for the department. The director of DHS assured the public that the agents will be equipped with "short-range Tasers and pepper spray and medium-range pellet guns, to deter attacks." Defending against AK47's with only Tasers, pepper spray and pellet guns, the officers will have no choice but to run, leaving the border

---

[264] "Obama Is Filling DHS with Amnesty Revolutionaries Backed by Soros," Sara Noble, Independent Sentinel, http://www.independentsentinel.com, December 6, 2013

[265] "DHS tells American border guards to run away from illegal immigrants hurling rocks at them, fleeing in vehicles," Neil Munro, The Daily Caller, http://www.dailycaller.com, March 8, 2014

unprotected. But, disarming Americans to make us defenseless seems to be part of the Obama/DHS plan now, isn't it?

Our now defenseless border patrol agents have more than armed drug smugglers and criminals to confront. They are confronting well-armed Mexican soldiers - on U.S. soil. Thanks to the investigative reporting of the *Judicial Watch Organization* we found out that Mexican military members have crossed the border into the United States 23 times in the Tucson and Yuma sectors of Arizona since 2010.[266] Department of Homeland Security records document 226 incursions by Mexican government personnel into the U.S. between 1996 and 2005. The latest incident reported by *Judicial Watch* occurred on January 26, 2014 when two Mexican soldiers held two of our border patrol agents at gunpoint after being discovered inside the U.S. about two and a half miles west of Sasabe, Arizona. A stand-off lasted 35 minutes before the Mexican soldiers retreated back across the border into Mexico.

The Mexican government claimed those two men were drug smugglers wearing military uniforms. The minister for press and public affairs at the Mexican Embassy said the two were "part of a counter-narcotics operation" and didn't know they were across the border. Some officials in the U.S. say the Mexican soldiers are not chasing drug smugglers. They are protecting cartel smugglers delivering drugs in the U.S. Where's the outrage? What is our government doing about this? There is no outrage, no media coverage, and no government action. Instead, our government continues to send virtually unarmed border security officers to the border - for what? To watch armed drug smugglers, Mexican soldiers and miscellaneous illegals entering the country, since they are unable to do anything including defend themselves. Our citizens are in grave danger and the federal government does not care.

A very troubling DHS activity related to illegal activity that we never hear about is the department's role in transporting children of illegal aliens smuggled into the U.S. to their illegal parents already living in the United States. Federal Judge Andrew S. Hanen called these actions *"dangerous and unconscionable...The DHS has simply chosen not to*

---

[266] "US Border Patrol Agents Held at Gunpoint by Mexican Military Inside US Borders," Freedom Outpost, http://www.freedomoutpost.com, April 7, 2014

enforce United States' border security laws."[267] It is important to note that these activities were happening long before the great Mexican-Central American child rush to the U.S. in which thousands of unaccompanied children were being smuggled across the border in 2014. The federal government's response was to disperse the children across America. This is wrong on so many levels:

- U.S. Border Officers are now mandatory baby-sitters leaving the border wide open for criminals, terrorists and drugs.
- These children will spread sicknesses to Americans.
- What is the cost of this orchestrated "humanitarian crisis?"
- Why doesn't the Obama administration have a problem with this?
- Why isn't anyone condemning Mexico for allowing this to happen? Then again, Mexico is most likely complicit in this "human trafficking."
- Why is no one concerned for the safety of these children? They are easy targets for abuse, molestation and even murder.
- It is important to note that <u>many</u> of these "children" are teenage boys and gang members. What's so humanitarian about giving gang members license to steal and kill?

As a matter of fact the indictment and subsequent conviction of a former U.S. Department of Homeland Security Officer of Inspector General (DHS-OIG) supervisor for falsifying documents and coercing other special agents to "impede, obstruct, and influence" a 2011 internal review of the DHS-OIG office sustains the accusations of disturbing DHS behavior.[268] Mr. Eugenio Pedraza did not properly investigate numerous cases: falsified reports; provided fraudulent documents; and failed to provide Border Agents with adequate training and supervision. Cases in question included: Border Patrol agents assisting in the "unlawful smuggling of undocumented aliens and narcotics into the United State

---

[267] "Judge claims DHS delivering smuggled children to illegal immigrant parents," Judson Berger, FoxNews.com, http://www.foxnews.com, December 13, 2013
[268] "Homeland Security Supervisor Falsified Documents on Border Investigations," Kristin Tate, Breitbart, http://www.breitbart.com, March 25, 2014

through several ports-of-entry in Texas." It saddens me to know that this is not a unique problem within the DHS. It is a corrupt culture that puts our honest border patrol agents in grave danger, as evidenced by DHS' "Rules of Engagement" and the death of Border agent Brian Terry.

The Department of Justice National Drug Intelligence Center produces annual "Drug Threat Assessments" providing vital information about Mexican drug cartel activity in the U.S. As Nicholas Ballasy reported in an article published by the *Daily Caller*, the NDIC 2011 assessment warned that Mexican based criminal organizations distributed most of the *"heroin, marijuana, and methamphetamine available in the U.S.* Drug cartels control the U.S./Mexico border which is the "primary gateway for moving the bulk of illicit drugs into the United States." The assessment also warned that *"border communities along both sides of the Texas-Mexico border are tantamount to living in a war zone in which civil authorities, law enforcement agencies as well as citizens are under attack around the clock."*[269] I would think that this department was very important providing critical information for law enforcement, but the 2011 assessment was the last report produced by the NDIC because The Department of Justice shut that department down "for budgetary reasons." That is ludicrous and puts border agents at even greater risk. It is another example of how our current government places rights and safety of illegal aliens above U.S. citizens - law enforcement and civilians.

While the Southern border states, certainly not the federal government, are focused on the Southern Border, the 5,500 mile Northern Border with Canada is virtually an open door for terrorist entry into the U.S. The Northern Border will never be addressed until a catastrophic event unfolds because enemies of America entered the country from Canada. When that happens, the government and the media will be shocked and the finger pointing in Washington D.C. will be working over-time. As always, it will be too late.

An October 2013 article by Suzanne Hamner published by *Freedom Outpost* asked the question: *"Which is more important: spending money to combat climate change/global warming or spending money on US*

---

[269] "DOJ shuts down National Drug Intelligence Center, no 2012 report released," Nicholas Ballasy, The Daily Caller, http://www.dailycaller.com, January 14, 2013

border security?" I as well as most Americans would answer that U.S. border security is more important, but the White House doesn't see it that way. The President believes global warming is definitely more important as evidenced by the budgetary fact that *"U.S. global warming spending is estimated to cost $22.2 billion this year...At the same time, the federal government will spend nearly $12 billion on customs and border enforcement this year."*[270]

We are funding countless global warming research programs and organizations based on erroneous studies and scientific methods that even United Nations scientists have admitted are inaccurate. Facts have proven that 36 of the 38 climate models and the claims of rising global temperatures are not reconcilable with current statistics. I'm sure you have noticed that the trendy phrase "climate change" has replaced "global warming." Why? Because Al Gore's global warming apocalypse is not true. As for "climate change," the climate has always changed – complete with extreme weather swings. Suzanne Hamner's article summarized: *"There is actual proof the US has an illegal immigrant problem through a poorly secured southern border that would allow terrorists to enter this country undetected, undocumented and unaccounted for; however, twice as much money will be appropriated to global warming which has no basis in scientifically proven fact, cannot meet the requirements for the scientific method, and scientists even admit the inaccuracy of their own models."* Ms. Hamner also makes the point that there are 35 Muslim jihadist terrorist camps in the United States that the government and mainstream media ignore.

Talk about a security threat - two Al Qaeda terrorists who admitted killing American soldiers in Iraq, were discovered living in Bowling Green, Kentucky as "war refugees." They were also living on government assistance (welfare) just like the Tsarnaev brothers (the Boston Marathon bombers). Arnold Ahlert, *Front Page Magazine* reported," *Unfortunately, these two men apparently represent the tip of a potentially deadly iceberg."* *"We are currently supporting dozens of current counter-terrorism investigations like that,"* said FBI Agent Gregory Carl, director

---

[270] The Daily Caller report quoted by Freedom Outpost, "White House Spends Half as Much on Border Security than on the Climate Change/Global Warming Scam," Suzanne Hamner, http://www.freedomoutpost.com, October 30, 2013,

of the Terrorist Explosive Device Analytical Center (TEDAC). House Committee on Homeland Security Chairman Michael McCaul (R-TX) implied that assessment was an understatement: *'I wouldn't be surprised if there were many more than that... And these are trained terrorists in the art of bomb-making that are inside the United States, and quite frankly, from a homeland security perspective, that really concerns me.'"*[271]

Brian T. Kennedy, President of the Claremont Institute, former director of the *Claremont Institute's Golden State Center* and its *National Security Project* has been and continues to warn us of the Need for National Defense. During a speech on March 4, 2014 at Hillsdale College's Allan P. Kirby, J. Center for Constitutional Studies and Citizenship, Mr. Kennedy reminded the audience of the April 16, 2013 terrorist attack at the Metcalf transmission substation near San Jose, California that disabled part of America's electrical infrastructure. The media was overwhelmed with the Boston Marathon terrorist attack which happened the day before on April 15, so little attention was given to this no-human injury attack.

Mr. Kennedy detailed the attack drawing attention to the highly skilled and organized military nature of the strike that lasted nearly an hour before police arrived. This was not a case of random vandalism. The terrorists cut underground fiber optic cables that disabled security and communications at the substation before assaulting the transformer and cooling system with high-powered rifles. Mr. Kennedy quoted John Wellinghoff, then chairman of the Federal Energy Regulatory as saying the attack was, *'the most significant incident of domestic terrorism involving [America's electrical] grid that has ever occurred.'* Obviously *it was a professional operation by skilled marksmen...with training in reconnaissance, stealth, and evasion."*[272]

Brian Kennedy's dire warning to protect the nations' electrical grid should be heeded by more than the handful of bipartisan Senators and

---

[271] "Homeland Insecurity: Al Qaeda 'Refugees' on Welfare," Arnold Ahlert, *Front Page Magazine*, http://www.frontpagemag.com, November 21, 2013

[272] "Early Warning: The Continuing Need for National Defense," Brian T. Kennedy march 4, 2014 speech at Hillsdale College's Allan P. Kirby, Jr. Center for Constitutional Studies and Citizenship in Washington, D.C. published in *Imprimis*, Vol. 43, No 3, March 2014

Representatives already recognizing, *"that defending America's electrical grid is an urgent priority…Given the potentially devastating consequence of failing to defend our sophisticated but vulnerable electrical grid, citizens might well wonder how it is that our government, which doesn't bat an eye at spending billions of dollars on the most frivolous and wasteful projects, fails year after year to do so."* These attackers have never been identified and are walking freely somewhere in America.

As the DHS turns a blind eye to illegal aliens now mandated by the White House to be called "undocumented Workers" flowing into our country, it is watching the TEA Party very carefully. I wonder why. There has never been a problem at TEA Party events, protests and rallies. Unlike the "Occupy" groups sit-ins complete with drugs, sex and crime, TEA Party events are lawful, respectful, non-violent and non-disruptive. During the May 2013 TEA Party-led rallies held across the country to protest the IRS' unfair targeting of conservative groups, armed DHS agents and vehicles were in attendance. Instead of tracking illegals, drug smugglers and potential terrorists, the DHS made a show of force at peaceful citizen group rallies in Missouri, Florida, California, Illinois and Indiana. The Los Angeles rally must have been a severe threat since DHS even had a helicopter there. Sadly, it appears that the government considers senior Americans, young American couples with children, and American disabled veterans peacefully congregating to raise a unified voice, more of a danger than illegal aliens and random free-roaming Islamic terrorists actually plotting to do us harm.

That is quite disturbing and brings to light the fact that the DHS is expanding its authority over local and state police departments. The Department of Homeland Security is looking like a "civilian military force," complete with military type vehicles and helicopters and military-style training. The department is purchasing millions of dollars of weapons and bullets. A civilian military force is not necessary for the protection of Americans from <u>outside</u> attacks. We have a superb professional military and every state has a standing National Guard for that. It is unnerving and I can see why more and more people feel that the government seems to be preparing for action against certain Americans – American citizens who refuse to march in lock-step with a lawless administration. Examples of this are growing all around the country at an alarming rate.

Why is the federal government quietly arming its civilian agencies while at the same time it is desperately trying to make it unlawful for citizens to have guns as guaranteed by the 2nd Amendment? Again, does "Big Brother" sound familiar?

- By February 2014 the **Department of Homeland Security (DHS)** had purchased over 2 billion bullets supposedly as practice rounds, claiming a big money savings to buy in bulk. Bullet purchases include:
  - Hollow point bullets that penetrate and fragment causing maximum damage to the body. They are used to kill – not stop people or for target practice.
  - Hornady .308 Winchester 168gr A-MAX TAP ammunition also known as "Zombie Hunter" bullets because they are for "deadly long range" firing. This ammo is used by hunters and snipers. It is not used for target practice.
- **The Internal Revenue Service (IRS)** responsible for the enforcement and collection of taxes for Obamacare has purchased firearms and ammunition.
- **The Environmental Protection Agency (EPA)** has its own police force complete with swat teams, armored vehicles and a variety of weapons and ammunition. The EPA has proven beyond a doubt that it is working hard to be the top citizen intimidation force in the country. Any agency that can remove an entire Wyoming city and give it to an Indian Reservation is pretty intimidating already. (See Part I-Government Agencies-EPA)
- **The Social Security Administration (SSA)** purchased 174,000 hollow point bullets for use at 41 locations across the country.[273]

---

[273] "Look What Other Federal Agencies Have Ordered Huge Amounts of Ammunition," Tim Brown, Freedom Outpost, http://www.freedomoutpost.com, August 15,2012

- **The Department of Education** has been purchasing firearms and ammunition since 2001, yet schools are "gun-free" zones and easy targets for terrorists.
- **The Department of Health and Human Services (DHHS)** responsible for the operation of the Affordable Care Act (Obamacare) has received firearms and ammunition.
- **The National Oceanic and Atmospheric Administration (NOAA)** purchased over a hundred thousand rounds from 2012 to 2014. What could the "weather" agency possibly need guns and ammunition for?
- **The United States Postal Service (USPS)** began soliciting firearms and ammunition suppliers in January 2014. The phrase "going postal" will likely have expanded meaning in the near future.

We are led to believe that the government is acting on our behalf and in our best interest but facts prove otherwise. Who is going to protect us from the growing number of federal employees with weapons? I can't imagine any government "oversight" system that could adequately monitor armed government workers considering that government agencies can't even keep track of employee credit cards. A good example of government and bureaucrat-controlled agency ineptness is the U.S. Park Police, the law enforcement agency that protects our National Monuments as well as the National Mall in Washington D.C. The Department of the Interior general inspector's office audited the Park Police and reported that the U.S. Park Police *"lost track of a huge supply of handguns, rifles and shotguns...We found credible evidence of conditions that would allow for theft and misuse of firearms, and the ability to conceal the fact if weapons were missing."*[274] The Park Police could not determine how many weapons were missing since they did not even know how many weapons they had. They did not have a policy or investigation procedure for missing weapons, and there was no firearms management at all! Keep in mind that this is the same police force

---

[274] "US Park Police lost track of huge supply of weapons, report says," published by Fox News.com with Associated Press contribution, http://www.foxnews.com, June 28, 2013

ordered to keep elderly veterans away from their WWII Monument during the government partial-shutdown in October 2013 while at the same time allowing illegal aliens to protest on the National Mall. Based on the lack of accountability promoted by the current administration, it is doubtful that anyone will be held responsible for this gross neglect.

Firearms and bullets are just the tip of the iceberg. Aside from small arms, the Department of Homeland Security is also equipped with serious weapons of war and is arming police forces around the country. Since the United States walked out on Iraq and is throwing Afghanistan to the wolves, the Defense Department is dispensing military equipment to law enforcement agencies at no cost under the **national military surplus program.**

So far, police departments around the country have received 165 MRAPS *(mine-resistant ambush-protected vehicles).* MRAPS are large armored military vehicles with gun turrets and bullet-proof glass. These vehicles are for war, not cruising down Main Street or serving warrants. *"Our decision to occupy Iraq seems to have morphed into a decision to have our police occupy our country."*[275]

Wouldn't it have made more sense to give vehicles like these to State National Guard units since they are the heavy-equipment forces activated to respond to disasters? But then again after reading what some of the National Guard units are training for, that may not be a good idea either. Jesse Hathaway of Media Trackers confirmed details of the Ohio National Guard 52nd Civil Support Team's training drill *"of a mock disaster where Second Amendment supporters with "anti-government" opinions were portrayed as domestic terrorists."*[276] In this training scenario, the Guard Unit was responding to *"a plot from local school district employees to use biological weapons in order to advance their beliefs about protecting Gun Rights and Second Amendment rights... junior high school employees poisoned school lunches with mustard gas, acting on orders from white-nationalist leader William Pierce."* As unbelievable as that is, the Portsmouth, Ohio police chief said that

---

[275] "Military Tools for Occupying Iraq Given to Police to Help Them Control U.S.," Political Outcast, http://www.political outcast.com, December 2, 2013

[276] "Ohio National Guard Training Envisions Right-Wing Terrorism," Jesse Hathaway, Media Trackers, http://www.mediatrackersd.org, February 10, 2014

the drill accurately represented "the reality of the world we live in." Seriously? In my world, reality is the fact that Islamists have established armed training colonies around the U.S. preparing for the formal call to jihad; Illegal aliens are roaming the country unmolested; warring gangs are ripping inner cities apart; and the government is becoming more and more oppressive toward American citizens. Just as Tea Party supporters and Christians are not threats, as the Administration wants you to believe, Second Amendment advocates are not "domestic terrorists" either.

I never would have guessed that the state of Utah was a potential war zone. As reported by the *Salt Lake City Tribune*, police in Utah have already received an MRAP, 4 grenade launchers, over 1,200 rifles, 45-caliber pistols, magazines, and weapon accessories valued at $2.8 million from the Defense Department. Unless Utah needs to protect itself from a state of Nevada invasion, or it plans to invade Idaho, why do the Utah police need such lethal military equipment?

South Carolina did not qualify for grenade launchers, but the city of Columbia did receive a 50-calliber machine gun ready MRAP vehicle. The Columbia Police Department said the vehicle will *"help protect SWAT team officers and the general public during dangerous confrontations. It's bulletproof, armored, and, as the name suggests, can even resist landmine explosions."* [277] Joshua Cook, author of the article, "SC Police Department Gets UN Blue Armored Vehicle that is Land Mine & IED Resistant," brought up a really good point. *"The question of course, is why a civilian police force needs or should have a military grade armored and arm-able vehicle. Such a 'tool' makes the government much, much more physically powerful than American citizens, increasing the risk of abuse, and the damage to civilians when that abuse occurs...Columbia's obtaining a MRAP is part of a wave of increasing police militarization. This wave occurs at a time in which violent crime rates have been steadily dropping for years, but at a time when political tension, dissatisfaction with the government, and attention to political and police abuse are at a high point."* Why are American civilian police departments being

---

[277] "SC Police Department Gets UN Blue Armored Vehicle that is Land Mine & IED Resistant," Joshua Cook, Freedom Outpost, http://www.freedomoutpost.com, November 13, 2013

armed with military resources including automatic weapons, MRAP vehicles, and unmanned drones when it is not for securing the border or to protect Americans from the criminal element of illegals? These weapons are poised against American citizens in their own country.

President Obama is considering gifting police departments with an additional 13,000 armored vehicles that the Pentagon won't need any more because the defense budget has been decimated. Since our military will soon be undermanned and underpowered, maybe he can call up and deploy random police departments to respond to an overseas crisis. Just a thought!

The president himself might have the answer. In 2008 President Obama said, **"We cannot continue to rely only on our military in order to achieve the national security objectives we've set. We've got to have a civilian national security force that's just as powerful."** Whoa! A civilian national security force as powerful as the military – that is a terrifying prospect. Doesn't anyone in government see the danger?

As if all that were not alarming enough, there are "questionable" people employed in leadership positions in the Department of Homeland Security (DHS) and other federal agencies and departments with access to confidential and sensitive information. Mohhamed Elibiary, DHS Advisory Council Member and key player in DHS policy is just one of these problematic people. For instance, when asked for "one" example of an Islamic country where non-Muslims are treated equally, Mohamed Elibiary responded, *"America, and yes I do consider the United States of America an Islamic country with an Islamically compliant constitution."*[278] Elibiary claims the Muslim Brotherhood (the Granddaddy of organized terrorism) is no threat to the U.S. He also compares "right-wing" Christians to the Muslim Brotherhood. How insulting is that?

More than insulting, villainous even, is the fact that the Department of Homeland Security promotes that image. DHS is on a mission to portray American Christians, Conservatives, and supporters of the U.S. Constitution as radical right-wing extremists thereby making them the real threat to our national security. Charles C. Johnson, *The Daily*

---

[278] "DHS Advisor Tweets: America an Islamic Country," Adam Kredo, The Washington Free Beacon, http://freebeacon.com, November 1, 2013

Caller, posted the DHS publication, *"Countering Violent Extremism Dos and Dont's."*[279] Here are a few excerpts guaranteed to raise your blood pressure:

- 2009 memo: DHS Office of Intelligence and Analysis 2009 Rightwing Extremism: *"Current Economic and Political Climate Fueling Resurgence in Radicalization and Recruitment,"* warning of the dangers posed by pro-life advocates, critics of same-sex marriage and groups concerned with abiding by the U.S. Constitution, among others.
- 2011 memo: DHS Office of Civil Rights and Civil Liberties notifies local and national law enforcement officials that it is Obama administration policy to consider specifically Islamic criticism of the American system of government legitimate.
  - The National Counterterrorism Center advises *"Trainers who equate the desire for Sharia Law with criminal activity violate basic tenets of the First Amendment."*
  - Discounting Justice Department evidence to the contrary, the DHS warned law enforcement against the *"conspiracy theory"* that many mainstream Muslim organizations have ties to, or are fronts for terrorist and Islamic political organizations whose desire is to establish Sharia law in America. The Justice Department has proven they do.

I read the two memos a few times, getting angrier each time. We have a big problem here when the very law enforcement and security agencies responsible for our national safety and security are <u>mandated to appease Muslims while demonizing Americans</u> who are any combination of: Conservative, Christian, pro-life, pro-traditional marriage, and pro-Constitutional law. If the government can totally transform traditional American values into terrorist threats while elevating Islam and its

---

[279] "Homeland Security guidelines advise deference to pro-Sharia Muslim supremacists," Charles C. Johnson, The Daily Caller, http://dailycaller.com, May 17, 2013

Sharia law to "protected" prominence, our nation will be lost. We are becoming foreigners in our native land - God help us all.

For the record and to save the NSA some time, I am Christian, conservative, pro-life, pro-traditional marriage, pro-Constitution, and pro-second amendment. I am all of these things. I also work, pay taxes, support a family, question the government (a right guaranteed by the First Amendment), respect all people regardless of race, religion, sexual preference or opinion, and promote capitalism as the antidote for poverty. I believe in moral absolutes. "Good," "evil," "right," and "wrong" are not optional concepts - they are real. I value the rule of law - divine and common; and I expect honesty and ethical behavior especially from elected leaders, public servants, teachers, and the clergy. I am not a racist, an Islamophobe, or a homophobe. And, I am not a right-wing extremist, a threat to anyone, yet alone a threat to the security of this country. As a matter of fact, I am just one of a majority of Americans from all walks of life who will no longer remain silent as our constitutional rights are blatantly being "stolen."

Robert Spencer is an expert on Islamic terrorism and has been warning us of the threat for years. He has published numerous books on the subject, provides volumes of information on his website, "Jihad Watch," and writes for "Front Page Magazine" (www.frontpagemag. com). A November 1, 2013 article published in "Front Page Magazine" confirms that Elibiary has access to the *Homeland Security State and Local Intelligence Communities of Interest* database containing intelligence reports for law enforcement agencies. I find that quite alarming. Elibiary was also a speaker at the 2004 conference paying tribute to the Ayatollah Khomeini, the "great Iranian visionary." How and why is this man a part of the agency responsible for our protection? And, scarier yet, how many more Elibiary's are there working for other federal agencies and departments?

The National Security Agency (NSA)   *www.nsa.org*

The National Security Agency is an interesting entity. The purpose of the NSA is to collect intelligence information, protect national security systems, and provide "critical strategic and tactical information." The agency's mission statement includes the paragraph: *"The Information Assurance mission confronts the formidable challenge of preventing foreign adversaries from gaining access to sensitive or classified national security information. The Signals Intelligence mission collects, processes, and disseminates intelligence information from foreign signals for intelligence and counterintelligence purposes and to support military operations. The agency also enables Network Warfare operations to defeat terrorists and their organizations at home and abroad, consistent with U.S. laws and the protection of privacy and civil liberties."*

The last line, *" consistent with U.S. laws and the protection of privacy and civil liberties,"* caught my attention because we learned in 2013 when classified information was released to the press by NSA contract worker Edward Snowden how the NSA was stepping all over our civil liberties by spying on us. President Bush's 2008 executive order number 12333 was enacted to implement 9/11 Commission recommendations and "maintain or strengthen privacy and civil liberties protections." I did not see a reference to President Obama's 2011 successful attempt to have those restrictions reversed. As Ellen Nakashima wrote in the Washington Post, *"The Obama administration secretly won permission from a surveillance court in 2011 to reverse restrictions on the National Security Agency's use of intercepted phone calls and e-mails, permitting the agency to search deliberately for Americans' communications in its massive databases, according to interviews with government officials and recently declassified material...The enlarged authority is part of a fundamental shift in the government's approach to surveillance: collecting first, and protecting Americans' privacy later."*[280]

The NSA has to walk a very thin line. On one hand it is disquieting to know that they can easily spy on us. On the other hand they have a tremendous responsibility to keep us safe from terrorism in the U.S. How do you possibly balance privacy and safety on such a massive scale? The NSA confirmed they record phone conservations but their sole focus is terrorism. They contend that the agency only scrutinizes

---

[280] "Obama administration had restrictions on NSA reversed in 2011," Ellen Nakashima, *The Washington Post*, http://www.washingtonpost.com, September 7, 2013

phone numbers and records with links to an investigation. The NSA is being criticized for possible spying without probable cause to which they counter that they do not have the time or manpower to casually go through random phone records without cause. The administration has recently instituted additional regulations to ensure citizen privacy but that will inhibit investigations costing the agency valuable time and resources. What will happen if an undetected attack occurs? Everyone will be shocked and the National Security Agency will be blamed, criticized and investigated for not preventing it. It's a "catch-22" for the NSA.

The National Security Agency has an enormous and continually growing database of information on Americans. The Department of Homeland Security also has a very large database of information. These two agencies can instantly access data on just about every American citizen in the country. Now add the Affordable Care Act/Obamacare Marketplace database (which is as secure as a broken window), the IRS databases, and the soon to be implemented Immigration database to create one expansive and exploitable source for all your private, business, medical and personal information that the government will keep safe and secure. Top officials and administrator's information will be protected, but our data can and will be stolen, manipulated and exploited by any bureaucrat with access. Under the guise of "keeping us safe" the government has the world's largest data surveillance system.

The federal government has an insatiable hunger for our personal information. CNET News reported that *"The U.S. government has demanded that major internet companies divulge users' stored passwords... which represent an escalation in surveillance techniques that has not previously been disclosed."*[281]

I am not feeling any safer as the government increasingly militarizes civilian law enforcement and security. Federalized Police departments with armored vehicles, sniper rifles, automatic weapons, and grenade launchers given the authority to swab our DNA, allowed unwarranted search and seizure raids, and allowed to monitor our personal lives does

---

[281] "Feds tell web firms to turn over user account passwords," Declan Mccullagh, CNET News, http://www.news.cnet.com, July 25, 2013

not a safer country make. Mistakes unintentional or not always happen. Data breeches do and will continue to occur. No, we are no safer at all.

President Obama orchestrated NSA's expanded authority to spy on Americans just as they spy on foreign officials but when this scandal came to light, the President told America that he was unaware of what was going on. The road up "Denial Mountain" is getting steeper and slipperier. We can add the NSA denial of knowledge to all the other scandals President Obama said he didn't know about; Fast and Furious, the IRS targeting of Conservative groups, spying on journalists, the NSA spying and wire-tapping phone conversations of foreign leaders and American citizens, the White House and State Department's roles in the Benghazi tragedy, and most currently the fact that millions of people have and will continue to lose their existing health care insurance under the Affordable Care Act. It seems Representative Joe Wilson was right after all.

In an effort to prevent another "Snowden" by ferreting out "untrustworthy" federal workers, our security agencies collected and shared "personal" information on thousands of Americans including Americans with no direct ties to the government at all. A list of 4,904 people and their personal information was dispensed to nearly 30 federal agencies including the IRS, the CIA, the NSA and even the FDA (Food and drug administration). These non-government people with no access to government information on the list included: firefighters, police officers, attorneys, employees of Rite Aid, employees of Paramount Pictures, the Red Cross, Georgetown University, and even a psychologist and a cancer researcher.[282] The only common thread between these people was that they had visited a website or purchased a book on how to pass a lie-detector test.

What about the highest-level government officials and employees leaking information all over the place? Vice President Biden and former CIA Director Panetta leaked classified Special Operations information on Navy SEAL Team 6 resulting in some Team member deaths. Between December 2011 and March 2012 the White House and State Department

---

[282] "Americans' personal data shared with CIA, IRS, others in security probe," Marisa Taylor, McClatchy Washington Bureau, McClatchy DC, http://www.mcclatchydc.com, November 14, 2013

(Hillary Clinton was still the Secretary of State) were complicit in providing classified information to *New York Times* chief Washington Correspondent David Sanger for a book he was writing, *"Confront and Conceal: Obama's Secret Wars and Surprising Use of American Power."* The White House and State Department gave up classified, confidential national security information to make Obama look strong against Iran during an election year.

The Freedom Watch organization has been investigating and through FOIA has obtained documents and emails that identify state department and administration officials complicit in yet another scandal. A great article by Patrick Howley published in the *Daily Caller* on October 23, 2013 identifies these people and provides a much more in depth look into corruption at the highest levels. Larry Klayman founder of Freedom Watch commented that Hillary Clinton and State Department Officials *"intimately participated in leaking highly classified national security information concerning U.S. cyber warfare capabilities and sources and methods, war plans against Iran...and other top secret information."*[283] Mr. Klayman feels these intentional leaks right before the 2012 elections were an attempt to portray the administration as tough on terrorism. He made a good point by noting that these "government" leaks are overlooked by federal authorities and the Justice Department, but non-administration leakers such as Edward Snowden (sensitive NSA information) and Bradley Manning and Julian Assange (Wikileaks) are actively pursued for prosecution by the same Justice Department.

I have a major problem with the fact that top government officials leak classified information for political gain - leaks that cost lives. It is criminal and the Justice Department just looks away. The DOJ was focused on subpoenaing Associated Press reporters' and a Fox News reporter's phone records. *Politico* featured famous investigative reporter Carl Bernstein's reaction to the AP subpoenas. Regarding President Obama's declaration of innocence – he knew nothing about the subpoenas, Bernstein said it was irrelevant if Obama specifically knew or not. *"It is known to the president of the United States that this*

---

[283] "Emails: White House, State Department coordinated with journalist on national security leaks," Patrick Howley, The Daily Caller, http://www.dailycaller. com, October 23, 2013

is the policy...To say there is no knowledge ... specifically about this in the White House is nonsense. This is a policy matter and this does go to the president... There's no reason for it beyond that which is nefarious."[284] Mr. Bernstein concluded by saying that this is dangerous and inexcusable behavior.

Government officials tell us that our personal information stored on government servers and websites is safe and secure; just as the passengers on the *Titanic* were assured that the ship was unsinkable! Increasing incidences of stolen government computers, espionage and government computers being hacked should concern every American. The epitome of hypocrisy is that the very government assuring us that our personal information is safe is itself hacking into our private accounts to access our personal information. A government that cannot "secure" its own data certainly cannot keep its citizens' data secure.

We must be vigilant with our personal on-line accounts for any signs of compromise. We have already seen banks, credit card companies, retail stores and social media sites including: Target and Neiman Marcus retailers, the SONY Corp, the New York Times, and NBC, Facebook, Microsoft Apple and Adobe hacked and customer information stolen. Unfortunately we are not able to monitor government "secure" websites where so much of our personal information is stored and stolen.

The Obamacare Health Insurance Marketplace web site is frightening. Cyber security experts have concurred that the website is not secure and can easily be hacked. The U.S. Army, the Department of Energy (DOE), the Department of Health and Human Services (DHHS) which is the department overseeing Obamacare, and others have been hacked. We will never be told the extent of the compromises or degree of the damage done. How safe are our energy resources and production facilities? What about water treatment and distribution facilities, and energy companies? Our energy and utility resources are targets. Can you imagine the chaos and crisis following a successful physical or cyber-attack?

Ironically, while the First Lady was vacationing in China singing the praises of "free speech," the President was finalizing plans to "relinquish

---

[284] "Carl Berstein rips White House over AP subpoena," Kevin Robillard, Politico, http://www.politico.com, May 14, 2013

oversight of the Internet Corporation (ICAAN) which assigns and maintains domain names and addresses for the Internet to "Global Governance." I was speechless! The United States and capitalism invented the internet. U.S. technology advanced it, maintains it, and protects it and our "freedom of speech." Now the president wants to sacrifice it on the altar of global governance (located in the United Nations chapel for anything that's not Christian or free). The United Nations is an organization that cannot manage humanitarian aid honestly. The U.N. has become one of the most corrupt organizations on the planet. One of the United Nations prized initiatives is establishing global gun control – actually American gun control since they don't seem to have a problem with jihadis having guns. The once great pillar of democracy has become the 6th pillar of Islam succumbing more and more to the OIC (Organization of Islamic Cooperation) made up of 56 Muslim states that make up the largest voting bloc at the U.N.

Muslim countries hate free speech and would love to control the internet. China doesn't like it either and they too would want control of the internet. The government of Turkey has blocked "Twitter" and tried to block "YouTube" because of recordings and postings alluding to government corruption. Turkish officials supported the bans citing national security concerns when in fact it was to prevent negative criticisms of the government. Can you picture countries like China, Russia, Libya or Saudi Arabia having any level of control over the world's internet? What is to stop the "global governance body" from censoring our free speech? Do we have to comply with foreign mandates? Our constitution says no foreign law is greater than our law and unfortunately, our laws along with our freedoms are being undermined by our own government.

Similarly, as the United States and the European Union (EU) get closer to a massive international trade agreement (like NAFTA on steroids), our commerce laws will be conditional to international trade and commerce laws. This scenario is just one more example of how important it is to support and defend our constitution. Can you imagine being subject to the whims of global governance?

That once laughable impossibility may be closer than we think. We, American citizens are literally being sold out by our own government officials and employees who have already sold their souls to the highest bidders of foreign governments and industries. James Bullard, the Federal Reserve Board President of St. Louis verbalized what so many in the government are working hard to attain. Speaking to the *Wall Street Journal* during a conference in Hong Kong, Bullard said, "*Attitudes in the U.S. are going to have to change because America will not permanently be the global leader.*"

By all indications, China has been accepted as the most probable world power that could gain financial control of America. Joel McDurmon warned us that since 2009 China has been cultivating "development zone" plans in which over $1 trillion of U.S. debt that China owns would be converted into direct equity investments - U.S. real estate, corporations and "profitable" infrastructure projects.[285] That would explain why the administration never seemed very concerned about being so deeply indebted to China. Chinese corporations are buying up American land at a frenzied pace. This is extremely troublesome. Chinese corporations are not independent like American corporations; the Communist Chinese government is involved in every aspect of Chinese business and finance. 43% of all corporate profits in China are from Chinese controlled companies. Though the government doesn't own the rest of the corporations, it still calls the shots.[286]

Chinese acquisitions in the United States of America include:

- The city of Thomasville, Alabama will "give" 40 acres of land to GD Copper USA which is a Florida-based subsidiary of Golden Dragon Copper Group as part of Alabama Governor Robert Bentley's economic development plan.
- A $620 million luxury condominium project in San Francisco
- A $1.5 billion condominium project in Oakland

---

[285] "China plans economic colonization with 'development zones' in US," Joel McFurmon, American Vision News, http://www.americanvisionnews.com, January 25, 2013

[286] "Chinese Buying Land in US Communities All Over America," Michael Snyder, Freedom Outpost, http://www.freedomoutpost.com, March 31, 2014

- Chinese purchase of Smithfield Foods included 460 large U.S. farms making them the top employer in communities across America
  - *"Smithfield Foods is the largest pork producer and processor in the world. It has facilities in 26 U.S. states and it employs tens of thousands of Americans. It directly owns 460 farms and has contracts with approximately 2,100 others. But now a Chinese company has bought it for $4.7 billion, and that means that the Chinese will now be the largest employer in dozens of rural communities all over America."*
- Chinese companies are investing in American businesses and new vehicle technology and buying property in Detroit, the U.S. automobile capital
- Sino-Michigan Properties LLC is planning to build "China City" on 200 acres of purchased land for Chinese citizens (that's Chinese citizens - not American citizens)
- A multibillion dollar giant "China City" is being planned on 600 acres of land on Yankee Lake in Sullivan County, New York. They eventually want to expand it to over 2,000 acres. I wonder how close that will be to "Islamberg," the independent Muslim city in rural New York.
- The construction of new-housing in California is on the rise and most of the buyers are Chinese.

Michael Snyder, author of the above reference article asked some very thought-provoking questions. *"So what happens when we get to the point when the Chinese government and/or Chinese citizens own 10 percent of all the real estate in the entire country...What about if we get to 20 percent or 30 percent? At what point will we be forced to admit that we have a major problem on our hands? Many of our leaders seem resigned to the fact that the future will be dominated by Communist China."*

Anyone who thinks that China is just a benign country stretching its legs in the world of economics and finance for the betterment of its people has not heard about the cyber-attacks on the U.S. or the purchases of key world ports and industries. I doubt many people have ever read what Qiao Liang and Wang Xiangsui, said in 1999. "*...If the attacking side secretly musters large amounts of capital without the enemy nation being aware of this at all and launches a sneak attack against financial markets, then after causing a financial crisis, buries a computer virus and hacker detachment in the opponent's computer system in advance, while at the same time carrying out a network attack against the enemy so that civilian electricity network, traffic dispatching network, financial transaction network, telephone communications network and mass media network are completely paralyzed, this will cause the enemy nation to fall into social panic, street riots, and a political crisis. There is finally the forceful bearing down by the army, and the military means are utilized in gradual stages until the enemy is forced to sign a dishonorable peace treaty.*"[287] Does this sound like an innocuous country?

The government is stealing our land right out from under us. Throughout the western states our federal (public) lands are being sold and given away to foreigners. The televised plight of one Nevada rancher's struggle with the federal government's Department of the Interior's Bureau of Land Management (BLM) is far more reaching than anyone could have imagined. The government has granted "grazing rights" to western ranchers for well over a hundred years but now it wants the ranchers and their ranches to disappear. Under the pretext of protecting the "desert tortoise" the government evicted rancher Cliven Bundy and his cattle from the federal grazing lands his family has used since the 19th century. When it was discovered that desert tortoises were just fine and as a matter of fact so over-abundant that the government had to eliminate some of them, the story changed. Then the claim was that Mr. Bundy owes the government over a million dollars in grazing fees, and, oh, by the way, the government can just take the land – no excuses necessary.

I do not know the legal ramifications of the situation, but what I saw on television was extremely disturbing. Armed agents and snipers with long rifles and automatic weapons surrounded the rancher and his family. They physically loaded up and took away a number of Mr. Bundy's cattle. One of Mr. Bundy's sons was Tasered. Another son was arrested for filming – documenting the government action while outside

---

[287] Unrestricted Warfare," Qiao Liang & Wang Xiangsui, 1999

of the illegally established "First Amendment Area" established by the BLM as the only area people could speak and protest. This government siege reminded me of how armed government forces stormed the Davidian Cult compound in Waco Texas during the 1990s and we all know how badly that turned out.

As news of the armed seizure spread, Americans from around the country headed to Nevada to support the Bundy family. National publicity made the BLM pause and the government decided to stop the siege most likely because there were too many witnesses. Unfortunately, this is not over and the worst is yet to come. Many mainstream news organizations broadcasted the same "talking points" that Mr. Bundy's Cattle have been grazing illegally on public lands for over 20 years. Sorry CNN, it's a lot more complicated than that simpleton explanation.

This event brought to light the U.S. government's intention to sell our federal lands outright or barter them to pay debt accumulated by the Obama administration. Solar Energy Zones could be the administration's rainbow to alternative energy utopia. The Chinese seem to share the same dream and are very interested in harvesting solar energy in the Western U.S. The takeover of American energy is being facilitated in Nevada by none other than Senator Harry Reid. Senator Reid's son attorney Rory Reid represented the Chinese firm ENN Energy Group that planned to build a multi-billion dollar solar facility near Laughlin, Nevada and also build on 9,000 acres in Clark County – coincidently where the Cliven cattle roam. Even though the Harry Reid and ENN deal seems to have been terminated in 2013, Senator Reid is still up to his neck in the Nevada land for energy program and has proven to the people of Nevada that he is not working for them.

Infowars.com published a report that" The Bureau of Land Management, whose director was Sen. Harry Reid's (D-Nev) former senior advisor, purged documents from its web site stating that the agency wants Nevada rancher Cliven Bundy's cattle off of the land his family has worked for over 140 years in order to make way for solar panel power stations...Deleted from the BLM.gov website but reposted for posterity by the *Free Republic*, the BLM document entitled 'Cattle Trespass Impacts' directly states that Bundy's cattle 'impacts' solar development...specifically the construction of 'utility-scale solar power generation facilities' on public lands." *Bizpac Review*'s article stated, *"...the feds were using the Bureau of Land Management to bully and intimidate ranchers like Bundy, pushing them off public lands in order to pave the way for lucrative 'green energy' projects backed by the Communist Chinese government and linked to Nevada Senator Harry Reid..."*

The same story is playing out in New Mexico where rancher Kit Laney who owns the Diamond Bar Ranch is just one of possibly thousands of ranchers being evicted from their lands across the Southwest for trespassing cattle and violations of water rights.

Why does the federal government think it is alright to have Chinese corporations controlling U.S. energy resources? This is an extremely perilous situation. Where is the outrage? Where are our elected officials? Is there anyone in D.C. not involved in deceit, theft, and the sale of America for personal gain? We really need some honest people in Washington and we need them immediately.

The Chinese in general are wonderful people who work very hard, take pride in success, contribute to American business and culture, and are truly happy in the United States. My problem is not with the Chinese people. I admire and cherish my Chinese friends and enjoy their company immensely. My problem is with the corrupt all-controlling Communist Chinese government. China is an aggressor nation and a documented human rights violator. Don't ever forget that while Chinese government officials are smiling in photo ops with our government officials, they neither consider us a friend nor a business partner. Whatever they do they have China's interests in mind. Washington needs to take a lesson in securing national interests.

Things are looking grim on the home front. Our national security and our individual freedoms are fading away like the color on an old postcard while many Americans are just sitting back watching reality TV shows and letting it all happen.

Peace through Strength: Foreign Policy
Is a Domestic Security Issue

Do you remember prior to the Obama presidency when some politicians and most liberals were insisting that American foreign policy was responsible for the rise in terrorism and the attacks on 9/11? Their mantra was that foreign countries did not like us and that our arrogant "super-power" attitude was despised around the world. That was back in the day when countries, ally or foe knew we meant what was said, we supported our allies, we stood up to enemies, and we did not hesitate to respond to threats. Countries like Israel and Poland could count on us. When Muammar Gaddafi of Libya saw the U.S. response in Afghanistan in 2001 and Iraq in 2003, he turned over his weapons of mass destruction fearing U.S. action against him. There were no negotiations, useless sanctions or empty threats. His impression alone of a "strong and powerful" United States of America is what compelled him to acquiesce. That is a perfect example of *peace through strength.*

Since 2009 the President and his administration have traveled the globe trying to turn enemies into friends by proclaiming that hey, the United States is no better than any other country. Unfortunately, their "Reset" policies have only turned friends into enemies and emboldened previously existing enemies. The President's world-wide "apology tours" to apologize to foreign countries for things the United States of America did in the past, his bowing to foreign kings, and my favorite, extolling the virtues of Islam in a speech in Cairo, Egypt with Muslim Brotherhood officials in attendance and declaring to the world that the U.S. is not a Christian nation, haven't worked out so well. As a matter of fact President Obama's foreign policy has been a total disaster.

Our traditional allies understandably do not trust us and we are financially indebted to China. The President literally threw in the towel on Iraq and Afghanistan after so much was sacrificed and then boldly supported the Muslim Brotherhood government in Egypt. The celebrated "Arab Spring" uprisings have destabilized the Middle East, empowered terrorist groups, and have caused the deaths of tens of thousands of people including four Americans murdered at the U.S. Consulate building in Benghazi, Libya. President Obama's infamous "red line" threat to Syria accompanied by pompous empty threats and his agreement to the Russian nuclear treaty with Iran literally handed Russia control of the Middle East. Obama's ridiculous tough talk and hollow threats against Russia that no country took seriously amounted to daring Putin to go all the way through Ukraine. His meaningless sanctions against a handful of wealthy Russians is a total embarrassment and is also a signal to China that we are not going to do anything if they decide to go after the islands they have targeted for decades. In 1952 China thought the U.S. was weak when it supported North Korea. This time it is correct that the United States is weak and will not act, and Iran and North Korea are laughing all the way to the bank knowing the U.S. won't do anything to stop their nuclear ambitions. In five years we have gone from the world's "Superpower" to the world's laughing stock.

Foreign Policy: The UN vs. the U.S.

I grew up under the illusion that the United Nations was a benevolent organization of countries working together for peaceful solutions and the betterment of all mankind. Imagine my surprise upon learning that the UN is now nothing more than a cesspool of corruption and politics.

The UN was established in 1945 with 51 member states. All were allies during the Second World War which had just ended. These were mostly European and Commonwealth countries and the nations of the Americas. The members considered themselves democratic "peace loving" nations bound together to prevent future aggression and for humanitarian purposes. The intergovernmental organization now is comprised of 193 member states claiming commitment to maintaining international peace and security, promoting human rights, fostering social and economic development, protecting the environment, and providing humanitarian aid in cases of famine, natural disaster, and armed conflict. As membership opened to more and more countries, the republic and democratic countries like the U.S. and its allies became the minority. Now Communist and Islamic countries have the majority of control.

When the non-democratic countries gained majority power, the UN began its "selective intervention" into internal and regional conflicts as well as "selective" human rights, "selective" speech and "selective" gun control. For instance:

- The UN considers lawful gun ownership by U.S. citizens a violation of human rights while at the same time doesn't have a problem with the member countries whose laws allow and promote the abuse and execution of women and even children.
- The UN condemns Americans opposed to illegal immigration and considers the deportation of illegal "immigrants" a human rights violation. The UN has no problem with the stringent immigration policies of other countries.
- The UN is openly hostile to Israel while siding with the Palestinians even though the Palestinians are bombing and firing rockets into Israel on a near-daily basis.
- The UN wants Christian speech restricted since it is offensive to Muslims but is silent as Muslims massacre Christians across the Middle East. I find the UN offensive.
- The UN wants "rich" Western countries especially the United States to increase financial support for worldwide programs without question even though the US already carries the bulk of the world's financial humanitarian aid and military intervention

expenses. At the same time select countries including wealthy Arab countries freely pick and choose what countries or areas they will support.

The list is endless. The U.S. and Israel are favorite targets at the United Nations where just about anything non-democratic, non-Jewish and non-Christian is protected and promoted. Condemning Israel for anything and everything has become a regularly scheduled event. I ask why we are still a member and financially support such a corrupt and morally bankrupt organization that is <u>nothing</u> like the organization that was founded in 1945?

Make no mistake about it, the United Nations is undermining our sovereignty and our current administration is making it easy for them to do so. UNESCO – the UN Educational, Scientific and Cultural Organization is a "global partner" with our Education Secretary Arne Duncan's "Common Core" education reform program that focuses on global society not Free American Society. The UN would like nothing more than to absorb our military forces into the UN Global Forces thereby ensuring no patriotic allegiance to the United States. For the betterment of mankind the UN is constantly pushing for the U.S. to pay "global taxes," and we should pay a lot. If you are not familiar with the United Nation's Agenda 21, know this, it is real and it is here. It is insidiously gnawing away at our private property rights, ownership and land use through environmental protection initiatives, regulations and taxes, levied by our own government to comply with the U.N. Agenda 21 agreement our President very quietly entered into.

There are two books I highly recommend whose authors take a candid look at the United Nations, presenting clear insight into the organization, people, issues, and the total dysfunction. I guarantee you two things after reading about this "mysterious and symbolic" icon anchored in New York City. One, you will have a better understanding of why the world is such a mess, and two, you will be quite angry.

- **The U.N. Exposed: How the United Nations Sabotages America's Security and Fails the World** by Eric Shawn, NY: Sentinel/Penguin Group Publishing, 2006

- □ Reporter Eric Shawn explains how the U.N. has failed its "original mission" and reveals "disturbing" aspects of the U.N. that are not reported by the media
- □ Author Introduction: *"I am disgusted by the fact that the altruistic efforts of so many U.N. staff members are undercut by the greed, corruption and ineptitude of the bureaucracy they serve..."*

- **Tower of Babble: How the United Nations Has Fueled Global Chaos** by Dore Gold, NY: Crown Forum, 2004
  - □ Dore Gold, former Ambassador to the United Nations has eye-witness knowledge of the organizational corruption and failures of the U.N.
  - □ Mr. Gold presents evidence that the U.N. turns a blind eye to mass murders, actually encourages terrorists, protects dictators and does not protect world security which was its primary purpose.

So What Exactly is the current United States Foreign Policy? I don't know – it keeps changing.

I went to the White House website (http://www.whitehouse.gov/issues/foreign-policy) looking for President Obama's foreign policies. The White House has the world neatly divided into regions and each region has a "policy." I did not see any official policy documents but snippets from Presidential speeches were dispersed between presidential photos, travel schedules, administrative officials' tweets, and "happy good news" articles about the President's endeavors. Links were provided so you could read the entire speech if so desired. Unfortunately it seems that vague, generalized, and often inaccurate "speech quotes" define our foreign policy. It's no wonder the world is in such chaos. The United States has replaced stalwart leadership and decisiveness with negotiating, submissiveness and appeasement.

For instance, President Obama's speech at the Palacio de La Moneda

Cultural Center in Santiago, Chile on March 21, 2011 defines our foreign policy in "The Americas" Region:

The President spoke of all North, Central and South American countries as a single America with common histories, heritages, interests and values. He speaks as if our Constitution is like the others when it clearly is not regarding equality and rights. Then he said, *"We're people of faith who must remember that all of us -- especially the most fortunate among us -- must do our part, especially for the least among us... We're citizens who know that ensuring that democracies deliver for our people must be the work of all...We are all Americans."*

What I take from that is we Americans (U.S. Americans) must pay our "fair share" throughout all the Americas and our fair share is always a lot more than anyone else's. I can't figure out what he meant by "our common history" and "our common heritage." We have nothing in common with Central and South America, and our (Republic) is not and never was like any of the other so called democracies which are in actuality Socialist and Communist governments.

President Obama's *New Strategy* for Afghanistan and Pakistan, March 27, 2009: *"We are in Afghanistan to confront a common enemy that threatens the United States, our friends and allies, and the people of Afghanistan and Pakistan who have suffered the most at the hands of violent extremists."* What? We were in Afghanistan to confront a common enemy, but we have since abandoned that country. As for Pakistan, they are part of the overall terrorism problem.

President Obama's take on the Middle East and Northern Africa were shared in a State Department speech on May 19, 2011. Referencing his 2009 Cairo, Egypt speech he claims to have developed U.S., Middle East and African assignation through mutual respect and interests. There was no mention of the Islamic countries accepting our values and way of life, but he spoke of this historic opportunity to show them that the United States "welcomes change that advances self-determination and opportunity whatever the perils. *"But after decades of accepting the world as it is in the region, we have a chance to pursue the world as it should be."*

"Perils" accompanying "this moment of promise" was an understatement. Presidential encouragement of the "Arab Spring" has cost the United States its most reliable ally in the region – Egypt. The celebrated Arab Spring has also been directly responsible for the deaths of tens of thousands of people struggling just to survive and couldn't care less about democracy.

President Obama's general foreign policy speech before the United Nations General Assembly on September 23, 2009 in which he touted America's shared destiny obviously was our nation's white flag of surrender to the global community: *"No one nation can or should try to dominate another nation. No world order that elevates one nation or group of people over another will succeed. No balance of power among nations will hold. The traditional divisions between nations of the South and the North make no sense in an interconnected world; nor do alignments of nations rooted in the cleavages of a long-gone Cold War."*

Whatever red lines are drawn by the President as well as sanctions instituted, condemnations issued, and threats of *"there will be consequences"* made, they are but a joke to all other nations. Regrettably, journalist Ronn Torossian is correct in saying: **"The Only World Leader Who Fears American Power Is Obama."**[288] No matter how the administration spins an issue they can't change the facts; and one fact is the administration's foreign policy is an abysmal failure.

The ideological Left cannot accept the historically proven fact that people and societies are different and therefore have different value systems, languages, religions and customs. Progressives want all people and countries to be on the same "level playing field" and then all would get along and work together for a better world. They seriously cannot figure out that what they consider normal or acceptable, is appalling to another culture. **World peace cannot be legislated no matter how much you hope for it and how hard you try.** Examples are abundant. So many countries including Iran, North Korea and pretty much the entire Middle East and Northern Africa thrive on tyranny, violence, deceit and brutality. No combination of money, technology, gifting, sweet-talk, concessions, appeasement, and negotiations will buy permanent peace.

---

[288] "The Only World Leader Who Fears American Power Is Obama," Ronn Torossian, posted on *Front Page Magazine*, http://www.frontpage mag. com, March 3, 2014

> **"It is fatal to enter any war without the will to win it."**
>
> —Gen. Douglass MacArthur 1952

The U.S. altruistically entered Afghanistan and Iraq to weed out terrorists and murderous regimes. Both were successful operations. Unfortunately the peacekeeping strategy was flawed and the perceived "need" to rebuild both countries and save the people by installing a democratic infrastructure was an impossible dream. Five years ago a new strategy was implemented to return control of the countries to their new governments, which are just as corrupt as the old ones were, and withdraw American troops. Withdrawal has turned into abandonment. The people that helped our forces topple the regimes and the most abused and at risk have been fed to the wolves. The Taliban are again controlling Afghanistan and Al Qaeda is being replaced by an even more demonic terrorist group – ISIS in Iraq. Terrorists, better equipped and funded than ever before are taking over the Middle East and Northern Africa. President Obama sacrificed a lot of blood and treasure in Iraq and Afghanistan implementing the same disastrous presidentially-directed strategy that President Johnson mandated during the Vietnam War. *"... On the battlefield itself, the Army was unbeatable. In engagement after engagement the forces of the Viet Cong and of the North Vietnamese were thrown back with terrible losses. Yet, in the end, it was North Vietnam, not the United States that emerged victorious."*[289]

As the U.S. left Iraq smoldering, Iraq's focus turned to rebuilding their once-again terrorist controlled state into a caliphate; one large and powerful Islamic nation created from numerous independent Arab countries. President Karzai of Afghanistan is probably looking for a country to retire to since his corrupt government cannot exist after the U.S. is gone and Afghanistan will once again return to the Dark Ages. After President Obama's successful destruction of Iraq and Afghanistan, his attention swung over to Egypt and the Arab Spring. As a U.S. Senator, Obama didn't want anything to do with toppling Saddam Hussein's

---

[289] "Tactical Victory, Strategic Defeat," Col. Harry Summers, *"Don't Tread on Me,"* H.W. Crocker, 2006

regime in Iraq, but he thoroughly supported toppling Egyptian president and our stable ally, Hosni Mubarek. He supported and celebrated the Muslim Brotherhood's takeover of the country. The only good thing to come out of that ugly situation was that the Egyptian military took the country back from the Muslim Brotherhood. The Egyptian military will restore order. Support of the Muslim Brotherhood by the president of the United States should have been alarming to every American. And as usual, the media virtually ignored the "dark" side of the Muslim Brotherhood and the fact that they are responsible for the deaths of thousands of Egyptians.

From Egypt the U.S. keenly followed the Arab Spring to Libya and the sudden critical necessity to overthrow Libyan President Muammar Gaddafi. The attainment of Libyan weapons of mass destruction and military weapons by terrorist groups seemed less of a concern to the administration than ensuring Gaddafi was destroyed by the rebels. A Libyan uprising was such an important issue for the administration that President Obama ordered military intervention without Congressional consent. It is interesting that at the time of his death, Gaddafi was ready to leave Libya but no one at the State Department would take that "3AM call" which all but guaranteed his death. After successfully destabilizing Libya, the U.S. State Department and the CIA began covert operations in Libya leading directly to the terrorist murders of U.S. Ambassador Chris Stevens and three other Americans in Benghazi. What is finally coming to light is that the Benghazi consulate was part of the covert plan to get Libyan weapons out of the country to Turkey, and from there to Syria and into the hands of the terrorist-supported Syrian rebels. The President, Secretary of State Clinton and UN Ambassador Rice all purposely lied to the American people that the attack was by a mob outraged over a stupid Muslim-insulting movie that no one had ever heard of. It may seem that the administration has successfully covered up the murders and the covert operations, but no matter how hard President Obama and Hillary Clinton wish and hope and try to hide this incident away, the American people will not forget Benghazi.

The media went silent when Libya was quickly devoured by Al Qaeda and other jihadists after the U.S. "pulled out." Leaving Libya in chaos and under terrorist control, our attention turned to Syria where all of a sudden it became "mission critical" to depose Syrian President Bashar al-Assad. It is interesting that the administration was ready for military intervention in Syria when President Assad crossed President Obama's "red-line" by using chemical weapons on his own people. There is still debate on that assumption since it is inconclusive whether the Syrian military or the rebels killed those civilians. The rebels we were supporting may have been responsible for the sarin gas deaths since they were definitely responsible for thousands of other civilian murders. Either way it put President Obama in an inconvenient situation. U.S. military intervention now would make the administration look foolish. This is when President Vladimir Putin of Russia stepped in with a solution for the Syrian problem. Putin put together a chemical warfare treaty in which Syria agreed to the destruction of its chemical weapons under United Nations supervision.

It was a ridiculous treaty. Why would Russia, an ally of al-Assad take America's interests under wing and suddenly be interested is brokering peace? Well, Russia now has a tremendous amount of influence not just in Syria but also with our traditional ally Egypt. Russian stock in the Middle East skyrocketed while U.S. presence and influence has all but disappeared.

Seymour M. Hersh wrote an extremely enlightening and comprehensive piece on the confusing series of events relating to President Obama's dealings with Turkey's Prime Minister Recep Tayyip Erdoğan and arming the Syrian rebels. The publication is "*The Red Line and the Rat Line*" published by *London Review of Books*, Vol. 36 No. 8, April 17, 2014, http.www.lrb.co.uk/v36/n08/seymour-m-hersh/the-red-line-and-the-rat-line.

Why did President Obama judge Hosni Mubarek of Egypt, Muammar Gadaffi of Libya and Bashar al-Assad of Syria monstrous humanitarian threats requiring immediate removal? I thought Kim Jong Un, the Supreme Leader of North Korea responsible for atrocities against his own people, tortuous executions of family members, and threatening nuclear attacks on neighboring countries and the U.S. would be considered a serious humanitarian threat. What about Iran? The President did not in any way support the Iranian uprising a few years ago in which numerous Iranians were killed. He considers

Hassan Rouhani the president of Iran as man he could negotiate with. Seriously? Negotiate with the country that threatens to annihilate Israel, is building nuclear weapons, has never complied with the United Nations, and supports Hamas and other terrorist groups to fight Israel and the United States. Majid Rafizadeh completely summarizes Iran in one single sentence: *"The goal of the Islamic Republic [of Iran] is to make some tactical changes to recover its economy, regain power, buy time and advance its nuclear program."*[290]

The Russian invasion of Ukraine was the next international incident fueled by a confused, indecisive, and morally bankrupt government, and I am not talking about Putin's Russian government. The U.S. had once again talked harsh, made threats, and then did nothing. The rest of the world quickly realized that President Obama was not going to do anything except talk tough. Unfortunately since our president is weak our country is also weak. Charles Krauthammer, most likely the smartest political mind in the country pointed out Obama's complacency. *"He said, any violation of Ukrainian territory is destabilizing, and that's not in Russia's interest. He is instructing Putin on what's in Russia's interest...I can assure you, Putin has calculated his own interests, and he's calculated that detaching Crimea from Ukraine and making it, essentially, a colony of Russia, is in Russia's interest – because he knows he has nothing to fear from the west, because it's not led by anybody. It used to be led by the United States."*[291]

China and Iran, both dictatorial aggressor nations love the impotence of the Obama administration. Russia's ability to casually walk-through another country while the rest of the world just watched will embolden both countries. China has been kept in check from expanding its maritime borders and intimidating Japan and the Philippines by a "strong" United States of America, but since America has turned into France, China will move militarily and Iran will terrorize the world.

Thinking about the debt we owe China makes me cringe, especially when I read what Chinese military officers like Lt. Gen. Liu Yazhou

---

[290] "Obama's Misconceptions on Iran," Majid Rafizadeh, *Front Page Magazine*, http://www.frontpagemag.com, March 7, 2014

[291] "Krauthammer on Ukraine: 'Everybody is shocked by the weakness of Obama's statement,'" Fox News "Special Report with Bret Baier," Foxnews.com, February 28, 2014

have said. *"...When a nation grows strong enough, it practices hegemony. The sole purpose of power is to pursue even greater power...Geography is destiny...when a country begins to rise, is should first set itself in an invincible position."*[292]

There has been a lot of seismic activity the past few years and I heard somewhere that they weren't all earthquakes. Some of the seismic events were Ronald Reagan, Margaret Thatcher, Winston Churchill, Franklin Roosevelt and George Washington rolling over in their graves. Not really, but quite understandable.

All the sacrifices to build a better world made during the 20th century have vaporized in a mere five years. You know things are extremely bleak when President Karzai of Afghanistan says *"We respect the decision the people of Crimea took through a recent referendum that considers Crimea as part of the Russian Federation."*[293] Fortunately for Afghanistan, Russia is re-investing in that country and offering development aid. The offensive part is that this is unfolding "in-your-face" while we, the U.S. are physically still in that country. Was that not the Russian military I watched on television in February 1989 leaving Afghanistan like a beaten puppy after nine years of an unsuccessful occupation of that stone-age country? Now the United States walks with its head down and tail between its legs.

Maybe this will wake up a few people – I sure hope so. As Europe, Asia and the Middle East crumble, Americans are sitting comfortably watching "reality" shows on television and obsessing over celebrity misbehaviors while Russia is planning to set up military bases in Latin America and Iranian warships are trolling off of the U.S. coast. In 2012 we learned that a Russian attack submarine with long-range missiles was casually touring the Gulf of Mexico right under our collective noses. It remained undetected for a few weeks. Earlier this year Yahoo news reported that a fully-armed Russian warship was docked in Havana, Cuba. Do you really think this is a good time to slash our military?

---

[292] "In the Words of Our Enemies," Jed Babbin, 2007 - Lt. Gen. Liu Yazhou statement in 2005

[293] "Afghanistan Supports Russia's Crimean Takeover, Welcomes Moscow Back Into Country," John Fund, National Review, http://www.nationalreview.com, March 24, 2014

If you want to know what Russians think about the U.S. and current events, check out Pravda, www.Pravda.ru. The editor in chief of the news outlets' Political Class section said: *"All statements of Obama, Kerry and other U.S. officials are boring and meaningless."* The editor then explained that there are two types of American politicians. *"The first one believes their own fairy tales, the rosy one about themselves and the dirty one about everyone else. The second type is the cynical one, they know that their words are not true, but say them anyway. I do not rule out that Obama belongs to the first type, but for us there is no big difference..."*[294]

The American media is complicit in covering up the truth about our President and his administration. The media was in a euphoric frenzy when President Obama made announcements such as: *He got Osama bin Laden, al-Qaeda is decimated, and the war on terrorists was virtually over.* Where is the media now? Why are they not showing us the devastating reality of what abandoning Afghanistan and Iraq has wrought? What exactly did 4,486 Americans die for? After a very successful surge, the president pulled the plug and let Afghanistan and Iraq drain back into the swamp of agony, death and despair. Former Army captain Matt Gallagher's question on Twitter hits the nail right on the head: *"Could someone smart convince me that the black flag of al-Qaeda flying over Fallujah [Iraq] isn't analogous to the fall of Saigon?"*[295]

President Obama entered office highly critical of the previous administration's foreign policy and deeply concerned about the world's collective opinion of the United States. He promised to end the wars, successfully negotiate with enemies, make the U.S. more likeable and improve our image abroad winning the respect of the world. Five years later, the world is afire.

- Victor Davis Hanson's assessment of Obama's foreign policy is frightfully accurate. *"Abroad, American policy in the Middle East is leaderless and in shambles after the Arab Spring - we've had the Syrian fiasco and bloodbath, leading from behind in Libya*

---

[294] "Obama: Boring and meaningless," Lyuba Lulko, *Pravda*, http://english.pravda.ru, February 24, 2014

[295] "U.S. Veterans despondent over al-Qaeda's resurgence in Iraq," Ernesto Londono, *The Washington Post*, http://www.washingtonpost.com, January 11, 2014

all the way to Benghazi, and the non-coup, non-junta in Egypt. This administration has managed to unite existential Shiite and Sunni enemies in a shared dislike of the United States. While Iran follows the Putin script from Syria, Israel seems ready to preempt its nuclear program, and Obama still mumbles empty "game changers" and "red line" threats of years past. We have gone from reset with Russia to Putin as the playmaker of the Middle East." [296]
Mr. Hanson pointed out that most of the Arab nations are anti-American. And, German and French leaders are still upset over Obama tapping their private communications. Japan, South Korea and Taiwan now see the U.S. as no longer a reliable friend.

- Sir Hew Strachan, advisor to the United Kingdom's Chief of the Defense and Oxford University professor assesses President Obama in his book "The Direction of War." Strachan writes, *"President Obama has been judged to be chronically incapable of conducting a coherent military strategy and has no sense of what he wants to do in the world."* [297]

- Daniel Greenfield wrote two hard-hitting articles on the current status of America. He points out that US foreign policy mirrors the United Nations agenda. *"Obama's America has turned a cold impartial face to its allies, aspiring instead to become the vessel of international organizations while assigning its morality to an international committee. American foreign policy is under international management and that transfers its decision process from D.C. to an international network of committees incapable of doing anything except worthless reports and denouncing Israel."* [298]

- In the second article, Greenfield writes: *"The collapse of the Pax Americana under Obama has freed up Russia and China to begin campaigns of territorial expansionism. Obama's failure*

---

[296] "Is Obama Still President?" Victor Davis Hanson, National Review, http://www.nationalreview.com, October 29, 2013
[297] "Obama is chronicle incapable of military strategy and clueless about he wants to do in the world according to top UK defense advisor," published in the *Daily Mail*, http://www.dailymail.co.uk, January 23, 2014
[298] "It Takes a Rogue Nation to Stop a Rogue State," Daniel Greenfield, *Front Page Magazine*, http://www.frontpagemag.com, March 4, 2014

to deter Russia in Ukraine will encourage China to use force as a solution to territorial disputes in the South China Sea...Those most immediately affected by the decline of the United States will be the Asian and European countries that outsourced their defense to the United States after WW2..." [299] Daniel surmised that the United States military will not be able to do much more than "peacekeeping missions."

Daniel Greenfield's words of warnings should be taken seriously. The U.S. needs to maintain a strong military to deter war. The U.S. should not interfere in all random local conflicts and human rights violations. The U.S. should have well-defined agreements and commitments that it can keep. The U.S. should act according to its own laws, not be bound by international law. He reminds us how England and France blindly followed the diplomatic path with Nazi Germany but Germany invaded all of Europe anyway and was well on the way to seize England before the U.S. entered the war. At the same time in America, diplomacy and sanctions on Japan contributed to an attack on Pearl Harbor on December 7, 1941.

---

[299] "What the Post-American World Will Look Like," Daniel Greenfield, *Front Page Magazine*, http://www.frontpagemag.com, March 21, 2014

ISLAM IN AMERICA

"Islam isn't in America to be equal to any other faith, but to become dominant. The Koran...should be the highest authority in America, and Islam the only accepted religion on earth."

—Omar Ahmad, 1988[300]

---

[300] Omar Ahmad - chairman of the Council on American Islamic Relations (CAIR) in California in 1988.
"Preachers of Hate: Islam and the War on America," Kenneth R. Timmerman, NY: Crown Forum, 2003

There have been innumerable measures taken in the United States since 9/11 to promote Islam as a "peaceful" religion. Political correctness has excused Muslim leaders and any criticism of Muslims no matter how factual, is deemed racist or bigoted. NEWSFLASH: Islam has not been hijacked. The Quran does not teach peace and tolerance! It does command believers (Muslims) to make war on Jews and Christians – wherever they are found. Peaceful co-existence is not an option. There is <u>no</u> "tolerance" for other faiths or people of no faith.

Two important points need to be made: (1) All Arabs are not Muslim, just as all Muslims are not Arab. (2) I am not an Islamophobe for speaking the truth about Islam. Truth is not situational and speaking factually about Islam or any other religion is not hate speech. This is not a call against all Muslims. It is a candid look at Islam and an assessment of the tenets of Islam defined by Muslims themselves that affect every Westerner as well as every non-Muslim worldwide.

We are told that radicalized (bad) Muslims have misinterpreted the Quran even though they consider themselves devout (real) Muslims following the commands of the Quran as they have for centuries. On the other hand, moderate "good" Muslims do not commit violence and murder but many of them do celebrate the deaths of infidels by the hands of "radicalized" Muslims. Muslims are not misinterpreting the Quran, non-Muslims are. Western culture's interpretation of religion based on the core fundamental concepts of a loving God, compassion, tolerance, forgiveness and salvation make it extremely difficult to understand Islamic culture.

Americans not familiar with Islam need to know a few things. Mohammad the sacred Prophet of Islam taught there is nothing holier than *jihad* (**war** - not internal struggle) and there are three options available to infidels (non-believers including Christians, Jews, Communists, and Atheists).

1. Conversion to Islam
2. Pay a tax acknowledging inferior status and subjugation under Islamic (Sharia) law
3. Death

Make no mistake, this is being taught in mainstream Islam today. As evidenced in Muslim-majority countries and communities, permanent "peaceful coexistence" is not part of their religion. Muslims who do not follow the violent commands of Mohammad are not reading a different Quran than the so called "radical" Muslims. They <u>choose</u> not to comply with the violent directives.

Islam is a theocracy - a government based solely around a deity and controlled by "clerics." There is absolutely no separation between religion and government. Islam, its ideologies, laws (Sharia) and government are one in the same. How do the U.S. government and the progressive guardians of separation of church and state reconcile that fact? How can Islam be accepted as a "religion" when by its own design it is a government? The theocracy of Islam has oppressed and brutalized millions of people and has spilled blood across the globe.

I used to buy into the myth that Islam was a peaceful religion co-existing with Christianity and Judaism. To my dismay I have learned the ugly truth about the "peaceful" religion. The quote at the beginning of this chapter, that Islam is not in America to be equal to any other religion, by Omar Ahmad, chairman of the Council on American and Islamic Relations (CAIR) is not a rare, off-the-cuff remark. It was made in 1988, years before the 1993 World Trade Center bombing and the 9/11 attacks. Ahmad's proclamation is common among countless statements made by so-called "moderate" Muslims here in the United States. You do not have to go to the Middle East to hear the rally cries of "Death to America!" And you won't hear about such things from our mainstream media.

Walid Shoebat (Palestinian-turned-Christian) agrees. *"Today, in response to what has become a mantra since September 11, that "true Islam is a religion of peace," I say no. I grew up there. I was there at the mosques, the Friday Madrassa, listening to sermons by Ikrima Sabri, tapes by Abdul Hamid Kishk. They taught only the destruction of the Jews and hatred of the West. To kill, to maim, to hate..."[301]*

My daughter was at college on that infamous day of September 11, 2001. She told me that while most of the students were shocked and saddened about the attacks taking place in New York and Washington,

---

[301] "Why I left Jihad," Walid Shoebat, 2005

Islamic students were celebrating. Loud cheers rang out as each of the World Trade Center Towers crumbled and fell to the ground killing thousands of people. I was perplexed. Many of the Islamic students were second generation "Americans" reaping the benefits of freedom, education and opportunity, so why would young people, naturalized citizens living here in the U.S. celebrate it being mercilessly attacked? Needing to reconcile that question, I began a thirteen year search for answers.

> *"Our enemy until the Day of Judgment is the Christians, what we call the Westerners or Europeans."*
>
> —Ali al-Timimi, Imam of the Dar-al-Arqam mosque near Washington DC

The *western misinterpretation* that Islam's Allah is the same as the Judeo-Christian God of the Bible masks the diametrically opposed religious doctrine between Islam and other religions. No matter how many times it is repeated - Allah and God are not the same. The Judeo/Christian God is a universal God who loves all people. The Quran's Allah has no love for unbelievers (infidels), and has conditional love for believers. The Quran's Allah orders Muslims to kill enemies; in the name of Islam – *"turning the other cheek,"* is a sign of weakness. Dissimilarities between the Bible and the Quran are numerous. Heaven in the Quran is a physical pleasure paradise with eternal virgins and "youths of perpetual freshness." The Biblical Heaven is a metaphysical place devoid of lust, power, riches, and other carnal desires. One of the biggest misconceptions is that the Quran preaches "tolerance" of other religions. It does not. And, it is important to note that Islam did not spread peacefully – it conquered by force, subjugation, and death. Former Muslim Walid Shoebat clearly warns: *"The very same Quran and Sunna that served as the rules of conduct in the seventh century remain the basis for Islamic law today."*[302] (The *religion of Islam* and *Islamic law* are indivisible and one cannot exist without the other).

Islam is not like any other religion. Christianity's God is powerful

---

[302] "Why I left Jihad," Walid Shoebat, 2005

because he is good. Islam's God is good because he is powerful. In Christianity, justice is righteousness. In Islam, justice means military and political supremacy of Muslims over non-Muslims. Violence by Christians in the name of God explicitly violates religious tenets. Violence by Muslims in the name of Allah explicitly fulfills religious tenets. In Christianity, the Bible contains "moral absolutes." In Islam, morality was established by Mohammad. Christians are encouraged to spread the word of the Lord. Muslims are commanded to be silent about their beliefs. In Christianity, love is the highest duty of Christians. In Islam, *jihad* is the highest duty of Muslims. I can confidently state no religion other than Islam promotes violence, genocide, and subjugation, all endorsed by their God. No other religion would celebrate the crashing of airliners into buildings, or the bombings of trains, hotels, and nightclubs to purposely kill civilians, or hijack a school to purposely terrorize and kill children (Beslan, Russia in 2004). Muslims worldwide including in America celebrate terrorism and death.

We would be wise to listen to men like Serge Trifkovic who said, *"The only way we can meaningfully judge the present and plan the future is by the example of the past. The problem of collective historical ignorance-or even deliberately induced amnesia-is the main difficulty in addressing the history of Islam in today's English-speaking world, where claims about far-away lands and cultures are made on the basis of domestic multiculturalists' assumptions rather than on evidence."*[303]

The Prophet Mohammed was familiar with Judaism and Christianity though not well-versed in either which explains his inaccuracies about both. He cherry-picked people and events in the Bible and cobbled together a new religion that really worked out well - for him. Muslims are forbidden to ever read the Bible (if they did, they would question their religion). Conveniently enough, when Mohammad decided to sack a city, or kill a man to take his wife, marry a six-year old girl, and order his followers to rape, pillage and murder, he would be visited by the Angel Gabriel who brought authorization from Allah to justify his desires. For instance Mohammad became a wealthy man because his followers were allowed to keep the ill-gotten gains they plundered

---

[303] *"The Sword of the Prophet: Islam History, Theology, Impact on the World,"* Serge Trifkovic, Boston: Regina Orthodox Press, Inc., 2002

from their slain victims, many of whom were defenseless women and children. Other captured loot was put into a common bank, from which Mohammad received one-fifth of all booty acquired. In Islam, to this very day, Mohammed is revered as the "perfect" man.

When the Prophet Mohammad could not win over the Jewish tribes of Mecca, Medina and Arabia, the century's old custom of slaughtering Jews began. As Islam grew, the Jewish population declined until no more Jews were in Arabia. After the Jews, Islam's eyes turned to the subjugation and slaughter of Christians and other non-believers. The lesson here cannot be overstated. **It is still happening right now** and at an accelerated pace. Muslims want Israel eradicated and Jews exterminated. They worked diligently alongside the Nazis during World War II hoping to make the "final solution" a reality. Why were they not war criminals like the Nazis they imitated and supported? Once Jews are eradicated; Christians will be next. There is no room for anti-Semitism in this struggle for survival. Western Christians must open their eyes to the plight of Christians and Jews in the Middle East. Our brothers are being massacred on a massive scale as the world governments sit silently idle.

Serge Trifkovic plainly states: *"Muhammad's practice and constant encouragement of bloodshed are unique in the history of religions. Murder, pillage, rape, and more murder are in the Kuran and in the Traditions 'seems to have impressed his followers with a profound belief in the value of bloodshed as opening the gates of Paradise' and prompted countless Muslim governors, caliphs, and viziers to refer to Muhammad's example to justify their mass killings, looting, and destruction."*[304] Mohammad set the "moral code" for all Muslims to emulate. That is problematic and explains behaviors we have a difficult time comprehending. I urge you to read real unbiased biographies of Mohammad, his life, and his teachings and you will get a glimpse of how and why Islam operates and why women are treated so badly in Muslim nations. You should also read the Quran/Kuran (An older English version is more accurate since the newer English translated versions have been edited so particular words don't seem so harsh to the sensitive Western reader.

---

[304] *"The Sword of the Prophet,"* Serge Trifkovic, Boston: Regina Orthodox Press, Inc, 2002

Islam's entire history is one of subjugation, conquest, and brutality. In the Fourth Century, there were over 30 million Christians living outside of Europe. With the advent of Islam, their numbers have consistently declined as the "peaceful religion" spread throughout the Middle East and Africa. As is the case today, subjugated people (*dhimmi*) are afforded protection under Islam as long as they pay the *jizya* (poll tax). If the tax is not paid, their property can be confiscated and they could be killed (legal Sharia "extortion"). It's strange, we only hear of the "persecution" of Muslims, not the persecution **by** Muslims (which is rampant). Political correctness and academic blindness have buried the real truths about Islam.

One myth that needs to be rebuked is that the Crusades were aggressive wars initiated by Christians only to persecute peaceful Muslims. Real history proves the Crusades were military responses to over three centuries of Muslim violence and subjugation (virtual enslavement) of conquered Christians. European Crusaders learned savage behavior from the tortuous actions of Muslim fighters against Christians and other non-Muslim enemies. History professor, author and media expert, Thomas F. Madden states: *"Muslims in the Middle East-including Bin Laden and his creatures-know little about the real crusades as Americans do. Both view them in the context of modern, rather than the medieval world...They were a desperate and largely unsuccessful attempt to defend against a powerful enemy."*[305]

As stated previously, Islam is not just a religion. It is an all-encompassing social and political system that controls every aspect of Muslim life. The Quran is the highest and only authority on life. It cannot be questioned, criticized, or evaluated. Any suggestion that the Quran has been altered or tainted in any way is offensive and heretical to Islam. Islamic (Sharia) Law is absolute and applies to everyone including the people of conquered lands. Apostasy (changing/converting faith away from Islam) is forbidden and punishable by death. Slavery is regarded as a permanent fact of life and slavery is alive and well today in places like Mauritania and the Sudan just as it has been for thirteen

---

[305] *"Crusade Propaganda: Abuse of Christianity's Holy War,"* Thomas F. Madden, National Review Online [quoted in *"The Sword of the Prophet,"* Serge Trifkovic, Boston: Regina Orthodox Press, Inc., 2002

centuries. *"There is no freedom of speech, thought, or religion in any Arab or Muslim nation."*[306] So where is the United Nations to intervene against rampant human rights abuses? Where are the feminist groups when Muslim women are beaten, tortured and murdered on a regular basis?

Former Muslim Walid Shoebat again clarifies: *"The hypocrisy is striking. Where are the accusations when it comes to true aggression? The world is basically silent when more than a million Sudanese are dead from starvation and mass execution. Silent when Christians die in Indonesia. Silent when Turks kill Cypriots...Why does the West remain silent about the horrific abuse and murder of women in Muslim countries?"*[307]

Muslims are taught to hate Jews and Christians. *"O ye who believe! Take not the Jews and Christians for your friends."* Jews are evil in the Quran and are *"the enemy of the Muslims"* (Surah 62:5). Christians are polytheists who worship false gods. **Make no mistake – Muslims consider all Jews and Christians the enemy and their mission is to establish a Caliphate -Allah's rule (Islam) worldwide.** *"Allah's object also is to purge those that are true in faith and to deprive of blessing those that resist faith..."* [Islam] (Surah 3:140-143). Unlike other world religions, Islam commands lying, stealing, and killing to promote Islam.

Christians have lived in the Middle East for over two thousand years - long **before** Islam was founded by Mohammad. Islam propagated with the blood of Christians and Jews and the historic oppression of non-Muslims by Muslims in the Middle East since the 7th century is a continuing human rights crisis but obviously not to the United Nations. Saudi Arabia, Pakistan and Egypt, three of our Middle Eastern "allies" who receive billions of dollars from the U.S. are high on the list of Islamic countries persecuting Christians. Other countries where violence and persecution of Christians is the norm include: Iraq, Afghanistan, Nigeria, Sudan, Mali, Libya, and Indonesia. Raymond Ibrahim, author and associate director of the *Middle East Forum* makes the point that three of these Islamic countries: Iraq, Afghanistan and Libya have been *"liberated thanks to U.S. forces,"* and Syrian rebels (terrorists) are being supported by the U.S. government. *"...the Obama administration recently tried to go to war with Syria on behalf of the "freedom fighters,"*

[306] "Why I Left Jihad," Walid Shoebat, 2005
[307] "Why I Left Jihad," Walid Shoebat, 2005

amazingly in the name of "human rights" (apparently the unsubstantiated rumor that Assad massacred people is enough for the U.S. to go to war, but the ongoing and well-documented massacres of Christians and other civilians at the hands of the opposition is not enough for the U.S. to stop supporting them.)"[308] Mr. Ibrahim warns, "Where the U.S. works to oust *secular autocrats, the quality of life for Christians and other minorities takes a major nosedive. Under Saddam Hussein, Qaddafi, and Assad, Christians and their churches were largely protected."*

Pillaging, torture, enslavement, and slaughter of Christians is real; it is happening now; it is disgraceful; it is not reported by the media; and it is ignored by the White House, the United Nations and the rest of the world.

In Iran, Persian, Armenian and Assyrian Christians live in constant fear under the Islamic Republic where Christian leaders are executed by the government. The Iranian secret police make arrests on false charges. Iranian Christian Hossein Saketi Aramsari was arrested in July 2013 and subsequently charged with "evangelism." *Mohabat News* reported that "*Conversion of youths and their families has become a major concern for the Iranian security authorities and Islamic leaders.*"[309] These Christians are arrested, jailed, tortured and abused to keep the truth from the Iranian people. American Christian Pastor Saeed Abedini has been in an Iranian prison for over a year and half for the crime of "practicing Christianity." The White House is deaf to the pleas and petitions to intervene on Abedini's behalf. The Obama administration has made it clear that they will do nothing to aid Christians in the Middle East, even if they are Americans.

A United Kingdom newspaper The *Telegraph* reported that a Christian man, Sawan Masih was accused of blasphemy and sentenced to death in Pakistan. He was accused of insulting the Prophet Mohammed which promptly triggered about 3,000 Muslim protesters to burn Christian homes and churches in the area called *Joseph Colony*.

---

[308] "*Confirmed: U.S. Chief Facilitator of Christian Persecution,*" Raymond Ibrahim, Front Page Magazine, http://www.frontpagemag.com, January 21, 2014. Originally published by National Review Online

[309] "U.S. Chose to Stay Silent on Muslim Persecution of Christians," Raymond Ibrahim, *Front Page Magazine*, http://www.frontpagemag.com, February 14, 2014

"In Pakistan even being accused of blasphemy is equivalent to being sentenced. The blasphemy laws in Pakistan are often used to settle personal vendettas."[310] Onan Coca reinforces that statement: *"Christians in Pakistan are routinely singled out for persecution by the active and violent Islamic militants who operate freely there. Attacks on churches are commonplace, and justice is often never found for victims of Islamic violence."*[311]

The story of a nine-month-old baby charged with attempted murder in Pakistan is not about Christian persecution, but it does illustrate the mentality and vindictiveness of a Muslim majority society. This baby Mohammad Musa was with his father and grandfather when a mob protest against gas cuts and price increases turned violent. An assistant sub-inspector claimed that the baby's whole family beat him up and since the baby was with them, he is guilty also. The baby was arrested, finger-printed, his hearing date was set and he was released on bail. Baby Mohammad's grandfather, Muhammad Yasin said, *"He does not even know how to pick up his milk bottle properly, how can he stone police?"*[312] How do you rationalize with people like this?

Massacres of Christians in Syria (by the very Syrian rebels that our government supports) escalated to horrifying levels in 2013. For instance, a Catholic priest and two other men were publically beheaded by Syrian rebels as numerous cell phones recorded the "joyous" event. In May 2013 the unstoppable Free Syrian Army attacked the Christian village of al-Duair massacring men, women, and many children. Then in October the ancient Syriac Orthodox Christian town of Sadad was attacked and 45 Christian men, women and children were tortured and killed. The town's churches were destroyed, never to be rebuilt. 9 children were killed and 27 others wounded when Islamic Syrian rebels (supported by the United States government) attacked St. John of Damascus Christian School. Syrian rebels also attacked the city

---

[310] "Christian Sentenced to Death for Blasphemy in Pakistan," Rob Crilly, The Telegraph, http://wwwtelegraph.co,uk, March 28, 2014

[311] "Pakistan Sentences Christian Couple to Death," Onan Coca, posting Eagle Rising, http://eaglerising.com, April 8, 2014

[312] "Baby Charged with Attempted Murder, Goes Into Hiding in Pakistan," NBC News, http://www.nbcnews.com, April 8, 2014

of Qamishi killing the city's Christians and clergy. They looted and destroyed the church and its possessions including a 2,000 year old icon. The Prophet Mohammad would be so proud of these soldiers of Islam.

Three separate Muslim bombings targeting Christians shook Iraq on Christmas Day 2013 as Christians gathered to celebrate the holy day. Most of the seven million Africans in southern Sudan are Christians (Anglicans, Protestants, and Catholics) and they are being killed by the Islamist forces of Khartoum. Entire villages are being destroyed by the Arab government.[313]

Brutality and murder are constants in countries ruled by Islamic law. In August 2009 after three Christian youths were accused of burning a Quran, eight Christians were burned to death and two others shot to death in Pakistan when an Islamic mob went on a rampage burning Christian's homes and shooting them as they fled the carnage. Clerics of the "peaceful religion" called for their deaths even though no proof of their guilt existed. You can be executed simply for being accused of defiling the Koran or any random imaginary blasphemy. *"The law is often misused to settle personal scores."*[314] In Mogadishu, Somalia, four men convicted of stealing, each had one hand and one foot cut off as punishment for their crimes. The sentences were handed down by the Islamic court. Christian convert Abdikhani Hassan was murdered by Al Shabaab Islamic militia members, and the al-Qaeda organization in Somalia has vowed to cleanse the country of Christians. Incidents like these are not occasional events; they are common occurrences where Islamic theocracy reigns.

NBC News has reported that the terrorist group *Boko Haram* is on a murderous rampage in Nigeria, Africa. In their quest to establish an Islamic state in northern Nigeria they are burning villages and killing innocent unarmed people. Their favorite targets are schools since they believe that is where "Western-style" education is taught. They killed 22 students at a school in the village of Mamudo in June 2013 and killed 29

---

[313] *"The Oppression of Middle East Christians: A Forgotten Tragedy,"* Walid Phares in *The Myth of Islamic Tolerance: "How Islamic Law Treats Non-Muslims,"* Edited by Robert Spencer, NY: Prometheus Books, 2006

[314] *"Eight Christians burnt to death in Pakistan after Koran is "defiled, "* Zahid Hussain, *The London Times*, http://www.timesonline.co.uk, August 3, 2009

students in the town of Damaturu in February 2014. Earlier in February Boko Haram killed over 200 people during two separate attacks.[315]

Onan Coca reported that Boko Haram executed a two-day attack on the Nigerian villages of Dikwa, KalaBalge, Gambulga and Gwoza murdering civilians including 200 students. *"The Islamic nations of the world have been unsurprisingly silent about the evil acts committed by Boko Haram. All of this is happening as Boko Haram strengthens its relations with other Islamic groups like Al Qaeda in an effort to entrench themselves in northern Nigeria...Islamic groups are terrorizing the populations in India, Pakistan, the USA, Iraq, Afghanistan, Syria, Yemen, Somalia, Kenya, Egypt, Libya, Nigeria and more."*[316]

Faith J.H. McDonnell's April 16, 2014 article in *Front Page Magazine* attributes the April 14, 2014 bombing of a bus station near the capital city of Abuja that killed 89 people and wounded 257 others to Boko Haram.[317] It is believed the bombing was planned to coincide with the first day of the Christian Holy Week. The president of Nigeria confirmed that Boko Haram seeks the *"eradication of Christians and the Islamization of Nigeria."* While our State Department is more concerned over poverty and "inequality" in Nigeria than the extermination of Christians the group's leader Abubakar Shekau clearly stated Boko Haram's mission to promote Islam and *"rid Nigeria of infidels."* Shekau told Nigeria's Civilian Joint Task Force, *"I swear by Allah's holy name that I will slaughter you. I will not be happy if I don't personally put my knife on your necks and slit your throats. Yes! I'll slaughter you! I'll slaughter you! And I'll slaughter you again and again."* Boko Haram does not have a problem with poverty or inequality – they just want to kill all Christians. Shekau also said that *"In Islam, it is allowed to take infidel women as slaves and in due course we will start taking women away and sell in the market."* Now, what part of those verified statements does the State Department not understand?

---

[315] "29 Boys Killed as Boko Haram Attacks Boarding School in Nigeria," NBC News, http://www.nbcnews.com, February 25, 2014

[316] "Islamic Extremists in Nigeria Slaughter 200 Christians," Onan Coca, http://eaglerising.com, April 14, 2014

[317] "Slaughter in Nigeria-Where Is the State Department?" Faith J.H. McDonnell, Front Page Magazine, http://frontpagemag.com, April 16, 2014

Even our "civilized" ally Turkey is again being heavily influenced by and slowly reverting back to Islamic control - remember the Ottoman Empire? Turkish Prime Minister Erdogan, if not sanctioning, is surely allowing Islamic jihad against Armenians, *"again causing their death and dislocation."*[318] Author Raymond Ibrahim is referring to the systematic genocide of Armenians by the Turks (Ottoman Empire) beginning in 1915 when the Armenian population was about 2 million people. By the end of World War I in 1918, an estimated 1 million Armenians had been exterminated and hundreds of thousands were homeless and stateless. In 1923 when the Ottoman Empire was replaced by the Republic of Turkey, *"virtually the entire Armenian population of Anatolian Turkey had disappeared."*[319] Islamic jihadis (linked to al-Qaida) from Turkey attacked the Christian Armenian town of Kessab in Syria. Eighty people were reported killed during the terrorist mortar attack on Kessab and surrounding villages as snipers targeted the townspeople. The terrorists returned to Turkey after the attacks. The Islamic jihadists attacked the Christian town again taking surviving Armenians hostage as well as desecrating the town's three churches and pillaging the empty homes. It was reported that Turkish artillery units supported the terrorists.

Raymond Ibrahim reminds us of how history repeats itself when you don't learn from it. *"Such is the continuity and interconnectivity of history. A century ago, Armenians fled to Kessab to avoid being massacred by Turkey. And today, their descendants are fleeing from Kessab - again, to avoid being massacred by terrorists aided by Turkey...the same story, the same enmity - Turkish to Armenian, or mores distilled yet, Muslim to Christian - lives on, even if in different contexts and formats."*

Women are favorite and easy targets for the courageous warriors of Allah. In Afghanistan, author Sushmita Banerjee wrote a book about escaping the Taliban, so they killed her. In Saudi Arabia (the wealthy civilized Arab country) where women are not allowed to drive, it is legal for a 90 year old man to marry a young girl. A three year old toddler was gang raped in that same civilized country. An eight year old girl in

---

[318] "Turkey's New Jihad on Christian Armenians," Raymond Ibrahim, *Front Page Magazine*, http://www.frontpagemag.com, March 27, 2014
[319] "Armenian Genocide," Educational Resources, http://www.armenian-genocide.org

Yemen who was sold to her forty year old husband bled to death on her wedding night from internal injuries. In the very same country a fifteen year old girl was burned to death by her own father. Another fifteen year old girl, this one in Syria, was gang raped and savagely slaughtered by the same Syrian rebels (our government supports) because she was a Christian. Two British girls, both eighteen years old were targeted in an acid attack in Zanzibar where they were school volunteers. They were both horrifically burned. And, in Bangladesh a fourteen year old girl was convicted of adultery after being raped by an older married cousin. Her sentence was to receive 101 lashes, but the little girl, Hena Akhter became unconscious after 70 lashes and she died in the hospital a week later. The United Nations reports that 5,000 women are victims of honor killings around the world, though the actual figure is probably much higher. The universal lack of concern is shameful and just what is the UN doing about it? Nothing.

Consider what has always happened to Christians and Jews under Islamic law in the Middle East and then take a look at Europe where an "Islamic crisis" is simmering just below the surface. Muslims first started going to Europe in the 1960s as "guest workers." As they have grown in power over the past four decades, so have their demands of the host countries grown. Assimilation into host societies has not and will not happen and the children of these Muslims grow up learning to hate the West. The population of Muslims living in Europe has grown enough for European Muslims to demand the institution of "*Sharia*" Law for Muslims instead of existing country laws. As Islam grows stronger in Europe, the demands will possibly overwhelm the established civil institutions until Islamic law reigns (that is the strategy). In Europe as in the United States, when Muslims cry discrimination, they are used to the progressive appeasement psyche that makes accommodations for their demands despite majority opinion, the law, and what is actually best for the country. The will of a minority prevails over the will of the majority. Tony Blankley challenges critics and the "disbelievers" of a radical Islamic threat in his book, *The West's Last Chance*. He clearly sees the crisis. *"We have thought ourselves into a position of near impotence. In much of the West, and particularly in Europe, there is a blind denial that radical Islam is transforming the world."[320]*

Mr. Blakely cites an organization, the Islamic Party of Liberation (Hizbut-Tahrir al-Islamiyya) that embraces the ideology of the original Muslim Brotherhood. They insist on the creation of a CALIPHATE to rule over all Muslims in **a borderless Islamic State**. ISIS in Iraq is working very hard to make that happen. The Islamic Party of Liberation has cells in forty countries; they support terrorism, protect terrorists, and hate America. They believe Israel does not have the right to exist. They also believe hijacking airplanes is permissible if the plane belongs to a country at war with Muslims (they already feel Israel and the West are at war with Islam). A March 2009 organization leaflet called for a declaration of "a state of war" specifically against America. You can imagine my surprise when the Islamic Group Hizbut-Tahrir *"Brandishing the Sword,"* held a conference at a suburban Chicago Hilton Hotel titled, "The Fall of Capitalism and the Rise of Islam" in July 2009. Is no one at all paying attention? Walid Phares noted, *" The aim of this conference is to recruit within the Muslim community in America...The Middle East governments go after them, but in the U.S. they are protected, so having a base here is going to help their cells around the world."[321]* Phares also said that Hizbut ut-Tahrir indoctrinates Muslim youths to prepare them for battle. Hizbut-Tharir is operating openly in America. They literally are telling us their plans about the ultimate goal to unite all Muslims under a Caliph to rule the world. They have ties to 9/11 mastermind Khalid Sheikh Mohammed and Al-Qaeda leader in Iraq, Abu Musab al-Zarqawi. But since Hizbut ut-Tahrir is not recognized by the State Department as a "known terrorist group," they are free to spew hatred and recruit as many future jihadists as they please.

The religion of Peace cannot be separated from the politics of Islam – they are one in the same. There is no free speech; there is only Islamic speech. Muslims and non-Muslims alike are forbidden to blaspheme and Sharia law demands retribution against all who blaspheme, or are accused of such. An example of this was the Danish cartoons crisis of

---

[320] *"The West's Last Chance,"* Tony Blankley, Washington DC: Regnery, 2005
[321] *"Islamic Supremacist Group Holds First U.S. Conference,"* Diane Macedo, FOX News.com, July 17, 2009

2005. Cartoons of Mohammad were originally published by a Danish newspaper, and within four months Muslims worldwide were incensed by the "blasphemy" against the Prophet. Violent protests (fascist mob action) resulted in massive property damage and death. The "tolerant" religion does not tolerate other cultures and religions, and absolutely cannot accept the concept of "freedom of speech."

Protesting Muslims first called for the Danish government to apologize for the free press cartoonists. The protests escalated demanding the death of the cartoonists, the boycott of Danish goods, and the burning of Danish flags. Watching news footage of protesters burning Danish flags across the Muslim world made me wonder how so many poor Muslims just happened to have Danish flags on hand. As usually happens, the protests turned to rage not only against the Danes, but against all Westerners resulting in the destruction of property including Christian churches, violence and deaths. The standard "Death to America" and "Death to Israel" chants took on a new ferocity.

Where was the outrage over the murders during this frenzy? How can it be that simple cartoons just as an untrue story in *Newsweek* magazine about a Quran being flushed down a toilet lead to such violence and death? American Muslims remained silent just as they have been silent about 9/11 and worldwide terrorism.

Fatwas were issued and the demand for the cartoonist's death was embraced by a number of "Islamic soldiers." The offended jihadists will not rest until he is dead. Cartoonists and journalists have consistently portrayed Christians in a negative light. It is insulting and offensive, but their right of freedom of speech is constitutionally protected. More importantly, Christians don't react in mob action threatening, terrorizing, and destroying property. The cartoons were just another excuse to mobilize Muslims against the West. I find it interesting that at every "spontaneous" Muslim rage rally, protestors are burning the offending country's flag as well as the American flag. Strangely there seems to be a limitless supply of American flags on hand for impromptu protests and burnings in the Middle East.

In November 2004, Dutch film director, producer, columnist, author, and actor Theo van Gogh was murdered. He was shot while riding his bicycle; he was shot again when he fell; then his throat was slit and a note attached to a knife was stuck into his chest. Van Gogh had received death threats for a film he did about Islamic violence against women. The man who assassinated him was Mohammed Bouueri, a Dutch Moroccan Muslim and self-described *jihadist*. The letter he attached to van Gogh's chest reflects the feelings of a multitude of radical and "not-so-radical" Muslims. "...*I surely know that you, O America, will be destroyed. I surely know that you, O Europe, will be destroyed. I surely know that you, O Holland, will be destroyed...*"

Considering what Europe endured under the oppressive boots of fascism, tyranny, and the Nazi regime during the twentieth century, it's unbelievable how easily European governments collectively are raising the white flag to Islam. And, even more astounding is how the U.S. government is blindly following suit. Appeasement empowered the monster that destroyed Europe during World War II. Barely a generation away from the horrors of subjugation and the deaths of millions, how can people now stand idly by and watch their freedom drain away <u>again</u>? What do you think Winston Churchill and people of Great Britain who survived the horrific war by refusing to surrender would think about Sharia courts in London, "no-go" zones, threats, extortion and increasing violence? They would be appalled. Was not the beheading of a British soldier in broad daylight in South East London which was heralded by Muslims in the UK and around the world a clue that Islam is taking over their country? UK cleric Omar Bakri Mohammed inspired the murder and praised it as a courageous and heroic act.

France and Germany also have "no-go" zones where non-Muslims dare not venture. Young Muslims filled with rage and hatred venture from their safety zones to pillage, rape, beat, kill and destroy property. Where is the anger? Much of the same is taking place in Denmark, Switzerland, and all across Europe. Political correctness has silenced non-Muslims. Anything offensive to Muslims can be prosecuted.

While the United Nations and the European Union bowing to Islamic pressure are busy trying to implement laws to criminalize speech critical of Islam and promote Islam in Europe and America, a jihadist website, "Islamic Socialist Net Work" operating out of the United Kingdom was posting "Wanted" posters to identify counter-jihad bloggers and Facebook users. Muslims in the UK, Australia and

Canada posted cash bounties for personal information to identify these enemies of Islam. They want anyone who supports counter-jihad dead.

The Organization of Islamic Cooperation (OIC) is just one of the Islamic organizations trying to create international laws to criminalize criticism of Islam. John DeMayo reported in October 2013: "*The Organization of Islamic cooperation -- and its 57 member states--has many objectives. All of the OIC's goals are focused on the domination of Islam and the shaping of international law to promote social, economic, cultural, scientific, and political and human rights that conform to Sharia or Quranic Law...This should not come as a great surprise to an America where our government is censoring media reports of acts of Islamic terror, purging references to Jihad and the term Islamic terrorists from terrorism training manuals and is now openly characterizing Christianity and Patriotism as dangerous extremism.*"[322]

Under the usual pressure from the OIC, the European Union (EU) is considering a new program of "direct surveillance" of any EU citizen "*suspected*" of being intolerant. Intolerant of Islam, that is. The proposal, "European Framework National Statute for the Promotion of Tolerance" compels the EU member state governments to create "special administrative units" to monitor individuals or groups expressing "intolerant" views. Audrey Russo wrote: "*European citizens are already habitually punished for expressing the "wrong views", specifically concerning Islam. Remember, it's all those citizens "suspected" of being "intolerant"...I guess it depends on who looks through Allah's microscope.*"[323]

Pamela Geller who is an expert on the Islamic grand plan and what is happening in Europe and America wrote an article about Abu Saqer (Leader of Jihadiya Salafiya (al-Qaida) in the Gaza Strip). Abu Saqer has a message for America and Europe. "*Islam is coming and there is no*

---

[322] "Organization of Islamic Cooperation Seeks to Silence Free Speech Globally Beginning With the US," John DeMayo, Freedom Outpost, http://www.freedomoutpost.com, October 25, 2013

[323] "Free Speech Alert: Islam Rips Ever Deeper into Europe," Aundrey Russo, Clash Daily, http://www.clashdaily.com, February 17, 2014

other choice." [324] Sager warned that after the battle with Syrian President Bashar al-Asad the thousands of foreign jihadists currently in Syria could turn their ire on other *"enemies of Islam,"* which include the U.S. and Israel. *"And we will raise the Islamic flag on every point on earth where Muslims live and we will chase all the enemies of Islam wherever they are. Even in the West, in Europe and the United States."*

How do you think the United States government would respond if "unprovoked" Muslim terrorists from Turkey, Tunis, Morocco, Algiers, and Tripoli were purposely attacking merchant ships from mostly Christian countries including the United States, to steal the cargo, ransom some of the crew and enslave others? I'm not sure how our government would respond now, but in 1801 President Jefferson sent the U.S. Navy and Marines to put an end to the savagery. They successfully freed captured Americans and trampled the terrorist forces ending Muslim pirating of American ships for quite some time.

Muslim aggression and violence is not a 20th century phenomenon. Muslim aggression and brutality have existed since Mohammad set the tone and it will continue as long as Islam exists. John Quincy Adams traveled extensively as an ambassador of the United States before becoming our sixth president. He was well acquainted with **Islam's perpetual war** and described Islam this way: *"In the seventh century of the Christian era, a wandering Arab of the lineage of Hagar, the Egyptian, combining the powers of transcendent genius, with the preternatural energy of a fanatic, and the fraudulent spirit of an imposter, proclaimed himself as a messenger from Heaven, and spread desolation and delusion over an extensive portion of the Earth. Adopting from the sublime conception of the Mosaic Law, the doctrine of one omnipotent God; he connected indissolubly with it, the audacious falsehood, that he was himself his prophet and apostle. Adopting from the new Revelation of Jesus, the faith and hope of immortal life, and of future retribution, he humbled it to the dust, by adapting all the rewards and sanctions of his religion to the gratification of the sexual passion. He poisoned the sources of human felicity at the fountain, by degrading the condition of the female*

---

[324] "Jihadist Leader Abu Saqer to USA: 'Islam is Coming and There is No Other Choice,'" Pamela Geller, Freedom Outpost, http://www.freedomoutpost.com, August 13, 2013

sex and the allowance of polygamy; and **he declared undistinguishing and exterminating war, as part of his religion, against all the rest of mankind.** *The essence of his doctrine was violence and lust; to exalt the brutal over the spiritual part of human nature.*"[325]

Even in the United States, most Muslim communities prefer separatism. They do not want to be part of the American nation. They do not want their children to accept American culture and values. They steadfastly hold on to Islamic law while at the same time use the American system to enhance their lives. The hypocrisy is they readily take what America can give them in the way of jobs, money, education, welfare, and freedom but they will never support America.

The Turkish government is building a huge mosque complex in Lanham, Maryland, near Washington, D.C. It will be "the largest and most striking example of Islamic architecture in the Western hemisphere." It is estimated that up to 80% of mosques in America have been built since the attacks in 2001 meaning a lot of Muslims are coming into the U.S. Muslims are flooding into Europe and North America and unlike other immigrants; they isolate themselves within their own communities where non-Muslims are not allowed. I am suspicious of the intent of this Muslim inundation into the U.S. considering they claim that since 9/11 the United States is hostile to Islam. So, why would Muslims choose to relocate there? I find it troubling that most of them have no intention of ever assimilating into their "chosen" country as evidenced by what Muslim leaders say and the never-ending civil rights accusations and law suits filed by Muslim organizations.

Another extensive Islamic Complex named *Islamic Village* is going to be built by the *Islamic Association of North Dallas* in Texas. This "Islamic Village" project has an innocuous name for yet another separatist "Muslim neighborhood." The village will be Muslim self-contained complete with: Quranic Academy, Suffa Islamic Seminary, residences, a social services department, a youth center, and a senior center.

The Assembly of Muslim Jurists of America (AMJA) will be training

---

[325] "John Quincy Adams on Islam," Dave Miller, Ph.D., (Blunt, Joseph (1830), The American Register for the Years 1827-8-9, New York, E&FGW Blunt),Apologetics Press, 2009

imams in "Islamic Home Finance in the West," with a focus on Sharia finance and implementing Sharia by force. Not coincidentally, *The Islamic Society of North America* held a conference in Dallas on June 15, 2013 to proselytize Sharia law in the U.S., and opponents to Sharia law were identified as "extremists." According to Muslim logic, since Sharia law is contrary to the constitutional law that we support, we, who reject Sharia law are the extremists - in our own country. We "extremists" will be condemned as intolerant "Islamophobes." The truth is that instituting Sharia law as public policy in the United States is an Islamic priority. In 2006 Sayyid Syeed, Islamic Society of North America (ISNA) founder and former Secretary General was recorded saying, *"Our job is to change the constitution of America."* How much clearer can it be?

Are you aware that our "ally" in the *War on Terror*, Saudi Arabia, has invested well over $87 billion since 1973 to infiltrate the United States with their fanatical "Wahhabi" philosophy of Islam? By 2011 the Saudi's (our ally) had established, and, or funded over 1,500 mosques, 200 colleges, and 200 Islamic centers. Wahhabism clearly states that Islam is the only true religion, Christians and Jews are infidels, and the West (America) is the cause of all Muslim adversity worldwide. Western democracy is rejected outright while *jihad* and martyrdom are embraced. While our children are being taught tolerance in school, Muslim children are being taught intolerance and the rejection of American values and democratic ideals. A Saudi school in Virginia founded in 1984 that teaches strict adherence to Islamic law received approval to expand its campus against the opposition of the community. The school's textbooks have traditionally celebrated militant jihad and martyrdom including a textbook teaching that killing adulterers and apostates is justifiable. Does the Department of Education audit what is taught in Muslim schools like they do to Christian schools? Do you really think that Muslim schools are going to follow Secretary of Education Arne Duncan's national "Common Core" educational program that all American public school children must endure? As a matter of fact, in Florida, a required Common Core high school history book contains an entire chapter on Islam and its virtues. No other religion is even mentioned. So is this the new educational norm?

The mother of a fourth grade student wrote a letter about what students in their public school district were being taught in social studies class. The letter published by Pamela Geller on January 20, 2014,[326] should be read by every parent. At this new public charter school where "Common Core" (Core Knowledge) dictates the curriculum, fourth graders were taught to proclaim in <u>Arabic</u>, "Allah is great." This concerned mother referred to the companion "parent book" for an overview of the course lesson. "*...I learned they were learning about Islam and were being told that Allah is great and that Muhammad was his prophet sent to earth...I looked at the book [parent guide] and read the rather large section on Islam, and was further infuriated. They were literally indoctrinating the kids with a message of how wonderful Islam is, how Allah is great, and how the big, bad Christians murdered thousands of them (without an account of what really happened in history).*"

In December 2013 a first grader at Helen Hunt-Jackson Elementary School in Temecula, California followed her teacher's assignment instructions to bring an item from home that represents a family Christmas tradition to show and tell the class about. Six year old Brynn Williams brought the star from the top of her family Christmas tree. She was explaining her family's tradition of putting the "Star of Bethlehem" atop their tree to remember the birth of Jesus at Christmas. She got one more sentence out, "*The three kings followed the star to find baby Jesus, the Savior of the world,*" when her teacher told her to stop talking and sit down. The teacher told her she was not allowed to talk about the Bible or recite any versus from it. The school stands behind the teacher's decision "to protect other students from being offended by Brynn's presentation."[327] The lesson here is that it is alright for teachers to offend some 6-year olds so that these children don't possibly offend other 6-year olds when none of the 6-year olds even know what "offensive" means. Actually, I'm offended that teacher is teaching 6-year olds!

Anything remotely connected to Christianity is banned from U.S. public schools, while it is fine for the schools to take American students

---

[326] "Parent of 4th Grader Writes Letter of Outrage over Islam Being Taught in Local Public School," Pamela Geller, posting on Freedom Outpost, http://www.freedomoutpost.com, January 20, 2014

[327] "First grader told to stop talking about Bible," Todd Starnes, Fox News, http://www.foxnews.com. January 14, 2014

on field trips to mosques, be given instruction on Islam, its superiority, and even made to pray. Henderson High School in Tennessee had to attend a mosque to participate in a three week "comparative religion course." The students each received a Quran. No other churches were visited - how is that for "comparative?" New York public schools are trying to add two new holidays to the calendar - Islamic holidays. So, in public schools, Christmas and Easter (Christian holidays) have been banished, but Muslim holidays are championed.

> *"Radical Islamic groups have now taken over leadership of the "mainstream" Islamic institutions in the United States and anyone who pretends otherwise is deliberately engaging in self-deception."*
>
> —Seif Ashmawi (late Egyptian-American newspaper publisher)

Non-Muslim college and university students are also being taught the tenets of Islam and evils of Western thought. You would not believe what university professors are teaching American kids. Here are just a few examples of the 101 professors David Horowitz chronicles in his book, "*The Professors*," that are teaching at American colleges and universities.[328]

- Professor M. Shahid Alam is an economics professor at Northeastern University. He considers America a Great Satan. He considers the 9/11 terrorists freedom fighters and compares them to America's founding fathers. He claims that America is the aggressor and says websites that criticize al Qaeda are "hate websites."

- Palestinian Professor Sami Al-Arian was a University of Southern Florida University professor. He was also the North American head of the terrorist group *Palestinian Islamic Jihad*. He is responsible for 2 non-profit organizations: *the World Islamic Studies Enterprise* and the *Islamic Committee for*

---

[328] "*The Professors*," David Horowitz, Regnery Publishing, Inc., 2006

Palestine, both groups raise money and recruit men for jihad in Palestine. Al-Arian founded the *National Coalition to Protect Political Freedom* specifically to oppose anti-terrorism measures in the United States. Thankfully Al-Arian was arrested in 2003. There is absolutely no doubt that he advocates *jihad,* and endorses the destruction of the West's cultural system especially the "Great Satan," America. He commends the killing of Jews and Christians.

- Professor Hamid Dabashi is an Iranian born professor of Islamic Studies at Columbia University. He claims that the Middle East is the victim of Western colonialism and condemns all Jews as vile oppressors (even the children). Not surprising, Dabashi teaches that Iran's theocratic regime is more democratic than the United States. He regularly cancels classes to participate in "anti-Israeli" protests which he encourages his students to attend.

- Professor Aminah Beverly McCloud is a Professor of Islamic Studies at DePaul University and follower of Louis Farrakan, the anti-white and anti-Semitic leader of the Nation of Islam. McCloud believes African-American Muslims are disregarded by Muslim immigrants from the Middle East. Professor McCloud resents Middle Eastern Muslims and feels they want to impose their interpretation of Islam on African-American Muslims. To me, since Islam originated in the Middle East and has been modified by the African-American Nation of Islam, the professor's attitude seems exceptionally arrogant and bigoted. Professor McCloud adds yet another dimension of hate to Islam the peaceful religion.

- Professor Joseph Massad assistant professor of Arab politics at Columbia University and Professor Ali al-Mazrui, humanities professor at the State University of New York and who is also the North American spokesman of the Islamic extremist group Al-Muhajiroun as well as the chairman of the Center for the Study of Islam & Democracy (which has been linked to the American Muslim Council that supports Hamas and Hezbollah) share the same view of Israel and the United States. Both men believe

Israel does not have a right to exist and there is no distinction between civilian and military targets. Do you find it a little strange that Professor Massad, a man who hates Israel teaches a course on Israeli politics? I surely do.

Freedom House Center for Religious Freedom released a report in January 2005 titled, "***Saudi Publications on Hate Ideology Fill American Mosques.***" The report is the culmination of over 200 books and other publications disseminated by Saudi Arabia from American mosques and bookstores. All publications espouse an anti-Christian, anti-Semitic, and pro-jihad message. One document from the Saudi government gives detailed instructions on how to "hate" Christians and Jews including never to greet them first; never imitate the infidels, and never become a citizen of the U.S. Other writings teach how to reject Christianity, **insist that Islamic law be applied, consider all non-Muslims as the enemy,** consider America as "hostile territory," and **how to prepare for war against America**: *"To be true Muslims, we must prepare and be ready for jihad in Allah's way. It is the duty of the citizen and the government."*

The Council on American Islamic Relations (CAIR) a purported "moderate Islamic organization" distributes *A Teachers Guide to Islamic Religious Practices* which raises the question, why would teachers need a guide on Islam when the public schools are not supposed to acknowledge religion at all? We know where many Muslim educators stand, so what are Muslim leaders (radical, moderate, and otherwise) really saying about Islam, America, and the West? Here is a minor sampling:

- 1996 Convention of the Islamic Association for Palestine: ***"Muslims sooner or later will be the moral leadership of America. It depends on me and you. Either we do it now or we do it after a hundred years, but this country will become a Muslim country."***

- The Muslim Council of Britain and the Muslim Parliamentary Association of the United Kingdom held a protest against the U.S. and Great Britain in May 2005. Popular chants, slogans and signs included:

- "USA, watch your back – Osama is coming back"
- "Kill, *Kill USA…*"
- "Bomb New York"
- "Your so-called democracy will fall under the sword of Allah. The Day of Judgment is coming."[329]

- Silicon Valley Executive **Omar M. Ahmad**, at the 1998 Islamic Conference in Fremont, California said, *"Islam isn't in America to be equal to any other faith but to become dominant. The Quran should be the highest authority in America, and Islam the only accepted religion on earth."*

- **Abdurahman M. Alamoudi** who is considered the most politically connected Muslim activist and son of a Yemeni businessman is an extremist and also a "terrorist" who endorsed al-Qaeda' killing of non-Muslims. He wants America conquered in the name of Allah. A frightening fact is that he created the MUSLIM CHAPLAIN CORPS in 1993, an organization to certify Muslim chaplains for the U.S. military under the <u>Saudi-funded</u> American Muslim Armed Forces and Veterans Affairs Council. This man was part of the development of an Islamic Awareness course for California public school children. The students (who are not allowed any knowledge or reference to Christianity) had to adopt Muslim names, wear Muslim clothes, make food sacrifices for Ramadan, memorize *suras* from the Quran, and recite Muslim prayers. They were also told that *jihad* is an enlightened "personal struggle." Most amazingly, the Ninth Circuit Court of Appeals which ruled the "Pledge of Allegiance "was unconstitutional because it contains the word "God," allowed this "religious" program because it exposed students to another culture. That decision is an example of activist judges making a mockery out of our Constitution. Alamoudi is a busy man. He was also an Islamic advisor to Hillary Clinton.

- **Ibrahim Hooper** is a Muslim convert and activist from Canada and a public spokesman for CAIR (Council for American Islamic Relations) who poses as representative of mainstream Muslim

---

[329] *"The West's Last Chance,"* Tony Blankley, Washington DC: Regnery, 2005

community. In1993 Hooper called for the U.S. to become an Islamic nation.

- In 2000, **Ahmad Abu Halabiya**, Palestinian FATWA Council said, *"Allah the Almighty has called upon us not to ally with the Jews or Christians, not to like them, not to become their partners, not to support them, and not to sign agreements with them. And he who doeth that is one of them, as Allah said, 'O you who believe, do not take the Jews and Christians as allies. Have no mercy on the Jews, no matter where they are, in any country... fight them wherever you are...whenever you meet them, kill them."* (5:51)The U.S. will fall unless it *"accepts the Islamic agenda..."*

- **Muzammil H. Siddiqi**, Harvard educated scholar and "foremost" authority on Islamic Law gives advice to Muslim Americans to participate in the legal/political system – But only in order to change America into a Muslim country.

- **Mustafa Carroll**: Executive Director of Dallas-Fort Worth, Texas CAIR told a crowd at the "Muslim Capital Day" event in Austin, Texas: *'If we are practicing Muslims, we are above the law of the land."* A representative of Louis Farrakhan's Nation of Islam told the crowd that Texas was an awful place and that Islam is the answer.

- **Sheikh Omar Bakri Muhammad**: Resides in Great Britain and calls for the restoration of "DHIMMA" (Jews and Christians can live under Islamic Law but <u>not</u> as equals and with severe restrictions). He also condones killing unbelievers. On his website, he urges young Muslims to join al-Qaeda: *"I believe the whole of Britain has become Dar-al-Harb [Land of war]. In such a state the Kuffar [non-believer] has no sanctity for their own life or property."*

- **Sheikh Yuseff Salameh**: (Palestinian authority) said Christians should become dhimmis under Muslim rule.

- **Sheikh Hamza Yusuf**, Muslim convert, teaches Islamic and Arabic Affairs in northern California: *"America has to learn...If you remain on the side of injustice [Israel] the wrath of God will come." "America stands condemned to suffer a very terrible fate."*

(September 9, 2001). *"I am a citizen of this country not by choice but by birth."* (1996)

When Muslim leaders are asked to condemn terrorist acts and violent acts against "non-Muslims," the standard reply is a stern denunciation of "all forms of terrorism" while pointing out that Islam forbids terrorism and any violence against "innocent" people or "civilians." *"Our religion is against terrorism."* BUT the point to remember is that Islam does not consider non-Muslims "innocents" or "civilians." And what we consider terrorism, they define as "legitimate resistance" or "justice." Muslim leader's public statements against terrorism are no more than "legal lies" which the media accepts as truth without question. When you hear a Muslim on a media outlet profess friendship with non-Muslim Americans and extol his patriotism and loyalty to America...he may be telling the truth or, he may be saying only part of the truth (kitman) or, most likely he may be lying outright (taqiyya). [330]   Abd al-Rahman al-Rasheed makes it clear: ***"Lying for the sake of the cause is moral and honorable."***

Raymond Ibrahim explains the concept. *"The Islamic doctrine of taqiyya permits Muslims to actively deceive non-Muslims - above and beyond the context of "self-preservation," as is commonly believed...* ***Taqiyya is of fundamental importance in Islam***. *Practically every Islamic sect agrees to it and practices it...We can go so far as to say that the practice of taqiyya is mainstream in Islam, and that those few sects not practicing it diverge from the mainstream...Taqiyya is very prevalent in Islamic politics, especially in the modern era."*[331]

Numerous Muslim organizations operate in the U.S. Some of the most powerful include:

- American Muslim Political Coordination Council which is comprised of:

---

[330] *"Taqiyya and Kitman: Role of Deception in Islamic terrorism,"* Islam Watch: Telling the Truth about Islam, American Congress for Truth, 16 March, 2007. (*Taqiyyya: How Islamic extremists deceive the West*, Dr. Andrew Campbell)
[331] *"Taqiyya* about *Taqiyya,"* Raymond Ibrahim, Daily Mailer, *Front Page Magazine*, http://www.frontpagemag.com, April 11, 2014

- □ American Muslim Alliance
- □ Council on American Islamic Relations
- □ Muslim Public Affairs Council
- □ American Muslim Council
- The Council of Presidents of Arab American Organizations
- American Arab Anti-Discrimination Committee
- The Arab American Institute
- The National Association of Arab Americans
- The Islamic Society of North America
- Muslim Student Association [Muslim Brotherhood "lite"] Operating on University campuses nationwide

So what are some of the things Arab/Muslim organizations do that most people never hear about? Well, in 1999 eight Arab organizations agreed on two main political goals: (1) Weaken U.S. support for Israel, and (2) Weaken U.S. anti-terrorism laws. In October 2000, seventeen Muslim & Arab groups marched on Washington, DC to protest U.S. support for Israel. They warned, or threatened to be more specific that America, *"would suffer a terrible fate if it did not divorce Israel."* They also wanted to voice support for the terrorist groups Hamas and Hezbollah.

The Islamic Society of North America (ISNA) founded an interfaith coalition called *"Shoulder-to-Shoulder"* for the purpose of pressuring state legislators to end promoting laws to stop foreign law from superseding the Constitution. Seven states have so far passed laws prohibiting foreign laws to take precedence over U.S. law. Their uninformed non-Muslim allies have swallowed the propaganda that these (now very necessary) laws are "an unnecessary, bigoted initiative that threatens all people of faith."[332] It should be noted especially by the other faiths allied with ISNA that (1) The ISNA is a U.S. Muslim Brotherhood entity, and (2) The "interfaith" coalition is being led by Sayyid Syeed the former Secretary-General of ISNA, and the very man seen in the 2006 documentary, *"The Grand Deception"* saying, **"Our job is to change the constitution of America."** Weakening U.S. law to

---

[332] "Islamists Mobilize Non-Muslims to Undermine Constitution," Ryan Mauro, The Clarion Project, http://www.clarionproject.org, 2013

allow for Sharia law is the goal to which they are committed – Do not be fooled!

A myriad of Muslim/Arab/Islamic organizations operate in the United States. They seem to be independent, but all of them are connected through ideology, leadership, financial operations, charities, and political aspirations. Many are directly tied to terrorist groups such as Hamas, Hezbollah, Palestinian Islamic Jihad, and even al-Qaeda. **All are tied to the "MUSLIM BROTHERHOOD" which operates in the U.S. under the front group "Muslim American Society,"** which is committed to the *"globalization of Islam through social engineering and violent jihad."* Yes, the same Muslim Brotherhood our President supported in Egypt during the "Arab Spring."

THE MUSLIM BROTHERHOOD: *"Allah is our objective. The Prophet is our leader. Qur'an is our law. Jihad is our way. Dying in the way of Allah is our highest hope."* [333]

Wahabbi Sunni Muslims founded the Muslim Brotherhood in Egypt in 1928. The brotherhood assassinated the prime minister of Egypt in 1948 and attempted to assassinate Egyptian president Gamal Abdal Nasser in 1954. Egypt banned the brotherhood but they remained entrenched in that country. The brotherhood expanded out from Egypt and over the past decades established power bases in Saudi Arabia, Jordan, Sudan, Syria, and throughout the Middle East. (The Muslim Brotherhood **created** Hamas, the Palestinian Islamic Jihad, and the Egyptian Islamic Jihad that merged with al-Qaeda). The Brotherhood assassinated Anwar Sadat in 1981 because he signed a peace agreement with Israel in 1979. Though the Brotherhood tries to present a more moderate political face, they have over 70 branches worldwide and have financial and political control over most of the Islamic terrorist organizations.

Speaking for the Muslim Brotherhood in Cairo, Egypt on December 10, 2005 during the "Universal Declaration for Human Rights Day,"

---

[333] *The Muslim Brotherhood's Statement*, www.ikhwanWeb.com, (Cairo, Egypt, December 12/10/2005), http://www.ikhwanweb.com, 2/5/2006

Muhammad Mahdy Akef's statement, *"Together Against Torture"* was recited: *"...we, the Muslim Brotherhood:*

1. *Join our voices to all the raised voices in our country and worldwide "Against Torture" and all forms of human rights violations such as: unwarranted arrests, arbitrary detentions, exceptional and emergency trials, and civilian brought before and tried by military courts.*
2. *Call upon the all the international organizations and institutions as well as the human rights organizations worldwide to play their role in the prevention and tracking down of all the forms of human rights violations..."*

The hypocrisy is astounding. This organization condemns the United States for "alleged torture" of terrorists when they exist to sustain terrorism and spread violence! Obviously their concept of "human rights" only applies to Western nations since they routinely torture, murder, pillage, incite violence, and teach intolerance and indiscriminate killing of all people who are not Muslim. Cases in point, the Christians in Darfur, Sudan are being systematically murdered by Muslims, but the Muslim Brotherhood does not consider this to be a violation of human rights. It was quite disturbing to learn that the Obama Administration insisted that members of the Muslim Brotherhood be invited to the president's speech to the Muslim World in Cairo, Egypt in June 2009. The Brotherhood was in attendance and embraced the President's warm message.

Canadian-born author Carolyn Elkins who immigrated to America and became a U.S. citizen posted an excellent article, "How Islam and the Muslim Brotherhood Have Helped Transform America," on February 26, 2014 on *Politichicks.tv*. She notes that the Muslim Brotherhood's number one goal is a global Islamic government.

***The process of instituting Sharia*, according to the Muslim Brotherhood:**

-**Settlement**: *Islam becomes part of the homeland it lives in*
-**Establishment**: *Islam roots organizations from which it grows*

311

-**Stability**: *Islam is stable in the new land*
-**Enablement**: *Islam is enabled by the people of the country into which it moves*
-**Rooting**: *Islam becomes resident -* entrenched *in the land it will subjugate*

It is not a secret plan. They have made their intentions clear - to Muslims while at the same time lying (another venerable tenet of Islam - **taqiyya**) to non-Muslims. Western non-Muslims are now aware of this deceitful tactic yet still act surprised and make excuses for Muslim behavior.

The Council on American Islamic Relations (CAIR) is a widely accepted "mainstream" Muslim group in the United States. CAIR puts on a happy Muslim-American face, and decries its purpose to be Muslim-American understanding and acceptance. Our government administrations either believe the shallow veil of partnership, or are afraid to expose CAIR and the other organizations for what they really are – subversive organizations intent on Islamizing America, not joining America. You only have to visit CAIR's website to learn about their obvious intent.

Since Hamas had come under too much scrutiny in the U.S. Hamas members convened in Philadelphia in 1993 to launch a new organization. CAIR is that national organization created by Hamas and the Muslim Brotherhood and launched in 1994 to covertly sabotage the American justice system. CAIR has successfully executed its mission to "pose" as a civil rights group protecting American Muslims when in **reality it is an arm of the Muslim Brotherhood and Hamas using the American legal system to destroy the American legal system.**

On 9/9/2001 CAIR board member, Hamza Yusuf said, *"This country is facing a terrible fate and the reason for that is because this country stands condemned. It stands condemned like Europe stands condemned because of what it did. And lest people forget, Europe suffered 2 world wars after conquering the Muslim lands."* CAIR board member, Siraj Wahhaj said, he prays, ***"America's democracy will crumble."***

CAIR is on a crusade to eliminate the U.S. Pledge of Allegiance especially from American schools. Unlike atheist groups who want the pledge banned because it contains the word, "God," CAIR wants it banned because the words "liberty and justice for all" are blasphemy under Islam. Pamela Geller explained that practicing Muslims cannot pledge allegiance to America because their only allegiance is to Islam. *"Liberty and justice for all is an assault on Islamic supremacism."*

"Ask the persecuted Christians living in Muslim countries about liberty and justice for all. Ask the Hindus living in Muslim countries about liberty and justice for all. Ask the Jews ethnically cleansed from Muslim lands about liberty and justice for all."[334]

CAIR's website posts "Action Alerts" to induce Muslims to get politically active to support their agenda. Templates of demands are preprinted for Muslims to sign and submit to U.S. politicians. Two examples of "Action Alerts" posted on CAIR's website:

- *ANTI-TORTURE: Reject Legalizing American Torture* in response to the October 5, 2005 House Bill citing an October 26, 2005 Washington Post article, that Vice President Cheney "...is proposing that Congress legally authorize human rights abuses by Americans."
- *CIVIL LIBERTIES*: Oppose Unsupervised Surveillance Powers In Patriot Act… Act today to secure your civil liberties!

It is vital to note that CAIR is well aware that they are lying but it serves their purpose of isolating Muslims in America to keep them distrustful of Americans. Is there anyone in the government gallant enough to call them out? I didn't think so.

Political acceptance, participation, and power are major goals of CAIR, the American Muslim Alliance, and the other Muslim organizations. The **American Muslim Council** website published "Know Your Rights" which included informative information for Muslims on how to obstruct security efforts including: Don't talk to the FBI; Don't open your door to the FBI; The FBI is looking for information to use against you and the Muslim/Arab community; and

---

[334] "Hamas-CAIR wants to remove Pledge of Allegiance, 'Liberty and Justice for all,' Allahu akbar!" Pamella Geller post, http://www.dcclothesline.com, February 19, 2014

it counsels Muslims to file complaints if they are subjected to additional security clearances. Twenty years ago the Muslim priority was to build mosques and schools in America; now the priority is politics. These Muslim organizations under the guise of "better understanding" are implementing a plot to disrupt, divide, and denigrate America. For instance they continually file lawsuits against the U.S. government for racial and religious discrimination. They are becoming more and more active in the political scene and work diligently to sway public opinion. They are increasing financial support to select political candidates. Muslim media regularly blames Zionist conspiracies and the Christian Right for discrimination and harassment. Virtually all Muslims in America are united in opposition to Israel and U.S. foreign policy. Many American Muslims are Black converts. Terrorist fund raising from U.S. mosques provide up to 40% of Hamas' budget. I'm just not seeing the better understanding and peaceful coexistence part of the Muslim-American plan.

A very important thing Americans need to understand is that al-Qaeda and other jihadists are very patient and very determined to kill Americans. Don't ever think that 9/11 was an isolated incident. Terrorists have not stopped planning attacks on the U.S. The 9/11 Commission Report little noted that additional al-Qaeda operatives were held in reserve for larger and more deadly operations in the U.S. than the 9/11 operation. Terrorist Sleeper Cells use Arab and Muslim communities as cover while living low profile lives until "activated." Al-Qaeda is not the only terrorist organization that is intent on harming America. Terrorist breeding grounds and sanctuaries are scattered across the country. Some Muslim enclaves are suspect and worthy of special attention. Islamic groups would consider any additional scrutiny as civil rights violations; I call it national defense.

- **Bridgeview, Illinois:** (Chicago, Illinois suburb) is also known as *"The American West Bank."* This Islamic community and mosque is Saudi (Wahhabi) financed; it supports Hamas; its approximate 2,000 members are mostly Palestinian Americans; it has been under FBI scrutiny for financial ties to three terrorist front groups: The Benevolence International Foundation, The Global Relief Foundation and The Holy Land Foundation.

- **Lackawanna, New York**: (Buffalo, New York suburb) is home to the Lackawanna Six cell, a group of Yemeni-Americans convicted of providing material support to al-Qaeda.

- **Jersey City, New Jersey**: An Egyptian Christian family was murdered in January 2005 after the father was threatened with death by Muslim members of a web site. Authorities ruled "no proof of a religious hate crime" even though a Coptic cross was carved into the wrist of one of the victims. According to our politically correct laws, this was not a hate crime.

- **Minneapolis, Minnesota**: In 2011 after a four year investigation, eighteen men were charged with providing material support to co-conspirators who intended to murder and kidnap Ethiopian and Somali government troops for the terrorist group al-Shabab. It is believed that twenty ethnic Somali men were recruited.

- **Columbus, Ohio**: Madrassah (Islamic school) in Masjid As-Salaamah mosque is being investigated for child abuse. Children ages 8-10 reported at their public day school (Mark Twain Elementary School in Westerville) that they had been chained to a wall by their wrists and ankles and beaten with a long stick for not learning their religious texts as instructed.[335] This is not unusual in Islamic schools but I think the pressure on local law enforcement by the Islamic groups and even our own Justice Department to drop it - will prevail. We can't let child abuse stand in the way of Islamic appeasement.

- **Dearborn - Detroit, Michigan**: There are approximately 500,000 Arab-Americans in Metro Detroit. The Muslim population is large enough now to demand the U.S. government allow them to be governed by Sharia law - not U.S. law.
  - A group of Muslims including the Council of Islamic Organizations of Michigan wanted U.S. Attorney Eric Holder to investigate the FBI for asking Muslims to inform on Islamic congregations even though the FBI's

---

[335] "Severe Child Abuse Alleged by Children at Ohio Mosque," published by the Clarion Project, http://www.clarionproject.org, November 5, 2013

investigations were properly conducted and based on reasonable cause. An *Investor's Business Daily* report posted on One News Now (www.onenewsnow.com) on June 5, 2013 said the FBI had been prohibited by the Justice Department from doing surveillance in all mosques since 2011.

▫ Dearborn is where Christians on public property at the annual Arab Festival in 2010 were harassed and literally stoned with rocks and bottles by angry Muslims because they did not allow Christians in this Muslim area. The police were of no help telling the Christians they should not have been there. The Christians were arrested and later acquitted. My question is how can Muslim police officers who support Sharia law not U.S. law enforce U.S. law they swore to uphold. Obviously, they can't and they don't. The incident was recorded on video though the media didn't report the story.

▫ Residents Terresa and Hussein Dakhlallah have been threatened and their property vandalized because they displayed an Israeli flag along with an American flag in their yard. People stood in their front yard with a gas can and lighter and threatened the couple that they would burn the house down. Their house has been hit with paintballs and when Terresa was putting up her Christmas lights she was told that if she lit them, "it would be the last thing" she would do.

▫ McDonald's paid $700,000 to members of the Muslim community to settle a lawsuit that accused McDonald's of falsely preparing food according to Islamic dietary law. There are two McDonald's in the U.S. that sell "halal" products - both are in Dearborn, Michigan.

▪ **Ft. Lauderdale, Florida:** The Masjid al-Hirjah mosque in Ft. Lauderdale is a hard line Wahhabi mosque. *The Muslim Civil Rights Center* works tirelessly to "increase public understanding and awareness of disparate treatment received by Muslims, especially by the media and policy makers" which seems a little ironic since the media and politicians paralyzed by political correctness easily comply with their demands.

- **San Diego, San Francisco, and Santa Clara, California:** The Islamic Society of Orange County is under Saudi control. Muzammil Siddiqi, the spiritual leader who is pro-Hezbollah and pro-Hamas, considers Hitler blessed by Allah, and didn't kill enough Jews. The Islamic Center of San Diego (Saudi controlled Wahhabi mosque) gave aid and comfort to two of the 9/11 Saudi hijackers.

- **Toledo, Ohio:** Was the scene of the February 2006 arrest of three men for conspiring to kill Americans and the president of the U.S.

- **Brooklyn, New York:** is the home of blind Sheik Ommar Abdel-Rahman's Al-Farouq mosque. Rahman was convicted for his role in the 1993 World Trade Center bombing and calls for followers to, *"extract the most violent revenge"* should he die in U.S. custody." [336]
    - Mohammed Siddiquee beheaded his landlord over a dispute which is quite acceptable to the Islamic community.

- **Hancock, New York:** The Islamic community on 80 acres of land decided to make their own town which they call **"Islamberg."** Their little town has its own mayor, deputy mayor, and town council. It even has a "graveyard" which I guess would come in handy to conceal evidence of indiscriminate honor killings or outright murders. This community rejects U.S. law and only abides by Sharia law. How does this fly? Remember the Waco, Texas compound and Ruby Ridge? The government considered these American citizens such a threat that they had to die, but they do not have a problem with radical Muslims setting up unlawful governments on American soil. Make no mistake this is not an isolated peace-loving "Islamic community." It is the Headquarters of a network of villages across the country. This **"Muslims of the Americas"** (**MOA**) network

---

[336] *FBI warns of attack if "Blind Sheik dies,"* Associated Press, Thursday, December 16, 2006, http://www/msnbc.com/id/16208506

has comparable towns and camps in at least thirty locations nationwide including: Texas, Virginia, South Carolina, Georgia, California and Tennessee. The MOA is a front for the radical terrorist group **Jamaat Al Fuqura** and has documented ties to al-Qaida. **MOA's mission is to train and create a jihad army in the United States**. *"The existence of dozens of Islamic guerilla warfare training camps located in rural neighborhoods throughout America, and the serious crimes they have already committed – and are planning to commit – should be of concern to all law enforcement officers."*[337] How can this be?

- **Brazoria County (near Sweeny), Texas:** *"Mahmoudberg"* hides on about 25 acres of heavily wooded land and is a Muslims of America network village. Compound member, Hussein Jones, conveniently enough is a police officer in the city of Freeport while the Brazoria County Police are not allowed inside the complex.[338]

- **WASHINGTON, DC** including the Maryland and Virginia suburbs is known as "The Wahhabi Corridor" and supports a number of mosques and Islamic centers.

- **Dar al-Hijrah** also known as the 9/11 mosque in Falls Church, Virginia is a hard line Wahhabi mosque and one of nation's largest. It is Saudi sponsored, raises funds for Hamas, and is a magnet for militant Islamists.

- **Dar al-Arqam Islamic Center** in Virginia seems sympathetic if not supportive of the jihad network. Imam Ali al-Timimi said, *"America is the greatest enemy of Muslims."* He celebrated 9/11 as the "Final Battle" between Islam and Infidels.

- **Ayah Dawah Prayer Center** in Laurel, Maryland is home to large number of Taliban supporters.

- **Tennessee: Masjid al-Noor** Islamic Association of Greater Memphis homepage: *"If any one desires a religion other than Islam (submission to Allah), never will it be accepted of him; and*

---

[337] "Twilight in America," Martin Mawyer, Law Enforcement Today, http://www.lawenforcementtoday.com, November 2012

[338] "Texas Police Double as Islamic Terrorist Militia," Pamela Geller, Freedom Outpost, http://www.freedomoutpost.com, February 24, 2014

in the hereafter. He will be in the ranks of those who have lost (all spiritual good)." [Qur'an 3:85][339]

- □ Imam Yasir Qadhi preaches (just as Mohammed did) that *"non-Muslims lives are forfeit and their property is legal for Muslims to take in jihad."*
- **Skyline Towers** near Washington D.C. is residence to numerous Saudi and Yemeni embassy workers. Many residents rejoiced on 9/11 and a large number of male residents left the complex immediately after September11, 2001. The media didn't consider this newsworthy.
- **Oklahoma City,** Oklahoma is home to the Islamic Society of Greater Oklahoma City mosque frequented by Islamic convert Alton Nolen, the man who beheaded one coworker and was trying to behead another when he was shot in September 2014. Nolen had converted to Islam while in prison.
  - □ A mere 20 miles from Nolen's attack in the name of Allah, Jacob Mugambi Muriithi a Muslim from Kenya was arrested for threatening to behead one of his coworkers. The intended victim said that Muriithi claimed to represent ISIS and ISIS kills Christians. When asked why ISIS kills Christians, Muriithi said *"this is just what we do."*[340]

A very serious and growing problem in this country that the media refuses to report is the time-honored Islamic tradition of "honor killing." Women and young girls are murdered daily in Islamic countries by a father, brother or other male relative because they brought shame to the family by being accused of a Sharia violation. In the United

---

[339] Homepage of Masjid Al-Noor, http://masjid-alnoor.org/menuItems/aboutIslam.aspx

[340] "Oklahoma Beheadings: Second Oklahoma Muslim Threatens To Behead Coworker Because 'This Is Just What We do.'" Inquisitr, http://www.inquisitr.com, September 29, 2014 and "Another Oklahoma Man, a Muslim, Arrested After He Allegedly Threatened to Cut Off Coworker's Head: 'This Is Just What We do,'" Dave Urbanski, The Blaze, http://www.theblaze.com, September 28, 2014

States, Muslim women are also being killed because they've become too westernized. For instance:

- In Michigan, Sanaz Nezami, twenty-seven years old died in December 2013 after being repeatedly beaten by her Islamic husband.
- Also in Michigan, Jessica Mokdad was killed by her step-father in May 2011 for not following Islam.
- Texas, 2008 - Sisters Amina and Sarah Said were murdered by their father for being too westernized. He then left the country.
- November 2013 - A young woman in Lincoln, Nebraska was attacked by her brother who was trying to kill her because she was a homosexual and brought shame to the family
- November 2009 Noor Almaleki died after being run over by her father for being "too westernized."
- Tampa, Florida 2011 - Fatima Abdullah was "honor-murdered" though her death was ruled a suicide - by beating her own face repeatedly on a coffee table. The Florida Family Association wants to know how she could have killed herself by repeatedly banging her face on a coffee table when the autopsy reported wounds to the back of her head, broken ribs and hemorrhaging around her ribs. She was treated horribly before she died and the only "witness" has left the country.
- Buffalo, New York 2009 - Aasiya Hassan was beheaded by her husband. She had recently filed for divorce and had an order of protection against him.
- Cleveland, Ohio 1999 - Methal Dayem was murdered. Her family was upset by her independence. Her crimes were working, driving, and worst of all, she backed out of an arranged marriage.
- Galveston, Texas 2014 - "Devout Muslim" James Larry Cosby murdered his 24 year old daughter and her homosexual lover. Islam strictly forbids homosexuality.

Google "honor killings U.S." and you will be disgusted with the volume of results. Honor killings are sanctioned by Islam. Death is a systemic tenet of the "peaceful" religion. How can Muslims possibly respect and tolerate non-Muslims when they are duty-bound to kill their own family members for Sharia infractions. Islam in general has no respect for life.

The Wahhabist philosophy of Islam has successfully infiltrated U.S. institutions including the military, the prison system, public schools and universities, the political system, law enforcement, and key government agencies including the Department of Homeland Security. They have also infiltrated the American business world. Their goal is to replace the U.S. Constitution with the Quran and turn America (and the entire West) into an Islamic state - the Caliphate.

Political correctness has handicapped the FBI since Islamic appeasement became standard government policy. In 1993 as foreign-based terrorism was increasing, FBI Director, Louis Freeh's focus was on "domestic" terrorism - militias, white supremacists, anti-abortion groups, and rightwing extremists. Twenty years later, The FBI and Department of Homeland Security are still focused on domestic terrorism and are feeling very threatened by conservatives and Christians. By 2001, FBI counter terrorism personnel were decimated to a mere 6% of total FBI personnel. Terrorism was prosecuted in the U.S. under civil law. The 1993 World Trade Center bombers were tried in civil court just like other common "civil" criminals – not the terrorists they were. I can only imagine how frustrating it is for FBI agents to work effectively with tied hands.

In Seattle, Washington the FBI ran bus ads as part of their terrorism awareness campaign. The ads showed pictures of sixteen "wanted" terrorists, and yes they were all Muslim. The government acquiesced and pulled the ads when Islamic groups cried discrimination saying they were concerned for the safety of Muslims. Pamela Geller, the American Freedom Law Center reacted, *"The FBI is putting Americans at risk by submitting to the outrageous demands of Islamic supremacists. It is not the fault of the FBI that the world's most dangerous terrorists are jihadists...So now opposing jihad terror is "anti-Muslim." Opposing Sept. 11 (New York), July 7 (London), March 11 (Madrid), Mumbai,*

Bali, Boston, Fort Hood, Kenya's Westgate mall, Nigeria, et al is anti-Muslim."[341] Walid Shoebat added, *"Posting the images of wanted terrorists is now the business of hate mongers and those who defend said terrorists are freedom's champions."*

Muslim "sensitivity" training became a high priority and the training was conveniently directed by Wahhabists. Arab linguists working for the FBI celebrated 9/11 attacks - the same FBI employees paid to protect the U.S. Post 9/11, Arab-American Muslims were hired as translators. Not one Arab speaking Jew was hired because the Arabs would not tolerate it. So, Muslims were investigating Muslims at the FBI – Just like Eric Holder's Justice Department investigating itself. The FBI foreign language squad has very serious flaws including little or no security clearances, leaks, thefts, and spies posing serious national security threats. According to Paul Sperry, *"Extremely sensitive information was deliberately withheld by translators."*[342] Secret documents and audio tapes have been stolen; copies of top secret documents are left unattended, laptop computers containing classified information just "go missing." The FBI lost 317 laptops between 1999 and 2002. Is this not insanity?

The interview of then departing FBI director Robert Mueller by Catherine Herridge, Fox News was covered by Pamela Geller in a *The D.C. Clothesline* article.[343] Mueller was asked what the greatest threat to America is, and his response was, *"Al Qaida in the Arab Peninsula, Al Qaeda in Iraq, Al Shabab, etc., terror in the homeland, homegrown terror." "Devout Muslims in America are our gravest security concern."*

As if the problems in our U.S. prisons were not bad enough already, prisons are being used as breeding grounds to recruit domestic terrorists. Muslim chaplains are preaching violence and converting thousands of inmates to Islam. Muslims are hiring Muslim chaplains to lead prayer and counsel prisoners. Not surprisingly, Islam is the fastest growing religion in the prison system. Don't you think that fact alone should

---

[341] "Seattle Bowing to Islamic Supremacists," Pamela Gellar, AFLC, AFDI, posted by Freedom Outpost, http://www.freedomoutpost.com, October 14, 2013

[342] "Infiltration," Paul Sperry, TN: Nelson Current, 2005

[343] "Outgoing FBI Director Warns Americans: Jihadists Here in America are most Serious Security Concern," Pamela Geller, Atlas, Shrugs, The D.C. Clothesline, http://www.dcclothesline.com, August 8, 2013

raise concerns? If Christianity was the fastest growing religion in our prison system, the media and the civil rights groups would be in frenzy, but they have nothing to say since it involves Islam. Imam Warith-Deen Umar was a Muslim cleric in the New York prison system. He recruited and trained chaplains and counseled thousands of inmates. Umar is not a preacher of peace and respect as Islam claims, but instead glorifies violence and incites prisoners against America. He saw African American prisoners as "natural candidates" and said that prison *"is the perfect recruitment and training grounds for radicalism and the Islamic religion."*[344] Umar said the 9/11 attacks were justified and the hijackers are martyrs, not murderers.

Our U.S. military is made up of service members of all nationalities and religions. There is an estimated 10,000-20,000 Muslims in the U.S. Armed Forces and there is a growing reality that for some of these Muslims, religion precedes duty to country. Army psychiatrist Major Nidal Hasan was proof of that when he intentionally targeted and killed 13 unarmed soldiers and wounded another 32 inside Ft. Hood, Texas in 2009. Hasan himself said it was an act of jihad, yet unbelievably, the administration made the disgraceful decision to label it "workplace violence" instead of the terrorist attack it was.

That should never have happened. Political correctness protected and promoted this openly hostile Muslim officer. Robert Spencer explained, *"The rules on the conduct of military officers were ignored. He was a terrible physician and had no business treating soldiers. Yet, because of where he came from, and how he prayed to his god, they promoted him and set him loose and ignored his open, very obvious jihadism."*[345]

Political correctness has mandated "culturally sensitive workplaces" when it comes to Muslim employees. The Council on American-Islamic Relations has been kind enough to prepare *"An Employers Guide to Islamic Religious Practices"*[346] to insure Muslim-friendly work environments.

---

[344] Warith Deen Umar, http://www.discoverthenetworks.org, 6/11/2009

[345] "Survivors of Fort Hood jihad massacre suing U.S. government for allowing jihad murderer Hasan to rise through ranks because of political correctness," Robert Spencer, Jihad Watch, http:www.jihadwatch.com, August 4, 2013

[346] "An Employers Guide to Islamic Religious Practices 1997/2005," http://www. cair.com. CAIR also has "A Teachers Guide to Islamic Religious Practices"

The Guide is more than suggestive policy - it is a demand on American employers. Muslim rights have taken priority at work and school. CAIR claims to be championing Muslim rights, but the real agenda is to "Islamize the workplace." For example, San Francisco International Airport constructed a prayer space exclusively for Muslims. This prayer space, paid for by taxpayers includes a cleansing facility since Muslims have to wash for prayers five times a day. I have two questions about this. Why was taxpayer money used to build a "religious" facility? And, can you imagine your employer building a chapel for Christians to go and pray five times a day?

So where does our government stand on the Islamic issue? Presidential words and actions indicate that Islam has attained unconstitutional "special status" in the United States.

- During President Obama's 2009 speech in Egypt in which he invited the "outlawed" Muslim Brotherhood to attend, he said, *"Islam has always been a part of American history."* NO, it has not! I can't even imagine where that astonishing statement came from. Islam has contributed nothing to America. No Muslims were part of our war for independence, construction of the Constitution and laws of the land. No Muslims built the country agriculturally, industrially, economically, or scientifically. During World War II, Muslim sympathies were with Hitler and the Nazis. No Muslims were part of the civil rights movement. The Brotherhood in the crowd he was addressing promotes jihad, honor killings, and dhimmitude. They only recognize *Sharia law* and are not bound by any other government or constitutional law. I haven't seen any Muslim hospitals, orphanages, or legal charities in the United States. I challenge you to think of a single positive contribution Islam has made to America.

- President Obama said, *"The USA is not a Christian Nation."* Again, the facts prove otherwise. The U.S. Constitution and laws are based on Judeo-Christian principles. Townspeople with common Christian values built churches and schools and taught their children ethical behavior. As towns grew into prosperous cities, "American values" such as personal responsibility, self-reliability, love of family and charity grew as well. Christians built hospitals and orphanages. Christians built schools to provide education, and Christians promoted charity. Christians opened and maintained shelters providing food, clothing, and safe places to live. Christians have always responded immediately to disasters providing money, materials, volunteer labor and emotional support. Christian abolitionists never stopped championing the end of slavery. The list could go on and on. Yes, Mr. President, the USA is a Christian nation though the government is working very hard to change that.

- Egyptian newspaper, *Al Masryalyoum* English Edition reported researcher Mohamed Hasanein Heikahl saying the U.S. has repeatedly supported the Muslim Brotherhood's ascendancy in Egypt.[347]

- In January 2011 President Obama sent former U.S. Ambassador Frank Wisner to Cairo to meet secretly with senior Muslim Brotherhood leader Issam El-Erian. This was before Egyptian President Mubarak's government tumbled during the "Arab Spring."

- June 2011 President Obama announced the U.S. was going to establish formal ties with the (terrorist organization) the Muslim Brotherhood.

- When the Muslim Brotherhood won control of Egypt after President Mubarak was deposed, President Obama did not hesitate to send billions of dollars in military aid including F-16 fighter jets to Egypt. After the Egyptian military correctly removed President Morsi from power, Obama cut hundreds of millions of dollars in military and other aid to Egypt.

- President Obama's State Department under Secretary Hillary Clinton reversed a ruling not to allow the Muslim Brotherhood founder's grandson into the U.S. The State Department collaborated with the Organization of Islamic Cooperation (a group of governments) "heavily" influenced by the Muslim

[347] "Exclusive: Obama agrees to meeting with Brotherhood, sources say," Moner Adib, Al Masryalyoum, http://www.egyptindependent.com, June 08, 2013

Brotherhood seeking to restrict American free-speech when it comes to negative criticism of Islam.

- The U.S. State Department excluded Israel from its "Global Counterterrorism Forum."
  Sources:
  "The Muslim Brotherhood's Man in the White House," Robert Spencer, *Front Page Magazine*, http://www.frontpagemag.com, October 23, 2013; "Exclusive: Obama Agrees to meeting with Brotherhood sources say," *Moner Adib, Al Masryalyoum english edition*, http://www.egyptindependent.com, June 8, 2013; "Obama: Islam has Always Been a Part of America's History," David Goetsch, posted on Patriot Update, http://www.patriotupdate.com, October 15,2013; "Obama Reaches Out to the Islamic Culture that is Strangling America," John DeMayo, Freedom Outpost, http://www.freedomoutpost.com, October 25, 2013; "It Won't Be Long Before Obamas' Islamic Radicalization Becomes Irrepressible in America," John DeMayo, Freedom Outpost, http://www.freedomoutpost. com, November 16,2013

- Remember when President Obama stated in an interview that there wasn't a "smidgeon" of evidence of wrong-doing at the IRS? That was in February 2014 and then in March 2014 it was reported that, "Mohammad Weiss Rasool, busted by the FBI several years ago for spying on behalf of al-Qaida, reportedly now works for the deputy IRS chief financial officer as a financial management analyst. Yes, you read that correctly. A convicted al-Qaida spy is gainfully employed by our government and is working at the IRS."[348]

- On May 26, 2013 President Obama said," *The best way to prevent violent extremism is to work with the Muslim American community - which has consistently rejected terrorism - to identify signs of radicalization and partner with law enforcement when an individual is drifting toward violence."* Wrong again Mr. President, they do not reject terrorism.

  - Robert Spencer, Director of *Jihad Watch* responded to the President's statement: "*The Muslim American community has consistently rejected terrorism? Four separate studies since 1998 have all found that 80 percent of U.S. mosques were teaching jihad, Islamic supremacism,*

---

[348] "More Islamic Infiltration," Allan West, updates@allanwest.com, March 17, 2014

> *and hatred and contempt for Jews and Christians ... And in the summer of 2011 came another study showing that only 19 percent of mosques in the U.S. don't teach jihad violence and/or Islamic supremacism.*"[349]

- As President Obama celebrated his 5th Ramadan dinner with select Muslims in the State Dining Room at the White House, he said that throughout our nation's history, *"Islam has contributed to the character of our country."*[350] He also said, *"Muslim Americans and their good works have helped to build our nation, and we've seen the results...Every day, Muslim Americans are helping to shape the way that we think and the way that we work and the way that we do business...And that's the spirit that we celebrate tonight - the dreamers, the creators whose ideas are pioneering new industries, creating new jobs and unleashing new opportunities for all of us."*

  - WHAT? That is crazy talk. Again, I challenge anyone to tell me exactly what Muslim good works have helped build our nation. Who are these dreamers and creators of new industries that he talking about? I find it extremely disturbing that the leader of the free world would make such erroneous statements unless he really does have a special attachment to Islam.

It's not surprising then, that our government complies with Muslim demands. Obsessive political correctness to be non-offensive (to select groups) is undermining our national security and creating additional risks to Americans. Politicians ignore evidence that profiling based on human characteristics is effective. But in an effort not to offend one particular group, little old ladies, small children, and disabled individuals are routinely selected for additional security screening at

---

[349] "Obama claims That Working With Muslim Brotherhood Will Bring Victory Over Terrorism," Pamela Geller, Freedom Outpost, http://www.freedomoutpost.com, May 26,2013

[350] "Obama Celebrates: 'Islam Has Contributed to the Character of Our Country,'" The Hill.com posted on Minuteman News.com, http://www.minutemennews.com, July 26, 2013

airports. Logic in no way enters the picture. "Selective equality" trumps security.

Our government is quietly being colonized with questionable political appointments, many now being made by President Obama. I am not questioning the race, religion, or heritage of these appointments. I am questioning the appointees' very real ties to suspected and even known terrorist related organizations and people. For instance, Faisal Gill was appointed by the Bush administration as the Senior Policy Advisor to the Under Secretary for Information Analysis and Infrastructure Protection at the Department of Homeland Security. The problem I had with this appointment was that Gill served as spokesman and "Director of Government Affairs" for the American Muslim Council which was founded by Abdurahman Alamoudi who was sentenced in 2003 to twenty-three years in prison for bringing more than a million dollars into the U.S. from the Libyan government. Alamoudi is also a supporter of Hamas and Hezbollah. Gill taught Muslim youth "political activism" at the Saudi sponsored Muslim Student Association's annual conference in Washington, telling students that they are in "*a critical position*" to cultivate [American] society for Islam. I am not at all comfortable with a ranking Department of Homeland Security member who has access to strategic information and is responsible for policy development that was not only associated with American Muslim Council, but acted in a teaching position to openly "promote" society for Islam.

David Hossein Safavian, an Iranian American lawyer and lobbyist was confirmed by the Senate in 2004 as Administrator for Federal Procurement at the Office of Management and Budget and was in control of $300 billion of annual government business contracts. Like Gill, Safavian is tied to Abdurahman Alamoudi the Hamas and Hezbollah supporter. As Chief-of-Staff at GSA, he made it easier for minority businesses including Arab immigrants to receive federal contracts. This is troubling because the GSA has access to over 1,600 government-owned buildings. The GSA contracts out to private janitorial, custodial, maintenance, and SECURITY firms including utility plants and NONE undergo FBI background checks. Since they are NOT federal employees, they do not even have to be citizens. Does that make any sense at all?

I remember when NASA was the awe-inspiring agency capable

of doing the impossible – putting a man on the moon. The missions, rockets, shuttles and all the astronauts were iconic. I clearly remember visiting Kennedy Space Center in Florida with some pretty excited kids. And I felt so lucky to be able to witness a launch – even if was just one of our Mars rockets and not a shuttle.

We no longer have space shuttles or any other way to reach into space. We the United States of America, once the undisputable leader of space research and exploration now has to pay Russia and other foreign governments to put our satellites in space and deliver our people to the International Space Station which we still spend billions of dollars on to maintain. When NASA's budget was thoroughly slashed, President Obama ordered NASA to use its revised funding for a "Muslim Outreach program." That is so bogus. Unless the US now teaches rocket launching technology to Muslims, what possibly does Muslim Outreach have to do with NASA?

Zahid Bukhari, Director of the Pew Foundation's Project, "Muslims in the American Public Square," and Fellow at the Center for Muslim-Christian Understanding, Georgetown University was interviewed on October 14, 2004 regarding Muslims in American Politics. Bukhari believes the National Islamic Shura Council, which consists of the leadership of all major organizations, should establish an effective secretariat in Washington, D.C. *"Inward unity and outward caring for the society will ultimately give the Muslim community an opportunity to lead America and influence American foreign policy toward the other peoples of the world." "Muslims in America are also more active politically and Islamically than are Muslims in any other country. These characteristics, plus being strategically placed in the belly of the sole super power of the world today, would* **give the Muslim community in America added effectiveness in its role as guardian for the future affairs of the Muslim world."** Did you get that? Mr. Bukhari clearly said "...give the Muslim community an opportunity to lead America and influence American foreign policy?" And he followed up by stating that "being strategically placed in the belly of the sole super power" would give Muslims in America (not American-Muslims) "effectiveness in its role as the guardian for the future affairs of the Muslim World." **They are** telling us what they are doing and what they plan to do and no one seems to care.

What a coincidence. We now have a new House caucus in Washington - the Ahmadiyya Muslim Caucus. Naseem Mahdi, the national vice president of the Ahmadiyya Muslim Community USA clearly stated their mission: *"We will not take the selfish approach that we will only talk about the rights of Ahmadiyya Muslims. We will talk about the rights of every human being, especially the rights of every believer."*[351] So, what is so bad about that statement, you say? The second sentence explains everything. Non-Muslims are not believers and are not considered human beings; therefore they are speaking ONLY about Muslim rights as prescribed by Sharia law.

The Investigative Project on Terrorism (IPT) published a very interesting article written by John Rossomando regarding Egyptian magazine, *Rose El-Youssef* December 22, 2012 article. The Egyptian magazine identified six "American Muslim activists" who are also Muslim Brotherhood operatives working with the Obama administration. These men have influence over U.S. policy and the Egyptian magazine feels that the Obama White House is the most important supporter of the Muslim Brotherhood.[352]

1. **Arif Alikhan:** Assistant secretary of Homeland Security for policy development
   a. A founder of the World Islamic Organization (identified by *Rose al-Youssef* as a Muslim Brotherhood subsidiary)
   b. *Rose al-Youssef* suggested he was responsible for the *"file of Islamic states"* in the White House and was the direct link between the Obama administration and the Arab Spring revolutions in 2011

---

[351] "Islam In Our Government: Muslims Get Their Own Official Caucus On Capitol Hill Backed By Obama," The *Washington Times*, News post by http://www.madworldnews.com, March 1, 2014

[352] "Egyptian Magazine: Muslim Brotherhood Infiltrates Obama Administration," John Rossomando, The Investigative Report on Terrorism, http://www.investigativeproject.org, January 3, 2013

2. **Mohammed Elibiary**: Member of the Homeland Security Advisory Council

    a. Denies having ties to the Muslim Brotherhood but the Egyptian magazine believes he may have *leaked secret materials* from Department of Homeland Security databases

    b. Participated in defining the Obama administration counterterrorism strategy

    c. Has record of criticizing successful terrorism prosecutions

    d. The magazine claims that Elibiary wrote President Obama's speech telling former Egyptian President Mubarak to leave office

It is frightening that this man advises federal, state and local law enforcement agencies on homeland security issues. As "Honest" U.S. media reports:

- *"Barack Obama and Mohamed Elibiary are engaging in taqiyya. They are deceiving the American people about Islam. They are deceiving them about our history."*[353] Also posted - Mohamed Elibiary's tweet on October 31, 2013: "America and yes I do consider the United States of America an Islamic country with an Islamically compliant constitution."

- *"...the Obama administration has repeatedly demonstrated that they will cater to the radical Muslim Brotherhood ahead of most American conservative and Christian groups so Elibiary has been allowed to spout out his Islamic ideology and is now warning Americans about their attitudes towards Muslims."*[354] Author Dave Jolly finds Elibiary's comments "alarming," and so does

---

[353] "Barack Obama's DHS Advisor Mohamed Elibiary: America is an Islamic Country," Tim Brown, Freedom Outpost, http://www.freedomoutpost.com, November 1, 2013

[354] "Muslim DHS Advisor Is Clear and Present Danger to America," Dave Jolly, Godfather Politics, http://www.godfatherpolitics.com, October 19, 2013

Michael Meunier, President of the Al-Haya Party in Egypt who said, *"I think the Obama administration should be ashamed to have had someone like this in their administration. This underscores the thinking inside the Obama administration."*

- Janna Brock brings to light yet another concern about this questionable member of the Department of Homeland Security Advisory Panel. Elibiary had the unmistakable *"R4BIA four finger salute"* symbol of the Muslim Brotherhood on his "Twitter" profile. Make no mistake - it does not stand for "Freedom4All" as is claimed. It is the Islamic symbol for world domination after crushing western democracy. *"The infiltration of all levels of American government is coming to fruition." This blatantly radical Islamic symbol is an affront to America, a reminder of who our enemy is. The enemy is Islam. And the enemy sits in the highest offices in the land, as a part of our highest security personnel."* Janna likens it as being led to slaughter by the people sworn to protect us. Take a good look at this symbol by Googling: "R4BIA four finger salute." You will notice that New York is written on that symbol as part of All THE WORLD the Muslims plan to conquer.

3. **Rashad Hussain**: U.S. special envoy to the Organization of the Islamic Conference
    a. *Rose El-Youssef* claims he maintains close ties with the Muslim Brotherhood network in America
    b. Participated in the June 2002 annual conference of the American Muslim Council formerly headed by convicted terrorist financier Abdurahman Alamoudi
    c. Organizing committee participant of the "Critical Islamic Reflection" with Muslim Brotherhood members Jamal Barzinji, Hisham al-Talib and Yaqub Mizra

4. **Salam al-Marayati**: Co-founder of the Muslim Public Affairs Council (MPAC)
   a. *Rose El-Youssef* links the MPAC to the international Muslim Brotherhood

5. **Imam Mohamed Magid**: President of the Islamic Society of North America (ISNA)
   a. ISNA founded by Muslim Brotherhood members
   b. Has given speeches and conferences on American Middle East policy at the State Department and **advises the FBI**

6. **Eboo Patel**: Member of President Obama's Advisory Council on Faith-Based Neighborhood Partnerships
   a. *Rose El-Youssef* states Patel maintains a close relationship with Hani Ramadan, grandson of the Muslim Brotherhood founder Hasan al-Banna
   b. Member of the Muslim Students Association which is the Muslim Brotherhood

Obama Appointee Azizah al-Hibri was appointed to the United States Commission on International Religious Freedom. Journalist Daniel Greenfield explains what an irony this is considering al-Hibri is a Muslim professor and granddaughter of a Sheikh *"who claims that the Koran inspired Thomas Jefferson and the Founders and that the Saudi criminal justice system is more moral than the American one."* She also believes that American law is inferior to the Koran, Islam does not need to be reformed, and America should reform to Islamic standards. *"Placing a woman who believes that American law is inferior to that of the Koran on an American commission to promote international religious freedom perverts the purpose of the commission and promotes religious tyranny instead."*[355]

---

[355] "Obama Appointee Claims Sharia Law Is Superior to American Law - Claims Founding Fathers Were Inspired By The Quran," Daniel Greenfield, published by Chic91160, Sharia Awareness Action Network, United States Defense League, http://www.usdl.info, July 1, 2013

Robert O. Malley was candidate Obama's foreign policy advisor in 2007 until he was fired when the public became aware of his "notorious" ties to Hamas, the PLO and other jihadist groups. Jump to 2014 and President Obama appointed Robert O. Malley senior director at the National Security Council (NSC). Mr. Malley advises the president on Middle East policy.

On the federal government social scene, a celebration was held in Washington, DC on February 25, 2014 to honor one Mr. Rached Ghannouchi, leading Islamic scholar and president of the Nahdha Party in Tunisia. Over 150 guests were in attendance including senior U.S. officials, diplomats, Middle East experts, media representatives, and Tunisian Nationals. Daniel Greenfield writing for *Front Page Magazine* sheds a little light on the special guest of honor.[356]

- During the Gulf War Ghannouchi said: Muslims now faced *"Crusader America,"* the *"enemy of Islam." "We must wage unceasing war against the Americans until they leave the land of Islam, or we will burn and destroy all their interests across the entire Islamic world."* After the Gulf War he applied for a U.S. visa but was denied.

- "Sheik" Ghannouchi blessed and praised the mothers of Palestinian suicide bombers. "The Palestinian woman, mother of the Shahids [martyrs], is a martyr herself, and she has created a new model of woman…"

- Ghannouchi said, that the Arab Spring *"will achieve positive results on the path to the Palestinian cause and threaten the extinction of Israel. I give you the good news that the Arab region will get rid of the bacillus of Israel…"*

This is a man deserving of United States government honors? **Does anyone in the federal government not associated with the Obama administration have a problem with any of this? They should!**

Of note, if you are so inclined to financially support the future

---

[356] "US Officials Attend Dinner Honoring Islamist Who Called for 'Unceasing War Against the Americans,'" Daniel Greenfield, *Front Page Magazine*, http"//www.frontpagemag.com, March 27, 2014

Barack Obama Presidential Library, I advise that you be careful to make sure that your donation is going to the correct organization since there are two Barack H. Obama Foundations:

1. New non-profit foundation headed by the president's friend, Marty Nesbitt was established to plan and build President Obama's presidential library.
2. The other non-profit Barack H. Obama Foundation (named for the President's father) is headed by the president's brother, Malik (Roy) Obama. At the same time the IRS was targeting and holding up for as long as possible non-profit 501(c)(3) status applications for conservative groups, Lois Lerner, IRA official who suspiciously invoked her 5th amendment right not to answer questions at a Congressional hearing on the matter had readily approved Malik Obama's foundation and even backdated the tax exempt status by thirty-eight months. Strangely and illegally I might add is the fact that the foundation had been soliciting donations as a certified U.S. tax-exempt organization for years. Tell me again that the IRS is not corrupt.

The foundation's website: www.barackhobamafoundation. org, describes the foundation as a humanitarian entity. The Jewish Press, www.jewishpress.com published an article on this foundation with a photo of Malik (Roy) Obama at a conference in Yemen in 2010. The significance of the photo, which no longer appears on the website, is that Obama is wearing a Hamas keffiya with the Arabic words, *"Jerusalem is ours-we are coming!"* The keffiya also includes a map which purports to be of 'Palestine. On the map, the Mediterranean Sea and the Jordan River are outlined in blue, beneath which is written the Palestinian Arab war cry: *"From the River to the Sea."*[357] President Obama had to know about his brother's foundation and affiliations; Malik (Roy) was the best man at Barack's 1992 wedding, and Barack was the best man at one of Malik (Roy's) weddings.

---

[357] "Obama's Brother, 'Best Man,' Dons Hamas Regalia," Lori Lowenthal Marcus, *The Jewish Press*, http:www.jewishpress.com, January 31, 2014

Unfortunately it doesn't end there. It seems that when Malik is not working at his Barack H. Obama Foundation (named after his father - not the president) he finds time to be the executive director of the *Islamic Dawa Organization* (IDO) which is a member organization of *The Union of Good (UG)*. *The Union of Good,* founded by Hamas in 2000 is an umbrella organization representing more than 50 Islamic fundraising groups worldwide with the purpose of transferring funds to Hamas. The *UG* headed by Muslim Brotherhood leader Yusuf al-Qaradawi was designated a terrorist organization by the U.S. Treasury Department in 2008: *UNION OF GOOD* (a.k.a. 101 DAYS CAMPAIGN; a.k.a. CHARITY COALITION; a.k.a. I'TILAF AL-KHAIR; a.k.a. I'TLAF AL-KHAYR), P.O. Box 136301, Jeddah 21313, Saudi Arabia.[358] The Islamic Dawa Organization has funded Hamas; "it still does and is part of the coalition of the Union of Good." Islamic Dawa Organization is listed as one of the affiliate organizations on the UG website complete with contact information to send contributions - for Hamas.

I was wondering why the IRS, the Department of Justice, the Department of Homeland Security and the State Department aren't investigating any of this and then I realized: The IRS is probably too busy harassing conservative groups and auditing critics of the President; The Department of Justice is too busy covering up department scandals, doing simulated investigations of the IRS and prosecuting conservatives; the Muslim officials at the Department of Homeland Security certainly won't investigate their own, and the State Department is too busy covering up Benghazi and protecting certain principal people, leaving no federal agency free to investigate. Hello Congress, this is where you're supposed to step-in.

The United States is under attack from within as well as from abroad. Islam is not an innocuous religion, nor should it be elevated to a position of prominence alongside Christianity and Judaism as a mainstream religion of the United States. **The Muslim agenda is to make Islam the only world religion and restore and enforce their Sharia law around the world.** Since Muhammad in the seventh century, this is, and has always been the goal of Islam.

---

[358] "Exposed: Obama Family Part of Secret Muslim Terror Operation," Freedom Outpost, http://www.freedomoutpost.com, February 1, 2014

Political correctness has crippled our government, institutions, schools, and workplaces, and is now compromising our very security. The only thing that has been hijacked is our Constitution. Politicians, lawyers, Muslim activists, the ACLU, and others have desecrated our founding principles and have manipulated our legal system for the advancement of their own agendas. The very core of our freedom and protection has been turned into a weapon to destroy our valued democracy and way of life.

Even Hollywood plays a part to promote the "peaceful" religion. Whether it is a commitment to political correctness, or intimidation by Muslim leaders, Hollywood presents a deceitful image of terrorism while ignoring the reality of Muslim terrorists. Daniel Greenfield posted an article, well worth a read on Front Page Magazine in which he identifies numerous movie storylines with Serbian, Russian, and even neo-nationalists of the Netherlands terrorists - not Muslim terrorists. *"In real life, terrorists are almost always Muslim. In the movie theater, they are anything but. America's fictional secret agents, covert operatives and rogue cops who play by their own rules have spent more time battling Serbian terrorists than Muslim terrorists."*[359] For example: *"When the Serbs aren't available, the Russians have to step in...When Jack Ryan: Shadow Recruit featured a terrorist cell in Dearborn, even though Muslims dominate the area, the villains were shown operating out of a Russian Orthodox church and getting their cues from a priest reading the Bible while the terrorists cried out, 'Slava Bogu' or "Praise God."* Imagine that.

---

[359] "Hollywood's Muslim Lies," Daniel Greenfield, *Front Page Magazine*, http://www.frontpagemag.com, January 24, 2014

> **Warnings**
>
> There are numerous Islamic experts we need to listen to. These people have seen the true face of Islam and are aware of the real Islamic plan. They have committed a great deal of time researching the issues and their findings should be taken seriously. It is a matter of self-defense and national security. Their collective voices are finally breaking through the media's *Muslim wall of silence*. Truth is not "hate speech."

- **Abdullah Al Araby**: Contributing author *The Pen vs. the Sword*, http://www.islamreview.com
  Dedicated to exposing the hidden side of Islam; the teachings that are deliberately omitted by Muslim activists in their attempt to spread the religion of Islam in the West. Some great articles by Abdullah Al Araby include:
  - *Islam: the Facade, the Facts*
  - *The True Face of Islam*
  - *Incredible Teachings of Mohammed*
  - *Being a Muslim's Wife*
  - *If Islam Ruled America*
  - *The Bible vs. the Quran*
  - *Nothing in Common*
  - *Masters of Deception-The Terror of Islam*
  - *The Islamization of American Schools*
  - *The Islamization of Europe*
  - *Apostasy in Islam – The Point of No Return*

- **Jed Babbin**: Former United States Deputy Undersecretary of Defense, author, and former editor of *Human Events*, Contributing editor, *The American Spectator*
  - *In The Words of Our Enemies*, (Regnery Publishing, 2007)
  - *Freedom's Foe: What Every American Should Know About the United Nations*, Green Hill Publishers, 2005

- **Claire Berlinski**: Journalist, academic and consultant who has worked in Britain, France, Switzerland, Thailand, Laos and Turkey. She has seen Islamic radicalism and terrorist indoctrination thrive in Europe and warns us that Europe's Islamic problem is our problem too.
  - *Menace in Europe: Why the Continent's Crisis is America's, too,"* New York, Crown Forum, 2006

- **Tony Blankley**: The late Mr. Blankley was born in London, United Kingdom and was an Executive Vice President with Edelman public relations in Washington, a Visiting Senior Fellow in National-Security Communications at the Heritage Foundation, co-host of the nationally syndicated radio program, *Left, Right & Center*, and an author.
  - *The West's Last Chance: Will We Win the Clash of Civilizations?* Regnery Publishing, 2005
  - *American Grit: What It Will Take to Survive and Win in the 21ˢᵗ Century* Regnery Publishing 2008

- **The Clarion Project**: Independently funded, non-profit organization committed to exposing Islamic extremism and promoting dialog by bringing together Middle East experts, scholars, human rights activists and Muslims to promote tolerance and moderation and challenge extremism. The Clarion Project website is a treasure trove of pertinent information [http://www.clarionproject.org]. They address Islamic issues head-on and work with Muslims who do condemn violence and call for reform. Clarion's movies address religious persecution, human and women's rights, jihad and the West, and Iran.
  - *Iranium:* What happens when Iran becomes nuclear
  - *The Third Jihad*: The danger radical Islam poses to the U.S. and the West
  - *Obsession*: Global jihad's goal of world domination and ministry of hate
  - *Honor Diaries:* Highlights the abuse of women including: genital mutilation, honor killings, acts of

violence, and gender inequality. Nine women's rights advocates expose the oppression of and violence toward women in Muslim-majority countries

CAIR went on a crusade to diminish the truth brought to light in the "Honor Diaries" calling it a campaign to smear Islam.

- **Gregory M. Davis**: Author and filmmaker who exposes the totalitarianism of Islam in its governance of all aspects of Muslim life – religious, political, and personal.
  - *Religion of Peace? Islam's War Against the World*, World Ahead Publishing, Inc., 2006
  - *Islam: What the West Needs to Know* Documentary – director: Bryan Daly, Gregory M. Davis, 2007

- **Steven Emerson**: Serves as the Executive Director of the **Investigative Project on Terrorism** (data and intelligence on Islamic and Middle Eastern terrorists groups). Emerson is one of the leading authorities on Islamist extremist networks, financing and operations and provides briefings to U.S. government and law enforcement agencies, members of Congress and congressional committees. He has testified before Congress numerous times on the terrorist networks of al Qaeda, Hamas, Hezbollah, Islamic Jihad, and worldwide Islamic militancy. http://www.steveemerson.com
  - *Jihad Incorporated: A Guide to Militant Islam in the U.S.*, Prometheus, 2006
  - *American Jihad: The Terrorists Living Among Us*, The Free Press, 2002

- **Brigette Gabriel**: Terrorism expert, journalist, author, commentator, activist, and founder of the **American Congress for Truth** (ACT) for America. ACT promotes citizen involvement and action to strengthen national security and defend American democratic values against the "assault of radical Islam." www.actforamerica.org

- <u>Frank Gaffney</u>: Founder and president of the **Center for Security Policy.** Mr. Gaffney is also a columnist at the *Washington Times, Big Peace,* and *Townhall,* and is a radio host on Secure Freedom Radio. He has an extensive knowledge of Islam and has been warning us about the Muslim Brotherhood's infiltration into the United States for quite some time.

- <u>Pamela Geller</u>: Founder, editor and publisher of Atlas Shrugs (www.atlasshrugs.com); President of the **American Freedom Defense Initiative** (AFDI) and **Stop Islamization of America** (SIOA); Columnist for *The American Thinker* and *World Net Daily.*
    - *The Post-American Presidency: The Obama Administration's War on America,* Pamela Geller, Robert Spencer and John Bolton, Threshold Editions; 1 edition 2010
    - *Stop the Islamization of America: A Practical Guide for the Resistance,* WND Books 2011. *This book was written since most parents *"have no idea that their children are being quietly indoctrinated into having a positive view of the most violent, oppressive, misogynist ideology on the planet today...Each individual must fight back, the book teaches you how..."* [Pamela Geller, January 2014]
    - *Freedom or Submission: On the Dangers of Islamic Extremism & American Complacency,* Create Space Independent Publishing Platform 2013

- <u>The Global Muslim Brotherhood Daily Watch</u>: (www.globalmbwatch.com)
  The (GMBDW) monitors Muslim Brotherhood activities, commentary, and historical background. *"The GMBDW represents neither a political nor a religious point of view and seeks only to present the best available and reliable information on the daily activities of the Global Muslim Brotherhood."* Steven Merley, an investigator and intelligence specialist is the editor of GMBDW and has authored several investigative reports,

contributes to counter-terrorism events, documentaries, and provides information to US agencies and non-governmental agencies.

- **Ayaan Hirsi Ali:** Somali-born Dutch politician living in seclusion due to death threats (from members of the "peaceful religion") because of her screenplay, *Submission* (for which Theo van Gogh was murdered by a Muslim in 2004) focusing on the brutality inflicted on Muslim women. She is a fellow at the American Enterprise Institute and has received several awards for her work on women's rights and human rights.
  - *Infidel*, Free Press, 2008
  - *Nomad: From Islam to America: A Personal Journey Through the Clash of Civilizations*, Atria Books, 2011

- **David Horowitz:** Founder of the David Horowitz **Freedom Center**, editor of the website *FrontPage* Magazine, writes for *NewsMax* magazine, and has founded the activist group, Students for Academic Freedom.
  - *The Professors: The 101 Most Dangerous Academics in America*, Regnery Publishing, Inc. 2006
  - *Unholy Alliance: Radical Islam and the American Left*, Regnery Publishing, 2006
  - *Obama and Islam*, David Horowitz and Robert Spencer (David Horowitz Freedom Center, 2010)

- **Raymond Ibrahim:** Associate director of the **Middle East Forum**, editor and translator of The *Al Qaeda Reader*, composes articles for *Jihad Watch* (www.jihadwatch.com), authors numerous papers on radical Islam, briefs governmental agencies, and has testified before the House Armed Services Committee on the educational/epistemological failures dominating American discourse concerning Islam. http://www.raymondibrahim.com
  - *The Al Qaeda Reader*, Broadway Books, 2007
    - Ibrahim translated previously unknown al Qaeda documents written in Arabic that he

says *"proves once and for all that, despite the propaganda of al-Qaeda and its sympathizers, radical Islam's war with the West is not finite and limited to political grievances-real or imagined-but is existential, transcending time and space and deeply rooted in faith."*[360]

◦ *Crucified Again: Exposing Islam's New War on Christians*, Regnery Publishing, 2013

- **Walid Shoebat:** Former member of the Palestinian Liberation Organization (PLO) who participated in violence against Israel and spent time in Jerusalem Central Prison. Shoebat's life changed in 1993 when he studied the Jewish Bible (Tanach) and recognized the truth about Judaism and Islam. He travels the country exposing anti-Semitism and Islamic hatred of Jews and Christians. http://wwwshoebat.com

  ◦ *Why I Left Jihad*, Top Executive Media, 2005
  ◦ *Why WE Want to Kill You*, Top Executive Media, 2007
  ◦ *Islam: What the West Needs to Know (Documentary – Director: Bryan Daly, Gregory M. Davis 2007)*
  ◦ *God's War on Terror*, Top Executive Media, 2008

- **Robert Spencer:** Director of *Jihad Watch*, author of eight books on Islam and jihad, as well as hundreds of articles on jihad and Islamic terrorism, and has led seminars on Islam and jihad for the U.S. Central Command, U.S. Army Command and General Staff College, a Department of Homeland Security task force, the FBI, the Joint Terrorism Task Force, and the U.S. intelligence community. He also spoke at a workshop sponsored by the U.S. State Department and the German Foreign Ministry, and has appeared on numerous cable news networks.

  ◦ *The Truth About Mohammad Founder of the World's Most Intolerant Religion*, Regnery Publishing, Inc., 2006

---

[360] *"The Al Qadea Reader,"* Edited and translated by Raymond Ibrahim, NY: Broadway Books, 2007

- □ *The Politically Incorrect Guide to Islam and the Crusades*, Regnery Publishing, Inc., 2005
- □ *Islam Unveiled: Disturbing Questions About the World's Fastest-Growing Faith*, Encounter Books, 2002
- □ *The Myth of Islamic Intolerance: How Islamic Law Treats Non-Muslims*, Prometheus Books, 2005
- □ *Religion of Peace? Why Christianity Is and Islam Isn't*, Regnery Publishing, Inc. 2007
- □ *Onward Muslim Soldiers: How Jihad Still Threatens America and the West*, Regnery Publishing Inc., 2003
- □ *Stealth Jihad: How Radical Islam is Subverting America Without Guns or Bombs*, Regnery Publishing, Inc. 2008
- □ *The Post-American Presidency: The Obama Administration's War on America*, Pamela Geller, Robert Spencer and John Bolton (Threshold Editions; 1 edition 2010)
- □ *Not Peace But a Sword: The Great Chasm Between Christianity and Islam*, Catholic Answers, 2013
- □ *Did Muhammad Exist? An Inquiry into Islam's Obscure Origins* (Intercollegiate Studies Institute: 1 edition, 2012)
- □ ***Arab Winter Comes To America,*** Regnery Publishing, 2014. *"The Arab Spring" uncorked a jihadist genie in North Africa and the Middle East. It is about to wreak its mayhem here, with renewed terrorism. Americans need to inform themselves of the threat – and ensure that their elected government in Washington takes action." "It is essential reading."*[361]

- ■ **Paul Sperry**: Investigative journalist, Hoover Institution fellow, and author.
  - □ *Infiltration: How Muslim Spies and Subversives Have Penetrated Washington*, Nelson Current, 2005

---

[361] Jihad Watch website: http://www.jihadwatch.org, April 14, 2014 – Robert Spencer's new book

- *Muslim Mafia: Inside the Secret Underworld that's Conspiring to Islamize America,* Paul Sperry and P. David Gaubatz, WND Books 2009

- **Eric Stakelbeck**: Author, Middle East and national security related authority, and terrorism analyst. As a correspondent, he interviewed world leaders and Islamic terrorists. He was a senior writer and analyst at the *Investigative Project on Terrorism,* founded by Steven Emerson. Eric is host of *The Watchman,* a weekly program on CBN News, and has been warning us about the Muslim Brotherhood for years.
  - *The Terrorist Next Door: How Government is Deceiving You About the Islamist Threat,* Regnery Publishing, 2011
  - *The Brotherhood: America's Next Great Enemy,* Regnery Publishing, 2013

- **Mark Steyn**: Canadian author and political commentator. http://www.steynonline.com
  - *America Alone: The End of the World As We Know It,* Regnery Publishing, Inc. 2006
  - *After America: Get Ready for Armageddon,* Regnery Publishing, 2011

- **Kenneth R. Timmerman**: Investigative reporter and contributing editor for *NewsMax.* His investigative work includes the exposure of intelligence wars, partisan bureaucrats, and the media. He exposed Iran's nuclear weapons program in 2006, exposed Osama bin Laden in 1998 in an article for Reader's Digest, and conducted a study on the unconventional weapons programs of Iran, Libya, and Syria. Timmerman is a columnist, has testified before Congress, and since 1987, has operated the **Middle East Data Project, Inc.** that provides investigative support and policy guidance to government agencies and private companies. http://www.kentimmerman.com
  - *Preachers of Hate: Islam and The War on America,* Crown Forum, 2003

- **Serge Trifkovic:** Serbian-American author and foreign affairs analyst. He was the foreign-affairs editor for *Chronicle* magazine, is a columnist for several publications, and is the director of the Center for International Affairs at the Rockford Institute. Trifkovic was a political consultant to Alexander, Crown Prince of Yugoslavia and former Yugoslav president Vojislav Kostunica, has testified to the Canadian House of Commons regarding the Balkans, and testified as an expert witness at the International Tribunal for the former Yugoslavia. http://www.trifkovic. mysite.com
  - *The Sword of the Prophet: Islam; History, Theology, Impact on the World,* Regina Orthodox Press, 2007
  - *Defeating Jihad: How the War on Terrorism May Yet Be Won, In Spite of Ourselves,* Regina Orthodox Press, 2006

- **Ibn Warraq:** Born in India to Muslim parents who migrated to Pakistan where as a boy, he attended a Madrasah and learned the Quran by heart. He is the founder of the **Institute of Secularization of Islamic Society**, a senior research fellow at the Center for Inquiry, and has spoken at the United Nations "Victims of Jihad" conference.
  - *Why I Am Not a Muslim,* Prometheus Books, 1995
  - *The Origins of the Quran,* Prometheus Books, 1998
  - *The Quest for the Historical Muhammad,* Prometheus Books, 2000
  - *What the Koran Really Says,* Prometheus Books, 2002
  - *Leaving Islam: Apostates Speak Out,* Prometheus Books, 2003
  - *Defending the West: A Critique of Edward Said's Orientalism,* Prometheus Books, 2007
  - *Why the West is Best: A Muslim Apostate's Defense of Liberal Democracy,* Encounter Books, 2011
  - *Koranic Allusions: The Bible, Qumranian, and Pre-Islamic Background to the Koran,* Prometheus Books, 2013

- **Geert Wilders:** Head of the Freedom Party (PVV) in the Netherlands. He has been warning the West for many years and has unjustly been labeled and condemned a racist for speaking the truth about Islam. He has had 24 hour protection for at least 10 years, since Islamists have vowed to kill him. He has a large group of European support but not publicly since opposing Islam in any way is a very dangerous practice there. Intimidation and threats have worked very successfully in Europe. Did Europe not learn anything from WWII? Wake up U.S. unless things change, this is our future.

- **Paul L. Williams:** Journalist, author, consultant, and adjunct professor of humanities and philosophy at Wilkes University and The University of Scranton. Williams was a consultant to the FBI and worked with Canadian officials to expose a plot to behead the Prime Minister and blow up parliament.
  - *The Al Qaeda Connection: International Terrorism, Organized Crime, and the Coming Apocalypse,* Prometheus Books, 2005
  - *Osama's Revenge: The Next 9/11, What the Media and the Government Haven't Told You,* Prometheus Books, 2004
  - *The Day of Islam: The Annihilation of America and the Western World,* Prometheus Books, 2007
  - *Crescent Moon Rising: The Islamic Transformation of America,* Prometheus Books, 2013

- **Bat Ye'Or:** Egyptian-born British scholar and author. Ye'Or focuses on non-Muslims living in the Middle East particularly Christian and Jewish dhimmis living under Islamic governments. She has written numerous articles, has provided briefings to the United Nations and the U.S. Congress.
  Ye'Or's works include:
  - *Islam and Dhimmitude: Where Civilizations Collide,* Farleigh Dickinson University Press, 2002

- □ *The Decline of Christianity Under Islam: From Jihad to Dhimmitude: Seventh – Twentieth Century,* Farleigh Dickinson University Press, 1996
- □ *The Dhimmi: Jews and Christians Under Islam,* Fairleigh Dickinson University Press, 1985

Even Al Qaeda is warning us! Al Qaeda's *Inspire* magazine publishes articles inciting violence, weapons-making advice and suggestions of targets in the U.S. and abroad.[362] A recent article found at: https://ia600601.us.archive.org/18/items/INSPIRE-12/INS-EH.pdf and reported on by Kerry Picket of *Breitbart,* suggests the use of car bombs inside the United States. The magazine's *Letter from the Editor* is very informative and very disturbing. Some of the editor's letter highpoints are:

- Whenever Al-Qaeda is mentioned, Americans think of vests and car bombs
- Americans fear vests and car bombs. They have seen the destruction in Iraq and Afghanistan
- There are many Feisal Shahzads (Pakistani-American citizens arrested for the attempted May 2010 car bombing in Times Square) living in the U.S. "yearning" to fulfill their jihad duty
- *"The American government was unable to protect its citizens from pressure cooker bombs in backpacks, I wonder if they are ready to stop car bombs!"*
- *"Therefore, as our responsibility to the Muslim Ummah in general and Muslims living in America in particular, Inspire Magazine humbly presents to you a simple improvised home recipe of Shahzad's car bomb."*

The article lists specific places and times to attack European targets including the Bastille Day Parade in Paris and soccer stadiums in England. As for America – first and foremost, it was suggested to target

---

[362] "Al-Qaeda Calls For Car Bomb Attacks on American Cities, Targets Abroad," Kerry Picket, Breitbart Big Peace, http://www.breitbart.com/Big-Peace, March 15, 2014

people not buildings by placing car bombs where many people are in attendance such as sporting events, election campaigns and festivals. You will notice in the article that his information is flawed (like the Air Force based in Chicago, for instance) but he does identify city names correctly. **The Suggested U.S. Targets:**

- **Washington DC** (the nation's capital) and **New York** since both are of symbolic importance to Americans. He notes that approximately 347,000 federal government employees and important government figures reside in Washington, DC. He goes a step farther and suggests that restaurants and bars along "M Street" would be good targets. He describes New York as the financial, cultural, transportation and manufacturing center of America.
- **Northern Virginia** because there is a large military presence. *"Almost all the military bases are based in this state, apart from the Air Force which is based in Chicago." Federal agencies including the Department of Defense [the Pentagon] and the CIA."*
- **Chicago** is a *"transportation hub important to global distribution and is the third largest inter-modal port in the world. It is also a center of world-wide commerce."* Targets include The Sears Tower and the Chicago Board of Trade.
- **Los Angeles** is the most populous city in California and the largest manufacturing center in the Western U.S. It also has "Hollywood" with a lot of high-profile personalities who visit restaurants on weekends.

Never forget that Islam is not "just" a religion. It is a religion embedded in a fascist government that controls every aspect of Muslim private and public life. I suggest that you do a little research on Islam for a clearer understanding of the "peaceful" religion. You will see how dangerous it is to blindly accept Islam simply as one of the world's religions.

- Jews have lived in now-Arab lands since the destruction of the "first Jewish Temple" in 586 BC

- Anti-Semitism is a mainstay of Islam
- Islam perpetuates a culture of "martyrdom"
- Mohammad married one of his wives when she was 6 years old and consummated the marriage when she was 9 years old
- Christian minorities were and still are being "sacrificed" in Africa and the Middle East
- Nowhere in the Islamic world today do non-Muslims have equal rights with Muslims (non-Muslims are *dhimmis* – inferior)
- Islam does not forbid the killing of innocents and justifies the killing of Jews because they are not considered civilians
- Islam spread through conquest - not peaceful evangelism
- There is no distinction between religious and civil authority
- The standard punishment for converting away from Islam is death

I am weary of hearing that Islam is a religion of peace, when it is obviously not. Again, I am <u>not</u> attacking all Muslims. There are Muslims who do reject Islam's hate, terror, *dhimmitude,* and global conquest who speak out and I applaud their efforts. They can and do separate themselves from the violence of Islam and strive to reform Islam. They are hated by other Muslims and Muslim organizations such as CAIR and they are even threatened with death. There are more Muslims who feel the same way but they are too intimidated and fearful of reprisals to speak out.

I am also tired of being told that there are "two" types of Islam. Both moderates and extremists read and learn the same Islam. Raymond Ibrahim clarifies this discrepancy. "...***mainstream Islam offers a crystal-clear way of life***, *based on the teachings of the Koran and Hadith...how does a believer go about "moderating" what the deity and his spokesman [Muhammad] have commanded? One can either try to observe Islam's commandments or one can ignore them: any more or less is not Islam - a word which means "submit" (to the laws, or sharia, of Allah)...are radicals "exaggerating" their orders? Or are moderate Muslims simply "observing reasonable limits" - a euphemism for negligence? - when it comes to fulfilling their commandments?"*[363]

---

[363] "Why 'Moderate Islam' Is an Oxymoron," Raymond Ibrahim, *Front Page Magazine,* http://www.frontpagemag.com, March 28, 2014

Mr. Ibrahim further explains that in the secularized West religious truth is subjective and even non-existent so any interpretation making the question *"What does Islam command loses all relevance."* So how do moderate Muslims (sincere Muslims who have submitted to the teachings of Allah) and accept that the teachings are "true" and should be obeyed "observe reasonable limits" when commanded to combat and subjugate non-Muslims. Even though most "moderate" Muslims do not engage in jihad directly, they are encouraged to support it indirectly (Money disguised as charitable donations) and propaganda (Islam is a "peaceful" religion). Keep in mind that radical - extremist Muslims do not consider themselves extreme at all. They are just following the commands of Allah and Muhammad.

Iranian-Syrian immigrant and now U.S. citizen Majid Rafizadeh shares his first-hand experience with us about Muslims born or raised in the United States. As they benefit from the freedoms and opportunities provided by the United States, many still judge the U.S. based on the Quran and their Islamic ideal - not our Constitution or western principles of human rights. The United States is not Islamic enough for them. Mr. Rafizadeh went on to explain how he thought a scholarly approach with Muslims regarding modern concepts of economies, politics, social values, and human rights, contradict Muhammad, the Quran and even modern Imams. He found out that *"since their evidence is not based on logic or science, and is rather based on what Allah, Muhammad, and the Quran say, it is extremely difficult to have any intellectual debate with proponents of Islamic principles in the United States or other Western countries."*[364]

There are two very important events taking place in the Middle East that the Western media is ignoring. In Gaza, the terror organization *Hamas* which is committed to the elimination of the state of Israel is training an entire generation of boys to be suicide bombers. Thirteen thousand high school students recently graduated from state sponsored paramilitary camps. *Hamas* Prime Minister Ismail Haniyeh spoke at the graduation ceremony: *"Beware this generation. This is a generation which knows no fear. It is the generation of the missile, the **tunnel** and the*

---

[364] "Lessons from Leaving Islamic Tyranny," Majid Rafizadeh, *Front Page Magazine*, http://www.frontpagemag.com, March 28, 2014

suicide operations." Interior Minister Fathi Hammad confirmed that the training was in preparation for the coming war with Israel.[365]

Fast-forward to the summer of 2014 when the "coming war with Israel" was launched. Hamas kidnapped and killed three Jewish teens and then began a massive assault on Israel with rockets. Israel put its "Iron Dome" defensive shield into operation saving the lives of countless Israelis and responded to Hamas with its firepower. It is important to note that Israel continually warned the residents in Gaza where they would strike Hamas giving the civilians' time to get out of the way. Unfortunately Hamas uses women and children as "human shields" and made the civilians stay in the line of fire to garner world sympathy and support when they showed pictures of their dead innocents. Israel AND Egypt destroyed numerous tunnels Hamas had constructed with aid money that was supposed to be for the people. Unbelievably Israel is constantly criticized for bombing civilians. Israel's Benjamin Netanyahu was correct when he said that *Israel uses missiles to protect its civilians while Hamas uses civilians to protect its missiles.*

United Nations actions leading up to and during this most recent crisis once again proves that the UN is corrupt and duplicitous in dealing with Israel. The UN school bombed by Israel was a storage facility for Hamas weapons and there is no way that UN personnel did not know that. To me the UN's is guilty of sheltering a terrorist organization and is responsible for the deaths at that location.

While *Hamas* thrives on hatred and violence, Egypt is turning in a very encouraging direction. If you recall, President Obama was very supportive of the Muslim Brotherhood government that came to power after the "Arab Spring" uprisings. Fortunately for Egypt and the rest of us, the Egyptian military removed President Morsi and his Muslim Brotherhood government from power. New elections will take place without Muslim Brotherhood involvement.

Egypt officially "outlawed" the Muslim Brotherhood in August 2014. The *Associated Press* reported "*Egypt's administrative court on Saturday dissolved the political party of the banned Muslim Brotherhood*

---

[365] "13,000 High School Boys Just Graduated 'Suicide Bomber' School in Gaza," Onan Coca, Eagle Rising, http://www.eaglerising.com, January 18, 2014

and ordered its assets liquidated..."[366] For the safety and security of our nation, the President and Congress need to do the same thing by officially declaring the Muslim Brotherhood a terrorist organization - since it is and rid our government of Muslim Brotherhood affiliated employees.

As reported by author Ryan Mauro, National Security Analyst and fellow with the Clarion Project, General El-Sisi commander of the Egyptian Armed Forces (and current head of state) is calling for an Islamic reformation. *"Religious discourse is the greatest battle and challenge facing the Egyptian people, pointing to the need for a new vision and a modern, comprehensive understanding of the religion of Islam-rather than relying on a discourse that has not changed for 800 years."*[367]

Mauro noted that El-Sisi did not identify Zionism or Western oppression as the greatest threat to Egypt. He accurately explained the situation as an ideological internal Islamic struggle. Independent interpretation of Islam ended by the year 1258 and finally in 2014, El-Sisi is calling for a critical examination of Islam and resulting reformation. He called for Egyptians to follow "true" Islam and be transparent to the world. El-Sisi has a lot of support. He is backed-up by Professor Ziauddin Sadar who said that Islamic doctrine is "frozen in time," and three of Islam's core pillars need to be reformed:

1. *Elevation of the Shari'ah to the level of the divine*
2. *Consequent removal of agency from the believers*
3. *Equation of Islam with the State*

This is a huge step toward confronting Islamic terrorism and stabilizing the Middle East. Unbelievably, President Obama who did not hesitate to support the Muslim Brotherhood government turned his back on the Egyptian military. This disastrous action was the key for

---

[366] Associated Press report quoted in article: "Muslim Brotherhood Dissolved by Egyptian Court," Freedom Outpost, http://www.freedomoutpost.com, August 11, 2014

[367] "Egypt's El-Sisi Boldly Calls for Islamic Reformation," Ryan Mauro, The Clarion Project, http://www.clarionproject.org, January 22, 2014

Russia to reclaim its influence in the Middle East. The debacle in Syria where our President again allied with "rebels" pretending to be freedom fighters blew the door to the Middle East wide open for Russia.

The Clarion Project promotes and supports Muslim Organizations that advocate Islamic reform.[368] These are some of the other organizations offering hope for the future of Islam, and unfortunately, they are deliberately ignored by the media.

- **Quilliam Foundation**: Counter-extremism organization that challenges anti-Western ideologies
  - **American Islamic Forum for Democracy**: Advocates U.S. constitutional principles and promotes separation of mosque and state, and create and promote deep reforms against political Islam.
- **Alliance of Iranian Women**: Advocates action against Iran to end abuse and The oppression of women
- **Free Muslims Coalition**: Committed to the elimination of Islamic extremism and terrorism and supports "secular" democratic institutions in the Muslim world
- **American Islamic Leadership Coalition**: Muslim alliance dedicated to the defense of the U.S. Constitution and religious plurality
- **International Quranic Center**: Believes that Islamic law should conform to human rights and does not consider the Hadith a reliable source of doctrine
- **Islamic Supreme Council:** With a focus on education, promotes non-Islamist and anti-extremist Muslims
- **National Council of Resistance of Iran**: Mission is to establish a "secular democratic republic" in Iran (separation of church and state).

Only Muslims can reform Islam by openly rejecting hate and violence. The proponents of reform walk a dangerous line. What other "religion" regularly exacts harsh punishment and even death on their own

---

[368] The Clarion Project : Challenging Extremism - Promoting Dialogue, http://www.clarionproject.org

members as well as non-Muslims? These brave people and organizations are the minority and need our support and encouragement.

Ask yourself when was the last time you heard American Muslims speak out against "honor killings" that are happening here in the United States with increasing frequency? How many have denounced the slaughter of Christians including the beheading of children at the hands of Muslims in Iraq or even expressed concern or sadness? Did CAIR or the American Muslim Alliance or the Islamic Society of North America release any comments yet alone condemnations? I heard only the usual silence - The hateful silence of consent.

How can the world including the U.S. and especially the President of the United States ignore the genocide of Christians in the Middle East and Northern Africa? How can anyone look at the videos and pictures of Christians including small children being brutalized, hunted down and murdered in Iraq taken by Allah's joyous and proud warriors and not see the real Islam? President Obama under the guise of responding to a humanitarian crisis didn't hesitate to attack Libya, but needed more time to assess the severity of the "potential" humanitarian crisis in Iraq as thousands of people (abandoned Christians) died. He couldn't even say the word "Christian."

In August 2014 while the President of the United States was on vacation, U.S. Congress was in recess, Europe was on holiday, and the United Nations was solely focused on condemning Israel for defending herself, the genocide in Iraq escalated as more and more people (Christians) were being slaughtered every day.

Non-Muslims must also stand up and speak out! They need the courage to speak the truth about Islam even if they are more comfortable with the term "radical Islam." Former British Prime Minister Tony Blair is standing up. During a keynote speech he publicly recognized Islamism as the *"greatest threat facing the world today."*[369] He told attendees *"Take a step back and analyze the world today: with the possible exception of Latin America, there is not a region of the world not adversely affected by Islamism and the ideology is growing."* With regard to the Egyptian military taking their country back from Muslim Brotherhood

---

[369] "Tony Blair: Fighting Islamism - A Defining Challenge of Our Time," The Clarion Project, http://www.clarionproject.org, April 24, 2014

control he said: "*on the fate of Egypt hangs the future of the region…The revolt of 30 June 2013 was not an ordinary protest. It was the absolutely necessary rescue of a nation.*" They need to support and encourage Islamic reformation. And, the federal government needs to accept the fact that we are not Islamophobes. We are also not the problem; we are not the haters; we will not surrender our freedoms; and we will not accept anything less than the liberties we have inherited through our Constitution.

Still having a problem identifying Islam as the "common thread" of terrorism? Check out the FBI's list of Most Wanted Terrorists at www. FBI.gov. The list was published in an article by Dean Garrison on May 4, 2013, "*FBI Most Wanted Terrorists*" … *30 Muslims and 2 Progressive Liberals. NO Right-Wing Patriots.*[370] No Right-wing patriots … Since the Department of Homeland Security is stalking the wrong people, can someone have them contact the FBI for the real list of terrorists!

Terrorist Trivia Time: What is the one thing the following murderers have in common?
- Pan Am Flight 93 bombers
- Air France (Entebbe) hijackers
- Achille Lauro Cruise Ship hijackers
- U.S. Marine barracks in Beirut, Lebanon bombers
- Israeli Olympic Team murderers
- Khobar Towers bombing in Saudi Arabia
- U.S. Embassy in Kenya
- U.S.S. Cole bombers
- Madrid Train bombers
- Moscow Theater murderers
- Beslan Russian School murderers
- 1993 World Trade Center bombers
- Sept. 11, 2001 NY and DC attacks hijackers
- Attempted Airplane "shoe" bomber
- Bali Nightclub bombing

---

[370] "FBI Most Wanted Terrorists … 30 Muslims and 2 Progressive Liberals. NO Right-Wing Patriots," Dean Garrison, The DC Clothesline, May 3, 2013, http://www.dcclothesline.com

- Attempted Airplane "under wear" bomber
- Beltway Snipers
- Bombay and Mumbai, India attackers
- Fort Hood murderer
- London Subway bombers
- US Embassy in Benghazi, Libya attackers
- Boston Marathon bombers
- Hamas using women and children as human shields
- ISIS beheading thousands of Christians including children in Iraq
- Beheading of a coworker in Oklahoma

Answer: ALL ARE MUSLIM.

The organization Wounded American Warrior (www.woundedamericanwarrier.com) published a definitive list of 21 murders by Muslims in the United States since February 2009. Most of these incidents were ignored by the mainstream media since violence and murder committed in the name of the "peaceful religion" are not the images they wish to portray

We are forbidden to "profile" terrorists, yet we have to allow TSA agents to grope elderly grandmas, small children and travelers with disabilities. We definitely have a problem here in the Land of the Free.

Words for Congress: If I had the opportunity to speak before Congress I would first remind them of their sworn oath to support and defend the Constitution against <u>all</u> enemies, foreign and domestic and then give them links to sign up for a Constitution course since so many obviously have no idea what it is or how it works. They <u>all</u> were hired to act on our behalf for our benefit and security and for the protection of our nation.

Dear elected leaders

With all due respect, your concerted efforts to neutralize the United States military will result in catastrophic consequences for the American people you have sworn to serve. So many of you blindly support a man seemingly committed to disarming America. A man with no military experience on any level; a loathing distain for the military he leads; and a man who thinks he knows more than the qualified military advisors that he fired. You have allowed ideology to rule rational thinking. During this serious period of global terrorism, it is disheartening to know that enemies of America are embedded within the government. It is no secret who some of them are (even I, a random nobody from the Midwest can provide names and positions). Neither political correctness nor job "insecurity" is an acceptable excuse for breaking your sworn oath; there is no ethical justification for doing so.

Maybe with all the political bickering, bloviating and back-stabbing you didn't notice that the Middle East is ready to explode and terrorism is on the rise. Please note Mr. President that al- Qaeda was never decimated. They have become stronger every day and al Qaeda along with numerous other terror groups are growing and spreading at an unprecedented rate. ISIS alone is proof of your failed foreign policy and foolish decisions. People in the Middle East and Northern Africa are dying by the thousands because America has abandoned them. Please read the history of the Vietnam War and focus on the carnage that ravished Southeast Asia when U.S. presidential foreign policy failure and American abandonment literally condemned millions of civilians to death. Has history taught you nothing?

General Carter Ham would know what to do. So would Rear Admiral Charles Gaouette and Major General Baker, but unfortunately you forced (fired) all of them out of the military because they were grounded in reality and did not subscribe to your "end the war no matter the cost" strategy. Those men were right and we desperately need them now.

It is your responsibility to ensure the protection of the American people and to uphold the constitutional laws in effect. For all elected leaders, government officers and agency appointees and employees - It is not your place to selectively decide which laws you will enforce and which laws you will not because you don't agree with them. It is also your responsibility to "secure" national security agencies from political appointments and employees of persons with ties to terrorist organizations and hostile, anti-American groups. Instead of protecting your country, you are giving these people license to write policy and regulations that protect their openly hostile constituents at the expense of American lives.

If your "job security" is determined by your allegiance to political allies and special interest groups, then your personal political aspirations trump your moral obligation to the citizens of the United States. If this is the case, you are not fit to hold any position in our government. Follow your conscience - not your party. Our lives depend on your decisions.

IMMIGRATION

Not like the brazen giant of Greek fame, with
conquering limbs astride from land to land;
Here at our sea-washed, sunset gates shall stand a
mighty woman with a torch, whose flame
Is the imprisoned lightning, and her name Mother of Exiles.
From her beacon-hand glows world-wide welcome; her mild eyes
command the air-bridged harbor that twin cities frame. "Keep,
ancient lands, your storied pomp!" cries she with silent lips.
**"Give me your tired, your poor,
Your huddled masses yearning to breathe free, the
wretched refuse of your teeming shore.
Send these, the homeless, tempest-tost to me; I
lift my lamp beside the golden door!"**

—Emma Lazarus, 1883

> *"Freedom hath been hunted round the globe. Asia and Africa have long expelled her. Europe regards her like a stranger, and England hath given her warning to depart. Oh, receive the fugitive, and prepare in time an asylum for mankind."*
>
> —Thomas Paine, *Common Sense, 1776*

Legal Immigrants

The United States is literally a nation of immigrants - **People who chose to come to America for a better life**. Legal immigrants have made major sacrifices to come to the U.S. Once here, they overcame hardships and discrimination, learned the English language, assimilated into American society, and worked hard to become U.S. citizens. I was reading through the American Citizenship Test and wondered just how well many native-born Americans would do on the test that covers American Government, System of Government, Rights and Responsibilities, History, Geography, and U.S. Symbols.[371]

Immigrants appreciate what America stands for; the very things we take for granted like freedom, liberty, and opportunity. Legal immigrants have an objectivity and respect for America that so many native-born Americans do not have. Immigrants can teach us a valuable lesson, and it would serve us well to listen to what they say. So, why did legal immigrants come to America, and what do they think about America now?

One immigrant I knew well was Stephen Francis Fitzgibbon who came to the United States from Ireland in 1914 when he was just seventeen years old. He joined three older brothers and a sister who had immigrated a few years earlier. In Ireland, jobs were scarce, and it was extremely difficult to support a family. When the United States entered World War I in 1917, Stephen joined the U.S. Army and was

---

[371] Civics (History and Government) Questions for the Redesigned (New) Naturalization Test, U.S. Citizenship and Immigration Services, effective October 1, 2008, www.uscis.gov

part of the American Expeditionary Force in France. After the war he proudly became an American citizen.

Foreign-born soldiers have fought and many have died for America since the Revolutionary War. As was the case with Stephen, legal immigrants today serving in the U.S. military are eligible for expedited citizenship. Approximately 31,000 foreign-born soldiers were serving in the U.S. armed forces in May 2009.[372] We are proud of and respect these brave men and women who risk their lives to become citizens of the United States of America.

I knew Stephen as a warm and wonderful Grandfather. He worked as a printing pressman, raised a family and made a good life in this "country of opportunity." I did not know as a child how hard it was for Irish immigrants at the turn of the twentieth century. Even though they faced discrimination and persecution, they persevered because America still offered freedom and the best life they could hope for. Though Grandfather never mentioned it, I know now that he experienced discrimination and he successfully overcame it. One of his brothers that had come to the United States could not deal with the prejudice and returned to Ireland. Irish immigrants were stereotyped as lazy drunkards even though they were hard working people. The truth is many of them labored on the hardest most unwanted jobs for minimal wages. Scores of immigrants started life in the U.S. living in unsanitary rat-infested ghettos. Even their religion was criticized and mocked. The Irish as well as Italians, Eastern Europeans, and most other immigrants overcame persecution and bigotry, and did not rely on or expect the government to support them. They persistently strove to make better lives for themselves and for their families. They became successful and valuable members of American society.

I know a woman who immigrated to America from Russia in 1990. She and her family were able to leave Russia after the breakup of the Soviet Union. Inessa was born in Saratov, a city near Stalingrad, USSR during World War II. Inessa's mother and family were originally from Kiev and had fled to Saratov as Hitler's troops invaded Russia. The family then moved to Moscow where Inessa grew up. Her father was a

---

[372] *"Immigrants have proud history of service,"* Military Times, 5/25/09 http://www.militarytimes.com/news/2009/05/MONDAY_ap-memorialday

military engineer and a hard line communist so her family had a better life than many in the USSR under Joseph Stalin. Inessa studied biology at Moscow State University and worked as a supervisor in a clinical lab. Inessa's husband, Anatoly earned a Ph.D. degree and worked on rocket and satellite components for the Russian Space Agency. He eventually was able to leave the Space Program to become a university teacher at the Science Institute. Their lives were better than many Russians. They had one child, a condo in Moscow, and a home in the suburbs.

So why would Inessa and Anatoly along with their teenage daughter abandon established careers and leave everything they had to come to America? The simple answer is "Freedom." The U.S. offered real liberty and opportunity. They worked hard to become United States citizens and are proud to be Americans.

Since Inessa and her husband grew up in the Soviet Union controlled by Stalin and the Communist Party, they know first-hand about Communism. And since they are Jewish, they also know first-hand about anti-Semitism. Anatoly's father was captured by the Germans during WWII. He survived the death camp only because the Germans considered him a Communist and did not know he was Jewish. Their daughter was first exposed to anti-Semitism in Kindergarten where she learned that Jews were still considered less important citizens. Even though their lives were better than other Jews in the USSR because of their Fathers' Communist Party positions, they still were subjected to anti-Semitism and discrimination.

The State told Russians that America was bad and was the enemy of the USSR, while at the same time Stalin and the subsequent Communist Party were starving, imprisoning, and killing the Russian people. The Communist regime used slogans like "equality," "freedom," and "brotherhood" while relieving the population of personal property and sentencing citizens to incarceration and forced labor at gulags. Because people were considered expendable, the death rate at those prisons was high and so quotas had to be established to replenish gulag slave labor. To meet those quotas, people were arrested and convicted of crimes they were innocent of and sentenced to hard labor at the gulags. For the lucky people who weren't imprisoned, life wasn't so great either. The economy was in permanent recession; goods and services were regulated and sporadically available. Since Communism like Socialism considers everyone equal, there is absolutely no incentive to work hard, excel, and be successful. And, no one escaped the watchful eyes of the KGB.

Russian-American communities in the United States have made significant contributions to our nation and they are sincerely concerned about their adopted country. They came from an oppressed society so they value liberty, freedom of speech, freedom of the media, freedom of religion, and the free market. They had NONE of these things that we take for granted in Russia. They understand the right of freedom of speech in the US, but do not understand why so many American university professors are literally "brainwashing" idealistic students with Socialist and Marxist doctrines. They clearly see that capitalism is the only system that provides freedom and prosperity.

Russians know all about communism, socialism, and fascism. They know censorship, oppression, and the dangers of single party control. Many see America now as standing with one leg in capitalism and the other leg in socialism. They see liberalism controlling the Democrat Party which follows the President in lock step. They remember very well what liberalism did to Russia. "Equality" and "change" seemed like a good idea at the beginning but then grew into a monster first stripping away property, then rights, and freedom a little at a time until they were gone. The media adulation and promotion of Barack Obama is unsettling to them. Obama seems more like a celebrity than a president. His every word and action is defended and disagreement and criticism are not acceptable. He easily coerces politicians and businessmen to do things his way. He blames U.S. business, the motor of the American economy for financial ills and blames the previous administration for all the country's problems. While Obama sees government regulation as the saving force of our economy, Russian-Americans see excessive government regulation as the road to socialism. They see the government creating laws to force businesses to conform to state programs. Government intervention and regulations continue to diminish the free market system.

Scores of Russian-Americans are uneasy with current events in America. They are wary of President Obama's open-arm policies with foreign dictators such as the late Hugo Chavez, the Castro brothers, and the fascist regimes of North Korea and Iran. They are offended when Obama apologizes to other countries for America and wonder how he could do that since it was America that saved and rebuilt Europe. It was America that has given Africa millions of dollars in food and medical aid. It is America that never hesitates to help any country in need.

Russian-Americans are patriotic Americans. They have a vested interest in the continued success and prosperity of America, and they have good reason to feel uneasy about the current political situation. Inessa's words of warning should be taken to heart: *"Why don't people want to learn? What happened in Russia is real, cruel, and can happen anywhere."*

Grace a Chinese immigrant friend of mine received her Ph.D. degree in Biochemistry from the Chinese Academy of Science in Shanghai, China where she held the position of Associate Professor at the Shanghai Institute. This position would have been the pinnacle of her career at the institute since the opportunity for career growth and advancement is limited.

She was offered a two-year appointment as a Research Associate in the laboratory of one of the world's leading virologists at a prestigious American university. With approval from the Chinese Academy of Science, she came to the United States in 1998 fully expecting to return to China in two years. Grace's husband and young son were also allowed to come to the U.S.

Once here, the family decided they wanted to stay in the United States. Grace had an extremely difficult time trying to get the Chinese Academy's approval to remain in the U.S. The Academy finally authorized her to stay when it was clear that she would have to return to China alone, since her husband and son would not leave the U.S.

She was reappointed in the virology lab where she conducted successful research, published numerous scientific articles and abstracts, was named on patents, and was promoted to the rank of full professor. Grace and her son became American citizens; and Grace's son, Steven has since graduated from college, has a good job, and a very promising career. His future in America is filled with unlimited opportunities. They came to the U.S. for opportunity and freedom they would never have enjoyed anywhere else. Chinese Americans diligently work and study and they have made outstanding contributions to America.

Ominously, since Grace has called this country home, she has noticed definite changes, and they are not for the better. As a Christian, she has witnessed the moral decline of our nation and the rise of greed and corruption. I never imagined the day would come when our great nation would be *internally* beaten down, as China was becoming more open and tolerant. Grace explained that the number of Christians in China is growing and the Chinese government now pays much more attention to education, science, and the lives of ordinary people.

Stephen, Inessa, and Grace are just a few examples of the millions of people who came to the United States to be a part of America and participate in this truly free and industrial nation. They identify with America. Legal immigrants work hard, pay taxes, and contribute to the nation financially, academically, and culturally. **They are what America is all about**.

Illegal Immigrants

Contrary to legal immigrants are *illegal aliens;* people who enter the country without a visa and also people who entered the U.S. on a valid visa that has since expired and they did not leave the country. Illegal aliens are labeled incorrectly as *"undocumented immigrants"* by the *politically correct* supporters of *illegal amnesty*. They are not immigrants; they are people who have broken the law. Real immigrants enter the country legally. Real immigrants come to the U.S. expecting to work and be self-sufficient. Real immigrants do not expect nor want the government to take care of them. Illegal immigrants on the other hand, do not want to be citizens but do want the rights and privileges of citizenship. They expect the government to take care of them; they expect free education for their illegal children and free medical care while many legal citizens still cannot afford health insurance or adequate medical care.

I understand and sympathize with the poor families who "illegally" enter the United States seeking a better life. But along with these harmless illegals, are felons, thieves, rapists, murderers, and terrorists. While the government fixes the illegal population in the U.S. at 12 million, other organizations including immigrationcounters.com publishes the number at over 24 million.[373] ImmigrationCounters.com "supports *legal* immigration and respect for all humanity yet highlights the significant impact of *illegal* immigration on America." The USA Political Action Committee estimates the number of illegal aliens at up to 20,000.[374] Front Page Magazine frontpagemag.com says the number of illegal aliens from Asia and the Middle East is increasing. They reported that in 2003 alone the Border Patrol apprehended 39,215 illegal aliens described as "other than Mexican" along the Southwest border, according to David Seminara, a Fellow at the Center for Immigration Studies, http://cis.org/ Illegal.[375] We seldom see any media coverage on the criminal activities of illegals even though according to immigrationcounters.com, there are 850,096 illegal alien fugitives and 519,161 illegal aliens incarcerated costing American taxpayers $29,281,321,211 since 2008. That "should" be newsworthy to the mainstream media.

Immigration Counters also stated that over 5 million babies have been born to illegal aliens since 2002. Well over 6 million children of illegal aliens are being educated in U.S. public elementary and high schools costing taxpayers almost $181 billion since 1996. These are astonishing statistics. Keep in mind that the figures cited were BEFORE the 2014 illegal invasion seemingly sanctioned by the White House. Do not expect honest information or accurate statistics from the government relating to the number of people and the exorbitant tax payer costs affiliated with the invasion, not to mention new and very serious national security and health threats.

The Minuteman Project (A well-established and effective citizen organization operating in the border states using volunteer resources)

---

[373] "Live Counters, News, Resources, Immigration Counters.com, October 19, 2013 Organization publishes illegal immigration numbers based on current government sources, private sources, research and analysis.

[374] USA Political Action Committee: US Securing America was established for Americans concerned about the security of the United States

[375] Illegal Immigration, Center for Immigration Studies, http://cis.org/Illegal, October 19, 2013

Eye On The Border, January 5, 2010 report published very troubling statistics compiled by Detective Ben Cardoza from the FBI and the Department of Homeland Security:[376]

- 95% of warrants for murder in Los Angeles, California are for illegal aliens
- 83% of warrants for murders in Phoenix, Arizona are for illegal aliens
- 86% or warrants for murder in Albuquerque, New Mexico are for illegal aliens
- 75% of people on "Most Wanted" lists in LA, Phoenix and Albuquerque are illegal aliens
- 24.9% of California detention center inmates are illegal Mexican nationals
- 40.1% of Arizona detention center inmates are illegal Mexican nationals
- 48.2% of New Mexico detention center inmates are illegal Mexican nationals
- 29% (630,000) convicted illegal alien felons fill U.S. federal and state prisons costing taxpayers $1.6 billion annually
- Over 53% of investigated burglaries in California, New Mexico, Nevada, Arizona, and Texas are perpetrated by illegal aliens
- Over 50% of all Los Angeles, California gang members are illegal aliens – from south of the border
- Over 71% of all apprehended cars stolen in Texas, New Mexico, Arizona, Nevada, and California in 2005 were stolen by illegal aliens or "transport coyotes"
- 47% of cited/stopped drivers in California do not have a driver's license, auto insurance, or vehicle registration and of those people, 92% are illegal aliens
- 63% of cited/stopped drivers in Arizona do not have a driver's license, auto insurance, or vehicle registration and of those people, 97% are illegal aliens

---

[376] Minuteman Project Eye On The Border: "Another Illegal Alien Fugitive Murderer Nailed at Border," January 2010

- 66% of cited/stopped drivers in New Mexico do not have a driver's license, auto insurance, or vehicle registration and of those people, 98% are illegal aliens
- Over 380,000 "anchor babies" (automatically become U.S. citizens) born in the U.S. to illegal alien parents in a single year and 97.2% of incurred costs are paid by U.S. citizens

News organizations rarely mention that 25% of the prison population is made up of illegal aliens. According to the USA Political Action Committee – Us Securing America[377] approximately 400,000 illegal alien criminals who were given deportation orders are still somewhere in the U.S. USAPAC and the organization, U.S. Illegal Aliens.com[378] presents some specific incidents that most Americans are unaware of:

- Federal agents arrested 2 Egyptians in May 2002 for trying to smuggle illegal Middle Eastern "immigrants" into New Jersey by way of Mexico. I wonder how many were not apprehended and safely made it into the U.S.
- Illegal alien, Saul Morales-Garcia shot a Las Vegas Police officer in December 2002. Garcia had already been deported, and illegally re-entered the United States again.
- Illegal alien, Enrique Sousa Alvarez was arrested in San Jose, California in June 2004 for kidnapping a 9 year old girl. He held her captive and repeatedly raped her for 3 days.
- Illegal alien, Adrienne George Camacho shot and killed Oceanside, California police officer Tony Zeppetella in August 2004. Camacho's criminal record included 4 felony convictions. He had been deported and re-entered the U.S. through California.
- Illegal alien Walter Alexander Sorto was repeatedly stopped for driver's license violations in Texas. Unfortunately the Houston

---

[377] USA Political Action Committee: "Us Securing America," Number of Children of Illegal Aliens in Public
Schools 6,239,061 May 15, 2009
[378] "The Dark Side of Illegal Immigration," Http://www.usillegalaliens.com, October 22, 2013

Police Department officers were forbidden from reporting his illegal residency status to federal authorities under "Sanctuary policies." I am not the least bit surprised to find out that Walter Sorto abducted, raped and murdered a Houston woman in 2004.

- Illegal alien Juan Leonardo Qunitero, previously deported for molesting a 12-year old girl murdered Houston police officer Brandon Winfield when the officer stopped to assist what he thought was a disabled motorist.

- Terry and Lisa Dilks of Iowa were murdered by two illegal aliens. Both had been arrested previously on drug charges but they were turned over to federal immigration agents and released.

The Examiner reported that 154 counts of child sex crimes were brought against illegal aliens in the state of North Carolina during the month of February 2014 alone. "That figure does not include all arrests of illegal aliens for similar charges, nor does it include conviction or sentencing data for those in the state illegally."[379] I find it unconscionable that government officials at all levels are more concerned about protecting the rights of illegal aliens than protecting our children.

"*Officer Down News*" maintains a website: http://www.officerdown. com publishing news and events about the police officers killed by illegal aliens. Without "*Officer Down News*," we would not know about these events since they are obviously not media important. When a police officer kills a person, it is instant and national news; yet when a police officer is murdered, there is mostly silence. The "Memorial Page" pays deserving tribute to these outstanding individuals.

Crime seems to be a common consequence of "Sanctuary Policies." To put it bluntly, sanctuary policies empower and protect criminals. I find it unfortunate that illegal aliens' rights take priority over the rights of American citizens especially now that the Justice Department under direction of the White House and the Department of Homeland Security have instructed law enforcement NOT to enforce many illegal-immigration laws. How many American citizens' civil rights will be

---

[379] "Illegal aliens charged with 150 child molestations in North Carolina last month," Dave Gibson, Immigration Reform Examiner, *The Examiner*, http://www. examiner.com, March 22, 2014

violated and how many Americans will die because the government prefers to protect illegal aliens over the citizenry that they are sworn to protect. This is so wrong.

An extremely disturbing crime organization that originated in El Salvador and then migrated to Guatemala, and Mexico has infiltrated America <u>via the Mexican border</u>. The **MS-13** gang (**Mara Salvatrucha 13**) is an extremely violent gang of illegal aliens that first appeared near Los Angeles, California in the late 1980's. They are heavily involved in drug smuggling, human trafficking and they have no problem killing people whether men, women or children. MS-13 has little fear of law enforcement and they have spread across the country to many major US cities. Besides their violent gang activities, there are increasing reports that terrorist organizations are now in contact with M-13 to provide "illegal" access into to the United States.

Then there is the *"La Raza"* movement ("The Race") made up of many immigrant groups. The mainstream "respectable" face of La Raza is the National Council of La Raza (The Council of The Race). The National Council of La Raza has received millions of dollars in tax payer funded federal grant money. *Human Events* published an interesting piece on the radical "Reconquista" agenda shielded by La Raza: *"Behind the respectable front of the National Council of La Raza lies the real agenda of the La Raza movement, the agenda that led to those thousands of illegal immigrants in the streets of American cities, waving Mexican flags, brazenly defying our laws, and demanding concessions."*

The radical and racist group, **"Movimiento Estudiantil Chicano de Aztlan"** (MECha) translates in English to "Chicano Student Movement of Aztlan. MECha and La Raza teach that the states of Colorado, California, Arizona, Texas, Utah, New Mexico, Oregon, and part of Washington are actually the Aztec homeland before Europeans came to North America and they want it back. That fictitious assertion would be humorous if MECha was not so dangerous. The MECha is one of the most anti-American groups in the country.

- A 2006 statement on the University of Oregon MECha website in 2006 describes MECha this way: *"Chicano is our identity; it defines who we are as a people. It rejects the notion that we ...*

should assimilate into the Anglo-American melting pot ..." The statement points out that Aztlan was the legendary homeland of the Aztecs which has expanded into the vast areas of the Southwest that were viciously stolen from Mexican people (they do not say the country of Mexico).

- The MECha founding principles listed in "El Plan Spiritual de Aztlan" (The Spiritual Plan for Aztlan): *"The spirit of a new people that is conscious not only of its proud historical heritage but also of brutal gringo invasion of our territories, we, the Chicano inhabitants and civilizers of the northern land of Aztlan from whence came our forefathers, reclaiming the land of their birth and consecrating the determination of our people of the sun, declare that the call of our blood is our power, our responsibility, and our inevitable destiny...Aztlan belongs to those who plant the seeds, water the fields, and gather the crops and not to the foreign Europeans..."*[380]

- MECha motto: *"For the Race everything. Outside the Race, nothing"*

Do these groups sound like benevolent people just seeking a better life in the United States? "Mainstream" Hispanic leaders confirm and support these ideologies.

- Richard Alatorre, City Councilman Los Angeles: *"They're afraid we're going to take over the governmental institutions and other institutions. They're right. We will take them over...We are here to stay."*

- Art Torres, Chairman of the California Democratic Party: *"Remember 187 -- proposition to deny taxpayer funds for services to non-citizens -- was the last gasp of white America in California."*

- Gloria Molina, Los Angeles County Supervisor: *"We are politicizing every single one of these new citizens that are becoming citizens of this country....I gotta tell you that a lot of people are*

---

[380] "Exclusive: The Truth About La Raza," Cn. Orwood, April 7, 2006, published by Human Events, http://www.humanevents.com, May 10, 2013

saying, 'I'm going to go out there and vote because I want to pay them back.'"

- Mario Obledo, California Coalition of Hispanic Organizations and California State Secretary of Health, Education and Welfare and awarded the Presidential Medal of Freedom by President Clinton: *"California is going to be a Hispanic state. Anyone who doesn't like it should leave."*

- Jose Pescador Osuna, Mexican Consul General: *"We are practicing 'La Reconquista' in California."*

- The national newspaper of Mexico, *Excelsior*: **"The American Southwest seems to be slowly returning to the jurisdiction of Mexico without firing a single shot."**

What the media does focus on are American citizens critical of illegal immigration. These Americans are labeled mean, uncaring racists. In the Southwest, American citizens banded together to patrol the border in defense of their homes and communities. The multi-ethnic citizen immigration law enforcement advocacy group, The Minuteman Project has been in action for ten years *"operating within the law to support enforcement of the law."*[381] These volunteer citizens watch the US-Mexican border for illegal aliens. The media has demonized members of this group of Americans as right-wing racists. To date the members of the Minuteman Project have acted honorably and within the law even though there have been instances of defamation and claims of civil rights violations – all of which have been discredited as attempts to disrupt the Project. It's unfortunate that the government doesn't spend as much time and resources monitoring illegals as they do American citizens like the members of the Minutemen Project. The Minutemen are an asset to the overburdened border patrol and should be respected as such. Check out their website at http://minutemanproject.com/

There are countless examples of illegal alien criminal activities. Illegal aliens and foreign criminals sneaking into our country put all of us at risk. The politicians know about this yet what is being done? Many

---

[381] The Minuteman Project, www.minutemanproject.com, founded by Jim Gilchrist in 2004 in response to the U.S. government's continual refusal to enforce existing immigration laws

politicians support amnesty. Blanket amnesty was granted by President Ronald Reagan back in the 1980s which only resulted in an **increase of illegal aliens**. Congress allowed "sporadic" fences to be built at some locations along the Mexican border. That is helpful, but it's like putting your finger in a hole in a dike. It does not fix the problem which our government leaders do not seem to take seriously.

The issue is not about keeping poor Latin and South American families out of the country. It is about keeping criminals and terrorists out. Since Mexico is the major springboard for illegal entry into the U.S. and many of the illegals are Mexican citizens, why is there no denunciation of the Mexican government? Are not Mexican citizens the responsibility of the Mexican government? Since millions of Mexican citizens are so unhappy with Mexico, why do they not protest and demand their government address their problems instead of protesting and demanding our government take care of them? **Why are American taxpayers responsible for supporting a foreign nation's citizens?** Maybe the Mexican government wants to rid the country of its poor and criminals so they do not have to financially support them. As a matter of fact the Mexican government publishes "guides" on how to sneak into the U.S.

In March 2009 Secretary of State Hillary Clinton told Mexican President Calderon and the world that America shares "co-responsibility" for the Mexican violence that is spilling over into the US. She based her claim on the illegal drug demand of Americans and Americans smuggling weapons into Mexico. She had plenty of blame for America, but did not mention that the Mexican government is totally corrupt, Mexico's economy is failing, and drug cartel violence is solely responsible for thousands of civilian deaths. There were over 1,000 civilian deaths along the Mexican border in January 2009 alone. She also failed to mention that Tijuana, Cuidad Juarez, Reynosa and Monterrey Mexico are under drug cartel control, and Phoenix, Arizona has been termed the "kidnap capital" of the United States because of drug-related kidnappings for ransom by armed Mexican kidnappers.

Mexican President Calderon did not address HIS country's problems, but he had plenty of criticism for the U.S. Calderon spoke before a Joint Session of Congress on May 19, 2010 condemning the state of Arizona for passing legislation to better protect the state from illegals streaming across the border. Political analyst John Lillipop defended Arizona's law as *"passing legislation which provides law enforcement officials with the tools needed to protect Arizona and her citizens from illegal invaders from the failed, third-world state of Mexico, and other nations more southerly."*[382] How did our elected officials sworn to protect and defend the Constitution respond to Calderon's attack? Democrat members of Congress responded with cheers and a standing ovation – Disgraceful!

Our southern border with Mexico is nearing the boiling point and all we hear is that we shoulder responsibility for the problems. Patriotic organizations such as the Minuteman Project are demonized for defending their homes and country since the government of the United States is unwilling to do so. While the press and civil rights activists are creating havoc in the Southwest putting Americans in danger and championing the rights of criminals who kill innocent American citizens, who is watching the United States-Canada border? The US-Canada border is "soft," and easily crossed. Canada does not have a notable record of screening foreigners and identifying and apprehending terrorists; and the US government doesn't seem concerned. That is a problem.

I would really like to know why "Sanctuary Cities" are allowed to exist. How can some federal laws be subjective and others discretionary? Why aren't mayors and other political leaders prosecuted for breaking the law when they totally disregard it by protecting illegals, and forbidding police departments from notifying ICE of illegal aliens? They must be liberals who get to pick and choose which laws they want to abide by. These people hold responsibility for countless unnecessary assaults and murders of many innocent people at the hands illegal aliens. There is nothing in our Constitution that allows rights to "illegal" aliens. Sanctuary policies directly violate our elected officials' oaths of office to *"support and defend the Constitution of the United States…and that I will well and faithfully discharge the duties of the office…"*

In light of the violence, death and insurmountable financial costs of illegal aliens invading our country, it was astounding to learn that in April 2009 some of our elected officials called for easing our immigration

---

[382] "To Mexican President Calderon: Can You Hear Us Now?" John Lillipop, http:// www.americanconservativedaily.com, May27, 2011

laws because illegal aliens were afraid to provide information for the 2010 census. They also called for the suspension of immigration raids. Logic dictates that illegal aliens are not supposed to be here, so why should they be counted on our U.S. census? And, why do we have immigration laws and departments such as ICE to enforce the laws and then forbid them to do their job, which is to apprehend illegal aliens? Law-abiding American citizens have no recourse.

Toni Preckwinkle, the Cook County Illinois Board President (Chicago) will not comply with federal immigrations laws. Illegal aliens are arrested for crimes and put in Cook County Jail. No other agency is notified, so these criminals "bond out" and flee never to face justice and answer for their crimes.

Elected and appointed officials are sacrificing innocent American lives to fulfill misguided principles to defend and protect law breakers, criminals, and even terrorists. But then again, they see a large voter pool and have no problem allowing illegal aliens to vote in our elections – illegally! Since illegals (and other non-citizens) are voting in elections throughout the U.S. don't let anyone tell you that we have "free" and "fair" elections. The federal government is well aware of this criminal activity yet no one is addressing the problem. Our current Attorney General supports amnesty and opposes voter ID cards so he certainly doesn't have an issue with it.

A Heritage Foundation investigation found that 180,000 "registered" voters in Florida may be non-citizens. The state can't check for illegal aliens who registered to vote because the federal government will not give Florida access to Immigration and Naturalization Service records to help identify illegals. Fox News reported in 2011 that *"Dozens of foreign nationals fraudulently voted in New Mexico elections, the state's top elections officials said after reviewing the state's voter registration rolls and a list of thousands of foreign nationals who have been issued driver's licenses."*[383] William Gheen president of Americans for Legal Immigration PAC stated: *"In the states of Texas, California, and Florida, this gives them the ability to control national electoral politics. The Democrats are registering and voting illegal immigrants en masse – especially west*

---

[383] "Foreign Nationals Fraudulently Voted in New Mexico Elections, State Official Says," Fox News, http://www.foxnews.com, March 16, 2011

of the Mississippi … No conservative is going to get elected to anything in this country in another five to ten years if we don't stop the massive theft of U.S. elections happening right now in America with illegal alien voters." [384]

It is time for Americans whether native-born or legal immigrants to pressure Washington DC to live up to its Constitutional obligation to defend the citizens of America. Too many Americans have died at the hands of illegal aliens, and it is a fact that foreign enemies and terrorists look for and many find ways into this country for nefarious reasons. It is a fatal assumption to think the government is doing its job to protect us. We must always be watchful and not afraid to demand the government abide by its own laws regarding illegals and national security.

For instance, who in the administration ordered the "Stand Down" of U.S. Border Patrol Agents during the government shutdown in October 2013 leaving our vulnerable southern border completely unprotected? Why would our government intentionally make it easier for terrorists to enter the country? A report by Janna Brock may hold the answer, and it has nothing to do with "budgetary issues or the shutdown." She quotes Shawn Moran, Vice President of the National Border Patrol Council: *"The politically-appointed class within the U.S. Border Patrol and in the U.S. Customs and Border Protection Agency are cooking the books to make it appear that illegal immigration is decreasing. This all started when Janet Napolitano said the border was safer than it's ever been."* [385] This is treasonous. Thank God we have the Minutemen on the border.

Jenna's article clearly explains that *"The cold hard truth is that every Islamic terrorist organization and state sponsor of Islamic terror knows the weakness that exists at American borders. The United Nations Office on Drugs and Crime (UNODC) recognizes both Mexican cartels as channels for entry by individuals from Africa and Asia entering the U.S. illegally, specifically mentioning Islamic terrorists originating from Somalia, most notably, Islamic jihadists Al-Shabaab, which has virtually taken over Somalia."*

---

[384] "Thanks to Democrats Masses of Illegals Are Voting in US and State Elections," posted by God Father Politics, http://www.godfatherpolitics.com

[385] "Why Have Border Patrol Agents Been Ordered To "Stand Down?" Janna Brock, Freedom Outpost, http://www.freedomoutpost.com, October 5, 2013

On September 17, 2013 CBS Los Angeles News published a list of "10 Illegal Alien Facts" concerning the Los Angeles, California area

1. More than 43% of all Food Stamps are given to illegals.
2. 95% of warrants for murder in Los Angeles are for illegals.
3. Less than 2% of illegals are picking crops – 41% are on welfare.
4. More than 66% of all births in California are to illegals on Medi-Cal and paid for by the U.S. taxpayers.
5. Nearly 60% of all occupants of HUD Properties in the U.S. are illegals.
6. More than 39% of California students' grades 1-12 are illegals.
7. 75% of LA's Most Wanted are illegals.
8. More than 50% of all gang members are illegals.
9. U.S. companies using illegals in 2005 profited over 2.36 Trillion dollars.
10. **U.S. Taxpayers are footing the bill for ALL illegals**.

Even with those FACTS, California Governor Jerry Brown signed the *Trust Act*[386] on October 5, 2013 prohibiting illegal aliens being turned over to U.S. Immigration and Customs Enforcement (ICE) unless charged or convicted of a "serious offense." I wonder how many more Americans will die at the hands of illegals who hadn't committed a serious crime - up to that point. I think murder is very serious and the government has no problem sacrificing legal, law-abiding citizens.

One advocacy group that rejects illegal immigration and is worth special mention is You Don't Speak For Me! (dontspeakforme. org). YDSFM! is an organization founded by Col. Al Rodriguez and Americans of Hispanic descent in response to "pro-illegal immigrant" advocacy groups that insinuate all Hispanic-Americans support their cause. YDSFM!'s policies support immigrants of all backgrounds who immigrate legally, obey the laws of the United States, and want to become part of American society. They are proud to be American citizens who do not support illegal immigration. You Don't Speak for Me advocates enforcement of immigration laws and securing the border.

---

[386] "California Makes U.S. Citizenship Obsolete," Arnold Ahlert, *Front Page Magazine*, http://frontpagemag.com, October 9, 2013

They do not support amnesty for illegals, and they clearly state that *"any organization or individual who does not espouse these core values does not speak for us."*

Legal vs. Illegal: A Tale of Two Immigrants, And Uncle Omar Makes Three

1. Christian Bueno-Galdos was seven years old when his family legally immigrated to the United States from Peru. The family embraced America and settled in New Jersey where Christian's parents raised him and his siblings. They abided by the laws of this nation and Christian loved his new country. He enlisted in the U.S. Army, became a U.S. citizen, and volunteered for two tours of duty in Iraq. This 25-year old army sergeant who had been awarded the Army Commendation Medal, Army Good Conduct Medal, National Defense Service Medal, Iraqi Campaign Service Medal, War on Terrorism Service Medal, Army Service Ribbon, and Overseas Service Ribbon was killed in Iraq along with 5 other servicemen in May 2009. This honorable young man gave his life for America. His memory and his sacrifice should be cherished.

2. Zeituni Onyango first came to the United States in 1975 from Kenya, Africa. She traveled back and forth from the U.S. to Kenya a number of times before coming to America in 2000 on a temporary visa. Zeituni applied for political asylum and public housing in Massachusetts in 2002. When asylum was denied in 2004, she was ordered deported but remained illegally in the country ever since. Zeituni then had back surgery and was able to move into a public housing unit for people with physical hardships. So how is a known illegal alien with no visible means of support able to stay in the U.S. living in public housing and receiving medical care – all paid for by U.S. taxpayers? For one thing, Immigration and Customs Enforcement (ICE) is occupied with apprehending illegal aliens with criminal records ahead of non-threatening immigration violators. Another reason may be that Zeituni Onyango is President Obama's aunt. I find this

situation quite troubling since the president of the United States is expected to uphold the laws of the land that he has taken an oath to abide by. Auntie Zeituni was granted political asylum in 2010 and her memoir, "Tears of Abuse," was published in March 2012. I wonder if the President has ever invited her to the White House for dinner. It's not like the taxpayers haven't been paying to feed her for the past 13 years anyway.

3. Onyango Obama came to the U.S. from Kenya on a student visa in 1963. When his visa expired in 1970, he did not leave the country. He was ordered deported in 1986, 1989, and again in 1992 after he lost his appeal; but he still did not leave. His "illegal" immigration status was not public knowledge until he was arrested for drunk driving in 2011. After his arrest he mentioned he would call the White House since his nephew is the president. Illegal alien Onyango (Uncle Omar) had a valid driver's license and a social security card. His drunk-driving case was "continued" for one year and was then dismissed. He claimed that his nephew Barack Obama stayed with him in Cambridge, Massachusetts for three weeks when he attended Harvard Law School. The White House claimed the President never met his uncle. It does not matter who is telling the truth since a judge (the same judge that approved Auntie Zeituni's asylum) granted Uncle Omar a "green card" and permission to stay in the U.S. As the news of this story spread in December 2013, the White House issued a clarification statement that oops, President Obama did indeed stay with Uncle Omar for a brief time in 1988 while attending Harvard Law School. After that visit, Obama only saw Uncle Omar every few months for a while. Continuing the clarification, the White House spokesman shared that the President hasn't seen Uncle Omar in 20 years and has not spoken to him in 10 years. I wonder how many other Obama's are in the country illegally.

These stories are representative of a sad fact in America today. We have wonderful and honest legal immigrants whose contributions to our nation should be celebrated. A September 14, 2013 article by Silvio

Canto, Jr. in the "American Thinker" summarizes legal immigration this way: *"Our family landed in the US without a penny...Upon landing in the US, our family was assisted by a church, individuals and lots of smiling faces who opened doors unconditionally. We never expected the US government to give us anything. Americans gave us freedom and that's what my parents were looking for."*[387]

And then we have illegal aliens who contribute nothing to our nation and only take from America. Responsible working Americans are providing for their health, education and welfare, and even paying for them to have attorneys and access to our legal system. This is just one example of the rights of non-citizens (illegal aliens) taking precedence over the rights of United States citizens. I don't see anything in our Constitution that guarantees illegals the same rights as citizens. And, I don't see anything in our Constitution that gives the President selective power over the Justice System to determine who can break our laws and who cannot.

Since June 2009 President Obama has talked about his plan to deal with the illegal immigration problem. He believes that undocumented immigrants (illegal aliens) should register, pay a fine, and then within time acquire the status of legal immigrants. A president of the United States of America, especially one with a legal background should above all people feel compelled to uphold the laws of the land, but then again many illegals vote (which is also illegal - and usually for Democrats who provide liberal entitlements). Amnesty for lawbreakers violates the law the president has taken an oath to support and defend.

The administration's selective disregard for upholding the law was highlighted by a 2014 *Center for Immigration Studies* report that out of nearly 722,000 "encounters with illegal or criminal immigrants," Immigration and Customs Enforcement (ICE) filed charges against less than 195,000 of them. Caroline May of the *Daily Caller* reported: *"According to ICE personnel, the vast gap between the number of encounters reported and the number of aliens who do not fall into the administrations narrowly defined criteria for enforcement, regardless*

---

[387] "The welfare state is way too big when I pay for your baby's birth," Silvio Canto, Jr., American Thinker, http://www.american thinker.com, September 14, 2013

of the criminal charges or the circumstances in which the alien was identified."[388]

Other key findings of the report:

- ICE arrests have declined 40% since the administration's "prosecutorial discretion" policies went into effect in June 2011
- The majority of "record breaking" deportations the administration cites are because ICE is credited with the removal of aliens apprehended by the Border Patrol
- 68,000 <u>criminal aliens</u> were released in 2013 (35% of all criminal aliens reported by ICE). The highest rates of criminal releases were in San Antonio, Texas, New York City, New York, Washington, DC, and Newark, New Jersey.

I was surprised to learn that over the last five years there was an increase of 2,458,000 foreign-born workers in the U.S. That is a 52% increase of foreign-born workers in contrast to an increase of 1,615,000 native-born workers.[389] I was dumb-founded to learn that the Treasury Department sent $4.2 billion of citizen taxpayer money to families of illegal aliens. A report by David North with the Center for Immigration Studies writes that this is a story *"about how our government works and how faceless, midlevel decision-makers can, and do, shape our basic policies, and how the courts are, in effect, powerless to do anything about it. This particular paying-the-illegals-to-stay pattern revolves around the Additional Child Tax Credit (ACTC) which is not so much a tax credit as it is an income-transfer program for low-income families, offering up to $1,000 per child to all resident families, including those of illegal aliens."*[390]

So, let me get this straight. The situation seems to be that legal taxpaying citizens finance the United States government to support illegal aliens: Financially through welfare programs and generous

---

[388] "Report: Obama administration released 68,000 convicted criminal aliens last year," Caroline May, The Daily Caller, http://www.daily caller.com, March 31, 2014
[389] "Under Obama: Job Growth 52% Greater for Foreign-Born Workers," Terence P. Jeffrey, CNS News, http://www.cnsnews.com, September 6, 2013
[390] "Paying Illegals to Stay," David North, Center for Immigration Studies, http://cis.org, October 2013

IRS managers; Provide free healthcare through Medicaid and other healthcare programs; Pay for their children's education; Subsidize college tuition for high school graduates; Allow illegal immigrants to protest in Washington D.C. and rally on the public mall while at the same time paying for security to keep WWII veterans away from their memorial. And they are the ones who are "frustrated," making demands and are *"Not going to take it anymore."*[391]

To learn more about the illegal immigration crisis (yes it is a crisis) and read the **facts** about illegal immigration, there are numerous organizations and websites you can access to read the truth that you will not hear from the media. These groups are committed to educating the American public about illegal aliens and the very real threat to our nation's security. Some of the organizations who work diligently to promote the truth include:

- Center for Immigration Studies (http://www.cis.org)
- The Heritage Foundation (myheritage.com)
- You Don't Speak for Me! (http://www.dontspeakforme.org)
- The Minuteman Project (http:/www.minutemanproject.com)
- Immigration Counters (http://www.immigrationcounters.com)
- The USA Political Action Committee (http:www.usapac.us)
- The Dark Side of Illegal Immigration (http://www.usillegalaliens.com)
- Human Events (http:www.humanevents.com)
- Numbers USA (http:www.numbersusa.com)
- Front Page Magazine (frontpagemag.com)

Native-born Americans simply take freedom and opportunity for granted. We were born into freedom and opportunity and did not have to struggle with oppression and tyranny. We need to talk with legal immigrants who came to the United States to work, learn, and contribute to their new home country. They can remind us why America is a great country. We need to oppose illegal immigration

---

[391] "They're Not Going To Take It Anymore: New Generation Of Immigrant Advocates Take Radical Approach," Elizabeth Llorente, Fox News Latino, http://foxnewslatino.com, October 16, 2013

and the leaders that promote "sanctuary" which blatantly disregards our laws. The word "illegal" is clear - There is no justification that makes "illegal" legal. Amnesty en masse for illegals is not a rational argument. It is a dangerous action not to mention criminally unfair to legal immigrants. I understand that it is virtually impossible to deport 12-20 million illegal aliens; but it is also irresponsible to grant blanket amnesty citizenship. "Permanent Residence" status allows illegals "out of the shadows," and legally into the workplace (where they claim they want to be). But then again, logic has no place in government. Citizenship status GUARANTEES access to the health and welfare system not to mention the establishment of a new voting bloc. Then again, using welfare to secure political positions of power, the legality of which does not matter, seems to be the current political priority - not the Constitution or legal citizens.

There is actually a third type of immigration taking place in our country. The United States has understandably been admitting refugees of "special humanitarian concern" (persons suffering religious or ethnic persecution - unless they are Christians) for a very long time. Unfortunately that humanitarian aid program has been hijacked and we receive refugees through the *Refugee Resettlement Program* whereby the <u>United Nations decides</u> who gets refugee status and what country those refugees are "assigned" to. Religious minority refugees such as Christians in the Middle East who are continually persecuted, abused and killed are not the refugees being granted asylum by the U.N. and resettled in the U.S. The refugees we are mandated to accept are Muslims from Middle Eastern countries such as Somalia, Sudan, Ethiopia, Iraq, Pakistan and Myanmar. Our own government is actually importing "radical" Islam and Islamic terrorists. How crazy is that?

Pamela Geller, President of the *American Freedom Defense Initiative* explains what the problem with that is: "*The Obama administration is importing whole Muslim communities from Islamic countries like Somalia. Many of these devout Muslims do not assimilate. They agitate for jihad, and many return to Somalia (or Pakistan, Afghanistan) for training. Why are we importing hostile invaders?* [392] Pamela points out that the

---

[392] "Welfare Jihad," Pamela Geller, post by Freedom Outpost, <u>http://www.freedomoutpost.com</u>, February 26, 2014

number of attacks by Muslims, commonly on women and homosexuals increases as Muslim immigration increases. Not coincidently, Muslim attacks are increasing in cities where large populations of Muslims have been imported through the "Refugee Resettlement" programs."

Tammy Bruce's March 2014 *Washington Times* article addresses President Obama's relaxed immigration rules for refugee asylum. *"Going out of your way to open the door to this country for people who have had terrorists associations is bad enough, but it doesn't stop there. Investor's Business Daily reports the Obama administration has rejected almost all the asylum requests from 20,000 Coptic Christians trying to flee Islamist persecution in Egypt."*[393] And, workers in the Israeli defense industry are now being denied U.S. visas. *"In other words, the Obama administration is making it easier for Muslims with terrorist associations to enter the country, while making it more difficult for persecuted Christians and Israeli Jews."*

Daniel Greenfield, Front Page Magazine adds: *"Maine's Somali Muslim settler problem is growing worse with gang violence and welfare abuse threatening the state. Governor LePage's efforts to make Maine's generous benefits system less attractive to Somali Muslim migrants who have swarmed the state seeking taxpayer handouts has led to protests from those same Somali Muslims."*[394] Mr. Greenfield quoted Fatuma Hussein, director of the Somali Women of Maine who said, *"It's a moral and human act to provide assistance and meet the vital needs of this population. The face of Maine is changing and so are our communities."*

It's not just Maine; the face of our country is changing. Instead of the once great and prosperous nation we had always been, we are turning into an "open borders" global welfare refugee state. We are supporting covert immigration by welcoming hostile refugees with insatiable demands. We are catering to immigrants expecting to live on welfare with no intention of ever contributing anything positive to America. As if we don't have enough problems with illegal aliens, we are now "importing" potential to probable enemies. I guess we are "a special kind of stupid" after all.

---

[393] "Obama's bizarre immigration rules," Tammy Bruce, *The Washington Times*, http://www.washingtontimes.com, March 6, 2014

[394] "Somali Muslim Migrants Protest Welfare Reform in Maine," Daniel Greenfield, *Front Page Magazine*, http://www.frontpagemag.com, January 12, 2014

We need to read and watch and keep current on the immigration situation. We need to contact Congress and voice our views. We need to identify the politicians and public officials who disregard the law and release illegals – to commit crimes again. Illegal aliens should be reported to ICE (Immigration and Customs Enforcement, a component of the Department of Homeland Security) even though many government officials hamper ICE's performance. The ICE website (http://www.ice.gov) provides information on illegal aliens including criminal activity, financial crimes, drug and contraband smuggling, etc. There are numerous websites that report on illegal activity. They invite survey participation and publish petitions for us to sign which they then forward to Congress and the White House. The border watch groups like Minuteman Project have proven that even those of us who do not live near a border can and should organize neighborhood watch groups. We need to know how to assist local, state, and federal agencies in battling illegal immigration. We need to stand by our Second Amendment right to bear arms not for mob-action as some fear, but for the very principle of self-defense guaranteed by our Constitution.

We must never forget U.S. Border Patrol Agent Brian Terry who was murdered in 2010 on the Arizona border by illegals working for a Mexican drug cartel. You would think the U.S. government would be aggressively involved in this tragedy, unless of course they had something to hide. Oh, yes they do want to hide the fact that Agent Terry was murdered with one of the very "walking guns" lost in the defective DOJ (Department of Justice) and ATF (Bureau of Alcohol and Firearms) "Fast and Furious" operation. In Terry's memory, we need to support John Dodson, the ATF whistleblower who has written a book on Operation Fast and Furious. Dodson has so far been prohibited from publishing his manuscript by the ATF citing a negative effect it would have on ATF's relationship with the FBI and the DEA. The investigation, or more accurately, the lack of investigation into "Fast and Furious," and the murder of Terry is outrageous as the Department of Justice and the Administration continue to block every avenue of responsibility.

We need to support Border States like Arizona struggling to enforce laws and protect its citizens without help from the federal government. Arizona is being attacked on two fronts: its southern border with Mexico and the very federal government whose top priority is to protect the citizenry from attack – foreign and domestic. The state of Texas has an incredibly massive border with Mexico. Governor Rick Perry has made it clear that the citizens of Texas are no longer going to wait for the federal government to do its duty to protect the Texas border. He has called up the National Guard to assist the severely under-manned and under-funded border patrol. What did Governor Perry get for being a leader, standing up for the citizens of Texas, and remaining faithful to his oath of office? He was indicted by Eric Holder's Department of Justice for a bogus abuse of power accusation. The juvenile administration strikes again.

We need to support real leaders like Governor Rick Perry, Governor Jan Brewer and Sheriffs' Joe Arpaio and Paul Babeu. We also need to keep pressure on our government officials to secure our borders, protect our citizens, and uphold our laws. Illegal aliens in the U.S. have become so comfortable with the current administration that they blatantly rally screaming that they are illegals' and they DEMAND amnesty. In October 2013 a group of illegals and immigrant-rights advocates shouting, *"Undocumented, unafraid"* shut down a federal detention facility in Phoenix, Arizona demanding Obama halt all deportations. The group then staged a march in Phoenix and tried to block the gates at the federal immigration enforcement office.[395] Just days after the Phoenix demonstrations, protestors in Tucson stopped "Operation Streamline" a program that convicts and jails illegals prior to deportation.

Do not forget the words of a few insightful U.S. Representatives[396]

- Tom McClintock – California: *"With respect to the pathway to citizenship, we should never forget that there is a pathway to citizenship. It is followed by millions of legal immigrants, right now, who are obeying all of our laws, respecting our nation's sovereignty, standing patiently in line, doing everything our country has asked of them to do to become Americans, and they are watching 11 million people trying to cut in line in front of them."*

---

[395] Illegal aliens in Arizona fight deportations, call on Obama to halt removals, *The Washington Times*, www.washingtontimes.com, October 15, 2013

[396] "Immigration Reform Quotes You Don't Want to Miss," Posted by Rachel Taylor, The Foundry, The Heritage Foundation, http://blog.heritage.org, June 28, 2013

- Matt Salmon – Arizona: *"I do not favor or support, nor will I vote for, a pathway to citizenship for people that are here who've broken the law. I would support – after we have developed a secure border – a mechanism for allowing those folks to work here in America…Everything that we should do should be based on good, sound policy and what's right for America."*

The next time you hear President Obama talking about his deep concern and respect for the American people, remember this: During the government shutdown in October 2013 when the National Park Service under direct orders from the president closed and barricaded all the national monuments in Washington DC (and around the country) he allowed an illegal immigrant protest on the also closed National Mall. Supporting the protesters were eight Democratic Members of Congress - fully participating in the protest rally. Does anyone but me have a problem with the fact that American citizens, legal immigrants, and elderly, World War II veterans who survived an atrocious war and watched friends and comrades die horrible deaths were "barricaded from their memorials while Illegal aliens were permitted to protest on the National Mall with the blessing of the President of the United States? I sure hope so!

Another unbelievable development in the "illegal" issue is the fact that the California Supreme Court granted illegal alien Sergio C. Garcia admission to the state bar so he will be able to practice law in California.[397] Though federal law prohibits law firms, businesses and public agencies to hire illegal attorneys, I am confident the Justice Department won't have a problem with an *illegal alien practicing United States law.*

This situation highlights a very real yet totally ignored system of organized subversiveness.

1. An illegal alien attorney has no problem suing for and subsequently winning admission to his "host" country's legal system.

---

[397] "California Court Permits Illegal Immigrant to Practice Law," Tim Brown, Freedom Outpost, http://www.freedomoutpost.com, January 3, 2014

2. The California Supreme Court did not "interpret the law" which is the court's function; they re-wrote the law to allow for illegal activity.

3. The federal government allowed this violation of the constitution to happen and the government agency responsible for enforcing U.S. laws turns a blind eye.

We need to remind our Congress that this action is illegal. We need to demand that Congress, the White House and the Justice Department uphold the law. We need to "call out" Presidential and Congressional "un-truths" and executive orders supporting illegals. We also need to petition the government against welfare immigration - illegal or legal.

We need to recognize legal immigrants, their commitment and contributions for the betterment of America. To highlight and honor legal immigrants that have contributed immensely to America, a trip to New York is in order. The Statue of Liberty and Ellis Island now preserved as the *Statue of Liberty National Monument* illustrates the honor and pride of legal immigration. Written records, visual documentation – photographs of legal immigrants arriving in the United States is humbling. Look at the faces of the immigrants in the photos and you will understand how difficult the journey to America was. You will also see the strength and fortitude of these "legal" immigrants who came to this country with nothing yet made America strong and successful.

Take a look around. You will see American citizens of all races, sizes, colors, and heritages. We may look different but we all have a common thread – we are Americans. We have different traditions and views (that's what makes us unique). Our ancestors as well as current immigrants made major sacrifices to be here. We Americans need to respect and support each other. We need to remember that WE are America. What we do will affect future generations and we have a responsibility to teach our children what being American means. If you cannot be a proud American, you should seriously consider finding another country and I guarantee that after experiencing citizenship in most of the rest of the world, you will return.

If America is so bad, why do so many people want to become citizens? Homeland Security Office of Immigration Statistics states that the number of people nationalized increased 58% from 660,477 in 2007 to a record 1,046,539 in 2008.[398] In the 1950s and 1960s, the average number of annual naturalizations was less than 120,000. The number rose to 210,000 during the 1980s and 500,000 in the 1990s. Legal immigrants clearly see something good in America.

Part of a foreign and defense policy expert Kim Homes' article that appeared in the *Washington Times* was quoted in an article by John Grimaldi. *"Those who believe in American Exceptionalism don't reject foreigners. They recognize what's unique about our history: a distinctive confluence of culture, government, and economy, and an ethos of personal responsibility that tamed the economy's wild horses and tempered the potentially anarchic tendencies of free people. These, not government action, gave rise to the wealthiest and most powerful nation on earth."*[399]

Theodore Roosevelt - The concept of immigration

"In the first place, we should insist that if the immigrant who comes here in good faith becomes an American and assimilates himself to us, he shall be treated on an exact equality with everyone else, for it is an outrage to discriminate against any such man because of creed, or birthplace, or origin. But this is predicated upon the person's becoming in every facet an American and nothing but an American...There can be no divided allegiance here. Any man who says he is an American, but something else also, isn't an American at all. We have room for but one flag, the American flag... We have room for but one language here, and that is the English language... and we have room for but one sole loyalty and that is a loyalty to the American people."

---

[398] U.S. Department of Homeland Security Office of Immigration Statistics: Annual Flow Report, March 2009

[399] "National Security: the threat from within, Political ideologues would undermine the basis of what made our nation great – American Exceptionalism", John Grimaldi, Association of Mature American Citizens (AMAC), http://www. amac.us, 2013

OBAMACARE

"A Government big enough to give you everything you need
is big enough to take everything you have."

—Thomas Jefferson

The "Health Care" issue has been debated for decades and we have now crossed the threshold into "nationalized medicine." To some this is a good thing. It would take us a step closer to being a true collective state in the global community making us more like Europe and many third world countries. I say it is a bad thing and will drag our country further down into the welfare abyss of corruption, bureaucratic control and patient abuse. The Affordable Care Act (forever to be known as Obamacare) was sold as the cure-all for America's health care crisis. It was presented in a pretty package guaranteeing health care to all. The concept sounded great. Who wouldn't want to be part of a nation that cares about the health of all its citizens? The reality is the government does not care about your health. They do care about holding onto power and expanding welfare for people already receiving government "assistance" including illegal aliens to buy votes. They also care about preserving their roles as social engineering advocates. Washington politicians will freely manipulate health care benefits and costs while **unelected bureaucrats will regulate the quality and quantity of health care for Americans**. Step by step and enforced by law, eventually we will all be required to accept whatever the government decides is best for us while our concerned leaders in Washington are exempt from Obamacare. They get to keep their first-rate health care plans. They have and will continue to have better health plans than the rest of us - a health care plan we do not have access to. If the politicians were required to be part of the same national system that they mandated for the rest of us, there would have been a lot more scrutiny about the healthcare bill instead of passing it without knowing what was in it

As it was, people with health insurance paid for it and were responsible for all costs not covered by the insurance. These same people were also already paying for Medicare and Medicaid, including the health care costs of welfare recipients and illegal aliens since the reality is no one can be denied medical treatment. Many employers provided insurance benefits at minimal cost to employees. Small business owners, independent contractors, and others purchased health insurance with premiums based on services needed, choice of doctors and hospitals, and cost.

Yes, the established health insurance industry had faults like denial of benefits for pre-existing conditions, limits of insurance, and disastrous personal economic consequences resulting from catastrophic illness expenses. And yes, the medical/insurance system needed reformation, but government controlled national health care is NOT the answer. Other plans had been discussed, but since they did not support the administration's view of national health care, they were disregarded. President Obama was not lying when he said that he would consider other health plans presented to him. The key words are "presented to him." All of the health care plans and proposals created by the Republican controlled House were immediately blocked by Harry Reid in the Senate ... so literally, no plans were ever "presented" to the President.

Politicians do not have our health and well-being in mind when they create monstrosities like the Affordable Care Act. They are the very people who pass laws that enable health care abuse in the first place. They are one reason that medical care is so expensive. The corrupt Medicare and Medicaid systems which consume over 20% of the national budget are a travesty. The Medicare system is like a giant legal "Ponzi scheme." It worked for a while, but now the recipients are beginning to outnumber the contributors and the system cannot be sustained. Other contributing factors to the high cost of health of insurance include excessive medical lawsuits that make malpractice insurance extremely expensive, and the inability to control drug costs.

I question how a government that can't honestly and effectively manage Medicare, can't secure our nation's borders, can't locate millions of illegal aliens, can't handle a hurricane, can't keep track of national security secrets, and can't stop spending our money foolishly can possibly manage a health care system. A great example of government ineptness is the bailout of GM. The government gave GM more money than the company was worth on the stock market only months before the company went bankrupt. The insult is that the politicians knew bankruptcy was inevitable for GM even with the bailout money. Government bailouts of private companies are examples of irresponsible and wasteful spending of our tax money. The government is not the entity we need controlling our healthcare.

Many Americans have no idea just how much a national health care program is really going to cost them. The financial cost (which will exceed the initial estimate of $1.6 trillion) alone will be devastating. There is no way our taxes will not be increased to pay for this program.

Now that the Affordable Care Act law is in effect, the administration and the Department of Health and Human Services which oversees Obamacare, are preparing Americans for the inevitably of tax increases that will be necessary to support this health care program. Aside from the financial cost, we will lose our option to purchase private insurance, and we will lose our choices in doctors, treatments, medications, and care even though President Obama promised time and time again that we would be able to keep our doctor, hospitals, and health plan. How can you justify the lies and deceit? How can anyone still trust anything Obama has to say? The President put HIS ideological and financially impossible health care vision above all facts and logic. The totally unforgiveable part of the Presidential lie is that he knew it was not true from the very first time he made the promise. The politicians that crafted, campaigned and promoted the ACA also knew it was a lie. For the record, the law was passed without one Republican vote and without being read by those who voted for its passage.

National Health Care has Consequences.

The "enlightened" government healthcare plan was sold as a great humanitarian leap forward. The government will take care of us and provide us with what we need. We will pay and pay and have no voice or choice in one of the most important issues of our lives – our health. Right out of the box, the plan mandated that everyone (legal residents) have health insurance. Welfare recipients and Illegal aliens will continue to receive free health care paid for by all of us. And the welfare rolls will rise since the health plan will cost many American jobs. Americans who still have a job whether full-time or part-time will pay as usual, and those same taxpayers will also provide the funds to subsidize the purchase of insurance for lower-income people who can't afford to pay for it. Government instituted penalties force us to comply with their mandate. Employers are required to "contribute" to the cost of health insurance which will adversely affect small businesses resulting in the elimination of jobs because the small business cannot operate with the health expense mandate. As we have been repeatedly told - we can keep our private insurance if we want BUT employers will be taxed at higher rates for choosing private insurance over the national plan. **Private plans will eventually be driven out of the marketplace** leaving only a single government health insurance program. When this happens, and it will, we lose complete control over our health care.

No matter how the administration portrays national health care, it is "socialized medicine." The fact is that public officials will be administering our health care. **They will decide** what doctors, treatments, and medications we will or will not get. There will be a single budget, and care and services will be rationed. We will have no choice but to accept the care and medications the "state monopoly" provides. **Our medical care will be based on politics not science**, and certainly not on what is best for us. Research incentives will be compromised, there will be no incentive to excel, and medical personnel will become complacent. We will suffer. In 2006 Deroy Murdock of *Human Events* clearly warned that, "*Patients in universal-care systems get cheated even worse than do students in failing public schools. While their pupils suffer intellectually, politically driven healthcare jeopardizes patient's lives.*"[400]

Another aspect of national health care never discussed is patient privacy. There will be a national medical database to store all of our medical records. The government and its unelected bureaucrat minions will have access to our medical histories, conditions, and treatments. They contend that our very personal information will be secure. That is another lie as evidenced by the Obamacare rollout website issues. There was and still is no reliable security program associated with the Government Insurance Marketplace website and system. It is like a "candy shop" for hackers and thieves. The truth is that the same government that cannot secure top secret national security data and CIA files will not be able to secure our personal life and health information. Our personal and private information will be able to be accessed at any time and can be used against us. That may sound a little conspiratorial, but just look how easy it was for an official in Ohio to access personal information on Joe the Plumber to smear his name because he asked a

---

[400] "*National Healthcare=Stethoscope Socialism*," Deroy Murdock, Human Events. com, http://www.humanevents.com, 8/24/2006

question Obama did not like. Government personnel as well as hackers will be able to access our most private information.

We only need to look at the national health care systems of other countries to see what is going to happen to us. These systems are portrayed as effective plans to provide health care to all and are embraced by national health care proponents. What these proponents do not tell us is that many of the national health care systems are failing and numerous countries are returning to the free market system for medical care. *"While enlightened Europeans seek out the success of privatization and free markets, national health care devotees in the United States would return us to the dark ages."*[401] Conrad F. Meier, The Heartland Institute gave us that warning back in 2005.

We should have also listened to the warning voices of people like Daniel Hannan, a British politician and member of the European Parliament. He knows about national health care first hand and told us how bad it is. He warned us not to go down that road. ***"...if your health system was that bad, why is the whole world knocking at the door to try and get in and use it? You get to choose a doctor; you get to choose the specialists. And if you are unsatisfied, you can go for better treatment elsewhere. And that's what is missing in the British system or in any state-run system."***[402] He stressed the fact that there is no remedy for problems and lack of quality care. Patients can't do anything about mistreatment or lack of care. People are supposed to be grateful for anything they get from the national health care system.

Britain's National Health Service is a national health care system funded by taxes to provide free and "fair" health care to its citizens. The NHS is obsessed with "equality," and that all people receive care. To meet this mandate, the NHS determines and regulates care and costs and also dictates the salaries of doctors and nurses. There is a shortage of doctors, hospital beds, diagnostic equipment, resources, and medications. The result of its national health care system is not quality

---

[401] *"My Turn: Health Care Revolution in Europe,"* Conrad F. Meier, late senior fellow in health policy for the Heartland Institute and editor emeritus, *Health Care News,* The Heartland Institute, April 01, 2005

[402] *Glenn Beck: "What Brits think of gov healthcare,"* The Glenn Beck Program, August 4, 2009

health care. It is inefficiency, rationed care, long waiting periods even for simple procedures, escalating costs, and tax increases. Statistics contradict the value of such systems. For instance, breast cancer kills 46% of women stricken with it compared to 25% in the U.S.; prostate cancer kills 57% of British patients compared to 19% in the U.S., and 10% of British patients died in hospitals.[403] Few people are aware of the British government's "postcode lottery," which supplies drugs to some cities, but not others. This function of national healthcare insures that people living in certain areas will <u>not</u> have access to certain medications. The bottom line on British National Care is that it is based on "cost-effectiveness" and the bureaucrats not the doctors decide which patients will receive care and medicines. Keep this in mind when you hear how great government health care is. For instance, it is not cost-effective for older patients to receive organ transplants and kidney dialysis, nor is it cost-effective for them to receive hip replacements, so they can, and will be denied. Patients have no recourse.

Horror stories of the British National Health Care System are countless. A few examples of the heralded British model illustrate what we can expect from national health care[404]

- Patients made to wait inside ambulances outside hospital emergency rooms for over eight hours to comply with a government rule that patients must be seen by a physician within four hours <u>after</u> entering a hospital
- The average waiting period for disabled children to receive wheelchairs is five months, though waits up to two years are not uncommon
- Cesarean Section births are denied because health bureaucrats deem them too expensive

---

[403] *"National Healthcare=Stethoscope Socialism,"* Deroy Murdock, Human Events, http://www.humanevents.com, 8/24/2006

[404] *"Bad Care After Good: Obama Seeks to Trade the U.S.'s Health Care Problems for Britain's Health Care Catastrophe,"* Jeff Emanuel, http://www.redstate.com, July 21, 2009

- The National Institute for Clinical Effectiveness (NICE) has the power to ration care and deny lifesaving and life-extending drugs, treatments, and procedures
- Heart surgery for a three-year old child was cancelled three times because of a lack of hospital beds
- A man with angina and on a heart bypass waiting list for 72 months was diagnosed with a chest infection. He subsequently suffered a heart attack that killed him. His widow received a letter from the cardiac department of Bristol Royal Infirmary a year after his death offering him an appointment for bypass surgery
- A 30 year old mother gave birth to her premature baby in a hospital bathroom because no qualified staff was available to assist her

Since "administrators" not doctors determine and authorize medical care, administrators have the power to determine care and deny care based on personal bias. No matter how we are told this would never happen, it will. They don't even have to justify a denial based on a medical reason. An example of this is Edward Atkinson of Norfolk, England who was "deleted" from a government hip-replacement surgery waiting list because he mailed pro-life literature to hospital employees. The hospital administrator said the material was objectionable so "We exercised our right to decline treatment to him for anything other than life-threatening conditions."[405] Mr. Atkinson cannot receive a hip replacement only because the administrator found his totally unrelated, personal views objectionable. That is a police state! I urge you to read **"Shattered Lives: 100 Victims of Government Health Care."** It is an extremely enlightening publication by the National Center for Public Policy Research.[406] The United Kingdom's *Daily Mail* newspaper

---

[405] *"National Healthcare=Stethoscope Socialism,"* Deroy Murdock, Human Events, http://www.humanevents.com, 8/24/2006

[406] "Shattered Lives: 100 Victims of Government Health Care," Amy Ridenour and Ryan Balis, The National Center for Public Policy Research, 2009

reported that the NHS is writing off cancer patients who are over 75[407] because they are just too old.

Dental care is a topic never addressed in the health care/insurance debate. Where does dental care/coverage fit into the picture? Anyone with dental problems can attest to how important dental care and coverage is. Take a look at Britain again for the answer. It is extremely difficult and getting worse for Brits to find an NHS dentist. Even with an NHS dentist, the patient could still be responsible for 80% of the treatment cost. *"Seven and a half million Britons have failed to gain access to an NHS dentist in the past two years (The population of the UK is 60 million)."*[408] People have actually pulled out their own teeth after enduring weeks of pain because they could not see a dentist.

Great Britain is slowly turning away from national health care to private, market-based health care because "Choice and competition... with money following the patient, competition between providers is intended to improve both efficiency and quality of care. Doctors, nurses, hospital and community services will be more responsive to patient needs."[409]*It comes as no surprise to learn that many Brits and other Europeans come to the United States for medical care. As a matter of fact, people from all over the world come to America for medical care and treatment."* National health care proponents and the media do not report such facts.

The health care problems in Great Britain are common in <u>all</u> government run national health care systems. Canada's National Health Care System is another model that was referenced by proponents in the U.S. Unfortunately the reality is very different than the image that was presented to us. The Canadian system goes a step further than Europe. It is illegal to operate commercial for-profit healthcare providers. But like Great Britain, Canada is moving away from the failed government

---

[407] "Too old to be given cancer treatment: NHS is writing off patients who are over 75," Jenny Hope, Mail Online, Daily Mail, http://www.dailymail.uk, January 26, 2014

[408] *"UK's National Health Care = Third World Dental Care,"* Professor Mark J. Perry's Blog for Economics and Finance, Monday, January 21, 2008

[409] *"Bad Medicine (National Health Care System in Great Britain),"* Allyson Pollock, *New Internationalist Magazine.* April 2003

health care system. In June 2005 the Canadian Supreme Court struck down a Quebec law banning private medical insurance on the basis that the long waiting lists violated patients, "liberty, safety, and security."[410]

The fact is Canadians who can afford to come to the United States for critical care, as was the case of a Canadian woman with a brain tumor who was told she had to wait six months for treatment. She mortgaged her home and came to the U.S. for immediate treatment – that saved her life.[411]

In October 2009, a Canadian baby whose mother was in labor for 40 hours during which time the umbilical cord wrapped around the baby's neck depriving him of oxygen. He was put on life support and the doctors said he would not live longer than three days, would not grow or urinate, or even move. The Canadian public health service mandated a January 20, 2010 deadline for the baby to recover or be taken off life support. The parents received a letter from the Alberta Health Services stating: *"There is no hope of recovery for Isaiah….Your treating physicians regretfully have come to the conclusion that **withdrawal of active treatment is medically reasonable, ethically responsible and appropriate….We must put the interests of your son foremost, and it is in his best interests to discontinue mechanical ventilation support."*[412] Reasonable? Ethical? Responsible? Appropriate? Those are the words used by the government to justify ending a helpless child's life.

The truth is, the baby has grown, moves his hands and feet, urinates, and opens his eyes. The doctors were wrong on all accounts. This story strikes me on a very personal level. It reminds me of when one of my nephews was born in 1991 with a deadly liver condition. After undergoing a liver transplant when he was a few months old, he developed a severe infection and was put on life support. The parents were told by doctors that: The baby could not survive; then, if he survived, he would be severely handicapped and blind. They strongly

---

[410] *"Canada's National Health Care System in Peril,"* Health News, http://www. health.dailynewscentral.com, 6/12/2005

[411] *"A Life and Death Situation,"* Patients United Now, http://www. patientsunitednow.com, 5/27/2009

[412] *"Mom appeals to government: Don't pull plug on my baby,"* Drew Zahn, World Net Daily, January 23, 2010

suggested the removal of life support. A single doctor said no – and would not allow the others to pull the plug. That baby, who wasn't supposed to live, recovered, grew up, graduated from school, drives a car, holds a job, and has enriched the lives of all who know him. The only difference between this American baby's story and the Canadian baby's story is that the American government did not interfere with his health issues and decisions.

Other examples of how the Canadian health care system really works:

- Patients diagnosed with cancer can wait up to three months to see an oncologist.
- The time it takes to see a specialist once a referral is obtained from the family doctor has risen from 3.7 weeks to 8.3 weeks.
- The time between the appointment with a specialist and actual treatment has increased from 5.6 weeks to 9.4 weeks.
- Waiting time for orthopedic surgery can be 40 weeks[413] (that is a long time to be in pain).
- The Canadian government sends high-risk pregnant women to the U.S. for prenatal care that is unavailable in Canada.
- Lotteries are held for people to "win" appointments to see general practice doctors.

So what are Canadians themselves saying about national health care? In August 2008 at the Canadian Medical Association annual meeting, both the outgoing president and incoming president of the organization were quite candid about the state of Canada's national health care system and neither man was complimentary. Sandy Szwarc, BSN, RN, CCP relates what the two key speakers had to say as was reported by the *Canwest News Service*.[414] Brian Day the outgoing president stated that over one million Canadians were on waiting lists for health care and five million people did not have access to a family

---

[413] "Canadian Health Care System Falling Apart," http://apatheticvoter.com, July 1, 2009

[414] *"Changing of the Guard – Bringing Timely Food for Thought,"* Sany Szwarc, Junkfood Science, http://www.junkfoodscience.blogspot.com, August 20, 2008

doctor. Canadian medical schools OECD (Organization for Economic Co-operation and Development) ratings were dropping. Canada ranked 26th out of 28 countries in doctors per population. Dr. Day said, *"In Canada we pay dearly to keep patients on waiting lists. This is illogical. Preventing patients from getting treatment is not my definition of preventive medicine…"* Dr. Day then said Canada's health care system should *"…embrace some private-sector initiatives,"* and thought public-private partnerships should be established to fund medical schools.

Incoming CMA president, Dr. Robert Quellet said healthcare costs have *"quadrupled in the last 20 years and the country's doctor-to-patient ratio has plummeted."* He said that the state of Canadian health care is "alarming," and *"we have one of the most costly and least efficient health systems of any industrialized country."* He concurred with Dr. Day that Canada's health care system needs private intervention.

I wondered why Canada's Newfoundland and Labrador Premier Danny Williams came to the U.S. in February 2010 for heart surgery. Could it be that he might not have lived long enough waiting for Canadian care? Or, could it be that Canada does not have the needed medical specialists, equipment, and aftercare that is readily available in the United States? Or, maybe he came (just like so many others) because the United States has many of the world's best medical doctors, equipment, facilities, and pharmaceuticals.

The French System of national health care is a network of financial crisis, mismanagement, abuse, corruption, waste, and a powerful physician and medical professional lobby that prevents any change or improvement. Research and development is not funded, and French pharmaceutical companies have not produced an advanced product in over 20 years. The French model is yet another system we do not want to imitate.

No real national health care debate would be complete without including everyone's favorite disingenuous filmmaker, Michael Moore whose so-called documentary "Sicko" promoted universal free health care by extolling the wonderful Cuban health care system. I am not sure where he got his information but the real Cuban health care system is nothing like he portrayed it. If you want the real story, I suggest you access the July 2007 National Policy Analysis article *"Sicko Presents False View of Cuba's Health System.*"[415] The reality is that the Cuban government controls all aspects of medical care. Private, non-governmental health facilities are illegal. This is the real Cuban health system:

- Long waits for patients at government hospitals
- Many services and technologies are available only to members of the Cuban party elite
- "<u>Foreign-only hospitals treat only foreign health tourists</u>" with <u>money to pay for it</u> while regular Cubans must use the inferior government hospitals and facilities
- Basic medicines like aspirin and antibiotics are limited
- There is a shortage of doctors – 1/5 of Cuba's doctors have been contracted out to Venezuela under an "oil-for-doctors" exchange program between Fidel Castro and Hugo Chavez
- Lack of medical equipment
- Lack of basic health goods such as beds, bed linens, and even food

Media outlets such as Canada's *National Post*, The *New York Times*, *Boston Globe*, *National Public Radio*, and 'Ihe *Chicago Tribune* have reported on the real situation in Cuba. Obviously Michael Moore missed those reports.

The National Policy Analysis article cites a 1997 joint letter by 18 exiled Cuban doctors who stated: *"We remain mystified as to why people of ordinary good will and faith would seek to find fault with the United States for the disastrous situation inside of Cuba, while failing to direct the blame squarely where it belongs – at the feet of Fidel Castro, who continues to rule our country with an iron fist after 38 years in power."* The doctors' also confirmed that the government directs scarce health resources to the regime's elite and to foreigners who can pay cash for services leaving the Cuban people neglected with little to no health care.

We could take a critical look at other countries with national health care, but we would just see more of the same. As a matter of truth

---

[415] *"Sicko" Presents False View of Cuba's Health System,"* Ryan Balis, policy analyst, National Policy Analysis, A Publication of The National Center for Public Policy Research, July 2007, http://www.nationalcenter.org

we already have an established government run health care system. This government controlled health care program operates on Native American reservations in our country and it is a disaster- a travesty that we never hear about. Native Americans have been the recipients of national health care for well over a century. Just look at how that system works and you will see what is in store for us. Lack of doctors, hospitals, medical facilities, equipment, resources, and medications are common factors of the government run health system. Native Americans are sick and dying and unable to get the medical care they need all because they are subject to a government run, bureaucrat administered health care system that is a failure. Congress should be investigating that situation – a government that truly cared about its people would.

If our health care system is so bad and other socialized (national) systems are better, why do so many foreign leaders and people with means come to the U.S. for medical treatment and surgical procedures? The simple answer is that America has the best medical care, doctors, resources, and research in the world because it is based on a free-market system. That is the only system that can and will produce quality doctors and medical professionals, superior medical technology and equipment, treatment, research, and medicines. Without the free market, medical research, treatment, and pharmaceutical advances will suffer resulting in poor quality health care and sicker people. How many people do you know or have heard of that traveled to say Europe, Canada, or anywhere else for that matter for medical care? I can't think of a single one.

We were told that the number of uninsured Americans was at a disastrous level. A Fox News Financial Report on June 2, 2009 reported an estimated 42 million Americans were without health insurance: 18 million were between the ages of 18 and 34 and 40% of them can afford health insurance but <u>chose</u> not to buy it; 10 million were illegal aliens; 8 million were children of which 50% are eligible to be covered under SCHIP (State Children's Health Insurance Program) but their parents chose not to participate; and the rest were children of illegal aliens who automatically became citizens because they were born in the U.S. SCHIP, created in 1997 was the largest expansion of tax-payer funded health insurance for children ever. SCHIP helps uninsured children get insurance coverage, at a tremendous financial cost, of course. Now here is the real surprise. *National Review* reports that researchers find *"no evidence that SCHIP actually improves health outcomes, or that the program addresses the systemic quality problems that confront even insured children."*[416]

So how many Americans were really without health insurance? Not as many as we were led to believe. How many Americans were temporarily without health insurance? How many Americans were on welfare (which is supposed to be temporary assistance – not a way of life) with no intention of ever getting off, and illegal aliens who don't care about health insurance because they will never have to pay for it? A FOXNews.com article reported that health care legislation doesn't technically cover undocumented workers but it does not contain any "mechanism" to deny them health care. The Federation for American Immigration Reform states that illegal immigrants already account for $10.7 billion of government health care expenditures.[417] So the cost of health care for illegals was not even included in the administration's health care system figures.

The Affordable Care Act is complex, constantly changing and totally incomprehensible. Many of the politicians that pushed the plan never read the thousand-plus page bill they committed to sign. They did not even know what was in it but assured us it was not a "government take-over of health care." We were told numerous times we could keep our doctors and insurance if we wanted to. But in the real world, penalties, and the government backed venues will eliminate private insurance until there is a single payer – government insurance program. Since health insurance is mandatory, the taxpayers will in addition to paying for their own health insurance have to subsidize (Senate health committee bill estimates over $700 billion in subsidies over 10 years)[418] low-income people to purchase insurance. Once the government has

---

[416] *"Does SCHIP Work? Obama wants to expand the program, but eliminating it would be best for all involved,* "Michael F. Cannon, National Review, http://www.nationalreview.com, February 2, 2009

[417] *"Bad Employer Bailout? Reform Could Fund Health Care for Illegal Workers,"* July 30, 2009, http:www.foxnews.com

[418] *"Individual Mandate: key to universal health coverage,"* Tom Curry, MSNBC, July 8, 2009, http://www.msnbc.com

total control over our health care, what is to stop unelected bureaucrats from dictating health and lifestyle choices, behavior, and the way we raise our children? Simple answer – Nothing. It is already happening.

A study by the Business and Media Institute summarized the problems with Obamacare and the media's championing of the president's plan in a document titled, *Uncritical Condition.*[419] They went a step further publishing suggestions to present the "Plan" in a fair and informative manner. The study's findings are extremely informative. The price tag of the Affordable Care Act still keeps increasing. The Congressional Budget Office estimated the initial health care bill would be at least $1.6 trillion and 36 million would still be uninsured. Network news organizations consistently reported lower costs and inflated the number of uninsured Americans. News organizations did not mention that the insurance program proposed by the administration would be just like the Medicare program. They also didn't mention that Medicare is plagued by corruption, is in financial turmoil, and is a big reason for our current escalating health care costs. You are hard-pressed to find a news story on the "flawed" Massachusetts health care reform program (mandatory health insurance premiums have risen 7.4%, 8-12%, and 9% consecutively the past three years); or the failed Hawaii health care program (that was cancelled only 7 months after it was instituted). Massachusetts and Hawaii along with the Native American reservation health care systems are evidence that government health care does not work.

The study also had suggestions for Americans to learn the whole story about national healthcare. They suggested the media be honest about the cost of such a plan. *"Journalists should also be skeptical of cost estimates from the government since they have been unreliable in the past."* Critics of the plan should have been allowed to present their point of view and substantiate their findings. Journalists and reporters should have reported on the problems with health care in Massachusetts and Hawaii, existing federal programs like Medicare, and national health care programs in other countries. They of course did not.

Critics of the administration's health care plan should have been

---

[419] *"Uncritical Condition: Network news fails to examine high cost and proven failures of government-run health care,"* Julia A. Seymour and Sarah Knoploh, Business & Media Institute, http://www.businessandmedia.org, 2009

listened to. Their claim that government insurance will "kill private insurance" was a credible warning. A public/government insurance plan (like Medicare) will not increase competition in the health insurance market and lower costs, as we have been told. It will do the opposite. There will be no competition. The government plan will consume private insurance, eliminate competition resulting in a government monopoly, and the costs will increase. Why would we want a "Medicare-like" national health care system when Medicare is a catastrophe? The government run Medicare program is corrupt, inefficient, wasteful, and costly. A national/government health care system is the same, but on a much greater scale.

How can a government that cannot control its own spending and continues to bury this nation under an insurmountable debt responsibly administer such a huge and important program? It can't. The bureaucrats could not even manage their July-August 2009 "Cash for Clunkers" program. Our Washington bureaucrats miscalculated the program budget and then erroneously estimated the number of government workers needed to administer the program. They had to borrow FAA employees including air traffic controllers to work for the clunker program. Was that a responsible and effective use of FAA air traffic controllers? I think not. While the administration was celebrating the program's "success" at stimulating the auto industry and the economy, car dealers were still waiting for the government promised money the program was designed to generate. The Cash-for-Clunkers Program should be remembered as another example of the ineptness of government involvement in the private sector. Keep in mind that the Cash-for-Clunkers program was a simple, straight-forward, and short-term program. It serves as another warning that the government is incapable of managing a national program especially one that costs trillions of dollars.

The Heritage Foundation is a great source for accurate information on the health care situation. The Heritage Foundation Center for Health Policy Studies commissioned the Lewin Group, a non-partisan health care policy and management consulting firm to examine the mammoth "American Affordable Health Choices Act of 2009 (H.R. 3200). The findings of the Lewin Group report are remarkably accurate. *This bill would establish a public health plan modeled on the Medicare program.*

The purpose of this plan is to compete (though realistically it would overwhelm and eliminate private health care insurance) with private health plans in a new "insurance exchange." **In summary, the Lewin report stated that 48% of privately insured Americans would leave private insurance, 56% of Americans with employer-based coverage would lose their current insurance, 80% of Americans in a new health insurance exchange would end up in the public plan, and 34% of the uninsured would still lack coverage. The report further stated that doctors would see payments decline by $31.7 billion because of the new public plan, and hospitals could see net annual incomes fall by $61.9 billion.**[420]

A Heritage Foundation Lecture from July 2001, *Perspectives on the European Health Care Systems: Some Lessons for America* provides insight into numerous European health care systems and presents a strong argument against national health care in America.[421] Another Heritage Foundation publication worth review is the June 25, 2009 *Medicare Administrative Costs Are Higher, Not Lower, Than for Private Insurance.* The definitive conclusion is that Medicare is not a good model to follow. Medicare's administrative costs are higher, not lower than private insurance.[422] The Heritage Foundation's investigation of Medicare is not a recent phenomenon as evidenced in a March 2004 publication titled, *Medicare's Deepening Financial Crisis: The High Price of Fiscal Irresponsibility* highlighting Medicare's problems and excessive costs. Their study concluded that the Medicare program alone will consume 24% of all federal income taxes by 2019 and 51% by 2042.[423]

---

[420] *"The Impact of the American Affordable Health Choices Act of 2009,"* The Lewin Group Report, July 28, 2009

[421] *"Perspectives on the European health Care Systems: Some Lessons for America,"* Robert E. Moffit, Ph.D., Philippe Maniere, David G. Green, Ph.D., Paul Belien, Johan Hjertqvist, and Friedrich Breyer, Ph.D., The Heritage Foundation, Heritage Lecture #711, July 9, 2001

[422] *"Medicare Administrative Costs Are Higher, Not Lower, Than for Private Insurance,"* Robert A. Brook, Ph.D., The Heritage Foundation, Web Memo, No. 2505, June 25, 2009

[423] *"Medicare's Deepening Financial Crisis: The High Price of Fiscal Irresponsibility,"* Robert E. Moffit, Ph.D., and Brian M. Riedl, Backgrounder published by The Heritage Foundation, No. 1740, March 25, 2004

The article also predicted eventual government restrictions on drugs, tighter drug formularies, even price-fixing in an attempt to control rising costs of the Medicare drug entitlement program.

As long as we're on the subject of Medicare, MSNBC.com published an article about Medicare fraud in Florida. Though Florida is highlighted, Medicare fraud is national, rampant, and steals an estimated 60 billion tax payer dollars a year. The December 2007 article by Mark Potter[424] exposes blatant fraud that rips off taxpayers and hurts honest patients, doctors, and legitimate businesses. Fraudulent companies repeatedly bill Medicare for medical equipment for fictional patients. In just one instance federal agents in Miami confiscated a single electric wheelchair costing $5,000 from an illicit company. Medicare was billed repeatedly for a total of $5 million dollars for that single wheelchair which was never delivered to a single patient.

Other schemes include patient identification theft which is used to bill Medicare for fraudulent services and items. Fraudulent doctors set up companies, then bill Medicare for three to four months, collect on invoices, and then shut down and move before the fraud is detected. Dishonest doctors and patients form complex networks of deceit and successfully defraud Medicare. The schemes are numerous, they constantly evolve and it seems that defrauding Medicare is relatively easy which begs the question, why can't Medicare (the government) monitor and control the security of a single health care entity? Since the government can't monitor one agency, how can it possibly manage a national health care network? It can't.

There is no guarantee of health care in the Constitution, and government interference into the free market is a dangerous step, but on the other hand, it would be inhumane to deny medical care to those who cannot pay for it. So what do we do about this? Contrary to what we are repeatedly told, most people do not have a problem subsidizing the poor. They do have a problem subsidizing a corrupt, inept system that provides for the poor's health care. We see corruption in the already government controlled health care programs, Medicare and Medicaid. How many billions of dollars have been lost through theft, fraud, and

---

[424] *"Blatant Medicare fraud costs taxpayers billions,"* Mark Potter, MSNBC, http://. www.msnbc.com, December 11, 2007

inept officials and administrators? How many billions of dollars could the government save by ending the corruption? We see Congressional corruption with "earmarks" and "perks" though they consider it a cost of doing business. There are always discussions about spending our money, but they never discuss ways to save our money. They see themselves as defenders of the poor and downtrodden, which should be a noble endeavor, but they are "defenders" for show. They pander to keep their positions and the benefits that go with them.

Why can't our legislators exert as much energy passing laws to find and eliminate corruption on national, state, and local levels, and to limit excessive lawsuits that are forcing doctors and hospitals out of business? We don't like the high cost of pharmaceuticals, and keep hearing how greedy and heartless the pharmaceutical companies are. National health care will eventually enforce the establishment of price controls on drugs. It sounds like a good thing, but reality is the pharmaceutical companies spend billions of dollars in research and development to get a single new drug on the market. We have become accustomed to getting "new" and "advanced" medicines. Price controls carry a price few people think about. There will be fewer new and improved medicines discovered, created, and put on the market. Our pharmaceutical advancements will come to a halt. This has been proven by countries that have national health care and price controls. They do not develop and market new products – the United States still does.

Administration, Senate and House proponents of the Affordable Care Act invested a lot of time and energy to convince Americans that there will be no "rationing" of health care. The problem with their argument is that the rationing of care and services is inevitable. As a matter of fact, Medicare is already rationing care. Home health care has proven to be an effective program that saves billions of dollars in health care costs. So instead of expanding such a successful and financially beneficial program, Medicare and Medicaid Services cut $34 billion from that program. Another $56.8 billion will be cut from the program to finance the Affordable Care Act.[425]

We were told there were no other alternatives. That also was not

---

[425] "Three Reasons Why Government Can't Run Health Care," Newt Gingrich, Human Events.com, http://www.humanevents.com, August 26, 2009

true. In Congress a number of proposals had been suggested. They were ignored and denied, guaranteeing they would never be presented for committee discussion and vote. A FoxNews.com report brought a few examples of this to light. *"Dozens of bills that aim to fill in pieces of the health care puzzle are floating around Capitol Hill. From allowing seniors to open health savings accounts, to increasing access to cancer screening procedures, to improving end-of-life care, many bills have languished in House and Senate committees with no action taken on them."*[426] Representative Paul Ryan's Health Care Freedom Act included provisions that would insure interstate competition and give families that do not have employer insurance $5,000 a year to buy insurance. Representative Nydia Valazquez introduced a bill for the establishment of small business cooperatives to fund health care plans. Several other reform proposal objectives included mutual insurance pools to reduce the cost of private health insurance, and expanding states' authority to disburse federal money. Dozens of sensible plans had been proposed but they were literally killed before ever being discussed by committee chairs, who were also national health care proponents. The same politicians who made sure these proposals were never heard then publicly criticized their opponents for not having an alternative plan.

In January 2010 C.L. Gray published an article titled, *Five Health Care Reform Solutions That Make Sense.*[427] Mr. Gray clearly and concisely outlined reforms necessary for health care reform (not health care replacement) that are realistic, make sense, and will not add to our tax burden. His steps for reform include: Selling insurance across state lines, allow people to purchase health insurance with pre-tax dollars, Health savings accounts, tort reform to end "abusive" medical litigation, and tax credits to cover the insured WITHOUT inflating our debt.

---

[426] *"Health Care Reforms Americans Will Never See,"* A series of health care proposals have been cast aside in Congress, the victims of chairmen with the power to decide which bills will be discussed and which won't see the light of day, www.foxnews.com, August 04, 2009

[427] "Five Health Care Reform Solutions That Make Sense," C.L. Gray, Fox News, foxnews.com/.../ci.Five+Health+Care+..., January 21, 2010

Health care plans and organizations for reform - NOT government controlled health care:

The Center for Health Transformation:
www.healthtransformation.net
A consortium of private and public leaders dedicated to creating and implementing an "intelligent" health care system to provide quality care and save money for all Americans. An intelligent health care system enables the individual (not the government) to make decisions and be responsible for his own health. It will advance overall health and improve quality of life. Healthier people lead longer lives, and lesser costs will save individuals, companies and governments billions of dollars. The mission of The Center for Health Transformation is to provide health solutions and policies to create better overall health and more patient choices at a lower cost.

The Heritage Foundation: www.heritage.org
An outstanding organization that extensively researched the issue and provided a library of reports and articles on national health care and provides options to reform our existing health care system – not replace it.

CATO Institute: http://www.cato.org
CATO is a public policy research foundation whose mission is to increase the understanding of public policies based on the principles of limited government, free markets, individual liberty, and peace. For example, Policy Analysis No. 613 includes: *"The answer then to America's health care problems lies not in heading down the road to national health care but in learning from the experiences of other countries, which demonstrate the failure of centralized command and control and the benefits of increasing consumer incentives and choice."*[428]

---

[428] *"The Grass Is Not Always Greener: A Look at National Health Care Systems Around the World,"* Michael D. Tanner, CATO Institute Policy Analysis No. 613, March 18, 2008

Americans for Prosperity: http:www.americansfor prosperity.org
An organization committed to educating the public on important issues including economic policy, health care reform, and exposing bad policies of our elected officials.

Patients First: http://joinpatientsfirst.com
An Americans for Prosperity Project focused on health care issues especially on patient rights and private health care.

Conservatives for Patient's Rights (CPR):
http://www.cprights.org
Another organization committed to patient's rights highlighting the debate on healthcare reform based on patient-doctor care, not government mandated care. Four important principles of PCR are choice, competition, accountability, and responsibility.

Media Research Center: http://www.mrc.org
Publications and panel discussions on "Real" health care reform. The Media Research Center closely monitors media reporting to expose disinformation, misinformation, and omission of pertinent facts and policies. They expose what the media is still not telling the American public about Obamacare. For example, they reported in July 2014 that the three big networks did not report the results of the Government Accountability Office (GAO) investigation of fraudulent Obamacare sign-ups.[429]

AMAC (The Association of Mature American
Citizens) http:www.amac.us
Has a five point plan for changes in our Health Care System that will provide coverage for all citizens at a lower cost for medical care using the free enterprise system (1/5th the cost).

---

[429] "The Liberal Media Keep Covering Up the Truth About Obamacare," (*The Washington Post* report) Media Research Center, http://www.mrc.org, July 31, 2014

Numerous comprehensive articles on health care have been published. One of these is, **National Healthcare – A Poison Pill,** (http://www.lowcostinsur.com), July 1, 2009: Common sense reforms including group insurance pools, uniform plans in all states, discounts/deductions based on income, state commissions for oversight, employer ability to deduct cost of individual insurance, limitations on lawsuits, and insurance rates determined by the market place – not politicians. A 2008 article worth reading is **What's Right with America's Healthcare System: Physicians and Patients from Around the World Come to US for Highest Quality,** Andrea Santiago, (http://healthcareers.about.com). The author discusses what is wrong with socialized and government owned healthcare systems that Michael Moore did not talk about in his documentary "Sicko." She mentions specific instances of problems with the Canadian and British healthcare systems, and explains why physicians trained in foreign countries willingly spend additional years training to be certified and practice medicine in America.

I am not a financial expert, but even I know of a simple way to reform Medicare that would save billions of dollars. Clean the Medicare House. Politicians and bureaucrats say they are committed to saving Medicare and providing the American people with a "fair" health care system. If that was true, they would reorganize Medicare by reducing the ineffective and inept administration and seriously prosecute fraudulent activities of dishonest administrators, doctors, vendors, and patients. They don't need to debate a new bill or pass new legislation to do that.

If the Administration and Congress would have listened to the people directly affected by the health plan they would have learned the reality of the health care situation. If they spoke with and listened to the Americans who carry the burden of health care costs and the doctors and providers who do have patient's best interests in mind, they would have learned that private insurance is not only what is preferred, but the only option that works. The free market – private sector will always do a better job than the government to provide services and administer health care. Attorneys have discovered a pot of gold with medical litigation. Excessive and even bogus lawsuits are major factors contributing to skyrocketing health care costs. This needs to stop, but no one in Washington wants to address that aspect of health care.

Remember when the President addressed Congress in September of 2009 demanding action on health care reform – his plan for health care reform. His presentation created more questions than answers. If you weren't skeptical about his health care plan before, you should have been extremely skeptical after that speech. Without restating President Obama's plan[430] I can say it is impossible to guarantee that millions of people without insurance will receive coverage, millions of people with insurance will get better coverage, health care costs will be lower, and the government will provide and run a health care system that will not cost the taxpayers anything. On top of all that good news, he also said that his plan would not cover illegal aliens. Unless illegal aliens just disappear, they will benefit from his health care plan – they cannot be denied medical treatment. Independent research organization, *The Center for Immigration Studies* published a report stating that a government-run health care program could *"benefit 6.6 million illegals and cost American taxpayers up to $31 billion."*[431] I heard all of President Obama's promises, but reality prevents me from believing him.

We had the best health care in the world. Reform, not government control was what we needed. Even though Obamacare is now law, we still need to stand up and make our voices heard. The list of people who lost their insurance and doctors is growing exponentially.

"If you like your health plan, you can keep it. Period."

—President Barack Obama

After the questionable passage of the Affordable Care Act, it was quite disturbing to see the White House web site posting: *There is a lot of disinformation about health insurance reform out there, spanning from control of personal finances to end of life care. These rumors often travel just below the surface via chain emails or through casual conversation.* **Since we can't keep track of all of them here at the White House, we're asking for your help. If you get an email or see something on the**

---

[430] Healthcare speech to Congress, http://www.whitehouse.gov, September, 9, 2009
[431] The Center for Immigration Studies, AMERIPAC (American Political Action Committee), Human Events Online, 9/11/2009, http://www.humanevents.com

web about health insurance reform that seems fishy, send it to flag@ whithouse.gov. Wow – reporting fellow citizens just because they hold a different or opposing opinion is what happens in countries like China, North Korea, Iran, Pakistan, and Russia, not in the United States! When President Obama was a "community activist" opposition and dissent were encouraged. It is hypocritical to label opposition to the government controlled health care plan as "mob action." Concerned citizens with the guaranteed freedom of speech to express legitimate grievances were and still are being criticized, denigrated, and reported to the government. That is unlawful. The U.S. Code 5 -552a states United States agencies, including the Executive Office of the President shall, *"maintain no record describing how any individual exercises rights guaranteed by the First Amendment unless expressly authorized by statute or by the individual about whom the record is maintained or unless pertinent to and within the scope of an authorized law enforcement activity."*

The government now boldly attempts to intimidate its citizens into silence. Where is the ACLU? Why are they silent when these First Amendment rights are being smothered? It seems the ACLU only champions free speech it agrees with. Where does the ACLU stand on the issue of government mandating the purchase of health insurance? I don't know - I haven't heard anything from them questioning the constitutionality of the government forcing citizens to purchase anything.

OBAMACARE: Politicians Lie, Numbers Do Not

(The promises of 2010 vs. the realty of 2014)

In 2010 we were promised that the overwhelming majority of Americans who had health insurance could keep their plans and doctors. In 2014 millions of Americans lost their insurance and millions more will lose theirs as the Affordable Care Act regulations are implemented.

In 2010 we were promised that health insurance premiums would go down at least $2,500 for every family. In 2014 Health insurance premiums are on average 41% higher and will continue to rise.

In 2010 we were promised that the Affordable Care Act would not "add a dime" to the deficit. In 2014 billions of dollars had already been added to the deficit.

In 2010 we were promised that the Affordable Care Act would create millions of new jobs. In 2014 millions of people are losing their jobs or forced into part-time work so the employer doesn't have to provide health insurance.

In 2010 we were promised that every American would have affordable health care. In 2014 Fifty million Americans are uninsured.

In 2010 we were promised no new taxes. In 2014 we saw over a half trillion dollars in new taxes.

In 2010 we were promised the ACA Healthcare website would be secure. In 2014 we saw numerous problems and massive security breaches.

In 2010 we were promised that the ACA would not affect Medicare. In 2014 at least $176 billion will be cut from Medicare.

*The above data is comprised from three sources of Obamacare information:

"Obamacare's Broken Promises: Four Ways Heritage is Showing How the Law is Bad for Americans," The Heritage Foundation, Members News, http://www.myheritage.org, winter 2014

"The Charts Obama Doesn't Want You to See," Amy Payne, The Foundry, The Heritage Foundation, http://www.heritage.org, April 11, 2014

"Broken Promises: The ObamaCare Story," Patrick Hedger, Josh Withrow, Julie Borowski, Logan Albright, Freedom Works, http:// www.freedomworks.org, 2014

HealthCare.gov: The Icing on the Obamacare Cake

The Foundry, part of The Heritage Foundation published a timeline of delays to illustrate the incompetency of the bureaucratic federal government. [432] The president who does not have authority to "make" or "change" or even "tweak" laws obviously feels he is above the law as evidenced by his legacy, Obamacare.

---

[432] "A Timeline of Obamacare Delays in Pictures," Kelsey Harris, *Front Page Magazine*, http://www.frontpagemag.com, March 24, 2014

- April 2013: 6 months prior to the absolute launch date of healthcare.gov, the White House said the Obamacare marketplaces won't be able to handle the menu of health plans promised.
- July 2013: Obama announces the delay of the employer mandate (all employers with 50 or more employees mandated to provide health insurance to full-time workers) for one year. Many employers have re-classified full time positions to part time because of the costly burden of Obamacare.
- September 2013: Obama administration announced that "small businesses won't be able to buy coverage on the online small business marketplace until November."
- October 1, 2013: HealthCare.gov is launched. It is plagued with major glitches and problems for which the government had to spend additional billions of dollars to try and fix the problems. Even with the "best" computer minds in the country working on this sacred project, problems persist including major security issues.
- October 23, 2013: The deadline for purchasing insurance coverage without a penalty is pushed up to March 31, 2014.
- November 14, 2013: President Obama's solution for the millions of Americans who already received insurance cancellation notices is to allow 2013 insurance plans "to be grandfathered in." This announcement led to the CEO, America's Health Insurance Plans statement: *"Changing the rules after health plans have already met the requirements of the law could destabilize the market."*[433]
- November 27, 2013: Obama delays the online business exchange for another year.
- December 1, 2013: Obama re-launches "HealthCare.org" claiming the website is fixed.
- December 18, 2013: Insurance companies agree to Obama's "request" to accept late registrations and payments. (As long as purchasers select an insurance plan by December 23rd and

---

[433] "A Timeline of Obamacare Delays in Pictures, "Kelsey Harris, The Foundry, The Heritage Foundation, http://www.blog.heritage.org, March 24, 2014

pay the premiums by January 10, 2014, they will have coverage effective January 1, 2014.

- December 23, 2013: Obama extends the deadline for insurance coverage to January 1, 2014.
- December 24, 2013: Obama gives more time (yet again he disregards the official deadline) to consumers who had technical problems and could not complete their applications by December 24th.
- February 10, 2014: Obama announced that businesses with at least 50 full-time employees are no longer subject to the employer mandate until 2016.
- March 5, 2014: President proclaims that the millions of Americas who lost their insurance can keep their old plans (If still available) through October 2016, avoiding a new round of cancellations during the 2014 election season.
- March 31, 2014 Deadline arrived and no information from the government about the enrollees, paid policies, or the number of people insured through Obamacare.

The Obama administration celebrated reaching the "goal" of 7 million people acquiring health care via the healthcare website. They would not release documentation to support that claim. 7 million people may have visited the website, but that is not proof that they all are insured or have paid the premiums to initiate insurance coverage. The White House celebration was very short and they are now quiet about the status of Healthcare.gov. I do not expect an honest accounting from this administration.

You need to keep in mind that even if your insurance did not change much in 2014, Obamacare is loaded with time-delayed financial land mines that will pop up periodically over the next few years. In the end you will see a change in the insurance you are currently happy with. In January 2014, Moody's Investor Service announced a "downgrade" for America's healthcare sector from "stable" to "negative" due to the Affordable Care Act.

Do you still consider Obamacare a good thing? National healthcare supports *selective punishment* for behaviors that bureaucrats "deem" undesirable. Undesirable behavior goes beyond medical care. How would we be guaranteed that our access to health care and treatment would not be affected by the personal bias of an administrator who has control over our healthcare? Tax-paying American citizens' behavior and health lifestyles will be analyzed and our medical care will be determined by bureaucratic administrators. These are just a few examples of what our healthcare future holds. That's what happens when the government and unelected bureaucrats have the power to control your life.

During a panel discussion about President Obama's healthcare endgame, Charles Krauthammer said, *"What the real objective of Obamacare is, to sever the relationship that people have now with employer-provided insurance and with their private insurance and also with the small group insurance so everybody ends up in the market, which is essentially controlled by the federal government. It is a semi-nationalization using the insurers as the middle man. But that's what it's about, and that was the objective in the first place, and that's why all the numbers are obscure, all the numbers are hidden..."*[434]

The Heritage Foundation published its healthcare proposal (one of numerous viable alternatives to the Affordable Care Act the federal government refused to even discuss). A 2010 publication, "Getting Health Care Reform Right" clearly presented the need for healthcare reform. Based on facts surrounding reform and the ACA, The Heritage Foundation presents a concise solution for healthcare reform - **Replacement**.

> **"The problem with socialism is you eventually run out of other peoples' money."**
>
> —Margaret Thatcher

---

[434] "Krauthammer: Obama's Plan is to Semi-Nationalize Healthcare," Melissa Clyne, Newsmax, http://www.newsmax.com, April 22, 2014, Charles Krauthammer on Fox News "Special Report" with Bret Baier

America

PART 3
WHERE DO WE GO FROM HERE?

"I am only one, but I am one. I cannot do everything, but I can do something. And because I cannot do everything, I will not refuse to do the something that I can do. What I can do, I should do. And what I should do, by the grace of God, I will do."

—Edward Everett Hale

Surviving in a Global Community

I realize and accept the fact that technology and the internet have connected the world as never before and there is no going back. We are stuck with the rest of the world, but that doesn't mean we have to accept cultural values and the demands of foreign governments that conflict with our values and our form of government.

The term "Global Community" is an oxymoron. There is no "global" assemblage of similar peoples with a common mind of cooperative spirit. There are ethnic, scientific, social, religious, and financial communities with common interests linked together by modern technology. A true Global Community is an unrealistic ideological concept because:

- Different languages, cultures, governments, ideologies and religions make a global community impossible
- All peoples, governments, and nations are NOT the same
- Democracy, Socialism, Communism, Fascism, Monarchy, Dictatorship, and Theocracy ARE very different and irreconcilable government ideologies
- Human rights are a globally "selective" concept. The human rights that we value are not the same human rights accepted around the globe
- Some countries ARE better than others

There are similar areas and groups of people and nations that have enough commonality to coexist peacefully, but only within their "common interest" environment – not globally. I am not suggesting that similar societies exist in isolation from the others. To co-exist with non-similar societies we must recognize and identify the differences, and interact with knowledge, understanding, and <u>caution</u>. Many nations outright reject our concept of free government with guaranteed rights and freedoms, human rights including life, respect, liberty, safety, and capitalism, the only proven economic system that works (and works very well). Since numerous nations reject our concept of these requisites and embrace anarchy, brutality and aggression, how can a "global community" exist?

The progressive attitude is that America should consider itself a part of the world community and no better than any other country. Americans are expected to accept and tolerate all people regardless of their ideologies and governments since we are all brothers sharing this planet. How can we set aside the values and ideologies that we embrace to mandatorily accept and tolerate "unacceptable" behavior of foreign peoples and nations? The so-called world community is a one-way street. We give – they receive. We tolerate – they do not. We welcome all people – they reject us. We provide science, health care, food, technology, military resources, financial and humanitarian aid, and disaster relief – they receive, expect more, and criticize America for not doing enough. Some would say that since America is a wealthy country (was a wealthy country) we are expected to support the world. Countries that do not accept western values quite obviously want only what we can provide and expect us to accept their values and governments, while they in no way tolerate our ideologies and way of life.

The 20th century was turbulent. Two world wars killed untold millions, and forever changed boundaries, social structures, governments and economies. Throughout that century, a single country ended both world wars, stood firm against Communism, rebuilt war-ravaged countries and never hesitated to provide world-wide aid. That country was America. This is not said with arrogance - it is an historical fact.

"In Germany, the Nazis first came for the communists, and I didn't speak up because I wasn't a communist. Then they came for the Jews, and I didn't speak up because I wasn't a Jew... Then they came for the Catholics, and I didn't speak up because I was a Protestant. Then they came for me, and by that time there was no one left to speak for me."

-Rev. Martin Niemoeller, German Lutheran Pastor
Arrested by the Gestapo in 1938

Honest News?

"Make yourself sheep and the wolves will eat you"

—Ben Franklin

Okay - now what? The very first thing to do is turn off the TV and pick up a book or newspaper or magazine or tablet and read about what is going on locally, state-wide, nationally or internationally. Or, at least watch current events on accurate and unbiased news channels. I used to always tune into CNN and MSNBC for news and events. Flipping around news channels after 9/11, I noticed that FOX News provided the most comprehensive coverage. Whereas the other news channels provided a lot of "opinion-coverage" pretending to be real news, FOX provided comprehensive and accurate reporting of the news. I do not understand why so many people have such a hard time distinguishing between news programs and analysis/opinion programs. For instance, *Hardball* with Chris Matthews on MSNBC is an analysis opinion program as is *The Factor* with Bill O'Reilly on FOX. FOX News is constantly criticized by the Left as a "Conservative" and "Republican" mouthpiece. I wish someone could explain that to me. FOX News presents the complete news and represents both sides of every story whether on "news" programs or "analysis" programs. The other cable news networks do not. Chris Matthews on MSNBC's *Hardball* literally attacks and mocks anyone and any group that disagrees with President Obama.

I prefer FOX News because they run important news stories other networks do not even mention. Unlike other news networks, FOX doesn't edit out important elements from their news broadcasts. For example, I listened to different news sources report on the horrendous story about schoolgirls kidnapped in Nigeria. The CBS report I watched, reported the kidnapping of the school girls by a terrorist group. FOX News reported the story accurately. Hundreds of "Christian" schoolgirls were kidnapped by the "Islamist" terrorist group Boko Haram who publicly said they were selling the girls into slavery for "Allah," (a practice sanctioned by the prophet Mohammad to punish infidel Christians that they didn't kill). By eliminating critical words of the story such as "Christian," Islamists," and "slavery" the story puts the blame on generic terrorists, not on Islamic teaching and Islamic sanctioned actions. I believe FOX News viewers are definitely more informed about current events than viewers of other networks.

People are finally waking up to the fact the most of the news media is biased to the Left. "Freedom of the press" was purposely written into our Constitution because we have historically depended on the media to report the <u>truth</u>. The media used to investigate our elected leaders and report any wrong-doing or suspicious behavior. They relentlessly used to question our officials on policy, issues and actions. Remember Watergate? The Founders considered the press the watchdogs of the Republic. Now it has been proven that the majority of journalists and news presenters are liberal, support and promote Barack Obama, and do not report on the president honestly and accurately. FOX News reports on all elected officials regardless of party. That is why the administration and the other news media organizations hate FOX and go out of their way to criticize and disparage the network just as they do to organizations and people who do not support the Obama agenda.

A perfect example of this is that FOX News never stopped investigating the Benghazi, Libya scandal. Yes, it is a scandal. FOX and its reporters have been mocked and degraded since first reporting on the attack of September 11, 2012. The administration with the mainstream media's help has been trying to bury this event ever since it happened with lies, falsifications and a major campaign to divert attention away from the administration by blaming "the Republicans" which is now interchangeable with the "it's Bush's fault" slogan as their standard non-answer line. The "Judicial Watch" Organization published emails they obtained only by suing for them under the Freedom of Information Act. It is interesting to note that it was a non-governmental organization and not Congress that was able to get evidence on the scandal. Those emails proved that the White House was duplicitous in a major cover-up. More documents will be forthcoming and the Benghazi issue is not going to go away even with the White House Press Secretary and the House minority speaker Nancy Pelosi continually minimizing the event and criticizing Fox News and Republicans for keeping this non-issue alive.

On the subject of President Bush, back in 2005 the *New York Times* and other media organizations openly mocked the president and his administration for warning that a premature withdrawal from Iraq would lead to destabilization and Islamic terrorists would try to establish their much anticipated "caliphate." The New York Times along with the rest of the mainstream media had nothing to say when the "Bush warnings" came to fruition in 2014 after U.S. troop withdrawal in 2011. Who can forget the media sensation promoting the "Bush lied, People died" campaign because Saddam Hussein's chemical weapons cache was not found? The same organizations obsessed with demeaning President Bush had nothing to report when Saddam's non-existent chemical weapons stored at the Al Muthanna facility in Iraq were seized by ISIS terrorists in Iraq. Besides standard munitions and random hazardous industrial chemicals, stockpiles of chemical munitions had remained stored at the facility where mustard gas, Sarin, Tabun and VX gas were weaponized.

Another example of media dishonesty is the lack of, or in most cases, the blackout of coverage on the IRS targeting of conservatives scandal. The IRS announced in June 2014 that coincidentally, the two years of IRS and Lois Lerner emails subpoenaed by Congress had disappeared during a computer crash in 2011. For the record, the government has a redundant backup system to store all data so the crash story is not plausible. The NSA can track and store personal information on every one of us simultaneously, but the IRS loses "selective" data. Maybe the IRS can request their missing data from the NSA. Claremont Institute fellow, John Hindraker commented, *"The Obama administration is lying, and lying in a remarkably transparent way."*[435] In the same article, author Matthew Vadum concludes, *"The media is onboard with the Democrats. The evening newscasts of the big three broadcasts last night all deemed the seven-way IRS computer crash unworthy of coverage, even as they had time for Harrison Ford's broken leg (NBC), a new technology for police car chases (ABC), and comedian Tracy Morgan's car accident (CBS). Just another day in Obama's America."*

Remember the media attack on *Chick-fil-A* when the company's president spoke out in support of traditional marriage? The mainstream media went out of their way to demonize Dan Cathy for his "personal" opinion which conflicted with the politically correct celebration of

---

[435] "The IRS's 'Lost' Email Deception," Matthew Vadum, *Front Page Magazine*, http://www. Frontpagemag.com, June 20, 2014

homosexual marriage. They broadcast protests by homosexual activists and statements by politicians including Chicago Mayor Rahm Emanuel who declared Chick-fil-A is not welcome in his city. They reported that the Christian owned company was to be boycotted. The media abruptly ended reports on Chick-fil-A when hundreds of thousands of supporters across the nation showed support for the company with record-setting food purchases.

The same mainstream media that was obsessed with Chick-fil-A did not report on the actions of one of the company's stores in Birmingham, Alabama during the terrible ice storm that paralyzed the South early in 2014. The owner of this particular store and his employees were stranded at the store because of the ice storm. Motorists were stranded all along the highway as well. This store owner, the restaurant manager, and the employees made hundreds of chicken sandwiches and walked through the freezing ice storm to highway 280, where they distributed them to stranded motorists. They also helped push cars off the road and kept the restaurant open all night providing warmth and facilities for weary motorists. In the morning Mark Meadows, the store owner and his crew fed as many people as they could. Mark refused to accept any payment for the food. Store Manager Audrey Pitt explained, *"This company is based on taking care of people and loving people before you're worried about money or profit. We were just trying to follow the model that we've all worked under for so long and the model that we've come to love. There was really nothing else we could have done but try to help people any way we could."*[436] These two Chick-fil-A stories are a good illustration of the hypocrisy of the liberal mainstream media. When a Christian corporation owner states his personal view that he supports traditional marriage, the media goes on a rampage making it a top "newsworthy" story. But, when owners and managers of the same "Christian" company act heroically by helping so many people, the same media goes silent and refuses to report the story.

Journalist Bernard Goldberg's book, "Bias: *A CBS Insider Exposes How the Media Distorts the News,"*[437] gives us a good look at the liberal

---

[436] "Media Ignores Chick-fil-A's Christian Charity in Ice Storm," Dave Jolly, Godfather Politics, http://www.godfatherpolitics.com, February 7, 2014

[437] "Bias: A CBS Insider Exposes How the Media Distorts the News," Bernard Goldberg, Washington, DC: Regnery Publishing, 2002

bias of network news corporations. Mr. Goldberg worked as a reporter and producer for CBS News for nearly thirty years and has won seven Emmy Awards. He has written op-eds for the *New York Times, The Wall Street Journal* and *The Washington Post*. He reveals in his book the news culture's mission failure to "provide objective and disinterested reporting." Mr. Goldberg is a proponent of honest and accurate journalism which is becoming harder and harder to find.

The Media Research Center: (MRC) www.mediaresearch.org has, since its founding in 1987 been the "media watchdog," whose mission is to expose propaganda and bias espoused by the left-wing national news media.

- **News Analysis Division**: Document, expose and neutralize liberal media bias. A team of news analyst experts monitor all major national news media.
- **The Business & Media Institute**: Dedicated to "Advancing the Culture of Free Enterprise in America" by promoting a fair portrayal of the business community.
- **The Culture and Media Institute**: Dedicated to "preserve and help restore America's culture, character, traditional values, and morals against the assault of the liberal media elite, and to promote a fair portrayal of social conservatives and religious believers in the media."

Some honest sources for news, current events and government include:

- **Canada Free Press**: www.canadafreepress.com (The best thing in Canada)
  CFP motto: "**Because without America there is no Free World.**" America and the free world must be guarded by all who believe in liberty
- **Fox News Channel**: www.foxnews.com News - (There really is a difference)
- **The New Republic**: www.tnr.com Journal of politics and the Arts

- **Real Clear Politics**: www.realclearpolitics.com News and current events
- **Human Events**: www.humanevents.com Established in 1944 Political news Contributors include: Charles Krauthammer and Thomas Sowell
- **National Review**: Semimonthly political news magazine founded by William F. Buckley, Jr. in 1955
- **National Review Online**: www.nationalreview.com Great contributors
- **The Washington Times**: www.washingtontimes.com Solid news reporting
- **Godfather Politics**: www.godfatherpolitics.com "For news the media refuses to print"
- **Politico**: www.politico.com Political news - national politics
- **American Thinker**: www.americanthinker.com Exploration of issues important to Americans
- **The Weekly Standard**: www.weeklystandard.com Great writers and commentary
- **The Daily Caller**: www.dailycaller.com Hard news reporting and news not reported by other media outlets
- **Breitbart News Network**: www.breitbart.com Founded by the late Andrew Breitbart * great news reporting continues his legacy
  - Breitbart Big Government: Political coverage, current issues, public opinion
  - Breitbart Big Journalism: Recent events
  - Breitbart Big Hollywood: Uncovers the Hollywood Left

"To put the world right in order, we must first put the nation in order; to put the nation in order, we must first put the family in order; to put the family in order, we must first cultivate our personal life; we must first set our hearts right."

—Confucius[438]

---

[438] "Confucius, Great Quotes from Great Leaders," Peggy Anderson, 1997

It Starts With Us

"Personal responsibility is the price of liberty"

—Michael Cloud

Responsibility: To affect meaningful change, we must be responsible. To demand responsibility from our leaders, we must be responsible ourselves. On a personal level we need to take responsibility for our words and actions. We must take responsibility for our very lives. It seems that over the past few decades, responsibility has been replaced with blame. It's easy - everything can be "excused." We can blame someone or something else for everything bad that happens to us.

We can make phone calls, check email, and program the GPS while driving. We don't need to be responsible because we have insurance to pay for our mistakes. We can spill coffee on ourselves and successfully sue the fast food restaurant where we bought it because it was too "hot." We can trip over own shoe laces, fall down in a store and then sue the store for our "self-inflicted" injuries. We can sue product manufacturers for injuries even though we used the product incorrectly. We can blame our adult shortcomings and problems on parents, guardians, teachers, and siblings instead of getting past what was and taking responsibility for our lives <u>now</u>. We can "buy off" our children with toys and amusements instead of spending time with them teaching values and responsibility. We can easily ignore homeless, hungry, and distressed people because we are too busy, and besides, "it's not my fault." We say let the government take care of them; and then we'll complain about tax increases to fund the government welfare programs.

Saying, "It's not my fault" does not absolve one's self of responsibility and that phrase needs to be eliminated from our vocabulary! It is our fault we hit the car in front of us because we were not paying attention. Spilling a beverage or falling over our own shoes is not anyone else's fault. We must stop blaming our parents for all of our problems. Grow up. As adults we are in control of our lives and we determine where our future goes. A very wise man said that children are gifts from God and they should be loved and cherished. They also need to be taught responsibility, morality, and to value themselves and others. It does not "take a village" to raise good kids. Children learn the most by spending time with their parents and family and feeling that they are loved. All the toys in the world will not make children develop into happy, self-reliant, successful and compassionate adults; watching and learning from their parents and family will.

Irresponsible personal behavior has consequences. That auto accident you caused created a real hardship on the other driver. The cost of products and insurance premiums increase to offset the millions of dollars paid out in ridiculous litigation cases. Guilt-ridden parents pay a fortune for therapy. Some children are unprepared for adulthood because of failing public school systems and inept teachers. Obnoxious, ill-mannered children not exposed to discipline grow up into obnoxious, ill-mannered adults. And children without parental involvement in their lives are at a much higher risk of dropping out of school, being influenced by drugs, gangs and criminal activity and end up struggling through life with a criminal record.

> *We must reject the idea that every time a law's broken, society is guilty rather than the lawbreaker. It is time to restore that American precept that each individual is accountable for his actions."*
>
> —Ronald Reagan

Righteousness: We need to be righteous. Righteousness is not an outdated virtue; righteousness is eternal. We need to adhere to principles of "right" behavior by "owning-up" and taking responsibility for our behavior. Only we can right our wrongs. Only we can take control of our lives and in doing so free ourselves to clearly see the world around us. Then we are able to establish lifelong priorities. The same wise man also told me, *"There is nothing more important than God, Faith and Family."* From that foundation compassion and empathy flow freely. We can help those in need - no matter our economic status. *"Pay it forward"* really does work. The more you have, the more you can help. Your words and actions will be noticed and remembered by others who in turn will act righteously. Churches and religious organizations provide great opportunities for you to get involved and help others. They can target local areas (your neighborhood) organizing and providing assistance for people in need. Financial support is only one way to get involved. Donations of time and physical work are greatly needed and are as important as money. Churches and religious organizations have historically proven to be more successful and efficient, mostly with volunteers providing aid and comfort to people in need than the Government ever has. Neighborhood and community centers provide much needed assistance also and are always in need of volunteers. We can be better and we can do better!

A very simple thing we can do is commend responsible behavior. Write a letter, send an email or call the supervisor or company of an employee who provided exemplary service. We need to acknowledge good behavior. We want people to realize that we recognize and appreciate responsibility and upstanding action. On the other hand, we need to contact the same manager, supervisor, or company to report irresponsible and unacceptable behavior or customer service. It is important that companies know how their employees are treating customers. <u>The same holds true for our government leaders and officials.</u> Contact government officials and your congressional representatives. Make them aware of your feelings and opinions on issues. Tell them what you are thinking - why or why not you support or disagree with an issue or a government policy. Also, don't hesitate to question their position on issues. Ask for an explanation. If you have a better idea, offer a suggestion. Most elected officials are extremely concerned about "pleasing" their constituents who hold the power to re-elect them.

The current financial crisis gripping our nation highlights irresponsibility on numerous levels. On a personal level, many people received "pre-approved" credit cards, auto financing, and mortgage forms in the mail. Wow, that was great! Not really. Credit card, car loan, and mortgage companies made borrowing as easy as turning on a light switch. Lax credit standards afforded millions of people the opportunity to purchase homes they really could not afford, cars they really could not afford, enormous HD televisions and electronic devices, and super-great vacations they really could not afford. We could easily justify our purchases. We were told by advertisements and companies that we "needed" and "deserved" these things. We became so consumed with the things we "deserved" to have that we became financially over-extended at a critical rate. Then, with the economic downturn (recession that has not stopped), millions of Americans found themselves in the position of being unable to repay their loans and they blamed the credit card and finance companies who made the loans. While it is true these companies do shoulder blame in qualifying buyers beyond responsible economic standing, the truth is the bulk of the blame rests on the buyer. For example, unless the "Vikings" from the Capital One physically forced you to make purchases on that credit card, then you are the only person responsible for creating that debt. You are the person who refinanced your mortgage at that wonderful 125% equity amount. Didn't it occur to anyone that 125% equity does not exist? Who is responsible to pay the loan amount over the true market value of your house? You are.

By the time we realized we were in financial distress, it was too late. An epidemic of financial crisis was rapidly spreading across the country. It seemed to begin with the housing market. It then spread through the major banks and lenders, cutting off credit which then affected business and manufacturing resulting in layoffs which continued to increase. How could this happen? How could so many people be in default when we were just being good consumers? We were just getting the things that we "deserved" to have. The story of how this financial catastrophe began, and who was responsible for it will be years in the making. Countless investigations, committees of inquiry and testimony, testimony, and more testimony will waste billions of dollars. Unfortunately only a few of the culprits, if any at all will be held accountable. Laid off workers, homeowners with subprime mortgages or those who purchased homes during the "high-end" of the housing boon are suffering. We need to watch the financial situation carefully. It is going to affect us the rest of our lives and our children's lives. It is important to stay aware of the news and demand responsibility on the part of the company executives who ruined numerous lives for their own personal gain. Demand responsibility from Union leaders who are quietly entrenched in the corruption pit. Irresponsible behavior of our elected officials in Washington created the subprime catastrophe, by forcing mortgage companies and banks to issue loans to people who clearly did not financially qualify for them. Borrowing was too easy.

Contact your Congressional officials, sign petitions, and support "watch dog" groups to demand honest oversight of government agencies to identify corruption resulting in the theft of our money. Demand that government agencies cut back and operate within their budgets like hard working Americans have to do. Many of us who still have jobs in the private sector have only gotten 1-2% salary increases, if any, the past few years. While working Americans and out of work Americans are struggling financially, how is it that government agencies and officials unabashedly feel they "deserve" substantial raises and bonuses. The latest example of this is the Veterans Administration (yet another Obama administration travesty). Veterans died because they were denied medical care and forced to wait unreasonably long periods of time just to make doctor appointments. Many of the lucky ones able to see a doctor received substandard care. While our veterans were dying because of criminally neglectful administrative operations, the Veterans Administration was handing out employee raises and bonuses like candy. This is despicable. If a private sector administration had secret/shadow lists to hide the deaths and criminal lack of care to ensure themselves better salary increases, the government would come down hard on that company and the Justice Department would not hesitate to investigate. Charges would be filed and people would be held accountable. The Justice Department obviously isn't compelled to hold government agencies and employees to the same standards. It's no wonder government employees feel insulated and safe from legal action and penalties for breaking the law. Nobody in government is "responsible" for agency operations.

It could be a long hard struggle for justice but we must stand firm and stay focused. Like the Benghazi scandal, the Fast and Furious scandal and the IRS scandal, the administration and Justice Department will not aggressively investigate and hold these public servants accountable. We must not forget about these scandals as the administration is hoping we will and keep reminding our elected officials that these scandals must be addressed and criminal behavior must be prosecuted.

Righteousness must be exercised daily. It is righteous to treat all people with respect; to help the less fortunate; to teach our children values; to protect others, and to stand up for our fellow Americans where injustice exists. How is it that even young children can unknowingly be righteous while so many adults cannot or will not? 9-year old Martin Cobb was killed while protecting his sister from a sexual assault on May 2, 2014 in Richmond, Virginia.[439] In March 2014, 11-year old Randez Brown died while trying to save his 7-year old sister after she fell into a creek in Charlotte, North Carolina.[440] 6-year old Dominick Burgos was killed on September 3, 2013 in Camden, New Jersey fighting a home invader that was attacking his sister.[441] These young children did not hesitate to respond to a crisis as many adults would have. They immediately tried to help someone in desperate need and tragically they died. These children are real heroes and should be honored and remembered. Adults have a lot to learn from them.

Honesty: Has taken quite a hit since our parents' generation. While Wall Street and some large corporations are guilty of operating dishonestly, lying, cheating and stealing have become epidemic since our government officials, sports celebrities, Hollywood icons, and even some of our teachers and clergy have been able to lie, cheat and steal so successfully.

Contrary to what we were led to believe over the past five years, the financial crisis President Obama "inherited" was not caused by President Bush. Bush made mistakes that worsened the situation but he did not create the financial grief. Back up to the mid-1990s when the Clinton Administration put immense pressure on banks to award more mortgages to the poor and minorities. They in fact <u>forced</u> mortgage lenders to lower the standards to open up home ownership to more people. Pressure turned into requirement, and Fannie Mae and Freddie Mac led the mortgage lender surrender of sound business practices. Mortgage applicant credit history and traditional down payments became irrelevant. Welfare payments and unemployment benefits became valid sources of income to qualify for a mortgage.

---

[439] Martin Cobb, The New York Daily News, May 2, 2014

[440] The one-year anniversary of the death Randez Brown, Charlotte Observer, http://www.charlotteobserver.com, March 2014

[441] Dominick Burgos, NBC News, http://www.nbcnews.com, September 3, 2013

Fannie Mae was obligated to mismanage the mortgage market. In 1999 Ron Brownstein of the *Los Angeles Times* praised the affirmative action lending practices of the Clinton administration as a success and said, *"Black and Latino homeownership has surged to the highest level ever recorded."* In retrospect, this government action was the initial assault of Government intrusion into the free market. It was a quiet, covert operation celebrated by the Left as a good thing.

Economists saw the danger and sounded the alarm, but their warnings fell on deaf ears. They predicted these risky loans would fail as soon as the housing market slowed. Bush Administration White House chief economist N. Gregory Mankiw warned in 2001 that government subsidies along with the issuance of loans to unqualified borrowers by Fannie Mae and Freddie Mac were initiating a huge risk to the financial system. Additional warnings by the Bush Administration were waved off by Congressional Democrats tightly affiliated with Fannie Mae and Freddie Mac. The two most stringent advocates for the financial soundness of the lenders were Senate Banking Committee Chairman Christopher Dodd and House Financial Services Committee Chairman Barney Frank. These two Committee Chairs led the charge for government intervention and regulation into the free market. They were fully aware of the situation and their irresponsible, unethical, and possibly illegal behavior should be investigated. They violated their sacred oaths of office. After the housing market bombed, the credit market closed and the stock market crashed, Congress pretended to be surprised, and no one was responsible, least of all Chris Dodd and Barney Frank. While millions of Americans suffer financially, these two have guaranteed pensions and excellent health insurance (not Obamacare).

President Bush didn't blame President Clinton and the Democrats for the problems he "inherited" from flawed Clinton White House policies. Bush is responsible for substantially increasing the national debt, though the War on Terror, Afghanistan and Iraq as well as the devastating damage of Hurricane Katrina created huge financial burdens. The Bush administration should have made a much bigger issue of the unsustainable housing market. As President, George W. Bush should have been more engaged. President Obama is not free from guilt either. His repeated claims that he "inherited" the financial crisis are not true. He did not fall off a cloud and land in the White House. He was a U.S. Senator and knew exactly what was going on. The penalty for the folly of politicians always falls on the taxpayers and we now owe an insurmountable debt. The administration decided which banks, automakers and corporations were "too big to fail," and mandated bail outs funded by the taxpayers. We are also saddled with the largest welfare debt in history. These are not the actions of a Government sworn to promote and protect our "general welfare."

Setting a dangerous precedent, the United States Government now sits on the top rung of our nation's financial ladder. The Government has no place in the private economy of the nation. Nowhere in the Constitution is the Government given authority to interfere or assume private business or enterprise. When you hear people say that it's not such a big deal – "the Government is paying for it," calmly remind them that WE according to our Constitution, are the Government and they are spending <u>our money</u>! Maybe that fact will hit home in the near future when our taxes spiral upwards since our disingenuous leaders will need more and more of our money to feed the insatiable welfare monster.

Our Founders placed a great deal of value on valor, courage, honor, and responsibility. These virtues did not just apply to personal behavior; they were expected to carry over into business and government. We need to aspire to their code of ethics. Good manners, honesty, courage, and responsibility should not be discretionary. They should become a natural part of ourselves and exercised every day. By our example our children will learn and grow. Our Founders acted in accordance to an unwritten code of ethical conduct that guided their personal lives, government and business. We need to follow our conscience and stand by our principles. We need to stand up for what is right whether it is popular or not. We need to learn from our children - we need to be honest.

"In matters of principle, stand like a rock."

—Thomas Jefferson

Tolerance: Is a commendable virtue if it is practiced honestly. Liberals worship "hollow" tolerance since there is no honesty driving it. They are tolerant only of others who share their view and ideology. They have no tolerance for anyone who doesn't embrace their vision. Our children are no longer taught respect, morality, virtue and responsibility in public schools. They are though bombarded with "selective" tolerance. Freedom of speech must conform to the prescribed standards of the Progressive cabal. All other speech is not free - it is hate speech, racism, or biased conservative speech. For example, if I was chanting that America is an imperialist, oppressive and evil empire while dancing on or burning the American flag, enlightened Progressives would consider it freedom of speech. On the other hand, if I was saying that America was a great country while waving a big U.S. flag, they would say I was oppressive, offensive and intolerant of non-U.S. citizens and other nations.

Likewise, if I wore a Tee-shirt with foul language or obscene graphics, I would be expressing my freedom of speech. But, if I wore a Tee-shirt with a Christian symbol, an American flag, or a conservative slogan, I would be offensive and intolerant. It was acceptable for a South American leader to proclaim to the world that white, blue-eyed American capitalists are the cause of South America's problems. But, it would be unacceptable for an American to say that Fidel Castro and the late Hugo Chavez were tyrannical dictators with no regard for their people and they are responsible for Central and South America's problems – which is the truth. If I were to dance half naked in a homosexual-pride parade, it would just be my right of expression. But, if I say that I support traditional marriage between a man and a woman, I would be a bigot espousing hate speech. Brendan Eich, co-founder and CEO of Mozilla was forced to resign from his own company simply because he made a personal $1,000 contribution in 2008 supporting the same-sex marriage ban in California. He personally supports traditional marriage. What does his personal view have to do with the Mozilla Company? Nothing except that political correctness has mandated his view as totally unacceptable. In the "new and improved America" we are not allowed to oppose same-sex marriage for any reason whether religious, biological or cultural, in either the public or private realm.

Liberals cannot accept and refuse to acknowledge the truth that most people who support traditional marriage are not homophobes. The Christian doctrine that denies homosexuality and supports traditional marriage in no way makes Christians bigots. Christians accept all people, including homosexuals as equal children of God not to be judged by man. Why is it so hard to understand that not accepting same-sex marriage because religious dogma celebrates marriage only between a man and a woman does not represent bigotry toward homosexuals? Marriage is not a government guaranteed right and the government has no business defining and re-defining marriage to accommodate political correctness. I firmly believe that most homosexuals just want to live their lives like everybody else. The liberal left homosexual rights activists are not helpful. They spotlight unreasonableness, exaggerate outrageousness, file flagrant discrimination law suits and do not represent most homosexuals. They are wrong to claim that marriage defines equality.

I am reminded of a trip to Disney World in Florida a number of years ago during "Disney Pride Week," an annual event that I never heard of. Most of the heterosexual couples there with children never heard about it either. The problem I have is that so many (not all) same-sex couples were loud, disruptive, and purposely touching, hugging, and feeling each other all over the place whether at the Disney Parks or other facilities and at numerous hotels. I do not care where they go and what they do except I do expect them as well as all adults to act responsibly around children. It seemed to me that the more children that were around, the louder and more insulting they became. It was quite awkward for many parents to have to explain why two men or two women were making out while walking down "magical" Main Street.

Since this is an annual sanctioned event at Disney World, why doesn't Disney have the decency to advertise it on their brochures so heterosexual couples <u>with children</u> can opt to go at another time? It is extremely unfair to families who take their children to the most "magical" and "innocent" place for kids, not to mention expensive, to be exposed to taunting and ill-behavior by many adults who demand respect but have no respect for others that are different from them. To me it is more proof that "tolerance" is a one-way street. Again I will clarify - I do not care how homosexuals live their lives or where they go and most homosexuals are fine decent people. I do mind irresponsible behavior, insults, crude language and even harassment by any adults in the presence of children. I am not advocating an end to this Disney event, just notice of when it takes place. It's probably a good thing that Walt Disney is dead since if he was still alive, the P.C. police would have to put him away and the government would be running Disney World, which reminds me of a Colorado baker who used to be able to think, act and operate his own business as he chose to do.

Do you remember the Christian baker in Colorado who was slapped with a discrimination suit after offending a same-sex couple by refusing to make a cake for their wedding? That baker, a principled man whose religious doctrine takes precedence in his life could not in good conscience support same-sex marriage in any way. The state of Colorado has no tolerance for Christian doctrine and so ordered this baker, Jack Phillips to take sensitivity training, immediately enact new policies for himself and his employees, and file quarterly reports with the State proving he has not rejected any business based on sexual orientation. Todd Starnes, author and Fox News contributor added, *"Think of it as reverse conversion therapy (or straight man's rehab) so that the state can mandate diversity through conformity."*[442]

Dan Calabrese, author of the article cited above explains how we wound up in this fascist state. *"...At first the Civil Rights Commission said you can have your beliefs but you can't hurt people. That sounds well and good, but it only applies to the extent that you see a reasonable definition of 'hurting people.' If a business contract between two parties is freely entered into, then either party must have the freedom to choose whether to enter into it."* Mr. Calabrese explains that by not providing a requested service, the vendor/provider is not hurting the requestor. It could be considered inconvenient, but not harmful. Jack Phillips no longer has a "choice" regarding his personal business. The state government assumed the power to control Jack and his business because his views are not consistent with theirs.

The government now determines what is good or bad and what is

---

[442] "Colorado baker who won't make [homosexual] wedding cakes ordered to sensitivity training," Dan Calabrese, The Best of Cain, Herman Cain (info@ hermancain.com) June 5, 2014

acceptable or unacceptable "personal" thought and behavior. This is a real problem. How did the government assume the power to censor personal opinion and religious belief? Corrupt politicians and liberal special interest groups outright reject and disregard our Constitution, bestowing on them-selves the power to control the United States government that now freely legislates the thoughts, words and deeds of Americans, once the "most free" people on Earth.

One person who will not sit idly back and watch our culture deteriorate is **Tammy Bruce**. Tammy is an Independent Conservative, radio talk show host, columnist and author. She is a significant and wonderful resource who honestly identifies and defines sensitive American cultural issues. Tammy was an active member of the liberal feminist establishment until she realized how corrupt and culturally damaging the liberal left really was. She had first-hand experience with the liberal left's agenda and is on a mission to enlighten Americans to the dangers actively at work in our children's schools, the media and the liberal homosexual community. Tammy is an enigma; a homosexual, pro-choice, pro-death penalty, gun-owning, voted for Reagan, conservative feminist. She is a warrior committed to fighting for the moral values of our nation and the souls of our children. She doesn't hesitate to single out cultural corruption that has become epidemic. Through her books Tammy gives us information we need to know in order to confront the plague of moral decay that has insidiously taken over our educational institutions, government, legal system, media and culture.

Tammy's first book *"The New Thought Police: Inside the Left's Assault on Free Speech and Free Minds,"* published in 2001, exposes how the liberal Left is silencing our rights in the name of "social equality." In her 2003 book *"The Death of Right and Wrong: Exposing the Left's Assault on Our Culture and Values,"* Tammy takes on the "facades of tolerance" and understanding. She provides a sobering look at how the liberal homosexual elite have hijacked our school system sex education programs and history courses. She addresses grave statistics on the rise of sexually transmitted diseases in teenagers and the inconceivable rise in suicide rates in teens and children. She clearly illustrates how liberal lawyers and judges are working diligently to remove morality from our laws and are making a mockery of our legal system. Tammy's 2009 book, *"New American Revolution: How You Can Fight the Tyranny of the Left's Cultural and Moral Decay,"* is a battle plan for every conservative. *"It's time to swing back the curtains and invite the light in. And that light is American Nationalism, perennially shunned by the Left, condemned by Socialists, and without any special interest group fighting for its rebirth. It has no legitimate advocates. And yet it is the very idea that will save not only our nation, but the rest of the world as well."*[443]

Christians in America need to come together in a united voice to tell the government and legislators who do the bidding of leftist and Muslim anti-Christian groups to "Stop." We have had enough of their censorship and their determination of allowable Christian speech. All Christian denominations must stand together against the government assault on our doctrines, beliefs, values, and speech. The final straw for me was when police were called to investigate the Attleborough Baptist Church for hate speech because of a sign in front of the church. The offensive, hate-filled sign which under pressure, the church did remove said, *"If you think there is no God, you'd better be right."* The single sentence was printed above flames.[444] Think about that simple message. There is nothing hateful or offensive about it. We need to support the Attleborough Baptist Church and all Christian Churches across this nation.

We need to talk to our clergy and members of our church communities. We need to stand firm against ever-increasing verbal, physical and legal assaults against our Faith. Our church leaders need to speak out for what is right and just. We cannot sit back and let our churches and our Faith be eroded by political correctness backed by the corrupt power of the government. During the American Revolution the Christian clergy did not take a timid back seat. The clergy cherished religious freedom and were thunderous voices against oppression. They championed freedom and many of them literally took up arms and led

---

[443] *"New American Revolution: How You Can Fight the Tyranny of the Left's Cultural and Moral Decay,"* Tammy Bruce, 2009, The Tammy Bruce Show, http://www.tammybruce.com/tammy/books

[444] "Church Teaches Bible, Police Investigate for Hate Speech," Onan Coca, Eagle Rising, http://www.eaglerising.com, May 28, 2014

others into battle against oppression. These men were heroes, willing to sacrifice their own lives for their religious beliefs and to ensure religious freedom for all Americans. I am not promoting an armed response; but I really do expect our clergy to step up with a unified voice for Christians across this nation. The time to speak up is now before our religious liberty is but a memory.

We need to remember the words of our Founders and the leaders that followed after them and we need to share their words with others. The Colonists were Christians who came to America for religious freedom. The Founders were Christians – even Ben Franklin though not a practicing Christian still held a firm conviction that God and Christianity were and always will be the cornerstone of this nation. Liberals cannot face the absolute truth that the Christian religion built this nation and our Constitution and laws are directly descended from it. Maybe we need to remind our pastors and clergy as well as our families and friends of the significant fact that Christianity indeed shaped this nation.

Words of warning from leading 18th and 19th century Americans Still ring true.[445]

- *"When you become entitled to exercise the right of voting for public officers, let it be impressed on your mind that God commands you to choose for rulers, just men who will rule in fear of God. The preservation of a Republican government depends on the faithful discharge of this duty;* **if the citizens neglect their duty and place unprincipled men in office the government will soon be corrupted, laws will be made, not for the public good, so much as for selfish or local purposes; corrupt or incompetent men will be appointed to execute the laws; the public revenues will be squandered on unworthy men; and the rights of the citizens will be violated or disregarded."**

  —Noah Webster

---

[445] "Republic vs. Democracy," The Free Republic, http://www.freerepublic.com, February 25, 2005

- *"It is impossible to rightly govern the world without God and the Bible."*

  —George Washington

- *"We have been assured, Sir, in the Sacred Writings, that 'except the Lord build the house, they labor in vain that build it.' I firmly believe this; and I also believe that without His concurring aid we shall succeed in this political building no better than the builders of Babel."*

  —Benjamin Franklin

- *"We have staked the whole future of American civilization, not upon the power of the government, far from it. We have staked the future of all our political institutions upon the capacity of mankind for self-government; upon the capacity of each and all of us to govern ourselves, to control ourselves, to sustain ourselves according to The Ten Commandments of God."*

  —James Madison

- *"The very existence of the Republic...depends much upon the public institutions of religion."*

  —John Hancock

The single, best-selling and most-read book in history is the **Bible**. There are many great books that elucidate the truths of Christianity and some of the lesser known ones include:

- **The Role of Pastors and Christians in Civil Government,** David Barton, 2003
- **The Heart of Christianity: Rediscovering a Life of Faith,** Marcus J. Borg, 2004
- **Separation of Church and State: What the Founders Meant,** David Barton, 2007
- **Evidence of the Truth of the Christian Religion,** Alexander Keith, 1834, Reprinted by Tolle Lege Press, 2011

- **Christianity For Skeptics**, Dr. Steve Kumar, 2012
- *Godforsaken: Bad Things Happen. Is There a God Who Cares? Here's Proof,* Dinesh D'Souza, 2012
- *What's So Great about Christianity?* Dinesh D'Souza, 2008
  - ▫ Author, Researcher and Filmmaker Dinesh D'Souza has three thoughtful books about Christianity. It is interesting to note that Eric Holder and his Justice Department charged Dinesh with campaign contribution violations for a twenty thousand dollar contribution during the 2012 election cycle. It was no coincidence that Dinesh D'Souza, a fearless critic of the Obama administration released a great documentary-movie, "*2016: Obama's America,*" in 2012.
- **The Christian Life and Character of the Civil Institutions of the United States,** Benjamin F. Morris, 1864, Reprinted by American Vision, 2007

Truth, the New Hate Speech

"*Truth is the new hate speech,*" is the name of an article published by The Black Sphere in response to bills working their way through Congress to criminalize hate speech. Leftists don't want to hear what people who do not agree with them have to say. "*The Leftists like to quiet people (who disagree with them). Quiet people don't question why freedom of speech only applies to people who think the way they do. Quiet people don't ask why gun control cities are the most dangerous cities in the world...so they can go on about the business of making us equal. Equally poor. Equally obedient. Equally defenseless...*"[446]

The Black Sphere (www.theblacksphere.net) is a very informative and refreshing website. Like Lloyd Marcus ("proud un-hyphenated" American), Kevin Jackson, founder and face of the Black Sphere, identifies himself as an "American," period. Kevin explains that many people assume that he started "*The Black Sphere* as some sort of racial

---

[446] "Congress' surprising definition of hate-speech," The Black Sphere, http://www. theblacksphere.net, April 23, 2014

response to the Left." It was not. Kevin Jackson explains that *"The one thing we all share is our individualism. We see a world where our differences are celebrated and not used to divide. We see a future where the people who represent us, represent us as Americans, and nothing else."* The Black Sphere team "wants to end identity politics, educating with satire and humor." It is a great website.

Hypocrisy Alert: The Southern Poverty Law Center, the number one "hate group" in America identifies Christians and Conservatives as hate groups no different than the KKK and Louis Farrakhan's Nation of Islam.

The Southern Poverty Law Center (www.splcenter.org) prides itself on "Fighting Hate - Teaching Tolerance - Seeking Justice." That sounds commendable but the fact is the SPLC very selectively identifies and labels hate groups - based on their ideology of "hate." The KKK and the Louis Farrakhan's Nation of Islam are true hate groups and they belong on the list. The New Black Panthers should be on the list, but I didn't see them there. Many of the groups listed on the SPLC website are labeled hate groups only because they do not agree with the liberal progressive agenda. For instance, the 9/11 Christian Center at Ground Zero has been designated a hate group and deemed anti-Muslim, but The Council on American Islamic Relations (CAIR) which is a Muslim hate group is nowhere on the SPLC's "hate map."

I noticed a disturbing trend in the SPLCs classification of Conservative and Christian organizations as "Hate Groups." Allegations of hate crimes are published and include *"hate group activities"* such as the distribution of organizational materials and sponsoring rallies (I believe that is called freedom of speech and is protected by the First Amendment - even if you don't agree with it). If you support legal immigration, you are anti-immigrant. If you are Catholic, check your parish church charter to see if it is practicing "Radical Traditional Catholicism." I had no idea the "traditional" Catholic Church was radical. Christian churches and groups including those radical Catholics are defined as Anti-homosexual and Anti-Islam.

The Southern Poverty Law Center has a designation labeled *General Hate.* General hate - what is that supposed to mean? Maybe the designated group had multiple hates and the SPLC could not determine which horrible offense was worse, so they decided that those groups just hate everything! Here are some of the organizations and churches that the Southern Poverty Law Center has listed under *General Hate*: The National Prayer Network, The Fundamentalist Latter Day Saints, The Christian Anti-Defamation Commission, The North Phoenix Tea Party, Agenda 21 Today, The Tony Alamo Christian Ministries and The Florida Family Association.

Many Christian churches and organizations as well as concerned citizen groups and Islamic watchdog groups (who are absolutely correct about the threat of Islam in America and the world) are declared Anti-Islamic hate groups: The Christian Action Network, The United States Defense League, American Freedom Defense Initiative, *Atlas Shrugs*, *Jihad Watch*, Concerned American Citizens, and Citizens for National Security.

The SPLC has determined that any organization supporting traditional marriage is a hate group, including: Catholic Family and Human Rights Institute (C-FAM), True Light Pentecostal Church, Catholic Family News and Ministries, The Family Research Institute, Christ the King Church, Illinois Family Institute, Truth In Action Ministries and unbelievably, the American College of Pediatricians.

One more intolerable hate category is *"Anti-Immigrant."* Anyone who supports "legal" immigration is anti-immigrant in the progressive world of the Southern Poverty Law Center. Did you have any idea that the American Border Patrol, U.S. Border Guards and Border Rangers, the California Coalition for Immigration Reform, Americans for Legal Immigration, and New Yorkers for Immigration Control and Enforcement (NYICE) are "hate groups?"

Maybe the Southern Poverty Law Center started out with good intentions, but it has completely gone off the rails. *"...we're tracking hundreds of potentially violent hate groups across the country with many members who are willing to shed blood for their cause. And we're providing key intelligence and training to help law enforcement combat violent extremists."* They are celebrating the fact that Attorney General Eric Holder revived the "Domestic Terrorism Executive Committee," to combat the "rising threat" of domestic terrorism. Well, that explains why the government has so much bad information and Christians and Conservatives are on the target list.[447]

Race has become a favorite weapon of the Left. Instead of uniting Americans as promised by Barack Obama, race is used as a weapon to divide Americans. This is not the vision Dr. Martin Luther King, Jr. lived and died for, and this path of division must be closed once and for all. The subject of race cannot be adequately addressed in a few paragraphs, but all Americans need to take a hard look at the subject. Questions we need to ask include:

- What can I do? Do I see people based on their words and actions instead of the color of their skin?
- Why does anyone listen to race-hustlers like the Rev. Jesse Jackson and Al Sharpton who have made very profitable careers inciting violence and promoting victimization?
- How many black children have to be killed by gang and "illegal" gun violence in cities such as Chicago before the government admits there is a massive problem that must be dealt with? President Obama did not hesitate to inject himself into the deaths of Trayvon Martin in Florida and Michael Brown in Missouri. Jesse Jackson, Al Sharpton and even Attorney General Eric Holder jump uninformed into media events of white-on-black death but have nothing to say about black-on-black death. Mr. President, "Why does it seem that black children in large cities are expendable – as long as they are murdered by black not white people?
- Discrimination is wrong so why is the government promoting it?
- Should we not be more concerned about people who really are being discriminated against instead of legislating "hate speech?" Words don't kill - hate does.
- Why aren't all murders hate-crimes? Why was the Justice Department so determined to charge (white/hispanic) George Zimmerman with a hate crime for killing black teen Trayvon Martin, but the murder of a 6-month old white baby in a stroller by black teens was not a hate crime?

---

[447] "Feds respond to SPLC, revive domestic terrorism working group," Richard Cohen, President, The Southern Poverty law Center, June 5, 2014

- Why is it so important to identify Barack Obama as a black president, not a black/caucasian president? Can't he just be "The President?"
- Why are white people called racists when they disagree with President Obama? Many people do not like his policies and governance which has nothing to do with the color of his skin. What do you call black people who disagree with the President?
- Why does the media fuel racial tension and identify most things in racial terms?
- How can white people even discuss race without being labeled bigots or racists?

Racists come in all colors, shapes and sizes. No matter how much the government tries to legislate racial thought, they fail. Children are not born racists. It is a learned attitude. Tolerance, acceptance and "color-blindness" need to be taught by parents, family, teachers, clergy and communities.

As a matter of fact, we Americans of all colors need to get it together. When we can identify ourselves as Americans without hyphenations we can curb racism. Our country will be facing major threats in the coming years and we need to be united Americans to survive.

John McWhorter is an Associate Professor in the English and Comparative Literature Department at Columbia University teaching Linguistics and American Studies courses. He is the author of a number of books, two of which focus on race relations in the United States. As an African-American, Professor McWhorter provides valuable insight about race issues all Americans must come to terms with. His 2001 book, *"Losing the Race: Self sabotage in Black America,"* spotlights victimization, separatism and anti-intellectualism. *"Authentically Black: Essays for the Black Silent Majority"* published in 2003 is a collection of essays exploring what it means to be black in America now. Among numerous topics presented, Professor McWhorter addresses racial profiling, getting past race, black leadership and diversity. These books are not just for black readers. They can benefit all Americans no matter their racial, social, political and economic background.

An issue that really bothers me is how badly black conservatives are treated. They are openly disliked and assaulted with racial slurs from both liberals and many African-Americans. Liberal Democrats regularly disparage and demean them. They are called traitors and "Uncle Toms" by black politicians and the general black public. For instance when Stacey Dash was hired as a commentator by Fox News, she was immediately attacked. Retired Lt. Col. Allen West stated, "*It never ceases to amaze; the duplicitous hypocrisy of the so-called "tolerant Left" and worse, the nastiness of the black community.*" This is despicable, yet why doesn't the government or the media acknowledge this racial bias? Where are Jesse Jackson and Al Sharpton when black conservatives are discriminated against?

To the surprise of most liberals there are a lot of black conservatives and their numbers are growing. As I mentioned in Part One, there are black Tea Party members and supporters though the media would never let that be known since the Left's official mantra is Tea Party members are white racists.

Black Conservative Americans

They are politicians, intellectuals, doctors, teachers, professors, authors, business owners and journalists. From different backgrounds and circumstances they have all become successful Americans. They are well aware of the past sins of the nation. They know of the pain of slavery and the sting of discrimination. Instead of dwelling on the past, they bear the burden of <u>discrimination by liberals and other black Americans</u> today to ensure a better tomorrow for minorities and all Americans. They clearly see a weakened America at this critical point in time. They acknowledge America's mistakes and yet move forward, committed to re-establishing our founding principles. They are true role models deserving the respect of all.

- **Allen B. West** is a former Congressman from Florida. He is also a retired U.S. Army Lieutenant Colonel having served in Operation Desert Storm, Operation Iraqi Freedom, and in Afghanistan. Col. West is a formidable champion for the

U.S. military and our veterans. He is a Senior Fellow at the London Center for Policy Research, a Fox News contributor, an author and writes for numerous media outlets. His 2014 book *"Guardian of the Republic,"* is inspiring. Allen is a refreshing conservative voice who will not back down from what is right. He has never, nor will he ever compromise his core values of family, faith, tradition, service, honor, fiscal responsibility, courage and freedom.

Regarding the incessant assault on black conservatives, Allen West said, *"Instead of engaging me, or others, based upon my thoughts, perspectives, ideals, and principles of governance, the debate becomes one of personal assault, and that includes my own family...I am more than willing to suffer the attacks, assaults, character assassinations, and lies in order to save my beloved Constitutional Republic, and strive to ensure a better future for my daughters. It is often a very lonely walk and there are times when I do not know if I can take another arrow. But then I am reminded of the dog tag around my neck with the verse from Joshua 1:9 (NIV)."* [Have I not commanded you? Be strong and courageous. Do not be terrified; do not be discouraged, for the Lord your God will be with you wherever you go.][448]

Take a look at Col. West's website at http://www.allenbwest.com

- □ **The Allen West Guardian Fund** (http://www.allenwestguardianfund.com) was established to support conservative military veteran and minority Republicans running for state and federal office.
- □ **The Allen West Foundation** (http://www.allenwestfoundation.org) was established to educate and inspire the next generation of conservative leaders among minority and veteran communities. It also supports organizations such as JROTC, Young Marines and NROTC.

---

[448] "Black conservatives afforded no safe quarter," Allen West, http://www.allenwest.com, February 7, 2014

- **Thomas Sowell** is a Senior Fellow at the Hoover Institution, Stanford University, California. Dr. Sowell is an economics professor, author and columnist. I admire Dr. Sowell as an economic genius as well as a social commentator providing exceptional knowledge of the American people. He is a man with timely opinions and advice well worth listening to. He has written numerous books including, *"Intellectuals and Society,"* (2009) in which he illustrates how *"Intellectuals as a class affect modern societies by shaping the climate of opinion in which official policies develop on issues ranging from economics to law to war and peace."* Visit Thomas Sowell's website at http://www.tsowell.com to learn more about Dr.Sowell and his writings. For increased understanding on specific subjects or general education, he has a wonderful "Suggested Readings" tab containing a list of his books as well as books he recommends by numerous authors covering a variety of subjects.

- **Dr. Ben Carson** (http://realbencarson.com) is a champion of education, hard work, and responsibility. He is a self-made American success story. From humble beginnings in Detroit, Michigan, he graduated from Yale University and The University of Michigan Medical School. Dr. Carson was a well-known pediatric neurosurgeon long before most of us met him after his keynote speech at The National Prayer Breakfast in February 2013 where he honestly commented on social and fiscal issues troubling our nation. Dr. Carson gained fame in the medical world when in 1987 he surgically separated conjoined twins joined at the head. He received the Presidential Medal of Freedom in 2008. Ben is not a member of any political party. *"If I were part of one, it would be called the Logic party."* Dr. Carson and his wife created the "**Carson Scholars Fund**" (http://www.carsonscholars.org) in 1994 which awards student scholarships for "academic excellence and humanitarian qualities." He has authored many bestselling books including: *"Gifted Hands"* (his autobiography), *"Think Big," "Take the Risk," "America the Beautiful"* and *"One Nation."* All are inspiring and are windows into the author's personal philosophy on life and faith in God. Ben Carson has a lot to say and we would be wise to listen to him.

- *"There's absolutely no reason at all that physicians and scientists, shouldn't be involved in things that affect all of us. We're people who've learned how to make decisions based on facts, empirical data, rather than on ideology, and one of the geniuses, one of the real things that made us a great nation, is that we brought people from all backgrounds into the legislative process."*

- When told he should just stick to being a doctor, he replied, "I mentioned the fact that five physicians signed the Declaration of Independence and were involved in the framing of the Constitution and the Bill of Rights and several things."

- *"And if you talk to most people, they mean well but they don't have much of a breadth of education, of knowledge, of understanding of what the real issues are and, therefore, they listen to pundits on television who tell them what they're supposed to think and they keep repeating that and pretty soon they say, 'Oh, well that must be true.'"*

- **Deneen Borelli** is an author, outreach director, Fox News contributor, columnist and frequent speaker at Tea Party rallies and events. Deneen's website *"Reigniting Liberty"* at http://www.deneenborelli.com is informative and insightful. Her 2013 book ***"Blacklash: How Obama and the Left Are Driving Americans to the Government Plantation"*** takes on the lies of "self-styled African American leaders" and calls for the community to break free from progressive policies holding them back. Deneen is the Outreach Director with Freedom Works, a grassroots organization that educates and mobilizes volunteer activists to fight for limited government. She was also a Fellow with Project 21 and manager of Media Relations with the Congress of Racial Equality. Deneen is an inspiration.

- **Republican Senator Tim Scott** is the first black U.S. senator from the South in well over a century. You would think that designation would be celebrated but, no, the liberal left, Democrats, and many black citizens castigate him as a "traitor" and "Uncle Tom" because he is conservative and a Republican. Tim grew up in a poor, single parent household in South Carolina. Knowing the importance of *"faith, hard work and living within your means,"* he became a very successful businessman. Scott was sworn in as a U.S. Senator from South Carolina in January 2013 and has never stopped trying to make things better for the constituents he represents and for all Americans. He believes in the American Dream and has presented numerous initiatives for economic freedom, school choice, energy development including offshore drilling, and tax reform. To minimize and demean Senator Scott's hard work, Representative James Clyburn criticized him for *"not voting according to the color of his skin."* That is another example of the political double-standard allowing Democrats to use racist language. Senator Scott deserves respect; not because of the color of his skin, but because of his actions, values and commitment to the people of his state. http://www.scott.senate.org

- **Lloyd Marcus** (un-hyphenated American) is an amazing man. *"I am not an African-American! I am Lloyd Marcus AMERICAN."* I first saw, and heard him speak at a Tea Party Express rally in 2010. His energy and enthusiasm are contagious. His passion and commitment to conservative values is commendable. Lloyd is an author, singer, songwriter, artist, volunteer president of the Deltona, Florida Arts and Historical Center, keynote speaker for the Tea Party, and the Chairman of the Conservative Campaign Committee. Lloyd grew up in the Baltimore Projects and saw first-hand how liberal programs failed the people they were supposed to help. He has rejected victimization of racism, rising to success because of the values and support of a loving family. In his 2010 book, ***"Confessions of a Black Conservative: How the Left has Shattered the Dreams of Martin Luther King, Jr.***

and Black America," Lloyd explains why conservatism works best for America. He supports this view in easy to understand terms through his own personal stories.

Lloyd published a thought-provoking article on his blog asking why liberals, Democrats and the main stream media remain steadfastly loyal to President Obama no matter how many times he breaks the law and no matter how many times he lies to the American people. *"The frightening inconvenient truth is the MSM, Democrat party and Obama consider American suffering and loss of life acceptable collateral damage to protect Obama and implement his agenda... What has emboldened Obama to continuously boldly go where no white president has gone before? The answer, his black skin suit-of-armor. Despite Obama's multiple crimes and misdemeanors against the American people and the Constitution, serious opposition to the first black president is simply not an option for many in the GOP and MSM [Main stream Media]."*[449]

You can access his writings and music on his website: http://www.LloydMarcus.com. Lloyd's 2014 CD, *"Lloyd Marcus: God, Country & Love,"* is an inspiring collection of songs. As an Army veteran himself, Lloyd passionately supports the **America's Mighty Warriors Organization,** www.AmericasMightyWarriors.org. *"America's Mighty Warriors' mission is to honor the sacrifices of our troops, the fallen and their families by providing programs that improve quality of life, resiliency and recovery."*

- **Alveda King** is an author, Christian minister, civil rights activist, and pro-life activist. She was a Senior Fellow at the Alexis de Tocqueville Institution and a former U.S. Congresswoman. Alveda is a Pastoral Associate of African-American Outreach for *Priests for Life*, the Catholic Church's Pro-life organization. Dr. Martin Luther King, Jr. was her uncle and she works tirelessly

---

[449] "Because He is Black, Americans Suffer and Die," Lloyd Marcus, http://www.lloydmarcus.com, June 6, 2014

to keep his message of peace alive. He would be so proud of the work she is doing.

- **Walter E. Williams** is a remarkable man with a biography worthy of the Presidential Medal of Honor (though that will not happen with President Obama in the White House). Dr. Williams has served on the faculty of George Mason University since 1980. He has also served on the faculties of Los Angeles City College, California State University Los Angeles, Temple University in Philadelphia and Grove City College, also in Pennsylvania. Dr. Williams holds a B.A., M.A. and Ph.D. in Economics. He has made scores of appearances on radio and television, serves on several boards of trustees/directors, has received numerous awards, has participated in debates, conferences and lectures, and has presented testimony before Congress.

  Mr. Williams has authored over 150 publications that have appeared in scholarly journals and prestigious print media. He is the author of 10 books including: *"America: A Minority Viewpoint," "The State Against Blacks," "Do the Right Thing: The People's Economist Speaks," "More Liberty Means Less Government," "Liberty vs. the Tyranny of Socialism," "Up From the Projects: An Autobiography, and Race and Economics: How Much Can Be Blamed On Discrimination?"* all highlighting important and critical social and economic issues.

  Walter E. Williams' web site contains a fountain of knowledge just waiting to be tapped. You can access his biography, syndicated columns, publications, courses and much more. He even provides a "Book Recommendation List" with books he has published and books by other authors. Along with the book list he provides a catalog of recommended websites. I urge you to visit his website at: http://www.econfaculty.gmu.edu/wew/.

- **Kevin Jackson** is an author, public speaker, radio host, political warrior, Tea Party supporter and founder of *The Black Sphere* (www.theblacksphere.net). Kevin injects energy, education and humor into the serious "political" world. He has been a part of the Tea Party since he spoke before 10,000 people at the April 15, 2009 Tax Day Tea Party rally in St. Louis. Missouri. Kevin's book, *"The Big Black Lie"* is inspirational. He escaped the "victimology" of Democrats and has an important message for fellow conservatives. Kevin Jackson is an educator and a shining star in the conservative movement. I look forward to hearing more from him. Remember Kevin's words, *"Magic doesn't protect the Constitution and our rights. We do!"*

- **Star Parker** is a true treasure. Through hard work, determination and faith in the Lord, she pulled herself up from the welfare abyss to become a successful independent woman who has dedicated her life to helping others. Star's 2009 book, *"White Ghetto: How Middle Class America Reflects Inner City Decay"* honestly illustrates the moral collapse of America. She proves that *"decaying social values, sexually transmitted diseases, fatherless homes and drug use aren't just problems for today's inner cities. It is the plight of America."* Her 2010 book, *"Uncle Sam's Plantation"* chronicles her life and the detrimental effects of the welfare system. Star is a syndicated columnist and is the founder and president of **CURE** (Center for Urban Renewal and Education).
  - **CURE** http://www.urbancure.org: CURE is a non-profit organization that addresses issues such as race, poverty, welfare, immigration, values and education. CURE's mission is to "build awareness that the conservative agenda of traditional values, limited government, and private ownership is of greater marginal benefit to low income peoples." CURE is a great organization that I enthusiastically support.

- **Larry Elder** has a BA in Political Science from Brown University and graduated from the University Of Michigan School Of Law making him a credible source of logic using evidence and reasoned analysis to expose inconsistencies and hypocrisy in our government, society-at-large and the media. He is an author and a nationally syndicated radio talk-show host. Larry was the host of the television shows, "Moral Court" and "The Larry Elder Show," as well as the recipient of numerous awards. Larry "engages political and cultural leaders in meaningful debates over race, government, personal responsibility and education."[450] He has created the **Larry Elder Charities**, a non-profit organization that gives financial support to individuals and organizations that can offer self-help non-government solutions relating to poverty, poor parenting, dependency and education.

Some of Larry's books, *"Ten Things You Can't Say in America," "Showdown: Confronting Bias," "Lies and the Special Interests That Divide America,"* and *"What's Race Got to do With It? Why it's Time to Stop the Stupidest Argument in America,"* deal head on with the most hotly-debated issues we face today. He is a champion for the America envisioned by our Founding Fathers: Limited government, more freedom, greater wealth, less taxes, less government dependency, more individual responsibility, education and border security. He also sees the need to clean up government agencies and special interest groups. And, he firmly states that the "essential" purpose of government is to protect its citizens. Visit Larry at www.larryelder.com

- **Herman Cain** is a financial expert, a successful business executive, a columnist, radio host, author, and a black Tea Party activist in Georgia. He was one of the investors that bought Godfather's Pizza and turned it into a very successful business. He left Godfather's Pizza in 1996 and became a senior economic advisor to Senator Bob Dole's presidential campaign. Mr. Cain was also the CEO of the National Restaurant Association. In 2005 Herman worked for *Americans for Prosperity (AFP)* a wonderful political advocacy organization. Unfortunately his bid as a Republican nominee for president was cut short by unsubstantiated 20 year old sexual harassment allegations. Herman Cain is a valuable source of business and political information and news. He is a

---

[450] Larry Elder Biography, http://www.larryelder.com

commendable American. Visit Herman Cain's websites at http://caintv.com and http://www.wsbradio.com/s/herman-cain.

- **Angela McGlowan** is a political and special interest contributor for the Fox News Channel. Angela is also the founder and CEO of Political Strategies & Insights (PSI), a government affairs, political strategy and public relations consulting firm. She served as director of Government Affairs and Diversity Development for Rupert Murdoch's News Corporation and was responsible for the development and implementation of "aggressive diversity initiatives" for the Fox Entertainment Group. I'll bet liberals hate to hear that! Angela has also served as director of **Outreach for the Better America Foundation** and conducted policy meetings with members of Congress. In her 2007 book, *"Bamboozled: How Americans are being Exploited by the Lies of the Liberal Agenda,"* she exposes the liberal plan to swindle the poor and minorities to support the Democrat Party. As a "Democrat-turned-Republican," Angela illustrates how the Republican Party best represents the values and interests of minorities.

- **David Webb** is a radio show host, commentator, columnist, and non-partisan political activist. The David Webb Show airs on Siruis XM Patriot 125 satellite radio. He also tapes an hour show titled David Webb's American Forum in which he hosts discussions with "notable" Americans before a live audience. David appears on Fox News, Fox Business, and CNBC. He is a columnist for *The Hill* and *Breitbart News*. David is extremely active in politics and a vocal proponent of fiscal responsibility. He co-founded TeaParty365 in New York City; is the spokesman for the National Tea Party Federation; and was named as a *"Time Magazine's Person of the Year"* (he was the protester representing the tea party movement). That is an amazing feat since according to the Left; the Tea Party is made up of white racists and bigots. David is a true patriot and you can check him out at http://www.davidwebshow.com and http://www.davidwebshow.com/american-forum.

- **Niger Innis** is a civil rights activist, spokesman for the Congress of Racial Equality (CORE), works with numerous organizations, is a lifetime member of the National Rifle Association (NRA) and is the Executive Director of The Tea Party.net (http://www.theteaparty.net). I have a feeling that liberals are having a hard time digesting that fact. Mr. Innis' leadership and experience are assets to conservative Americans.

Additional organizations:

Black Conservatives Fund (BCF) http://BlackConservativesFund.com: A grassroots political action committee committed to the support of "principled" black conservatives running for office. Their mission is to educate black voters on "how liberal progressive politicians like President Barack Obama have failed them," time and again.

American CurrentSee http://www.americancurrentsee.com: *Dare to be Independent and Free*: An innovative and free digital magazine for America's new generation of black conservatives - influenced by black American thinkers like Dr. Ben Carson, Rev. A.R. Bernard, Thomas Sowell, Herman Cain, Armstrong Williams, Juan Williams and Mia Love. American Current-See is dedicated to "dialogue on subjects from the best way to seize the debate inside the black community from the liberals to embracing a new agenda of economic opportunity, moral leadership and freedom from suffocating government."

There are countless black Americans who have, and continue to strive to make America the great country envisioned by our Founders. They are from different walks of life but have faith, belief in moral absolutes, and great confidence in the future of our nation. They are committed to a stronger America for all the generations to come.

Conservatives and Christians, regardless of race, political party and gender cannot afford to wait any longer for things to "get better." As we have seen the past five years, "hope and change" were highly overrated. The clock is nearing Midnight and if we don't confront the liberal progressives controlling our government, schools, healthcare, and even the environment, the America we know will be lost. We must remember that ALL actions, even seemingly insignificant ones have consequences. The people we elect to office do affect our lives.

Presidential policies and the corrupt use of "Executive Actions" lead to lawlessness. And remote, foreign policies also affect us. An assault against one Christian denomination is an assault on all. The government is counting on inter-denominational strife and division to keep Christians from uniting. The government is counting on racial tension and division to keep the races from uniting. The government is counting on angering middle and lower class citizens to blame and hate the upper class and big-business in order to create financial chaos and an angry mob mentality which will empower the government police state. A liberal government is a dangerous government and the bigger and more powerful it grows, the harder it is to keep within the constraints of the U.S. Constitution, which is the <u>only</u> true law of the land.

Public Schools in America: Censoring Education with Common Core?

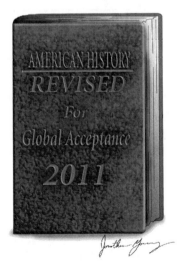

Besides selective tolerance, what else are our children learning, or more accurately, not learning in school? Our public elementary and high schools are in crisis and it's not just a financial one. Teachers' Unions and the Federal Department of Education have diminished, not improved the quality of public education in America.

At Pershing High School in inner-city Detroit, the kids learned that they can violently abuse each other and if the teacher interferes by trying to stop the fight, she can be fired and even charged with child-abuse. You may have seen this incident on television. Two boys were fighting; crashing into desks and vehemently hitting each other while their 30 year old female teacher begged them to stop. School protocol required her to use her walkie-talkie to call security. But since her walkie-talkie did not work and she feared for the boys' safety as well as the safety of the other kids in class, she hit one boy on the back with a broom to break up the fight. She was immediately fired for striking that boy. *The Daily Caller reported, "Striking a student with a broom is a violation of state laws against corporal punishment. That means the teacher has not only lost her job, she could also be charged with child abuse."* [451] The mother of the boy hit with the broom was extremely vocal about the teacher's actions as she showed reporters where her son was hit (no visible marks), but she had nothing to say about her son violently beating another boy.

In the Chicago Public Schools where sex education for kindergartners was mandated in 2013, a new "Afro-centric curriculum" has been introduced to work in conjunction with the "Common Core" educational system. The Afro-centric curriculum is linked to the website, *TheAfrican.com* whose publisher regards the United States as a "Zionist-occupied enemy territory," and refers to "fake Jews." The curriculum includes inaccurate historical information such as Martin Bernal's book, *The Black Athena* in which he claims that the Greeks stole much of civilization from black Egypt. Since "social justice" reigns supreme in Chicago, it is not surprising to learn that the 8th grade literacy unit, titled, *"Being an Advocate to Social Justice,"* directs students to the American Civil Liberties Union website; includes the poem, *"Racism is Around Me Everywhere;"* and even presents cartoons from *LeftyCartoons.com.* Students in Chicago will still be deficient in math, reading, history, values and respect, but they will be well educated about sex and prepared for a future in community activism.

---

[451] "Inner City Teacher Tries To Break Up Horrifically Violent Fights, Gets Fired," Robby Soave, The Daily Caller, http://dailycaller.com, May 6, 2014

The *L.A. Times, Huffington Post* and *Political Outcast* reported that the Gervais School District in Oregon has updated its "human sexuality policy" and beginning in the Fall of 2014 they will make condoms available to all high school and middle school students. That means 6th graders will be treated and taught the same as seniors in high school. If you are the parent of an 11 year old in middle school, do you think free condoms and more sex education will keep your young child from having sex? The school district decided to implement this program after a survey indicated that 7% of the high school girls had "experienced pregnancy," and 42% of students said they never or sometimes used protection. Why are public schools obsessed with increasing sex education when statistics prove that the more students are taught about sex and given free condoms, the higher the rates of teen pregnancies, abortions and sexually transmitted diseases?

Political Outcast's Mark Horne commented on the logic of the plan. *"So, because we can imagine preventing pregnancies by condoms, some people decide that encouraging the use of condoms will discourage pregnancy. This is bad reasoning... But if you want to decrease pregnancy why not discourage sex? The age of consent in Oregon is 18...And what does this have to do with 11-year-olds?"*[452] Now would be a good time to read Tammy Bruce's book, *"**The Death of Right and Wrong: Exposing the Left's Assault on Our Culture and Values.** She extensively addresses the subject (crime) of school culture regarding children and sex.

There has been a lot of debate about the "Common Core" State Standards education program pushed by the Obama administration. Proponents of common national standards feel that it will improve the quality of education and they herald it as a base for instructors to teach standardized reading and critical thinking. Opponents of course, disagree. They believe that educational standards must be the responsibility of state and local communities. They also strongly feel that mandated national standards fail to empower individualism and creativity. The states that already have higher standards will have to lower them to meet the Common Core standards.

Many, and with good reason, see Common Core as another federal

---

[452] "School Board Decides to Encourage Pre-Teens to Make Babies," Mark Horne, Political Outcast, http://www.politicaloutcast.com, June 6, 2014

power grab resulting in more federal control over the individual states. Federal law prohibits the federal government (including the U.S. Department of Education) from "exercising any direction, supervision, or control over the curriculum, program of instruction" or selection of "instructional materials."[453] The Department of Education bypassed the law by making Obama's "Race to the Top" funding and Bush's "No Child Left Behind" waivers contingent on each state's "adoption" of Common Core. More accurately, the states are blackmailed into "adopting" Common Core or they face losing federal funding. The federal government through the Department of Education now has control of the educational curricula, testing assessments, and standards of education for the nations' children, kindergarten through 12th grade. In the world of private business that would be extortion. Parents have lost what little control they had over their children's public school education.

The State of Indiana's "pre-Common Core state standards were ranked among the highest in the nation."[454] Indiana officially left the Common Core national standards in April 2014 and has been threatened by the federal government that the state's No Child Left Behind waiver will be revoked and thereby the states' federal funding will be affected. Even though Indiana's education standards and testing scores are higher than the Common Core requirements, the Obama administration/ Department of Education claims the state of Indiana does not meet Common Core expectations. Indiana has just proven that the federal Common Core program is not "state-led" and not "voluntary" as the administration claims. Forcing states to "lower" their education standards to the federal level proves that logic does not exist in the Department of Education. Other states have made the same move away from Common Core and they too are facing federal wrath.

The Daily Caller published an interesting report released by *Mission Readiness* which is a non-partisan national security organization made

---

[453] "Why Common Core is Bad for America," Jonathan Butcher, Emmett McGroarty and Liv Finne, The Washington Policy Center, http://www.washingtonpolicy.org, May 17, 2014

[454] "Indiana's pre-Common Core state standards were ranked among the highest in the nation," The Heritage Foundation, Heritage Blog, http://www.blog.heritage.org, April 18, 2014

up of senior retired military leaders. The report stated that nearly 75% of Americans age 17 to 24 *"do not meet one or more of the basic qualifications to join our nation's armed forces." "The report makes clear that one of the biggest obstacles is the failure of our schools to prepare them academically. Mission Readiness found that not only are too many young people failing to graduate, many of those who do graduate lack the foundational skills necessary to take their place in the military or the modern workforce."*[455]

I have read articles about how ridiculously confusing the new math system is, and how age-inappropriate some reading materials are. I am suspect of Common Core because of the federal government's liberal influence in the education of our children. If you read any of Tammy Bruce's books, *"The New Thought Police: Inside the Left's Assault on Free Speech and Free Minds," "The Death of Right and Wrong: Exposing the Left's Assault on Our Culture and Values,"* and *"New American Revolution: How You Can Fight the Tyranny of the Left's Cultural and Moral Decay,"* you will be astonished at how the liberal/progressive agenda has taken over our public schools and is negatively influencing our children. David Horowitz's book *"The Professors"* illustrates the negative progressive educational agenda devouring our institutions of higher education.

I will continue to investigate and monitor the Common Core issue and I recommend you do the same. Since I am not an educator I must count on reliable non-partisan data to understand and assess the program. I found helpful information on of all places, About.com. Under the School-Age Children section was an article titled, **"What are Common Core State Standards and the Arguments for and Against Them"** by Katherine Lee.[456] *"It will be some time before we know the full effect the Common Core State Standards has on schools and on student learning and performance. In the meantime, what's clear is that there is a lot of passion on both sides about what students need to succeed and*

[455] "How Common Core Affects our National Security," The Daily Caller, http://www.dailycaller.com, April 28, 2014

[456] What are Common Core State Standards and the Arguments for and Against Them: The facts about Common Core and pros and cons of these standards," Katherine Lee, About.com, http://www.childparenting.about.com, May 17, 2014

learn in school. If both sides of the issue can keep the improvement of education and increased support for children a priority as CCSS and school curricula get sorted out, it will be all the better for children and our future."

The article suggested parents learn as much as possible about Common Core and they should also speak to other parents. It is imperative that parents know what is being taught to their children. The same article also listed the following "good sources of information" on Common Core:

- *Common Core Standards* by Derrick Meador, expert on teaching at About.com
- *What are Some Pros and Cons of the Common Core Standards?* also by Derrick Meador, Ask.com
- *What Are the Common Core State Standards?* by Amanda Morin, Kids & Learning Activities Expert at About.com
- Video - Ethan Young, Farragut High School student, Knox County, Tennessee making a case against CCSS, http://www.theblaze.com
- Video - Kenneth Ye, also a Farragut High School student arguing against CCSS, http://www.examiner.com

The Education Action Group Foundation (EAG) is a non-partisan non-profit organization focusing solely on education. **EAGnews.org** is the news service website of EAG dedicated to education reform and school spending research, reporting, analysis and commentary. Kyle Olson, the publisher of EAGnews.com has made two documentary films, has appeared on the Fox News Channel, NPR and MSNBC and is a contributing writer for Townhall.com.

Every day the Education Action Group Foundation (EAG) highlights the need for a student-focused education system that is financially sustainable and will put us on a firm footing to compete globally in the future. EAG's perspective on education reform includes issues such as the government's failure of responsible quality education in many communities across the nation. That failure is evident by bleak test scores and out of control spending that does nothing to improve education. EAG insists that the educational system make students the top priority by ensuring quality teachers, adequate supplies, support and current technology instead of focusing on teacher union contracts and demands. Parents need to decide on the best school option for their children and schools need to be allowed more control over their budgets and personnel decisions.

Back in 1989 Albert Shanker, former AFT president, made the following observation and as you will see, not much has changed with public education over the past 25 years. *"It's time to admit that public education operates like a planned economy, a bureaucratic system in which everybody's role is spelled out in advance and there are few incentives for innovation and productivity. It's no surprise that our school system doesn't improve: it more resembles the communist economy than our own market economy."*[457]

As parents, grandparents and guardians we need to know what our children are being taught at school. We must be involved with our schools, teachers and curriculum. We must question actions, policies and ideologies of the school district. We need to know what text books and other books are mandatory reading. We need to know what school field trips are planned, and why. What is the educational benefit of the particular field trip? For instance, I am reading about more and more school field trips to Islamic mosques. As a parent I would want to know why children who are not allowed to sing Christmas songs or make any mention of the Christian religion on school grounds are brought to Muslim churches and made to pray to Allah and even wear Muslim garb. The tired old liberal response that field trips to mosques give kids a chance to see and experience other cultures doesn't work anymore. Children are brought to mosques for exposure and recruitment to the Muslim religion, which goes against every public school policy prohibiting religious expression at school. It's time to demand an end to field trips to Islamic mosques. They do not provide educational or cultural value. The Islamic religion continues to be accepted and promoted in our public schools and it has to stop.

---

[457] EAG News: Our Perspective, Albert Shanker, http://www.eagnews.org, May 4, 2014

"Empowering Parents" Focus on the Family (http://www. focusonthefamily.com)

Focus on the Family is a Christian organization and an excellent resource for parents and families especially now as children face moral obstacles daily at school, on television and from social media. Focus on the Family provides a wealth of information on family topics and has numerous free downloadable "how-to" guides. One of the most recent guides is *"Gender-Confusing Messages in Schools."* http://focusonthefamily.webconnex.com/co-truetolerance2014?utm.

Now we must also question web site access on school computers. What web sites are accessible to students and just as importantly, which ones are blocked? Case in point, Andrew Lampart a senior at Nonnewaug High School in Woodbury, Connecticut was using the school's computers to prepare for a class debate on the subject of gun control. He could not access the pro-gun *National Rifle Association* website, but he could get on anti-gun and gun control websites such as *"Moms Demand Action"* and the *"Newtown Action Alliance."* Searching for the state of Connecticut political parties, he was able to access the State Democrat website, but the state GOP website was blocked.

Thinking this strange, he decided to check on access to conservative and religious websites. Christianity.com and the Vatican websites were blocked, but he immediately gained access to Islam-guide.com. Regarding websites on "abortion" issues, he quickly was able to access Planned Parenthood and Pro-Choice America, and needless to say, "right-to-life" groups were blocked. Andrew concluded, *"They're trying to, in my opinion, shelter us from what's actually going on around the country and around the world by blocking these websites. It should be the other way around. The websites should be unblocked so that students can get different viewpoints from different sides of each argument."*[458] Exposure to intellectual data from both sides used to be a tenet of comprehensive educational development.

Many parents feel timid and too insecure to question teachers,

---

[458] "High School Student Uncovered Something 'Appalling' When He Tried to Access NRA and Conservative Websites," Editorial, The Political Insider, http://www.thepoliticalinsider.com, June 19, 2014

principals and school board members. Parents need to connect with other parents harboring similar questions and concerns. Then, parents as a unified force can feel empowered to confront the school or school board and demand that their questions and concerns are addressed. The academic elite feel only they know what is best for children and many educators, feeling superior to parents, ignore and talk down to them like they speak to the children. They will not tolerate disagreement, questions or suggestions for improvement. Many teachers think of themselves as enlightened visionaries all the while towing the union line and chanting the union's talking points. Newsflash: Teachers unions are not concerned about what is best for the children. They are concerned about keeping membership and making money.

Many teachers, schools and school boards want no parental involvement in the students' academic lives. The child might develop an open mind and would then question the teacher. Parents are allowed into the sacred arena only when there's a behavioral problem such as a student bringing a plastic water gun to school, or a student wearing a tee-shirt with an American flag on it. Those are two of the horrendous things liberal school administrators and teachers have no tolerance for, and to think that most people believed all teachers put their students first.

Stuck with "Bad" Teachers:

Los Angeles Superior Court Judge Rolf M. Treu ruled that current teacher tenure statutes violate the California Education Code and deprives students of their right to an education. Stephanie Simon of Politico reported, *"The statutes permit too many grossly incompetent teachers to remain in classrooms across the state - and found that those teachers shortchange their students by putting them months or years behind their peers in math and reading."*[459]

Judge Treu stated that all judges *"should focus on the law when*

---

[459] "A Defeat for Terrible Teachers in California," Katrina Trinko, The Daily Signal, June 10, 2014 quoting Politico reporter Stephanie Simon, http://www.dailysignal.com

making decisions, ignore politics and personal opinion." Michael Hausam reporting for the Independent Journal Review reiterated, *"... the functional impossibility of firing 'grossly ineffective' teachers and the resultant letting-go of 'competent' ones especially in low-performing schools, keeps the kids from getting the quality of education to which they are entitled."*[460] Needless to say, the teachers union is appealing the ruling, but if enough people publicly stand behind Judge Treu and his decision, and demand the state put children - not teachers first, the ruling will stand and set a precedent for other states to look at their tenure laws. It is a good first step in improving education in America.

National School Choice: Parents need to know there are options

- Traditional Public Schools: Open Enrollment Options so parents can select the best school for their child.
- Public Charter Schools: Tuition free independent public schools open to all children. Students are chosen through lottery selections.
- Magnet Schools: Tuition free public schools operated by school districts providing specific curriculums like math, science, engineering and arts.
- Private School Choice: Created by individual states to allow parents to use state-funded scholarships, refundable tax credits or corporate funded scholarships to send their children to private schools. Programs vary by state - Some allow funding for all children, others are specifically for low and, or middle income families.
  - School Choice Indiana: Indiana has been a leading force for school choice and has adopted a voucher program for children from kindergarten through high school. The Institute for Quality Education in Indianapolis,

---

[460] "California Judge Rules Against Teacher's Unions and His Perspective is Incredibly Refreshing," Michael Hausam, Independent Journal Review, http://www.ijreview.com, June 10, 2014

Indiana is a non-profit organization whose mission is to improve "the quality of education for all Indiana students." (http://schoolchoiceindiana.com)

▫ Online Learning - Virtual Schools: Internet-based academies teaching students primarily through an online curriculum with the same academic standards as traditional public schools. These schools can be: state-run, district-run public schools, charter schools, magnet schools, or private schools.

  ▪ K12 - Online education (http://www..myinfo.k12.com): Very interesting information on their website. Online lessons work in conjunction with in-home instruction and teacher contact and guidance.

▫ "Blended Learning" Online education is combined with traditional classroom attendance learning.

▫ Homeschooling: Educating children at home has been a steadily growing phenomenon in the United States. All states permit homeschooling and many states require standardized testing, curriculum approval and professional evaluation of students. Many homeschooling families in certain areas have organized into local or regional groups to augment in-home learning and provide social opportunities for the students.

The National School Choice Week organization, which actually operates all year long, is a non-partisan, non-political public awareness initiative to inform the public and empower parents to be able to "choose" the best educational environment for their children. During one week each January, National School Choice Week organizes thousands of events and activities across the nation to highlight and promote the need for effective education options for ALL children. It also allows "participants to advance their own messages of educational opportunity, while uniting with like-minded groups and individuals across the country." Events are independently planned by a very diverse coalition of individuals, schools, education groups and organizations.

The 2014 National School Choice Week sponsored 5,500 events in all 50 states and even over 100 events abroad. It generated over 3,000 positive news stories for participating schools; reaching about 100 million people. Political leaders from both parties including 22 U.S. governors and 49 U.S. mayors spoke for school choice. Millions of people across the nation - students, teachers and parents learned about educational opportunities.[461] The 2015 National School Choice Week will be January 25-31, 2015.

I urge you to check out their website at http://www.schoolchoiceweek. com. National School Choice Week welcomes all questions, comments and feedback. You can contact the organizers directly:

- Andrew Campanella, National School Choice Week president email: campanella@schoolchoiceweek.com
- General inquiries email: schoolchoiceweek.com
- For information about your school's involvement - email Kristin Weiers, Manager of School Relations: kristen@ schoolchoiceweek.com
- For information about your organization's involvement email - Will Green, Manager of coalitions and external relations: will@ schoolchoiceweek.com
- For media inquiries - Israel Ortega, Director of Communications and Media Relations email: israel@schoolchoiceweek.com

You Tube:

- Watch what organizations are saying: http://youtu.be/ toNCET985KM
- Watch what schools are saying: http://youtu.be/jBkEy6yuPzg

Some of the organizations supporting National School Choice Week:

- Black Alliance for Educational Options: http://www.baeo.org

---

[461] National School Choice Week, http://www.schoolchoiceweek.com

- Children's Scholarship Fund: http://www.scholarshipfund.org
- Foundation for Excellence in Education: http://www.excelined.org
- Families Empowered: http://familiesempowered.org
- KIPP Foundation: Magnet Schools of America: http://www.kipp.org
- National Alliance for Public Charter Schools: http:// *www.* **publiccharters.***org*
- New Schools Venture Fund: http://www.newschools.org
- Students First: A Movement to Transform Public Education: http://www.studentsfirst.org
- Center for Education Reform: http://www.edreform.com
- Thomas B. Fordham Institute: http://www.edexcellence.net
- The Friedman Foundation for Educational Choice: http://www.edchoice.org

National School Choice Week is a great organization committed to the best education for every child. They provide information on education options and empower parents through a national support network of other parents, teachers, educators, schools and organizations all working together for the betterment of education for our children.

Civics Courses Need to be Taught in the Classroom: Author F. J. Rocca wrote a wonderful article clearly defining the most basic terms every American student and adult should know.[462]

Liberal: ORIGINALLY and at the time our country was founded, the term Liberal applied to *"those who believed in and defended the rights of individuals over the power of tyranny."* There were no collective rights of groups. The meaning of the term, *"The People"* meant each and every individual citizen whose rights are lawfully protected. Unfortunately the term liberal has strangely evolved to identify progressive groups and enlightened humanitarians who promote increased government control which always results in the loss of individual freedom.

---

[462] *"A Civics Lesson that Desperately Needs to be Taught in Elementary School Again,"* F.J. Rocca, Freedom Outpost, http://www.freedomoutpost.com, March 16, 2014

Pure Democracy: The term "pure democracy" is completely misunderstood since it does <u>not</u> denote individual rights. It is the apparatus used by a majority to strip away rights of the individual. It is a collective form of government, whereas "the people" means a group of persons - not individuals. Democracies function by direct vote of the people, simply meaning the majority rules whether for good or for bad. Without a republican foundation (not referring to the GOP) like our government, pure democracy is mob rule, or as our Founding Fathers called it, "mobocracy." Only a government cemented by a solid constitution with built-in checks and balances can insure the rights of each individual citizen.

Take for example how Liberals hate the Second Amendment and are working diligently to impose ever-increasing gun control laws to nullify it. Most people do not understand the detrimental consequences if they were to succeed. The Founders specifically worded that amendment making its meaning crystal clear. Citizens' right to arms is the final defense of a "free" populace to protect ALL their rights under the Constitution. History has proven time and time again that when citizens are disarmed, the government expands in power and corruption. Even the most seemingly-secure governments can be taken over by special interest groups (mob mentality) imposing their desired definition of laws and government regulations on all citizens. Disarming the populace guarantees total government control. Outlawing legal gun ownership will not curb gun violence. Violence will increase since thugs and mentally impaired people will continue to illegally have and use guns. Actually it will be easier for them to kill since they will know their victims are unarmed and cannot defend themselves.

Take an honest look at the tragic spree shootings that have occurred over the past few years. All had one common element - the shooters were mentally impaired and they should not have had weapons. In all cases, if legally armed citizens were present, fewer people would have died. Logic shows that mental illness is the culprit and that is where the government should be focusing, not attacking law-abiding Americans. The same holds true for gangs. Where the government outlaws legal gun ownership, law abiding citizens are not safer. Armed thugs control the streets and the violence is appalling. Instead of making more victims out of law-abiding citizens, why is the government focus not on illegal guns and gang activity. Armed criminals don't even feel safe in some of our cities.

True Republic: A True Republic is rule by law and guarantees the rights of the individual including the right of "due process" as defined by its Constitution. The United States of America has a republican form of government. Individual citizens vote for people to represent them. The Constitution and its' amendments are the laws containing the set of rules the government and the citizens are obligated to adhere by. F.J. Rocca hit the nail on the proverbial head when he wrote, *"Politicians who endlessly advocate what they call "democracy" are trying instead to insure their own power against the very democratic principles they preach. They want power. They want power and once they get it, are unlikely to care much about individual rights."*

All elected officials swear an oath of allegiance to defend and protect the Constitution which includes the "inconvenient" covenant to abide by the law. It really upsets me to see a growing trend by liberal politicians emboldened by powerful special interest groups to accept and enforce only the laws they agree with. For instance, per the Constitution and established law it is illegal for non-citizens to vote in U.S. elections. Liberal politicians don't like that law so they blatantly disregard it, just as they ignore other illegal immigration laws. They feel entitled to break the law to win votes, and votes mean more power. The real reason Democrats fight so hard against photo ID laws to prove citizenship to be able to vote is because they would lose an enormous block of illegal voters. It is a sad commentary on America when illegal aliens have more rights including medical care, food and housing while homeless American veterans wander the streets with nothing.

It is also against the law for the President of the United States to unilaterally release five high value terrorists (not prisoners of war since they represent no legitimate country) without a thirty day notice to Congress. The current administration and liberals in the government with power and a penchant for abiding only by the laws they agree with, are racking up violations of the law at an incredible pace. I do not understand why Congress isn't more involved in this matter and we should be very vocal about Washington's obligation to adhere to the laws.

Unfortunately President Obama, who wanted his legacy to be National health care (laws were broken to get Obamacare passed) and desperately wanted to be liked around the world, is going to be remembered only as the "lawless President." Samuel Adams words have come to fruition. ***"…It does not require a majority to prevail, but rather an irate tireless minority keen to set brush fires in people's minds…"[463]*** Minority special interest groups, liberal politicians, businessmen and academics endorsed by the current administration and federal government are steamrolling Americans across the country.

The United States of America is a republic not a democracy. So when you hear people refer to America as a democracy, please step up and remind them that the U.S. is a republic. If they demand proof, here are some Constitutional heavy hitters to set the record straight:[464]

- *"Remember, democracy never lasts long. It soon wastes, exhausts, and murders itself. There never was a democracy yet that did not commit suicide."*

  —John Adams

- *"Democracies have ever been spectacles of turbulence and contention; have ever been found incompatible with personal security or the rights of property; and have, in general, been as short in their lives as they have been violent in their deaths."*

  —James Madison

- *"A democracy is a volcano which conceals the fiery materials of its own destruction. These will produce an eruption and carry desolation in their way. The known propensity of a democracy is to licentiousness which the ambitious call and the ignorant believe to be liberty."*

  —Fisher Ames

---

[463] Samuel Adams quotes, http://www.brainyquote.com/quotes/
[464] "Republic vs. Democracy," United States Constitution, The Free Republic, http://www.freerepublic.com

- *"In democracy ... there are commonly tumults and disorders ... Therefore a pure democracy is generally a very bad government. It is often the most tyrannical government on earth."*

  —Noah Webster

- *"The experience of all former ages had shown that of all human governments, democracy was the most unstable, fluctuating and short-lived."*

  —John Quincy Adams

- *"A simple democracy...is one of the greatest evils."*

  —Benjamin Rush

Hillsdale College: Constitution 101- "America's Declaration of Independence and Constitution are the twin pillars of American Liberty"

As mentioned in Part One, Hillsdale College is committed to the Constitutional principles of individual liberty and limited government guaranteed by our Constitution. Hillsdale College President Dr. Larry Arnn has launched a major national campaign to educate millions of Americans about the Constitution and what it means for all of us now. **"Constitution 101" is the cornerstone online course of this national educational effort and is absolutely FREE to everyone.** The course easily works around your schedule and it will be one of the most informative and beneficial learning experiences you could undertake.

Constitution 101 is just one of the many courses offered by Hillsdale College dedicated to Constitutional education which is sadly lacking in America today. It is imperative that we know our history, the Constitution and our legally guaranteed rights to be able to protect our liberty and secure our freedom which honestly is being attacked, and not-so-slowly being destroyed. I applaud Hillsdale College and urge you to check out their website to learn about their commendable mission to educate everyone who wants to learn. Aside from the numerous free courses offered, the college hosts many other programs including: Constructive Alternatives; the Hoogland Center for Teacher Excellence - seminars on civics and history for high school teachers; National Leadership Seminars; the Allan P. Kirby, Jr. Center for Constitutional Studies and Citizenship in Washington, D.C.; and publishes *Imprimis*, an extremely informative monthly newsletter available free on line or in hardcopy.

- **https://hillsdale.edu**: Hillsdale College official website
- **https://online.hillsdale.edu**: Complete information and registration for Hillsdale College on-line Constitution courses

Conservatism vs. Liberal Ideology

Hold steadfast to your beliefs and values. Let no one force you to relinquish them. Michael Reisig wrote an article on the differences between political conservatism and liberalism that should make you proud to be conservative. "*...liberal ideology in America appears to continually be attempting to "create" truths, rather than establish principles. You can't create new truths for every generation, you have to apply established values/principles that you adapt to new circumstances – it's the consistency that's important here – the refusal to compromise to satisfy particular stratums of society or dissatisfied new generations...*" [465]

Allen West (http://www.allenwest.) compiled an interesting list of questions to ask a liberal progressive.[466] A few of his questions are:

1. "If former President George W. Bush was un-American for adding $4 trillion to the national debt, then what is President Barack Hussein Obama who is on his way to adding $8 trillion - and still has two more years to go?"
2. "If as Obama states, *'we leave no man behind,'* [referring to the deserter Bowe Bergdahl traded by Obama for 5 high value terrorists] then what of Marine Sergeant Andrew Tahmooressi

---

[465] "The Terrible Ideology of Liberals," Michael Reisig, Eagle Rising, http://www.eaglerising.com, May 5, 2014

[466] "5 questions to ask a liberal progressive," Allen West, http://www.allenwest.com, June 19, 2014

[marine in a Mexican jail], Pastor Saeed Abedini [imprisoned in Iran] and Kenneth Bae [imprisoned in North Korea].

3. "When the average price of gasoline hit $2.50 a gallon, liberals and their media accomplices went apoplectic ... on George W. Bush. So why silent now, when it's $3.67?"

4. "If it is racist to disagree with the proven failed policies of... Barack Hussein Obama, then what is it when liberal progressives disrespect, dismiss, denigrate, demean, disparage, discredit and seek to destroy black conservative Republicans...?"

Erosion of the Virtues and Ideals that
Created Western dominance:

Journalist Bruce Thornton gives us a warning: *"The astonishing wealth of the West, more widely distributed than in any other civilization, the abandonment of religion as the foundation of morals and virtues, the transformation of political freedom into self-centered license, and the commodification of hedonism that makes available to everyman luxuries and behaviors once reserved for a tiny elite, have made self-indulgence and the present more important than self-sacrifice and the future. Declining birthrates, a preference for spending on social welfare transfers rather than on defense, and a willingness to beggar our children and grandchildren with debt in order to finance these entitlements – all bespeak a people whose wealth deludes them into thinking that they can imprudently ignore the future and indefinitely afford these luxuries that in fact insidiously weaken the foundations of our social and political order..."*[467]

Ambrose Evans-Pritchard, international business editor of the *Daily Telegraph*, UK leaves us with words of encouragement: *"To the American people I bid a fond farewell. Guard your liberties. It is the trust of each generation to pass a free republic to the next. And if I know you right, you will rouse yourself from slumber to ensure exactly that."*

---

[467] "Western Arrogance and Decline," Bruce Thornton, *Front Page Magazine*, http://www.frontpagemag.com, March 17, 2014

Good news and accomplishments

The Economy:

It's difficult to come up with positive news about the economy and try as I may, I cannot think of any economic accomplishments the past few years. Good news I do have is that organizations such as The Heritage Foundation offer sound solutions on economic and tax policies that would restore our economy to a healthy productive state. More than 100 policy experts contribute to the Heritage Foundation with specific plans to accomplish that goal. The Heritage Foundation *"Saving the American Dream"* plan outlines specific and workable reforms and cuts to numerous areas of government to cut spending and rein in the debt. The largess and scope of the federal government must be reduced. For instance, Heritage Foundation economists have extensively researched the housing market issue and can prove that government-sponsored entities like Fannie Mae and Freddie Mac warp the housing market and cost taxpayers trillions of dollars.

The government has no right or financial privilege to be in the housing business. The Heritage economists summary findings: *"We found that removing the government guarantee from housing finance should have a minimal impact on the overall U.S. economy – and it would likely result in lower housing costs, less personal debt, and higher personal income."*[468] The answer is not to replace Fannie Mae and Freddie Mac with new improved government programs, the solution is to eliminate them completely and encourage private investment and innovation. That alone would result in much needed reforms at the Federal Housing Administration (FHA).

Energy Independence:

We must speak out about our energy problem! It is imperative that we become energy independent since we can no longer afford economically

---

[468] "How to Free the Housing Market from Government – and Lower Your Mortgage Payments," John Ligon, The Foundry, The Heritage Foundation, http://www.heritage .org, February 18, 2014

or politically to be reliant on foreign oil. Take a look at what's happening around world. The Middle East oil cartel is very unstable and may not last much longer. Russia can shut-off Europe's oil supply at any time which is a pretty good reason Putin isn't worried about Europe telling him what to do. Alternative energy sources such as wind mills and solar panels are great except they are only economically feasible in very limited areas. No matter how hard the government and environmentalists wish and hope for "alternative" energy to replace fossil fuels, the fact is that even after they've wasted billions of our tax dollars on green energy we are no closer to that reality.

The next time someone lectures you about how his electric car is helping to save energy and the environment, kindly remind him that "electricity" is not a natural resource. It needs to be produced and that is usually by burning fossil fuels including coal. So while the President is running the coal producers out of business which also contributes to unemployment, he is effectively plugging a much needed resource. His actions are currently and will continue to increase the cost of fuel for everyone.

We do not have the technology and money to replace oil with windmills and solar panels. Sorry, but we do have an abundance of oil and natural gas, so much of that "bad" stuff that we could be energy-independent within years. On-shore and off-shore drilling for oil and natural gas, fracking and clean coal is what we have and what we need to put us on the road to energy independence. It is more than an economic decision; it is a national security necessity. I'm not advocating the end of alternative energy research and development. I see alternative energy as local or regional resources. For instance, you need rushing water to efficiently produce hydro-energy which is not available everywhere. The southwest deserts do not have water but there is a lot of sun where solar power could be harnessed. The problem is that energy would only be available locally. On the Plains, miles of open land can accommodate the enormous amount of space needed for windmill farms, and wind is in abundant supply. Environmentalists do not consider "consequences." The environmental geniuses that pushed wind power are very quiet since finding out that windmills kill thousands of birds - Another costly "Oops." The bottom line is that the average American cannot afford alternative energy; and since the government is purposely making oil and gas more expensive for consumers, we soon won't be able to afford what we have now for our energy needs.

Besides supporting the coal industry, we need to back realistic energy resources promoted by organizations such as **Americans for Prosperity** who thankfully will not cease promoting the Keystone XL Pipeline. Why does the administration so vehemently oppose the pipeline which would create 42,100 average annual jobs over a one to two year construction period, open our path to energy independence, and will not have a major impact on the environment as environmentalists hysterically claim? As reported by Amy Payne, *The Foundry* – The Heritage Foundation, their own State Department impact reports have concluded *"that the pipeline...to deliver up to 830,000 barrels of oil per day to Gulf Coast refineries would pose no significant environmental risk and would not contribute substantially to carbon dioxide emissions."*[469]

We were told over and over how beneficial biofuels were for us when the government mandated "environmentally-friendly" ethanol production. Oops, it turns out that ethanol production and use has had disastrous consequences as Amy Payne reports, *"The mandate promised less dependence on foreign oil, lower fuel prices, and fewer greenhouse emissions. Instead of delivering on these promises, the mandate delivered concentrated benefits to politically connected producers and high costs to America's energy consumers."*[470] We need to support the groups pressing for oil independence and press our representatives to vote likewise.

We need to be vigilant about what is going on with the national economy as a whole and energy is an enormous part of our economy. Take the time to research alternative plans. The **Consumer Energy Alliance** (http://www.consumerenergyalliance.org) is a great place to start for information, education, advocacy and action. We need to phone, write, email, and tweet our Congressional representatives, the

---

[469] "What's Actually Good for the Environment May Surprise You," Amy Payne, The Foundry, The Heritage Foundation, http://www.heritage.org, April 22, 2014

[470] "What's Actually Good for the Environment May Surprise You," Amy Payne, The Foundry, The Heritage Foundation quoting Nicolas Loris, a Heritage Foundation Herbert and Joyce Morgan Fellow, http://www.heritage.org, April 22, 2014

President, the Environmental Protection Agency, and the federal Bureau of Ocean Energy Management. Drill today or tomorrow we'll pay – and pay dearly.

The Healthcare Crisis: Obamacare is not the answer

Getting Health Care Reform Right - The Heritage Foundation[471]

Contrary to President Obama's claim that there were no alternative plans to his Affordable Health Care Act plan, Heritage Foundation was one of several groups that publicly offered alternative plans.

Facts: Obamacare is unpopular, unworkable, and unaffordable, subverts doctor-patient relationships, limits patient choice, centralizes control, increases costs, creates two new entitlements, and it will cost taxpayers nearly $1.8 trillion over the next 10 years. Obamacare transforms the healthcare system into a centralized federal government system, and "reduces states to mere vehicles for implementing federal policy." Americans are now required under penalty of law to purchase "federally approved" health insurance.

Solutions: Recommendations (Summary recommendations from Heritage Foundation Solutions 2014 policy recommendations).

1. Repeal Obamacare based on Congressional Budget Office projections that the ACA will cost taxpayers $1.8 trillion over the next ten years even though President Obama claimed it would reduce the budget. The ACA also gives the Department of Health and Human Services (DHHS) unrestricted power to impose new regulations that will not allow patient choice, will increase premiums, and millions more people will lose their existing insurance.

2. Reform the tax code to equalize tax liability for both employer-based insurance and individual coverage insurance. Each state

---

[471] "Solutions 2014: Expert Analysis, Powerful Messages, Winning Policies," The Heritage Foundation, http://www.solutions.heritage.org

should have a "high-risk" pool to ensure people with pre-existing conditions can still obtain affordable health insurance.

3. Make health insurance portable (Change employer-based health care from a "defined-benefit" to a "defined contribution). This would permit people to "maintain ownership of their insurance" no matter where employed.

4. Allow free markets to supply insurance and health services that people want and need. The ACA defines health insurance plans and many people are paying for services that they do not want and will never use.

5. Since Medicaid cannot provide quality health care, Medicaid beneficiaries should have access to private health insurance.

6. "Protect the right of conscience and unborn children." The government should not have the power to make people pay for actions that violate their ethical and religious beliefs. There should be a permanent law prohibiting taxpayer money be used to pay for abortions or health coverage that includes "elective" abortions.

In 2014 the **American LegacyPac** created the **"Save our Healthcare Project"** to challenge Obamacare's detrimental effects on health insurance coverage and benefits, skyrocketing premiums, and failed websites. This citizens-group chaired by Dr. Ben Carson demands that healthcare be centered on doctor-patient relationships - not government-patient relationships. The Project has alternative suggestions and ideas, educational information and videos and maintains a citizen's petition to "Save our Healthcare." You can directly access the website at www.savingourhealthcare.org or email info@americanlegacypac.org for information.

The **Manhattan Institute for Policy Research: "Rhetoric and Reality – The Obamacare Evaluation Project"** has also done a tremendous amount of research on Obamacare and publishes reports on its performance, or lack of. Their website also maintains an "Obamacare Impact Map" showing the cost of Obamacare state by state. www.manhattan-institute.org/html/obamacare

The **Christian Seniors Association (CSA):** Published a common sense "Simple Health Care Plan" to replace Obamacare. The "Eight-Step Health Care" Plan includes the restoration of $716 billion stolen from Medicare by the government to fund Obamacare. Tax-deductible individual health insurance as well as tax-deductible medical costs including doctor visits will encourage better health. Expand tax-deferred Health Savings Accounts (HSA). Since competition results in lower costs, more choices and improved quality of services, insurance companies need to compete "across state lines." Subsidize pre-existing conditions as well as low-income people to be able to purchase health insurance. Medical malpractice lawsuit awards must be capped since these lawsuits are a big reason why health care costs are so expensive.

The Christian Seniors Association is a wonderful resource for seniors providing information and expert advice on issues of concern for seniors such as health, healthcare, finances, and consumer protection. Visit the CSA website at: http://www.christianseniorsassociation.org

If you know people who still think Obamacare is the way to go, you might want to give them a few more facts about it:

- The Internal Revenue Service (IRS) that oversees and enforces Obamacare is the same IRS that targets political opponents, conservative and Christian groups, has purposely destroyed incriminating evidence of criminal activity, and spends billions of dollars on perks, raises and bonuses. Contrary to President Obama's claims, it is a real scandal and it is criminal.
- Obamacare health insurance exchanges are required to give the IRS your personal information under the guise of health insurance tax assessment.
- If you received a subsidy amount above what you should have even though it most likely was their error, you will be required to pay it back. The Foundry reported in May 2014 that at least one million people are getting an incorrect subsidy amount.[472]
- Remember when VP candidate Sarah Palin was crucified by the administration and the media for warning about

---

[472] "Yes, Some People Will Have to Pay Back Their Obamacare Subsidies," Amy Payne, The Foundry, Heritage Foundation, http://www.blog.heritage.org, May 21, 2014

Obamacare "death panels?" She was right - just look at the Veteran's Administration (VA) scandal. Bureaucrats and agency employees decided who got medical attention and when. 40 veterans at just one facility in Phoenix, Arizona died either waiting for care or because they were denied care. There could be 1,000 or more deaths across the country at other VA facilities. This is what happens when the federal government is in control and this is what will happen with Obamacare.

Christian America

The Supreme Court ruled in May 2014 that *prayers said to open town council meetings do NOT violate the Constitution*. This decision reaffirms the court's 1983 ruling upholding opening prayers in the state of Nebraska legislature. **That court said prayer was part of the nation's fabric, not a violation of the First Amendment.**

March for Marriage: In June 2014, thousands of people rallied on Capitol Hill to support traditional marriage. The people who attended this "March for Marriage" event were not homophobes; they were simply pro-traditional marriage. There was very little media coverage of the rally compared to massive media coverage of "same-sex" marriage protests and homosexual parades. It is refreshing to see that people are starting to stand up for what they believe in – in defiance of political correctness. These events will increase across the nation to inspire, support and spread the word that we are here, we are staying, our numbers are growing and we will no longer be bullied into silence and forced to embrace ideologies that we do not believe in.

The Manhattan Declaration: A Call of Christian Conscience

In September 2009 a delegation of Orthodox, Catholic and Evangelical Christians met in New York. Individual Christian clergy and lay people acting not as representatives of their respective organizations but representing Christians from around the country who decided it was time for Christians to unify and make a stand. The resulting effort of this unique delegation was the *"Manhattan Declaration: A*

Call of Christian Conscience" published on November 20, 2009 with the signature of every delegate.

"We act together in obedience to the one true God, the triune God of holiness and love, who has laid total claim on our lives and by that claim, calls us with believers in all ages and all nations to seek and defend the good of all who bear his image. We set forth this declaration in light of the truth that is grounded in Holy Scripture, in natural human reason... and in the very nature of the human person. We call upon all people of goodwill, believers and non-believers alike, to consider carefully and reflect critically on the issues we here address as we, with St. Paul, commend this appeal to everyone's conscience in the sight of God...Because the sanctity of human life, the dignity of marriage as a union of husband and wife, and the freedom of conscience and religion are foundational principles of justice and the common good, we are compelled by our Christian faith to speak and act in their defense."[473]

Summary of affirmation:

1. All people possess inherent rights of equal dignity and life
2. Marriage is the union of a man and a woman which has from the beginning of history been regarded as the most fundamental institution in society
3. Religious liberty is an inherent freedom

The signers officially proclaimed their obligation to defend these Christian truths and pledged to each other and all Christians to speak and act accordingly – no more silence.

All Christians need to check out the Manhattan Declaration website at http://www.manhattandeclaration.org. Read about the original Christian delegates' representative of all denominations who drafted the declaration and the growing list of clergy and laypeople who have added their names to the declaration. The profound words of those committed to protect the Christian religion and the dignity of every human being inspires a sense of hope and faith for the future of Christians in America. I am confident that after exploring the website

---

[473] "Manhattan Declaration: A Call of Christian Conscience," The Manhattan Declaration Organization, http://www.manhattandeclaration.org

you will not hesitate to join this growing force of Christians by adding your name to the declaration.

CURE: Center for Urban Renewal and Education – The Black Pastor Network

Star Parker founder of CURE has created a wonderful new program to empower black churches and the people they serve. Under the guidance of William Allen, the "Black Pastor Network" is a council of African-American pastors committed to "reach & teach influential black churches to stand up for their values." Many black pastors and Christians are ostracized because they believe that marriage is between one man and one woman; they support life - not abortion; and they know that welfare damages the freedom and dignity of every person. William Allen is a professor of Political Philosophy at Michigan State University. He has written numerous books regarding America's founding, the uniqueness of America, and the government which was established to preserve the individual above the state.

The Black Pastor Network is a model for all Christian Churches to embrace. View the website at www.cure.org or email: star-parker@urbancure.org. All Christians need to support each other. Our pastors and clergy are called to take the lead.

Priests for Life: A ministry of support for the pro-life movement and a member organization of the *Gospel of Life Ministries*. Their mission is two-fold: (1) To galvanize the clergy to "preach, teach and mobilize people more effectively in the effort to end abortion and euthanasia," and (2) provide guidance and offer a wide variety of activities to engage clergy and lay persons of all faiths and ethnicities to protect the "most vulnerable members of the human family." Fr. Frank Pavone is the national director for Priests for Life and works closely with the pastoral staff which includes **Dr. Alveda King**, (Rev. Martin Luther King, Jr.'s niece) who is a dedicated pastoral associate and tireless voice promoting the sanctity of life. The number of educational programs and outreach organizations is amazing. The Priests for Life website is well worth a look. http://www.priestsforlife.org. You can contact them by email: mail@priestsforlife.org.

Coalition of African American Pastors (CAAP): is a national organization of Black pastors. CAAP was represented at the 2014 "March for Marriage" event in Washington, D.C. When asked his opinion on the "end game" to redefine marriage, Rev. Owens replied, "It's a terrible slippery slope. They intend to turn this whole society as if we have no gender. It's terrible that this president has started this country on an immoral course. This is the most immoral president we've ever had."[474]

The UN vs. the Vatican: In May 2014 the Vatican was called before a United Nations committee hearing to answer charges that the Catholic Church's opposition to abortion and its 2,000-year-old doctrine against abortion constitutes a violation of the *UN Charter Against Torture*. So, the selective human-rights obsessed UN is saying that opposing abortion constitutes torture, but abortions (especially late term that virtually rip the fetus apart) are not torture. The Vatican's response was immediate: "*...goal is to prevent children from being tortured or killed before birth, as is stipulated in the 'Convention'...For example, in Canada, 622 living babies were delivered after failed abortion attempts, between 2000 and 2001. Some methods of late-term abortions constitute forms of torture, particularly in the case ...where the fetus, still alive, is dismembered to be pulled out of the womb in pieces.*" The Vatican was right to stand up to the hypocritical United Nations.

Crisis Magazine: http://www.crisismagazine.com is a lay (non-clergy) organization created to inform and educate the Catholic community. "*It is imperative that the entire Catholic community in the United States come to realize the grave threats to the Church's public moral witness presented by a radical secularism, which finds increasing expression in the political and cultural spheres...we see the need for an engaged, articulate and well-formed Catholic laity endowed with a strong critical sense...and with the courage to counter reductive secularism which delegitimize the Church's participation in public debate about issues which are determining the future of American society.*"

---

[474] "Black Pastor on Obama: 'This is the Most Immoral President We've Ever Had,'" Tim Constantine, The Capital Hill Show, http://www.tpnn.com, June 20, 2014

Social Values

I never paid much attention to beauty contests and the like because I always felt they were disingenuous. Society expresses to girls that inner beauty is what counts while at the same time idolizes physical beauty emphasized by Hollywood and beauty contests. This year though good stories have come out about a few of the Miss USA contestants that are worth noting:

- The winner and Miss USA 2014 is Miss Nevada Nia Sanchez. Aside from being beautiful, Nia holds a fourth-degree black belt in taekwondo and promotes the importance of women being able to defend themselves.
- Miss Indiana, Mekayla Diehl drew a lot of attention for being a "normal" size. Mekayla proved on live television that you do not have to be skinny to be beautiful. She is also an advocate for child abuse awareness since she was sexually abused as a child.
- Miss North Dakota, Audra Mari overcame bullying in high school by competing in ice hockey.
- Miss Pennsylvania, Valerie Gatto brought a very special message. Valerie was "a product of rape." Her mother was raped at knifepoint resulting in pregnancy. Instead of abortion her mother chose life. Valerie advocates educating women about sexual assault and as quoted in *Today.com,* she said, "*I believe God put me here for a reason. To inspire people, to encourage them, to give them hope that everything is possible and you can't let your circumstances define your life.*" Well said, Valerie!

American Exceptionalism

The simple phrase "*American Exceptionalism*" makes liberal heads explode. They react with disgust and even rage. They do not accept American Exceptionalism calling it a myth or a conservative fairy tale. For example, Michael Lind of the New America Foundation published an article, "*The Case Against American Exceptionalism,*" in which he claimed that American Exceptionalists are no-nothing boastful boobs "not allowed to peep beyond borders, to learn from the successes and mistakes of people in other countries."[475] He omits one important fact - After WWII the success of "other" countries like Japan, South Korea and throughout Europe was possible only because of the United States.

Kim R. Holmes' article in the *Washington Times* perfectly refutes Michael Lind's assessment of American Exceptionalism. We don't reject foreigners. Foreigners substantiate our exceptionalism. *"They recognize what's unique about our history: a distinctive confluence of culture, government and economy, and an ethos of personal responsibility...These, not government actions, gave rise to the wealthiest and most powerful nation on earth."*[476] Immigrants confirm the "truth" that America is exceptional - meaning different from all other countries.

The central claim to American Exceptionalism is not that the U.S. is better than other countries. It is different from other countries and being different is what made America successful. Post World War II Europe is proof of America's Exceptionalism. Kin says of the U.S. *"...It carried most of the military burden for the alliance of free nations that contained the Soviet Union. Our allies trusted America because they knew it was different from other powers victorious in war: It was a liberator, not a conqueror."*

Kim Holmes is a former Assistant Secretary of State, a current fellow at the Heritage Foundation, and author of a must-read book, "**Rebound: Getting America Back to Great**" published in 2013.

Defining American Exceptionalism for Michael Lind, Oliver Stone and other liberal minds: It is ironic that we unenlightened "no-nothing boastful boobs" know the definition of American Exceptionalism whereas Mr. Lind and his colleagues are so off the mark. This is why learning "history" is so important! Liberals define American Exceptionalism as uninformed arrogance by people who feel that America is bigger, better, stronger, and of all things, good; whereas they know better and America is oppressive, militaristic, imperialistic, and bad. They judge America in terms of personal ideology and as

---

[475] "HOLMES: Why the fear of American Exceptionalism?" Kim R. Holmes, the *Washington Times*, November 13, 2013
[476] "HOLMES: Why the fear of American Exceptionalism?" Kim R. Holmes, the Washington Times, November 13, 2013

supporters of the world community - no country is better than any of the others, and not even "facts" can alter their view.

The facts are: The Founders, well-versed in world history and government knew they were creating something new and of "extraordinary significance." Charles Murray proves in his book, **American Exceptionalism** that *"for the first century after the Constitution went into effect, European observers and Americans alike saw the United States as exceptional, with political and civic cultures that had no counterparts anywhere else."*[477] "Foreigners not just Americans described and continue to describe America as *"being unlike all other countries and peoples."* America is not equal to other countries. It is different. It always has been and if the time ever comes when America is just another country, then America will cease to exist.

Nick Adams' book *"The American Boomerang: How the World's Greatest 'Turnaround' Nation Will Do It Again,"* takes a look at America through the eyes of an Australian who explains why America is exceptional and what America means to the free world.

Nick shares the sentiment of British Prime Minister Margaret Thatcher: *"What's good for America is good for the world."* If America is weak, the world is weak. When America is strong, the world is also strong. *"The world becomes a much more dangerous place when America is weak. Everyone in the world should care about America staying number one."*[478]

When asked what makes America exceptional during an interview with Jamie Glazov, *Front Page Magazine*, Nick stated the positive things that made our nation unique: *"Individualism...Patriotism...Optimism...Limited government, God...Faith..Life...Bold...Brave. Equality of opportunity, not equality of income. Choosing extraordinary over mediocre. It's about seeing the world in terms of good and evil, right and wrong – not rich and poor, strong and weak. **American Exceptionalism is God over man and man over government."***

"Falling in Love with America Again," by Jim DeMint current

---

[477] "American Exceptionalism: An Experiment in History," Charles Murray, American Enterprise Institute, http://www.aei.org June 27, 2014

[478] "The American Boomerang," Jamie Glazov, *Front Page Magazine*, http://www.frontpagemag.com, June 11, 2014

President and CEO of the Heritage Foundation is another great book. Through real-life examples, he brings people ("hands-on citizens") working together toward the shared goal of returning to our founding principles and restoring and protecting our economy and culture. "... *each of us regardless of political party, age, race, religion or ethnicity must rediscover the power we represent. The country's future is at risk, not just because of constant pressure from 'the Bigs' (big government, big banks, big labor, big education and big Wall Street cronies), but because so many of us fear it's too late to solve problems so huge....*" It's not too late and we can do it.

After 9/11 when Americans were questioning their country and society in general, Dinesh D'Souza's 2003 book "**What's So Great about America**" reinforced the sentiment that *"America is the greatest, freest, and most decent society in existence."* He illustrates why American ideals and patriotism should be embraced and why Americans should be proud.

America: Imagine the World Without Her

Dinesh D'Souza and Gerald Molen (Academy award winning producer of Schindler's List) released their movie, *America: Imagine the World Without Her* in July 2014. This well researched and documented film comes at a perfect time as our nation stands *"at the crossroads of hope or disaster, whose destination will soon be decided."* Dinesh takes 21st Century Americans "into the future by first visiting our past."

We Ride to DC: Fixing America starts with the truth

Anyone familiar with investigative filmmaker Dennis Michael Lynch's (DML) films *They Come to America* and *They Come to America II* will be excited to see his 2014 release, *We Ride to DC*. DML focuses on the mainstream media's distortion of the truth by ignoring the facts. This film will encourage Americans to get involved. Dennis Michael Lynch is the founder and CEO of **TV360Media** specializing in the production and distribution of digital films. Mr. Lynch is dedicated to "truth" and sharing truth with the American people. As such, when you purchase one copy of his film, you get two free to share with others. The truth is not just for a few - it is for all who want to hear. Check out <u>www.</u>

weridetodc.com to learn about this film and the DML organization. www.DMLDAILY.com is DML's online magazine for up to date information on what's happening in America.

> *"The only thing necessary for the triumph of evil is for good men to do nothing."*
>
> —Edmund Burke

Organizations and Resources

American Center for Law and Justice (ACLJ) http://www.aclj.org
The ACLJ concentrates on Constitutional and human rights in the U.S. and around the world, provides legal services and supports training law students to protect religious liberty and human rights. *"The ACLJ is pro-life and dedicated to the ideal that religious freedom and freedom of speech are inalienable, God-given rights for all people."* The ACLJ does not charge for its services. I think this is a most commendable organization all conservatives can support.

American Enterprise Institute: (AEI) http://www.aei.org
A private, nonpartisan, not-for-profit institution dedicated to research and education on issues of government, politics, economics and social welfare. AEI founded in 1938 has some of America's "most accomplished policy experts." AEI is dedicated to serving leaders and the American public through research and education on important issues. The American Enterprise Institute conducts research through seven primary research divisions:

1. Economics
2. Foreign and Defense Policy
3. Politics and Public Opinion
4. Education
5. Health

6. Energy and the Environment
7. Society and Culture

Americans for Prosperity: http://www.americansforprosperity.org
Organization committed to educating citizens about economic policy
and supporting those citizen activists to advocate for public policies
supporting the principles of entrepreneurship and fiscal and regulatory
restraint. Americans for Prosperity strongly supports:

- Cutting taxes and government spending
- Stopping government intrusion into the economic lives of
  citizens
- Watching for and exposing government waste, fraud and abuse
- Removing unnecessary government barriers to entrepreneurship
- Restoring fairness to the Judicial system

AFP's network includes all 50 states relentlessly educating citizens
on their individual elected official policy platform and voting record
and mobilizes citizens to *"effectively make their voices heard in public
policy issue campaigns."*

CATO Institute: http://www.cato.org
A public policy research organization dedicated to the *"principles of
individual liberty, limited government, free markets and peace."* CATO
scholars and analysts conduct independent, nonpartisan research on a
wide range of policy issues.

Christians United for Israel (CUFI): http://www.*cufi*.org
Speak up for Israel...*"For Zion's sake I will not keep silent, for Jerusalem's
sake I will not remain quiet til her righteousness shines out like the dawn,
her salvation like a blazing torch"* (Isaiah 62:1)
Israel is under constant threat from Hamas and a never-ending
list of terrorist organizations. Israel like the United States is a defender
nation not an aggressor nation, no matter how much the U.N. and
mainstream media push the Palestinian agenda of victimization. Israel
is in the right and Christians need to stand by her side.

Citizens United: http://www.citizensunited.org
"Dedicated to restoring our government to citizen control."

- Citizens United Productions (CUP): Produces fact-based documentaries.
- Citizens United Foundation (CUF): Dedicated to making Americans aware of public policy issues relating to *"traditional values: strong national defense, Constitutionally limited government, free market economics, belief in God and Judeo-Christian values, and the recognition of the family as the basic social unit or our society."*
- The Presidential Coalition: Educates Americans on the necessity of *"principled conservative Republican leadership at all levels of government."*
- Citizens United Political Victory Fund: Supports "true" conservative candidates running for federal office.

Concerned Women for America (CWA): http://www.cwfa.org
Legislative Action Committee of informed and involved women - Mothers, Grandmothers, daughters committed to *"Upholding Life and Liberty for our Families and Nation."*

Constitutional Coalition: http://www.constitutionalcoalition.com
Focusing on the Declaration of Independence and the Constitution, the Constitutional Coalition's mission is to educate Americans about our Constitution, *"acknowledging absolutes as the basis for our laws and God as the giver of freedom..."*

Faith and Freedom Coalition: http://www.ffcoalition.com
"Freedom regards religion as the companion in all its battles and all its triumphs as the very cradle of its infancy and the source of all its claims... because religion alone is the safeguard of morality, and morality is the best and surest pledge for the survival of freedom."

—*Alexis de Tocqueville*

The Faith and Freedom Coalition believes *"that the greatness of America lies not in the federal government but in the character of our people - the simple virtues of faith, hard work, marriage, family, personal responsibility, and helping the least among us...Never before has it been more critical for us to speak out for these values...the Faith and Freedom Coalition is committed to educating, equipping, and mobilizing people of faith and like-minded individuals to be effective citizens..."*

Faith and Freedom Coalition Standing for American Principles:

- Respect for the sanctity and dignity of life, family, and marriage as the foundations of a free society
- Limited government, lower taxes and fiscal responsibility
- Education reform - putting children first
- Help the poor, needy, and "those who have been left behind"
- Free markets and free minds to create opportunity for all
- Victory in the struggle with terrorism and tyranny while supporting our democratic allies including Israel

Family Security Matters: http://www.familysecuritymatters.org
"Engaging American Families in our Nation's Security"
As the name implies, securing the safety of families is a top priority. Numerous well-known writers and journalists contribute to Family Security Matters on a variety of subjects including Radical Islam in America - which is a priority.

Fellowship of the Minds: http://fellowshipoftheminds.com
Conservatives from different backgrounds coming together for interesting political, cultural and economic news and commentary.

Freedom Center: http://www.freedomcenter.org, email: info@ horowitzfreedomcenter.org
The David Horowitz Freedom Center is dedicated to the defense of free societies. *"The Freedom Center combats the efforts of the radical left and its Islamist allies to destroy American values and disarm this country as it attempts to defend itself in a time of terror...Combining forceful analysis and bold activism, the Freedom Center provides strong insight into today's*

most pressing issues on its family of websites and in the activist campaigns it wages on campuses, in the news media, and in national politics..." Freedom Center has over 4 million pamphlets in circulation and has produced several widely reviewed and influential books.

- **Academic Bill of Rights:** The Freedom Center maintains a special focus on protecting students from indoctrination and intimidation on college campuses. The Center gives a voice to Conservative students and supports academic freedom for students.
- **Freedom Center Students**: The "online hub for conservative students" The Center supports students with "intellectual ammunition" and speakers, and connects students from different campuses.
- **FrontPage Magazine**: The Center's online journal of news and political commentary is linked to over 2000 other websites. Shillman Fellows in Journalism making major contributions to the news journal include: Raymond Ibrahim, Bruce Bawer, and Daniel Greenfield
- **"The Point"** is a FrontPage Magazine blog run by Shillman Fellow Daniel Greenfield.
- **DiscoverTheNetworks.com**: Is "the largest publicly accessible database defining the chief groups and individuals of the Left and their organizational interlocks."
- **Jihad Watch:** The website run by author Robert Spencer that "traces the efforts of Islamic radicals" whether it be terrorism abroad or domestic activities to "infiltrate and subvert Western institutions and civic life." Jihad Watch is a critical and reliable resource for honest and current information.
- **Israel Security Project:** Reports from Jerusalem on the Middle East. Caroline Glick, director of the project is an editor and syndicated columnist for the *Jerusalem Post*. Glick was a captain in the Israel Defense Forces (IDF), and a Foreign Policy Advisor to Prime Minister Binyamin Netanyahu.

- **TruthRevolt**: The newest Freedom Center program whose goal is to "unmask leftists in the media for who they are." TruthRevolt is run by Shillman Senior Fellow Ben Shapiro.

FreedomWorks: http://www.freedomworks.org An organization with over 6 million American members desiring less government, lower taxes, economic freedom, free markets and individual liberty. "Preserving liberty depends on all Americans having access to their elected officials - not just special interests. FreedomWorks holds Washington accountable to the citizens that put them in office."

Focus on the Family: http://www.focusonthefamily.com is a global Christian ministry dedicated to families. Focus on the Family has extensive resources to share with and support parents and families including featured websites, books, literature, and documentaries. In May 2014 Focus on the Family released a great documentary, *"Irreplaceable: What's Wrong With the Family and What Do We Do About It?"*

Heritage Foundation: http://www.heritage.org
A research and educational institution to formulate and promote conservative public policies based on the principles of free enterprise, limited government, individual freedom, traditional American values, and strong national defense. The Heritage Foundation is committed to the preservation of our founding principles and an America *"where freedom, opportunity, prosperity and civil society flourish."*

The Heritage's Research Institutes are devoted to developing policies that will strengthen our economy, society and America:

- **The Institute for Economic Freedom and Opportunity**: To promote a strong economy
  - The Thomas A. Roe Institute for Economic Policy Studies
  - The Center for Trade and Economics
  - The Center for Data Analysis

- **The Institute for Family, Community, and Opportunity**: To promote a stronger society
  - The DeVos Center for Religion and Civil Society
  - The B. Kenneth Simon Center for Principles and Politics
  - The Center for Health Policy Studies
  - Domestic Policy Studies
- **The Kathryn and Shelby Collum Davis Institute for National Security and Foreign Policy**: To promote a stronger America
  - The Douglas and Sarah Allison Center for Foreign and National Security Policy
  - The Margaret Thatcher Center for Freedom
  - The Asian Studies Center
  - International Studies

The Heritage Edwin Meese III Center for Legal and Judicial Studies, the Center for Policy Innovation, and the Research Editing staff work closely with the Heritage Institutes.

The Heritage Foundation's *Solutions 2014: Expert Analysis, Powerful Messages, Winning Policies* is a free down-loadable publication "of today's best conservative policy recommendations for those fighting on the front lines of political life, whether by running for office or simply being an active citizen in their community." http:// www.solutions.heritage.org

Hoover Institution: http:// www.hoover.org
The Hoover Institution on War, Revolution and Peace at Stanford University in California is a public policy research center "devoted to the study of economics, politics, history, and political economy - both domestic and foreign - as well as international affairs. With its eminent scholars and world-renowned library and archives, the Hoover Institution seeks to improve the human condition by advancing ideas that promote economic opportunity and prosperity and secure and safeguard peace for America and all mankind."

Judicial Watch: http://www.JudicialWatch.org, email = info@ JudicilWatch.org

"Because no one is above the law"

A conservative, non-partisan educational foundation promoting transparency, accountability and integrity in government, politics and the law. *"Judicial Watch advocates high standards of ethics and morality in our nation's public life and seeks to ensure that political and judicial officials do not abuse the powers entrusted to them...through litigation, investigations, and public outreach."* Using "freedom of information" laws and other tools, Judicial Watch investigates and uncovers misconduct "by corrupt government officials and litigation to hold to account politicians and public officials who engage in corrupt activities."

- Public education and outreach programs for American citizens including Judicial Watch publications *The Verdict* and special reports to make the public aware of "abuses and misconduct by political and judicial officials, and advocates for the need for an ethical, law abiding and moral civic culture."
- Open Records Project: Provides training and legal services on how to effectively use the Freedom of Information Act and other open records laws to ensure accountability in government.

Judicial Watch's investigation of the Benghazi, Libya attack of September 11, 2012 is commendable. Even with the Obama administration's campaign of obstacles and lies, the Judicial Watch team relentlessly dug for the truth about the attack. Judicial Watch was able to obtain cover-up documents through the Freedom of Information Act that even Congress had been unable to secure. The Judicial Special Report, "The Benghazi Attack of September 11, 2012 Analysis and Further Questions from a Diplomatic Security Service Regional Security Officer and Special Agent," is a comprehensive report on the facts surrounding the deaths of four Americans. During a Congressional hearing on Benghazi, Secretary of State Hillary Clinton dismissed their deaths by saying "What difference at this point does it make?" [how they died]. Hillary, it makes all the difference in the world.

Leadership Institute: http://www.leadershipinstitute.org
Founded in 1979, the Leadership Institute recruits and trains conservatives for working with the government, politics and the media. "The institute strives to produce a new generation of public policy leaders unwavering in their commitment to free enterprise, limited government, strong national defense, and traditional values."

Manhattan Institute for Policy Research:
Development of ideas to foster economic choice and individual responsibility from rigorous research on challenging public policy issues such as: taxes, health care, energy, crime, the legal system, homeland security, urban life, education, race, culture and more.

- *City Journal* is the Manhattan Institute's quarterly magazine that presents a wealth of information to every American.

Students for Life of America: (SFLA) http://www.studentsforlife.org
"Pro-Life" students whose mission is to end abortion by educating other students about the issues of abortion, euthanasia, and infanticide. They identify and support pro-life student leaders with training and resources for success and promote student activity with other local colleges and national organizations.

The Tea Party: The Tea Party is a national grassroots movement of millions of Americans of all political parties, races and religions who share a common belief in the principles and values that made this nation great. The Tea Party is not a single national organization. It is comprised of numerous Tea Party groups from across the nation who are united in principle and speak with a cohesive voice. It's kind of like separate colonies uniting to form a single force (country) while keeping their individual identities. Sound familiar?

The Tea party promotes the "American Dream" of which freedom is the very foundation. The guiding principles of freedom to achieve the American Dream include:

- Constitutionally Limited Government assures personal freedom and our Constitutionally guaranteed rights
- Free Market Economics - Economic Freedom to grow jobs and provide opportunities
- Fiscal Responsibility to ensure a debt-free future for our children and grandchildren

Major Tea Party groups:
- Tea Party Patriots: http://www.teapartypatriots.org
  - "Envision a nation where personal freedom is cherished and where all Americans are treated equally, assuring our ability to pursue the American Dream."
- Tea Party: http://www.teaparty.org
  - "We stand by the Constitution...We serve as a beacon to the masses that have lost their way, a light illuminating the path to the original intentions of our Founding Fathers. We must raise a choir of voices declaring America must stand on the values which made us great."
- Tea Party Express: http://www.teapartyexpress.org
  - Since 2009 the Tea Party Express has made 8 national bus tours plus several regional tours hosting over 400 rallies. "We are committed to identifying and supporting conservative candidates and causes that will champion tea party values and return our country to the Constitutional principles that have made America the 'shining city on a hill.'"

Vision to America: http://www.visiontoamerica.com
VA is a division of Christian Worldview Communications, LLC and its purpose is to restore America to the Christian Republic created by our Founding Fathers. "America was once a light to the world-a place God blessed with liberty and prosperity. Today, Americans are taught that the Almighty State has all the answers. As a result, our God-given liberties are being traded for a false sense of security. It is our Vision to see Americans once again recognize that we are endowed by our Creator

with certain unalienable rights and that this Creator is the God of the Bible."

Wall Builders: http://www.wallbuilders.com *"Presenting America's forgotten history and heroes with an emphasis on our moral, religious, and constitutional heritage"*

Wallbuilders mission: Exert a direct and positive influence in government, education, and the family by (1) educating the nation concerning the Godly foundation of our country; (2) providing information to federal, state, and local officials as they develop public policies which reflect Biblical values; and (3) encouraging Christians to be involved in the civic arena.

In 2014 Wallbuilders hosted a Congressional Pastor's Briefing in Washington D.C. for the purpose of supporting "courageous and patriotic" ministers who will provide leadership and speak out on pressing issues whether spiritual or temporal. The new "Black Robe Regiment" of Pastors and ministers meet with Senators and Representatives to discuss issues of faith.

Young Americans for Liberty: (YAL) http://www.yaliberty.org
A pro-liberty organization with over 500 chapters and 162,000 activists on American college campuses. "The mission of YAL is to identify, educate, train, and mobilize youth activists committed to 'winning on principle.' Our goal is to cast the leaders of tomorrow and reclaim the policies, candidates, and direction of our government."

- **YAL Statement of Principles:**
  "We are the Young Americans for Liberty. We recognize the God-given natural rights of life, liberty, and property set forth by our Founding Fathers. Our country was created to protect the freedoms of the individual and be directed by We the People... We welcome limited government conservatives, classical liberals, and libertarians who trust in the creed we set forth."

CONCLUSION

Therapists will tell you that anger and resentment are normal emotions. I will add that it's the expression of those emotions that defines the person. You should be angry and frustrated at what is happening in our country today. Put your anger, resentment and frustration to productive use. Stop complaining. Learn the issues. Learn about the politicians who will be representing you. Remember that actions do speak louder than words. "Hope and Change" sounded wonderful in 2008 but too many people did not look beyond the teleprompter, resulting in the chaos we have today.

Regardless of political party, all elected and appointed officials must be held accountable. No more excuses. We want what our Founders wanted and sacrificed to bequeath to us: A smaller federal government whose main purpose is the security and protection of United States citizens, economy and institutions; State and local governments free to regulate their own affairs without the blackmailing arm of Washington, DC; and free enterprise based on the capitalist economic model – the only one that can ensure economic success and prosperity.

Lower taxes generate higher revenues. Period. The tax burden on the working middle class is exhausting, and indiscriminately taxing the wealthy to finance out-of-control spending is not the answer. How long can the working middle-class hold on? How long do you think the wealthiest 1% of taxpayers can sustain paying more federal income taxes than the bottom 90% of taxpayers? *With success comes wealth; with wealth comes investment and growth; with investment and growth comes an economically strong country.* Yes, a lot of wealthy people are "not so nice," but you can't discriminate because you dislike or envy someone.

Many wealthy people fund charities, scholarships, hospitals, research and development and create jobs. Without investments by the wealthy people, all these things wither. We need to champion meaningful tax reform, whether that is a "fair tax" or a "flat tax." Equality is being able to have the opportunity to work to support your family unencumbered by excessive taxation. Equality is not spending your life supported by government money and benefits. Do not forget, "nothing is free," and every cent the government spends comes from us. We have to manage and account for our money at home and we have to demand Washington do the same – it is our money they are wasting!

The government's job is to protect religious freedom, not deny and destroy it. The government including the President and every other government official are bound to abide by and enforce Constitutional laws as long as they exist. The Constitution provides no waivers for picking and choosing which laws to obey. And do not be misled that gun control is the answer to violence in this country. If guns are removed from law-abiding citizens the only ones with guns will be the thugs, terrorists, and of course, the government.

Learn about America and the people who created and built it. Learn what life is like in other countries and you will see that no country has the opportunities provided here. The more you learn, the more you will see that the U.S. must change its current course. U.S.S. America is teetering on the brink of a whirlpool and it won't take much more for her to go over the edge. It will be difficult to save her, but we must for the sake of our children, our grandchildren and for the free world. Get angry, stay angry. Direct your attention and energies to solving our problems and strengthening our nation. We were known as the "silent majority," allowing ourselves to be bullied, threatened and intimidated into silence. Well, no more silence! We must stand up and seek out others who support this nation and its constitution. We must reject government corruption, waste and political correctness. We must assess, discuss and promote solutions.

We must reject the politically correct response of "contrived outrage" that we are affronted with on a daily basis. No more pretending to be offended or shocked and no more accepting insincere empty apologies from politicians, leaders and government officials who cannot "feel" our pain. It is annoying when Hollywood celebrities do it, but it is insulting when coming from the government. President Obama was not surprised, shocked and outraged at the scandals landing on the steps of the White House. He knew what was happening. Secretary of State Clinton was not outraged over the Benghazi attack and does not feel the pain of the mothers of the murdered men. The very same people who do not hesitate to "condemn" others and other countries need to take a look inward before jumping on the condemnation train. All these "catch" words are so overused that they have become meaningless. I don't see the point to call a news conference to announce and condemn an event (like Russia invading Ukraine or when terrorists go on a rampage) when you are not going to do anything about it. To them condemnation is acknowledgment for their success. Domestically, condemning people and threatening to destroy their career if an apology is not made for something they did or said is so juvenile and pointless. Unfortunately, too many Americans are truly "stuck on stupid."

There used to be a time when we were taught that "name-calling" was not nice which is probably why liberals embrace that activity. If you stand up for your rights, your faith, your family and your country, expect to be verbally assaulted. Don't take the bait - shake it off. The liberal vocabulary of disparagement is limited, so they just repeat the same words over and over. Tell yourself: I am not a "racist" for criticizing President Obama. I am not a "domestic terrorist" because I believe in my Second Amendment rights. I am not a "National Security threat" because I am a Christian and a Conservative who will no longer be silent. I am not a "traitor" because I will expose government corruption. I am not "Anti-American" for supporting the Constitution. I am not a "religious fanatic" because I believe Jesus Christ died for my sins. I am not a "war monger" because I support our troops and am so grateful to them. I am not a "homophobe" because I believe in the sanctity of marriage between a man and a woman. I am not a "greedy capitalist" because I believe in the free market and personal responsibility - not entitlement. I am not a "separatist" because I oppose illegal immigration and Sharia law. I am an American.

We must listen to the warnings of others. The threats they warn us of are real and extremely dangerous to our freedom and way of life. As our fathers and fore fathers did, we must commit to the security and success of each other and our exceptional nation. David Boaz has great advice for us: *"In 1776, 1950, or now, there's never been a golden age of liberty, and there never will be. People who value freedom will always have to defend it from those who claim the right to wield power over others…And, in today's world that means more than a musket by the door. It means being an active citizen."*

Armed with knowledge and fortitude and with *"a firm reliance on the protection of Divine Providence, we* must *mutually pledge to each other our lives, our fortunes, and our sacred honor."* In the words of great American hero Todd Beamer, one of the passengers on hijacked United Airlines Flight 93 who saved countless lives by sacrificing his own life to deny terrorists from completing their mission on September 11, 2001,

"LET'S ROLL"

God, grant me

The Serenity to accept the things I cannot change

The courage to change the things I can

And the Wisdom to know the difference.

CPSIA information can be obtained at www.ICGtesting.com
Printed in the USA
LVOW06s1619071015

457323LV00002B/416/P